D1188165

REAL ESTATE

INFORMATION
SOURCES

REAL ESTATE

INFORMATION
SOURCES

Janice B. Babb

Beverly F. Dordick

[
Librarian and Assistant Librarian
National Association of Real Estate Boards
Chicago, Illinois
]

Series Editor
Paul Wasserman, Professor and Librarian
Graduate School of Business and Public Administration
Cornell University, Ithaca, N.Y.

GALE RESEARCH COMPANY · BOOK TOWER · DETROIT, MICHIGAN

LIBRARY OF CONGRESS

CATALOG CARD NUMBER

63-16246

CONTENTS

CONTENTS

CONTENTS

PREFACE

Modern day managerial processes grow ever more complex. One consequence is that the number of agencies and published resources which supply factual data necessary for rational decision-making constantly mounts. In many fields, the types of resources are quite varied and numerous. But the practitioner, the student and the librarian working in these fields often lack an organized and comprehensive guide to the available resources, and, as a consequence, the opportunity to apply the maximum amount of factual data toward problem-solving is all too frequently lost.

REAL ESTATE INFORMATION SOURCES is the first in a series planned to aid in overcoming this deficiency in basic business research tools. To be known as the "Management Information Guide Series," each volume will be devoted to a general subject of wide interest to business and professional men. These works will provide leads to information and information resources by classifying, describing, and indexing key books, periodicals, and other published resources, as well as organizations and facilities, which make up the total information apparatus of each of the fields to be covered.

Paul Wasserman
Series Editor

INTRODUCTION

A definition of the real estate business as it is today seems desirable as an introduction to this source book, primarily because of the widely-held impression that the listing and selling of houses constitutes the real estate business. In actuality, however, a large body of literature on the highest and best use of real property, appraisal of value, finance, development, and management of property to create an "income stream" for the investor has been developed during the last forty years by experts in the field. This literature covers the theory, methods, and results of the use of real property.

Appraisers and property managers evaluate and lease all types of property, including institutional property and those properties suitable only for a special use. While heavy construction is not a part of the real estate business, knowledge of its special requirements is necessary for the planning and development of such uses. Real estate experts necessarily play a role in the planning of all types of improvements. Performing the property management function demands a thorough familiarity with the requirements that will provide the most useful buildings and the highest return on investment. Selection of site, most profitable use of a site, specialized requirements of particular uses, and management of the improvement once constructed are highly interrelated.

Only the real estate, its utility or investment use, is covered in this source book. Those property types which normally are so specialized as to demand a professional management group, such as restaurants and hotels, are treated only in terms of the real estate, construction requirements, and return on investment. The operation of a business as a property use is not of interest beyond the point of return on investment. It is within the framework of this definition that the sources following were compiled.

The literature of planning and real estate overlap extensively. The effect of planning and regulation on value and transfer of real property is obvious. This sourcebook does include those references on planning as it directly affects the development and use of real property; e.g., zoning is based on planning decisions and urban renewal includes an extensive literature on planning and regulation of property use. General discussions of planning principles are not within the scope of this source book.

With a few exceptions, this compilation does not contain references to articles in periodicals. However, the general list of periodicals, with its annotations (Appendix A), and the lists of specialized periodicals at the end of each section will direct readers to this body of literature. Pertinent indexes of periodicals have been cited, as well.

No effort has been made to give complete coverage to Congressional hearings, state documents, and bulletins of state agricultural experiment stations. As in the case of periodical literature, the compilers have attempted to indicate bibliographical and index tools through which such items may be found.

Publications cited have been limited almost entirely to those in English issued in the United States, Canada, Great Britain, Australia, and New Zealand.

December 1962

Section 1

GENERAL

Alonso, William. A MODEL OF THE URBAN LAND MARKET: LOCATION AND DENSITIES OF DWELLINGS AND BUSINESSES. Unpublished Ph.D. thesis, University of Pennsylvania, 1960.

California. University. Real Estate Research Program. CENTRAL CITY PROPERTY VALUES IN SAN FRANCISCO AND OAKLAND, 1950 TO 1960, by Paul F. Wendt. (Research Report 18). Berkeley: 1953. 52p. tables, charts. pap.
> Part I. Movements of land values and related variables. Part II. Relationship between land value changes and accessibility.

Casey, William J. REAL ESTATE DESK BOOK. New York: Institute for Business Planning, 1961. 315p. tables.
> A ready-reference manual of practical information on real estate investments, taxation, forms of ownership, conveyancing, etc. Appendix: REAL ESTATE INVESTMENT TABLES.

Davies, Pearl Janet. REAL ESTATE IN AMERICAN HISTORY. Washington, D.C.: Public Affairs Press, 1958. 232p.
> "This is a history of real estate ownership in the United States and of the business which serves it." Traces history of the National Association of Real Estate Boards.

Fisher, Ernest M. URBAN REAL ESTATE MARKETS: CHARACTERISTICS AND FINANCING. (NBER. Financial Research Program. Studies in Urban Mortgage Financing No. 3). New York: National Bureau of Economic Research, 1951. 186p. tables, charts.
> Describes the several related markets for the different types of real property that, taken together, make up the real estate market.

Goldsmith, Raymond W. THE NATIONAL WEALTH OF THE UNITED STATES IN THE POSTWAR PERIOD. (National Bureau of Economic Research Studies in Capital Formation and Financing No. 10). Princeton, N.J.: Princeton University Press, 1962. 434p. tables, charts.
> Comprehensive, detailed estimates of the national wealth and its components since 1945. Land and various types of real property discussed as components.

Goldsmith, Raymond W. A STUDY OF SAVINGS IN THE UNITED STATES, 3 vols. Princeton, N.J.: Princeton University Press, 1955. tables, charts.
> Wealth estimates, 1897 to 1949. Includes detailed statistics on real estate holdings and mortgage debt. Land and structures values as components of national wealth in volume III.

Hoyt, Homer. ONE HUNDRED YEARS OF LAND VALUES IN CHICAGO; THE RELATIONSHIP OF THE GROWTH OF CHICAGO TO THE RISE IN ITS LAND VALUES, 1830-1933. Chicago: University of Chicago Press, 1933. 519p.
"This study was undertaken because there seemed to be no comprehensive data available to show the cyclical fluctuations of land values in any American city and because the knowledge of the past movements of land prices seemed to me to be indispensable for any rational real estate investment policy."

Keiper, Joseph S., et al. THEORY AND MEASUREMENT OF RENT. Philadelphia: Chilton Co., 1961. 194p. tables, charts.
A technical study of the origin and development of land-rent theory and its relation to contemporary economic problems; analyzes real property values in the American economy.

Olcott, George C. and Company. OLCOTT'S LAND VALUES BLUE BOOK OF CHICAGO AND SUBURBS. Wilmette, Ill.: 1911-
"The figures on the maps ... are the unit of values per front foot, for inside lots not coming under the corner influence in every block in the city and suburbs. The unit used is for lots 125 feet in depth, except for the high priced lands in the downtown section of the city where a depth of 100 feet is used. Tables for determining the value of lots of a different depth than the unit are printed ... Rules for determining corner values."
Use and height symbols. Each map (unless a fractional section) covers a section and one-half. Issued annually.

REAL ESTATE ANALYST SERVICE. St. Louis, Mo.: Roy Wenzlick Research Corp., 1932-
Fifty-nine bulletins and studies issued annually in several series: Agricultural Bulletin, Appraisal Bulletin, As We See, Construction Bulletin, Mortgage Bulletin, Real Estate Analyst, Real Estate Trends, Real Estate Tax Bulletin. Analyses and statistical compilations on vacancies, construction activity and costs, mortgage markets, farm values, foreclosures, and local economic activity, etc. Annual index.

REAL ESTATE MARKET. Washington, D.C.: National Association of Real Estate Boards, Department of Research, 1300 Connecticut Ave. N.W., zone 6.
Spring, 1962, issue was the 73rd real estate market research study. Residential, commercial, industrial, and land-farm property covered. "Information on supply and demand factors, on prospects for the future, and on trends in price, rate of transfers, and levels of rents and vacancies." Issued semi-annually.

Real Estate Research Corporation. REFERENCE VOLUME OF SIGNIFICANT ECONOMIC DATA FOR REAL ESTATE, MORTGAGE LENDING AND BUILDING. Chicago: 1949-   tables, charts. pap.
Statistics in three main sections: Production-Income; Investment-Consumer; Basic Real Estate Factors. Issued annually.

Regional Plan of New York and Its Environs. LAND VALUES; DISTRIBUTION WITHIN NEW YORK REGION AND RELATION TO VARIOUS FACTORS IN URBAN GROWTH, by Harold M. Lewis, et al. (Engineering Series, Monograph no. 3). New York: 1927. 72p. tables, diagrs.
Distribution of land values and factors that influence land values.

Shapiro, Irving D. AN ECONOMIC BASIS FOR REAL ESTATE DEVELOPMENT.
Unpublished Ph.D. thesis, Columbia University, 1960.

Urban Land Institute. DYNAMIC FACTORS IN LAND VALUES, by Homer
Hoyt. (Technical Bulletin no. 37). Washington, D.C.: 1960. 15p. illus.
pap.

Urban Land Institute. THE URBAN REAL ESTATE CYCLE — PERFORMANCE
AND PROSPECTS, by Homer Hoyt. (Technical Bulletin no. 38). Washington,
D.C.: 1960. 16p. pap.

U. S. Bureau of the Census. CENSUS OF HOUSING. Washington, D.C.:
Government Printing Office.
    (For annotation, see entry in RESIDENTIAL PROPERTY section).

U. S. Department of Agriculture. Agricultural Research Service. LAND OWN-
ERSHIP IN THE GREAT PLAIN STATES, 1958; A STATISTICAL SUMMARY, by
Roger W. Strohbehn and Gene Wunderlich. Washington, D.C.: Government
Printing Office, 1960. 80p. tables, charts, map. pap.
    Results of a 1957-1958 survey on characteristics of landowners
    and trends in ownership patterns for ten states.

Wenzlick, Roy. Real Estate in 19-   ; Forecast for Subscribers. REAL ESTATE
ANALYST.
    Issued annually as the first number of the year.

Wickens, David L. RESIDENTIAL REAL ESTATE, ITS ECONOMIC POSITION
AS SHOWN BY VALUES, RENTS, FAMILY INCOMES, FINANCING AND
CONSTRUCTION, TOGETHER WITH ESTIMATES FOR ALL REAL ESTATE. New
York: National Bureau of Economic Research, 1941. 300p. tables, charts.
    Data on values of urban residential properties, the relation of
    these values to mortgage debts, current rentals, construction,
    income of occupants, rates of obsolescence of properties, terms
    of financing and sources of funds.

Zuckerman, Solly, et al. LAND OWNERSHIP AND RESOURCES; A COURSE
OF LECTURES GIVEN AT CAMBRIDGE IN JUNE, 1958. Cambridge, England:
Department of Estate Management, Cambridge University, no date. 136p. ta-
bles, charts.
    Published in co-operation with the Cambridge University Estate
    Management Club.

Bibliographies

ACTION. URBAN RENEWAL BIBLIOGRAPHY, comp. by Katherine McNamara.
New York: 1954. 313p. pap. processed.

BULLETIN OF PUBLIC AFFAIRS INFORMATION SERVICE. New York:
Public Affairs Information Service, Inc., 1915-
    Issued weekly with five periodic cumulations each year culmi-
    nating in an annual cumulative volume. Cites books, periodical

articles, pamphlets, government documents, and miscellaneous
reports. See such subject headings as Farm ownership, Farm
tenancy, Housing, Industrial districts, Land values, Landlord
and tenant, Real estate business, Real estate management, Real
property, Rent, Suburban development.

BUSINESS PERIODICALS INDEX. New York: H.W. Wilson Co., 1958-
Issued monthly except in July, with periodic cumulations including annual cumulative volumes. Approximately 125 periodicals
covered. See such subject headings as Real estate business, Real
property, Mortgages, Home ownership, Insurance, Mortgage,
Banks and banking - Mortgage departments, Land tenure, Land
values. Preceded by the INDUSTRIAL ARTS INDEX.

California. University. Real Estate Research Program. CALIFORNIA REAL ES-
TATE BOOKSHELF. Berkeley: 1962. 149p. pap. processed.
Previous editions in 1952 and 1959. A comprehensive bibliography of 333 annotated references; classified arrangement with
author and title indexes.

Council of Planning Librarians. BIBLIOGRAPHIES BRIEFLY NOTED. Oakland,
Calif.: 6813 Thornhill Drive, zone 11, 1960-
No. 3 ... July 1962 first issue since Sept. 1960.

EKISTICS; ABSTRACTS ON THE PROBLEMS AND SCIENCE OF HUMAN SETTLE-
MENTS. Doxiadis Associates, 24 Strat, Syndesnou, Athens, Greece. 1956-
Monthly.

EXCHANGE BIBLIOGRAPHIES. Council of Planning Librarians. Oakland, Calif.:
6318 Thornhill Drive, zone 11, 1958-
Subscription may be placed for 10 consecutive bibliographies issued in about 18 months or bibliographies may be purchased separately.

Government Affairs Foundation, Inc. METROPOLITAN COMMUNITIES: A BIB-
LIOGRAPHY. Chicago: Public Administration Service, 1956. 392p.
Includes annotated references on land use, real estate values
and valuation, housing demand. Supplement, 1955–57 compiled
by Victor Jones and Barbara Hudson, 1960. 229p.

Illinois. University. College of Commerce and Business Administration. REAL-
TOR'S BOOKSHELF, A BACKGROUND FOR REAL ESTATE LEADERSHIP, comp.
by the Department of Education, National Association of Real Estate Boards.
Urbana: 1949. 56p. pap.
Approximately two hundred annotated references.

INDEX OF ECONOMIC JOURNALS, 5 vols. Homewood, Ill.: Published and
distributed for the American Economic Association by Richard D. Irwin, 1961.
Covers 1886 through 1959; arranged in twenty-three main categories, including land economics, housing, natural resources, agriculture.

INDEX TO AMERICAN DOCTORAL DISSERTATIONS, comp. for the Association of Research Libraries. Ann Arbor, Mich.: University Microfilms.
> An annual compilation of all doctoral dissertations accepted by American and Canadian universities. Contents arranged by subject and by institution, with author index. Dissertations on real estate and related subjects usually listed in Economics section. Issued as final number of each volume of DISSERTATION ABSTRACTS.

Port of New York Authority. Library Services Section. A SELECTED BIBLIOGRAPHY OF THE PORT OF NEW YORK AUTHORITY, 1921-1962. New York: 1962. 110p. pap.
> Indexed.

U. S. Department of Agriculture. Library. LAND OWNERSHIP, A BIBLIOGRAPHY OF SELECTED REFERENCES, comp. by Annie M. Hannay, et al. (USDA Bibliographical Bulletin, No. 22). Washington, D.C.: Government Printing Office, 1953. 292p. pap. processed.
> 2,969 citations, classified arrangement, author and subject indices. Includes foreign material.

U. S. Housing and Home Finance Agency. PUBLICATIONS. Rev. May 1962. Washington, D.C.: 1962. 15p. pap. processed.

U. S. Small Business Administration. REAL ESTATE AND INSURANCE, by Bob A. Hedges, et al. (Small Business Bulletin no. 65). Washington, D.C.: Government Printing Office, 1962. 16p. pap.
> An annotated bibliography of government and nongovernment publications, with lists of periodical titles and trade associations in the fields.

U. S. Small Business Administration. A SURVEY OF UNIVERSITY BUSINESS AND ECONOMIC RESEARCH PROJECTS - A COMPILATION OF FACULTY AND DOCTORAL RESEARCH PROJECTS IN BUSINESS AND ECONOMICS COMPLETED OR IN PROGRESS IN UNIVERSITY SCHOOLS OF BUSINESS AND DEPARTMENTS OF ECONOMICS DURING THE ACADEMIC YEARS 1957 THROUGH 1961, prepared by Stella Traverr. Washington, D.C.: Government Printing Office, 1961. 642p. pap. processed.
> Includes sections on urban land, housing, real estate, agriculture, natural resources, industrial development, regional planning and development.

Urban Land Institute. URBAN REAL ESTATE RESEARCH. Washington, D.C.: The Institute, 1959-
> Issued as parts of the Research Monograph series: No. 1 covers 1946-1958; No. 3 covers 1959; No. 5 covers 1960. Annotated bibliographies and inventories of research in progress. Also discusses areas in which research is needed.

Wasserman, Paul, et al, eds. STATISTICAL SOURCES, 1st ed. Detroit: Gale Research Co., 1962. 296p. processed.

Bibliographies (continued)

Identifies primary and important secondary sources; classified
arrangement; national rather than regional and local emphasis. Includes sections on the real estate business, real estate
loans, public lands.

Section 2

THE REAL ESTATE BUSINESS

GENERAL

Commission Rates; Digest of Schedules on Sales, Exchanges, Leases, Appraisals and Management in Important Cities. BUILDINGS, annually in the December issue.

Gross Hours and Earnings of Production Workers, by Industry. EMPLOYMENT
AND EARNINGS, a table appearing in each issue.
    Statistics for the group, Finance, Insurance and Real Estate.

International Real Estate Federation. American Chapter. REALTOR STUDIES
IN FOREIGN COUNTRIES; A BRIEF SUMMARY OF REAL ESTATE PRACTICES
AND INFORMATION THERETO AS REVEALED DURING STUDY TOURS CON-
DUCTED WITHIN THE COUNTRIES, comp. and ed. by Eugene P. Conser.
Chicago: 1961. 46p. pap. processed.

(Statistical tables on the number of individuals engaged in the real estate business, with a subgrouping for operative builders.) MONTHLY LABOR REVIEW,
each issue.

Triester, Stanton L. The Role of the Real Estate Man. p. 3-21. In Friedman, Edith J., ed. REAL ESTATE ENCYCLOPEDIA. Englewood Cliffs, N.J.:
Prentice-Hall, 1960.

U. S. Bureau of the Census. CENSUS OF BUSINESS. 1935. CONSTRUCTION
INDUSTRY, 3 vols. Washington D.C.: Government Printing Office, 1937.
    Vol I: Work performed, personnel, payroll, and cost of mate-
    rial, by states and cities and by kinds of business;
    Vol II: Employment by months, and by occupational groups, by
    states and cities and by kinds of business;
    Vol III: Types of construction, comparisons between 1929 and
    1935, and miscellaneous data; Work performed by type of con-
    struction, location, size grouping of establishments by value of
    work performed. Data for United States, geographic divisions,
    states, cities of 500,000 or more inhabitants.

U. S. Bureau of the Census. CENSUS OF BUSINESS: 1935. REAL ESTATE
AGENCIES. Washington D.C.: 1937. 39p. tables, pap. processed.
    Establishments, commissions and fees, personnel and payroll by
    geographic divisions and states. Funds were provided by the
    Works Progress Administration.

GENERAL (continued)

U. S. Bureau of the Census. CENSUS OF BUSINESS, 1939; VOLUME 4: CONSTRUCTION. Washington D.C.: Government Printing Office, 1943   397p.

U. S. Bureau of the Census and U. S. Bureau of Old-Age and Survivors Insurance. COUNTY BUSINESS PATTERNS. Washington, D.C.: Government Printing Office.

> Published in 1951, 1953, 1956 and 1959. United States Summary, County Totals; 2: New England States, 3: Middle Atlantic 4: East North Central, 5: West North Central, 6: South Atlantic, 7: East South Central, 8: West South Central, 9: Mountain, 10: Pacific. Employment and payroll data by industry groups for those reporting units covered by Old Age, Survivors and Disability Insurance Program. Editor's Note: Many real estate salesmen are "independent contractors" and not included.

U. S. Internal Revenue Service. STATISTICS OF INCOME. Washington, D.C.: Government Printing Office, 19-   . pap.

> Annual compilation; real estate category divided into real estate except lessors of real property other than buildings and lessors of real property except buildings. Balance sheet and income statement data, including costs of sales and operations and expenditures for advertising. Sole proprietorships, partnerships, and corporations covered.

Yearbook of Real Estate and Management. BUILDINGS, issued annually as the December issue.

> Includes annual digest of suggested local real estate board commission rates in major cities, salesmen and managers', and percentage lease tables, and a list of state license law officials.

LICENSING

All fifty of the United States, the District of Columbia and five of the provinces of Canada license real estate brokers and salesmen. A list of the licensing agencies and their addresses appears in Appendix C. Printed lists of licensees are usually issued annually by these agencies. Rules and regulations under which licenses are granted and, in many cases, additional study materials for applicants are available from the respective agencies.

Arco Publishing Co., Inc. REAL ESTATE SALESMAN AND BROKER, ed. by Jacob E. Kronick. (Arco Text for Job and Test Training Series). New York: 1959. various paging. pap. processed.

> A study manual for applicants for real estate licenses. Discussion and a trial examination; Real estate and assessment glossaries.

LICENSING (continued)

"Constitutionality of License Laws. p. 366-91 In Semenow, Robert W. QUES-
TIONS AND ANSWERS ON REAL ESTATE, 4th ed. Englewood Cliffs, N.J.:
Prentice-Hall, 1961.
Discusses and cites cases involving real estate licensing.

Kaufman, John J. ILLINOIS REAL ESTATE BROKERS' AND SALESMEN'S EXAM-
INATION REVIEW MANUAL. Fox River Grove, Ill.: University Outline Publications, 1961. 95p. pap.

(List of State License Law Officials) BUILDING. Annual, in the December
issue.

National Association of License Law Officials. 1961-1962 SUMMARY ON LI-
CENSE LAW STATISTICS. Pittsburgh: 603 Berger Building, zone 19, 1962.
3p. pap. processed.
A report on the states and the District of Columbia, giving
numbers of broker and salesman licenses issued in 1962 (including those for branch offices) and numbers of examination
applicants (with percentages for passing and failing examination).

National Association of Real Estate Boards. License Law Committee. ORGAN-
IZATION OF STATE REAL ESTATE COMMISSIONS. Chicago: 1962. 3p.
pap. processed.
A tabular summary.

National Association of Real Estate Boards. License Law Committee. REQUIRE-
MENTS FOR REAL ESTATE BROKER'S LICENSE. Chicago: 1962. 5p. pap.
processed.
A tabular summary.

National Association of Real Estate Boards. License Law Committee. REQUIRE-
MENTS FOR REAL ESTATE SALESMAN'S LICENSE. Chicago: 1962. 4p. pap.
processed.
A tabular summary.

National Association of Real Estate Boards. License Law Committee. SUG-
GESTED PATTERN REAL ESTATE LICENSE LAW AND SUPPLEMENTARY RULES
AND REGULATIONS, 2d ed. Chicago: 1961. 52p. pap. processed.
First edition issued in 1958.

Ripley, Ralph P. STUDY GUIDE FOR REAL ESTATE LICENSE EXAMINATIONS.
Englewood Cliffs, N.J.: Prentice-Hall, 1962. 56p. forms. pap.
A general guide, suitable for study for the examinations of all
states and the District of Columbia.

Semenow, Robert W. QUESTIONS AND ANSWERS ON REAL ESTATE, 4th ed.
Englewood Cliffs, N.J.: Prentice-Hall, 1961. 602p. tables, forms, diagrs.,
map.
Most widely-used general study aid for applicants in preparing
for license examinations.

LICENSING (continued)

Semenow, Robert W. REAL ESTATE LICENSE LAW REQUIREMENTS FOR THE 50 STATES. Englewood Cliffs, N.J.: Prentice-Hall, 1961. n.p. tables. pap.
>   The requirements presented in tabular form. Distributed with the author's QUESTIONS AND ANSWERS ON REAL ESTATE.

Westcott, Ray D. THE REAL ESTATE PRIMER ... WITH TYPICAL "ALL-DAY" EXAMINATION FOR REAL ESTATE BROKERS AND SALESMEN, 1963 ed. Temple City, Calif.: 9643 Longden Avenue, 1962. 266p.
>   Designed for use by applicants for California real estate license as an examination study manual. Revised frequently.

PRINCIPLES AND PRACTICE

Atkinson, Harry Grant and Frailey, Lester E. FUNDAMENTALS OF REAL ESTATE PRACTICE. New York: Prentice-Hall, 1946. 459p.
>   Revision and expansion of material issued in 1939 by the National Association of Real Estate Boards for use of Association members and their employees as a text in evening classes. Twenty-one lessons, each with suggested readings and points for discussion.

Brede, William J. CREATIVE THINKING IN REAL ESTATE. New York: Harper, 1959. 296p.
>   "Stories of the ingenuity, imagination, skill and integrity of brokers and principals in realty negotiations." Case histories of experiences of successful Realtors.

Brede, William J. O.K. — IT'S A DEAL! ODD TALES ABOUT REAL ESTATE. New York: Early Brothers, 9 Rockefeller Plaza, zone 20, 1946. 96p. pap.
>   "Selected stories of the fortunes and foibles of brokers and principals in property negotiations, which reveal the habits, idiosyncracies and variable moods of those who sell, own, finance and lease real estate." Taken largely from the author's newspaper columns.

Brown, Robert K. and Sturgess, A. H., Sr. REAL ESTATE PRIMER. Englewood Cliffs, N.J.: Prentice-Hall, 1961. 249p.
>   Presents the various aspects of real estate brokerage for the salesman; includes chapters on listing, advertising, sales contracts, closing. Appendix I: Real estate terms and phraseology.

Case, Frederick E. REAL ESTATE. Boston: Allyn and Bacon, 1962. 511p. tables.
>   Organization of the real estate business, functions of the executive, and the specialized branches of the business. A revision of MODERN REAL ESTATE PRACTICE, 1956.

Fisher, Ernest M. and Fisher, Robert M. URBAN REAL ESTATE. New York: Henry Holt, 1954. 502p.

PRINCIPLES AND PRACTICE (continued)

An approach to the principles of real estate "in terms of the physical, legal, social, and economic forces that bear upon it." Intended for the student and the professional man.

Friedman, Edith J., ed. REAL ESTATE ENCYCLOPEDIA. Englewood Cliffs, N.J.: Prentice-Hall, 1960. 1458p. illus., tables, forms.
Fifty-two chapters in twelve sections. Contributions by over fifty experts, brokers, lawyers, title officers, tax specialists, bankers, etc.

Hoagland, Henry E. REAL ESTATE PRINCIPLES, 3d ed. New York: McGraw-Hill, 1955. 538p.
A general treatise relating the subject of real estate to such fields as economics, finance, law, history, taxation, and government. Intended as an introduction.

Holmes, Lawrence G. and Jones, Carrie Maude, eds. THE REAL ESTATE HAND-BOOK. New York: Prentice-Hall, 1948. 783p. tables, charts, diagrs., forms.
Explanation of all kinds of real estate transactions and their execution. Intended for individuals in the business and related fields. Includes bibliography and glossary.

Husband, William H. and Anderson, Frank R. REAL ESTATE, 3d ed. Homewood, Ill.: Richard D. Irwin, 1960. 577p.
Emphasizes the implications of the practical aspects of real estate activities. References at chapter ends.

INTERNATIONAL REAL ESTATE FEDERATION CONGRESS, AMSTERDAM, JUNE 2-8, 1962. Amsterdam: Netherlands Real Estate Association, 1962. 80p. illus.
FIABCI Congresboek Van het xiiie. Internationale Markelaars-congres 4-6 Juni 1962 te Amsterdam. Program in various languages.

Martin, Prestan. REAL ESTATE PRINCIPLES AND PRACTICES. New York: Macmillan, 1959. 434p. tables, charts.
A text that emphasizes financing, Federal programs, and real estate developments within the new patterns of rapidly expanding urban areas. Questions, problems, and references at chapter ends. Traces the cycle of urban real estate from subdivision through demolition to redevelopment.

Morrison, Donald T. WEAVER SCHOOL OF REAL ESTATE; AN INTENSIVE COURSE IN THE FUNDAMENTALS OF THE REAL ESTATE BUSINESS WHICH SHOULD GIVE A MAN OR WOMAN THE EDUCATIONAL BACKGROUND FROM WHICH TO OPERATE ANY TYPE OF REAL ESTATE BUSINESS SUC-CESSFULLY. Kansas City, Mo.: 1958. 530p. illus., plans, forms, diagrs.

National Association of Real Estate Boards. ANNALS OF REAL ESTATE PRAC-TICE. Chicago: 1923-1930.

PRINCIPLES AND PRACTICE (continued)

Proceedings and reports of general sessions and division meetings at annual convention. Divisions: Appraisal, Brokers, Cooperative Apartment, Farm Lands, Home Builders and Subdivi-
ders, Industrial Property, Mortgage and Finance, Property Management.

National Association of Real Estate Boards. Committee on Education. A BAS-
IC COURSE IN REAL ESTATE. Chicago: 1961. 130p. pap. processed.
Prepared for the use of member boards.

National Association of Real Estate Boards. Committee on Education. THE
PLACE OF REAL ESTATE IN OUR EXPANDING ECONOMY; PROCEEDINGS
OF A CONFERENCE CO-SPONSORED BY THE NATIONAL ASSOCIATION
OF REAL ESTATE BOARDS AND THE COLLEGE OF BUSINESS ADMINISTRA-
TION, UNIVERSITY OF FLORIDA, NOVEMBER 10, 1950, GAINESVILLE, FLA.
Chicago: 1951. 39p. pap. processed.

National Association of Real Estate Boards. Committee on Education. REAL
ESTATE FUNDAMENTALS; A SET OF FIFTEEN LECTURE OUTLINES, ed. by
faculty members of the Department of Real Estate at the University of Florida.
Chicago: 1958. 46p. pap. processed.

National Association of Real Estate Boards. Committee on Education. REAL
ESTATE PRACTICE; A SET OF FIFTEEN LECTURE OUTLINES, ed. by John T.
Bonner, Jr. Chicago: 1959. 46p. pap. processed.

National Institute of Real Estate Brokers. FIFTY YEARS OF REAL ESTATE.
(Brokers Institute Bulletin Service). Chicago: 1953. 63p. illus. pap.
Ideas, ideals and interesting real estate transactions of Joseph
Laronge upon completion of fifty years in the real estate busi-
ness.

National Institute of Real Estate Brokers. THE PACE OF PROGRESS; REAL
ESTATE TRENDS AND OPPORTUNITIES IN THESE CHANGING TIMES. (Brokers Institute Bulletin Service). Chicago: 1955. 63p. illus. pap.

National Institute of Real Estate Brokers. REAL ESTATE SPECIALIZATIONS.
(Brokers Institute Bulletin Service). Chicago: 1962. 63p. pap.
Industrial and rural; counseling, appraising, management, in-
surance, mortgage banking, home building and urban renewal.

North, Nelson L. and Ring, Alfred A. REAL ESTATE PRINCIPLES AND PRAC-
TICES, 5th ed. Englewood Cliffs, N.J.: Prentice-Hall, 1960. 504p. tables,
charts, diagrs., map.
Presents the facts of real property ownership and discusses the
principle commercial and financial transactions involved in the
ownership and transfer of real estate. First edition by Benson
and North, 1922. Appendix includes amortization and yield
tables, measurement tables, check lists on drawing sales contract, closing.

PRINCIPLES AND PRACTICE (continued)

Prentice-Hall, Inc. THE ENCYCLOPEDIC DICTIONARY OF REAL ESTATE
PRACTICE, rev. ed. Englewood Cliffs, N.J.: 1962. 533p. illus. tables,
forms, diagrs.
> Over thirteen hundred entries, including the terms encountered
> in various fields of real estate practice, such as accounting,
> advertising, law, and office management, and information on
> Federal laws and regulation, taxation, sales techniques. In-
> cludes more than two hundred specimen forms.

Prentice-Hall, Inc. THE PRENTICE-HALL TREASURY OF MONEY-MAKING
REAL ESTATE IDEAS AND PRACTICES. Englewood Cliffs, N.J.: 1962. 366p.
illus., tables, forms.
> A collection of materials and methods used by successful real
> estate men throughout the country. Includes advertising, busi-
> ness letters, listings, etc.

PRENTICE-HALL REAL ESTATE GUIDE. Englewood Cliffs, N.J.: Prentice-Hall,
1953-   . illus. looseleaf.
> A looseleaf service issued in monthly parts, intended to serve
> as an operating and an instructional manual. Concise, accu-
> rate information in eighteen sections, including selling, ad-
> vertising, Federal taxation, appraisal, management, state prop-
> erty taxation, financing, rent control. Indexed.

Ratcliff, Richard U. REAL ESTATE ANALYSIS. New York: McGraw-Hill,
1961. 342p.
> A text for professional training and professional services in
> the solution of real estate problems. Investment aspects of
> real estate activity emphasized.

Ring, Alfred A. QUESTIONS AND PROBLEMS IN REAL ESTATE PRINCIPLES
AND PRACTICES. Englewood Cliffs, N.J.: Prentice-Hall, 1960. 242p. pap.
processed.
> "Intended to serve as a guide to the study and mastery of real
> estate principles and practices." Recommended as a workbook
> for REAL ESTATE PRINCIPLES AND PRACTICES, 5th ed. Ques-
> tions gathered in years of teaching real estate survey courses.

Spilker, John B. REAL ESTATE BUSINESS AS A PROFESSION, 3d rev. and
enl. ed. Cincinnati: John S. Kidd and Son, 1949. 524p. tables, diagrs.,
charts.
> Traces the history and evolution of the real estate business and
> its elevation to a professional level; licensing, real estate law,
> management, appraisal, investments, and housing. Part I: Prin-
> ciples and practice; Part II: Appraisal; Part III: Management;
> Part IV: Investments; Part V: Housing.

STANDARD COURSE IN REAL ESTATE Series. New York: Macmillan, 1924-
1927.
> Standard Course in Real Estate. Outlined by the Joint Com-
> mission Representing The National Association of Real Estate

PRINCIPLES AND PRACTICE (continued)

Boards, The United Y.M.C.A. Schools and the Institute for
Research in Land Economics and Public Utilities. Part of LAND
ECONOMICS SERIES, edited by Richard T. Ely.

Babcock, Frederick Morrison. THE APPRAISAL OF REAL ES-
TATE. 1924.

Clark, Horace F. and Chase, Frank A. ELEMENTS OF THE
MODERN BUILDING AND LOAN ASSOCIATIONS. 1925.

Ely, Richard T. and Morehouse, Edward W. ELEMENTS OF
THE LAND ECONOMICS. 1924.

Fisher, Ernest McKinley. PRINCIPLES OF REAL ESTATE PRAC-
TICE. 1926.

James, Harlean. LAND PLANNING IN THE UNITED STATES
FOR THE CITY, STATE AND NATION. 1926.

MacChesney, Nathan William. THE PRINCIPLES OF REAL ES-
TATE LAW; REAL PROPERTY, REAL ESTATE DOCUMENTS AND
TRANSACTIONS. 1927.

Nelson, Herbert U. THE ADMINISTRATION OF REAL ESTATE
BOARDS. 1925.

Unger, Maurice A. REAL ESTATE, PRINCIPLES AND PRACTICES, 2d ed. Cincinnati: South-Western Publishing Co., 1959. 710p. tables, diagrs., forms.
The economics of real property and the techniques of handling
real property transactions for practitioners, students of business administration, and consumers.

Van Buren, DeWitt. REAL ESTATE BROKERAGE AND COMMISSIONS - LAW
AND PRACTICE. New York: Prentice-Hall, 1948. 349p. forms.
The fundamental principles of land ownership and of agency.
Written as a text for real estate license applicants, real estate
attorneys, and practicing real estate men.

Vidger, Leonard P. SELECTED CASES AND PROBLEMS IN REAL ESTATE.
Belmont, Calif.: Wadsworth Publishing Co., 1963. 197p. tables. pap.
Forty-nine case problems on such real estate subjects as finance,
law, housing demand, and investment; presented to supplement
textbook study and discussion. References at end of each.

Weimer, Arthur M. and Hoyt, Homer. PRINCIPLES OF REAL ESTATE, 4th ed.
New York: Ronald Press, 1960. 716p.
An introduction to the study of real estate with stress on the
principles rather than practice. Emphasis on the decision-making process in the real estate business. Indicates the place of
real estate in the economy and the relationship of the real estate business to other areas of business administration.

Whitmer, Robert E.   Public Relations in the Real Estate Business.   p. 1380-
403 In Friedman, Edith J., ed. REAL ESTATE ENCYCLOPEDIA.   Englewood
Cliffs, N.J.: Prentice-Hall 1960.
>   Discusses real estate board membership, community service,
>   employee relations, the use of signs, and reproduces sample
>   letters.

ORGANIZATION AND MANAGEMENT

Branch Offices: Good or Bad?   MONEY MAKING IDEAS FROM FELLOW
REALTORS, No. 42, October 1961   (entire issue).
>   A collection of statements by Realtors on branch real estate
>   offices.

California Real Estate Association.   THE MODERN CONCEPT OF REAL ESTATE
ADMINISTRATION.   Los Angeles: 1958.   48p.   illus.   pap.
>   Written for 11th annual Educational and Sales Conference.
>   "To serve the Realtor who wishes to measure the value re-
>   ceived from each of the everyday costs of operating a real
>   estate brokerage office."

California Real Estate Association.   REAL ESTATE OFFICE MANAGEMENT.
Los Angeles: 117 West Ninth Street, zone 15, 1962. various paging.   tables,
charts, forms.   looseleaf.
>   Material collected and published for the Association's 1962
>   Real Estate Office Management Conference.   Section I: Plan-
>   ning your Real Estate Brokerage Operation; Section II: Plan-
>   ning your Real Estate Office Policies; Section III: Hiring
>   and Developing Qualified Real Estate Sales Personnel;   Section
>   IV: Developing Real Estate Office Systems and Procedures.

California Real Estate Association.   SELECTING, TRAINING, AND REDUCING
TURNOVER OF REAL ESTATE SALES PERSONNEL;   A SURVEY OF CURRENT
PRACTICES IN REAL ESTATE OFFICES IN CALIFORNIA, by Fred E. Case.
Los Angeles: 117 West Ninth Street, zone 15, 1957. 48p. charts, forms.   pap.
>   Presented by the Educational Committee at the 1957 Educational
>   and Sales Conferences.

California Real Estate Association.   SUCCESSFUL REAL ESTATE OFFICE POLI-
CIES AND PROCEDURES.   Los Angeles: 117 West Ninth Street, zone 15,
1959.   77p.   pap.
>   A guide for developing an office manual.   Includes personnel
>   practices for salaried and sales employees and policies on list-
>   ings, advertising, and selling.

ORGANIZATION AND MANAGEMENT (continued)

California Real Estate Association. YOU AND YOUR REAL ESTATE BUSINESS.
Los Angeles: 117 West Ninth Street, zone 15, 1959. 144p. tables, charts.
pap.
>Papers by sixteen Realtors on administrative and sales supervi-
>sion, organizational policy, and leadership.

Doris, Lillian, THE REAL ESTATE OFFICE SECRETARY'S HANDBOOK. New
York: Prentice-Hall, 1953. 430p. forms.
>A manual covering such general subjects as punctuation, tele-
>phone manners, and postal information and specialized real
>estate matters such as special files, typing real estate instru-
>ments, and assisting in various real estate activities.

Florida Association of Realtors. HOW TO SELECT GOOD SALESMEN. (Real
Estate Research Project No. 3). Orlando, Fla.: 1962. 35p. pap. processed.
>Concerned with the use of written intelligence, interest, and
>personality tests.

Hefti, Wilma C. HOW TO KEEP REAL ESTATE OFFICE RECORDS. Englewood
Cliffs, N.J.: Prentice-Hall, 1954. 178p. illus., forms.
>A guide for setting up an efficient system of records covering
>listings, advertising and prospects, closings, etc., and for
>analyzing records and statistics to increase business.

Hefti, Wilma C. REAL ESTATE OFFICE BOOKKEEPING SIMPLIFIED. Englewood Cliffs, N.J.: Prentice-Hall, 1958. 334p. tables, forms.
>A "guide for setting up a complete and comprehensive set of
>books in a real estate office ... how to prepare financial
>statements." Covers single and double-entry systems and trust
>accounts.

Hershman, Mendes. Form of Organization for Real Estate Activities. 45-76
In Friedman, Edith J., ed. REAL ESTATE ENCYCLOPEDIA. Englewood Cliffs,
N.J.: Prentice-Hall, 1960.
>Discusses single proprietorship, general and limited partnerships,
>corporations, joint ventures, and trusts; lists advantages, dis-
>advantages, and tax aspects of each.

How to Train New Salesmen. MONEY MAKING IDEAS FROM FELLOW
REALTORS, No. 22, October 1956 (Entire issue).
>A collection of statements by Realtors.

Institute of Real Estate Management. THE REAL ESTATE MANAGEMENT DE-
PARTMENT: HOW TO ESTABLISH AND OPERATE IT. Chicago: 1958. 135p.
forms.
>"Authoritative information on the implementation and operation
>of a management department within the framework of the general
>real estate organization." Sample forms: p. 96-135.

Ledig, Alma S., et al. MAKING MORE MONEY FROM YOUR REAL ESTATE

ORGANIZATION AND MANAGEMENT (continued)

PRACTICE; A NEW SIMPLIFIED SYSTEM FOR THE EFFICIENT AND COOR-
DINATED OPERATION OF YOUR REAL ESTATE OFFICE. Chicago: University
Printing Co., 1410 East 62nd Street, zone 37, 1955. 111p. illus., diagrs.,
forms.
> Records and accounting office systems and equipment, especially
> designed and integrated by the University Printing Company and
> the Shaw-Walker Company.

McMichael, Stanley L. HOW TO OPERATE A REAL ESTATE BUSINESS. Englewood Cliffs, N.J.: Prentice-Hall, 1947. 455p. tables, forms.
> A manual on establishing a real estate office and running it
> as an efficient business. Appendix includes forms, monthly
> payment tables, mensuration, etc.

Mandel, H. Robert. How to Operate an Appraisal Office. p. 806-35 In
Friedman, Edith J., ed. ENCYCLOPEDIA OF REAL ESTATE APPRAISING.
Englewood Cliffs, N.J.: Prentice-Hall, 1959.

Murray, Jean Grissom. The Modern Real Estate Office. p. 22-44 In Friedman, Edith J., ed. REAL ESTATE ENCYCLOPEDIA. Englewood Cliffs, N.J.:
Prentice-Hall, 1960.
> Discusses location factors, size and equipment of the office,
> personnel and departments, and office manuals.

National Association of Real Estate Boards. Department of Research. REAL
ESTATE SALESMEN: QUALIFICATIONS, COMPENSATION, ADVANCEMENT.
Washington, D.C.: 1962. 44p. pap. processed.

National Institute of Real Estate Brokers. EVERYDAY REAL ESTATE; OFFICE
FACILITIES, POLICIES, PROCEDURES AND PAPERWORK ARE IMPORTANT IN
EFFICIENT OPERATION OF BRANCH OFFICES, NEIGHBORHOOD AND SMALL-
ER-TOWN OFFICES. (Brokers Institute Bulletin Service). Chicago: 1959. 63p.
illus. pap.

National Institute of Real Estate Brokers. TRAINING AND FINANCING SALES-
MEN. (Brokers Institute Bulletin Service). Chicago: 1955. 63p. pap.

National Institute of Real Estate Brokers. THE MODERN BROKER'S OFFICE;
INSIDE STORY. (Brokers Institute Bulletin Service). Chicago: 1954. 63p.
illus. pap.
> Practices and procedures.

National Institute of Real Estate Brokers. OFFICE IDEAS AND PROCEDURES.
(Brokers Institute Bulletin Service). Chicago: 1950. 61p. illus. pap.
> Book Two of THIS BUSINESS OF REAL ESTATE.

National Institute of Real Estate Brokers. OFFICE PLANNING AND DESIGN.
(Brokers Institute Bulletin Service). Chicago: 1960. 63p. illus., plans. pap.
> Cover note: with more than 150 photos and floor plans.

ORGANIZATION AND MANAGEMENT (continued)

National Institute of Real Estate Brokers. OFFICE POLICIES AND PROCEDURES. (Brokers Institute Bulletin Service). Chicago: 1959. 63p. illus. pap.
"Selected examples of rules covering specific problems and situations as well as the daily routine of the real estate profession." Reprinted from policy books of real estate brokers.

National Institute of Real Estate Brokers. OPERATING PROCEDURES OF A SMALL REAL ESTATE OFFICE. (Brokers Institute Bulletin Service). Chicago: 1948. 57p. illus. pap.

National Institute of Real Estate Brokers. SALES MEETINGS. (Brokers Institute Bulletin Service). Chicago: 1951. 46p. illus. pap.
Miami Beach Sales Meeting panel; sales contests, bonus plans, panel meetings procedures.

National Institute of Real Estate Brokers. SELECTION AND TRAINING OF SALESMEN. (Brokers Institute Bulletin Service). Chicago: 1961. 63p. illus. pap.

National Institute of Real Estate Brokers. TESTED TALKS FOR SALES MEETINGS. (Brokers Institute Bulletin Service). Chicago: 1957. 63p. illus. pap.

National Institute of Real Estate Brokers. International Traders Club. TRADE OFFICE SYSTEMS AND PROCEDURES. Chicago: 1960. 36p. forms. pap. processed.
Information on filing systems, salesmen's training, etc.

Pension and Profit Sharing Plans. MONEY MAKING IDEAS FROM FELLOW REALTORS, no. 41, July 1961 (entire issue).
A collection of statements by Realtors on two forms of benefits for real estate salesmen and office personnel.

Real Estate Salesmen's and Managers' Surveys. Reported in the Yearbook of Real Estate Management, the December issue of BUILDINGS magazine.

Ryan, W. J. "Insurance in the Real Estate Office." p. 1330-364 In Friedman, Edith J., ed. REAL ESTATE ENCYCLOPEDIA. Englewood Cliffs, N.J.: Prentice-Hall. 1960.

Setting up an Exchange Department in Your Office. p. 79-91 In National Institute of Real Estate Brokers. REAL ESTATE TRADER'S HANDBOOK. 1st rev. ed. Chicago: 1956. 152p.

Smith, Ray. REAL ESTATE BROKER'S OPERATING HANDBOOK. Dayton, Ohio: Real Estate Broker's Digest Service, 3114 East 3rd Street, zone 3, 1958. 288p. illus. charts, forms.
A handbook on real estate office operations covering such topics as staff selection and training, sales management, salesman compensation, and policy books.

ORGANIZATION AND MANAGEMENT (continued)

U. S. Department of Commerce. Bureau of Foreign and Domestic Commerce. ESTABLISHING AND OPERATING A REAL ESTATE AND INSURANCE BROKER-AGE BUSINESS, by Warreb F. Hickernell, et al. (Industrial Small Business Series No. 26). Washington, D.C.: Government Printing Office, 1946. 137p. illus., tables. pap.
> Includes chapters on forms of organization, budgeting for capital requirements, and licensing. Originally as a U.S. War Department Education Manual.

VOCATIONAL OUTLOOK AND GUIDANCE

Chronicle Guidance Publications. REAL ESTATE SALESMAN. (Chronicle Occupational Briefs No. 55R; 1-63-10). Moravia, N.Y.: 1958. 4p. illus. pap.
> A vocational guidance pamphlet prepared principally for use at the high school level.

Durst, Seymour B. and Stern, Walter H. YOUR FUTURE IN REAL ESTATE. (Careers in Depth Series). New York: Richard Rosen Associates, 1960. 159p.
> Describes the various branches of the real estate business and provides a check list for self-evaluation.

Headington, Robert C. REAL ESTATE MANAGEMENT — POTENTIAL CAREER FIELD. (Arizona Business Bulletin, vol. 8, No. 9). Temple: Bureau of Business Services, Arizona State University, 1961. p. 1-6. pap.

Institute for Research. REAL ESTATE AND INSURANCE BUSINESS AS A CAREER. 537 South Dearborn Street, zone 5, 1960. 24p. pap.

U. S. Bureau of Labor Statistics. EMPLOYMENT OUTLOOK FOR INSURANCE AND REAL ESTATE AGENTS AND BROKERS. (Occupational Outlook Report Series). Washington, D.C.: Government Printing Office, 1961. 10p. illus. pap.
> Reprint of 301-10 of the 1961 OCCUPATIONAL OUTLOOK HANDBOOK, (Bulletin No. 1300-50).

National Association of Real Estate Boards. THE CHALLENGE OF REAL ESTATE; YOUR CHANCES FOR SERVICE AND PROFIT IN A DYNAMIC FIELD, prepared by the Department of Public Relations in conjunction with the Department of Education. Chicago: 1959. 24p. illus. pap.
> Outlines the career possibilities in the various branches of real estate; discusses education and the real estate man in his community.

National Association of Real Estate Boards. PREPARING FOR THE REAL ESTATE BUSINESS. Chicago: 1950. 4p. pap. processed.

VOCATIONAL OUTLOOK AND GUIDANCE (continued)

National Association of Real Estate Boards. REAL ESTATE: A CAREER WITH
A BRIGHT FUTURE, by John G. Davis. Chicago: 1962. 4p. pap. processed.
>   Reprinted from the February 1962 issue of the JOURNAL OF
>   COLLEGE PLACEMENT.

National Association of Real Estate Boards. Department of Public Relations.
THE REALTOR JUNIOR PROGRAM FOR YOUR BOARD; A CONTINUING
STORY OF GROWING BENEFITS. Washington, D.C.: no date. 4p. pap.
>   "A method of acquainting high school students with the real
>   estate calling and Realtors."

Science Research Associates, Inc. REAL ESTATE AGENTS; CAREER PROSPECTS
FOR REAL ESTATE AGENTS ARE GOOD FOR THOSE WILLING TO WORK ON
COMMISSION AND MEET TOUGH COMPETITION. (Occupational Brief No.
169). Chicago: 1961. 4p. illus. pap.

Women's Council of the National Association of Real Estate Boards Committee
on Education. THE STATUS OF WOMEN IN REAL ESTATE. Chicago: 1962.
19p. tables. pap. processed.
>   Based on a survey by 1959 Standing Committee on Education,
>   Beryl McClaskey, Chairman. Role of women in the real estate
>   business. Characteristics of brokers and saleswomen: age,
>   marital status, education, income, size of office, training,
>   qualifications and attitude.

REAL ESTATE BOARDS

Bouma, Donald Herbert. AN ANALYSIS OF THE SOCIAL POWER POSITION
OF THE REAL ESTATE BOARD IN GRAND RAPIDS, MICHIGAN. Unpublished
Ph.D. thesis, Michigan State College of Agriculture and Applied Science,
1952.

California Real Estate Association. BOARD OFFICERS' INFORMATION AND
PLANNING MANUAL. Los Angeles: 117 West Ninth Street, zone 15, no
date. n.p. illus. pap. processed.

California Real Estate Association. MANUAL OF PROCEDURE FOR LOCAL
REAL ESTATE BOARDS AND LOCAL BOARD OFFICERS IN RELATIONSHIP TO
THE CALIFORNIA REAL ESTATE ASSOCIATION AND NATIONAL ASSOCIATION
OF REAL ESTATE BOARDS, comp. and ed. by Eugene P. Conser. Los Angeles:
117 West Ninth Street, zone 15, 1955. 70p. pap. looseleaf.
>   Revised pages issued periodically.

Detroit Real Estate Board. A SURVEY OF FUNCTIONS, SERVICES, FINANCING,

REAL ESTATE BOARDS (continued)

STAFFING OF THE TWELVE LARGEST STATE ASSOCIATIONS OF REALTOR BOARDS, WITH COMPARATIVE TABLES, EXPLANATIONS. Detroit: 1957. various paging. tables. pap. processed.

Executive Officers Council of the National Association of Real Estate Boards. BASIC OPERATING POLICIES OF REAL ESTATE BOARDS. Chicago: 1962. 38p. tables. pap.
> Cover note: A COMPLETE COMPILATION OF INFORMATION OBTAINED IN 1960 AND 1961 SURVEYS OF MORE THAN 300 REAL ESTATE BOARDS OF ALL SIZES.

Executive Officers Council of the National Association of Real Estate Boards. BOARD-OWNED OFFICE HEADQUARTERS. Chicago: 1957. 40p. pap. processed.
> 34 boards and state associations. Comparison of costs for construction or purchase, yearly operating costs, physical description, floor plans, method of financing.

Executive Officers Council of the National Association of Real Estate Boards. EXTENSION COURSE IN REAL ESTATE BOARD ADMINISTRATION, 16 vols. Chicago: 1960.
> Home study course consisting of 16 lessons, sent on weekly basis. Some of the topics covered: Constitution and by-laws, fiscal management, Written communications, Servicing your members, The care and feeding of problem members. Enrollment limited to volunteer secretaries and paid employees of local boards and state associations.

Executive Officers Council of the National Association of Real Estate Boards. WHO'S WHO IN THE EXECUTIVE OFFICER'S COUNCIL. Chicago.
> Data on type of executive officers (volunteer or paid), number of board members in different categories, phone, address, whether or not the board has multiple listing service. Issued annually.

Foy, Frank J. REPORT ON OVERSEAS FACT FINDING TOUR, 1960, 3 vols. Victoria, Australia: Real Estate and Stock Institute of Victoria, 1961. pap. processed.
> Title on cover: Real Estate Administration Overseas; Fact Finding Tour, November and December 1960. By the General Secretary Real Estate and Stock Institute of Victoria and the Real Estate and Stock Institute of Australia. Close study of six local boards, two state associations and the Federation in the United States, Great Britain and Canada. Vol. 3 cover title: Real Estate Administration Overseas, Fact Finding Tour on Multiple Listing.

National Association of Real Estate Boards. COMMENTARIES ON THE CODE OF ETHICS, by Eugene P. Conser. Chicago: 1959. 36p. pap. processed.
> Originally published in REALTOR'S HEADLINES in 1958 and 1959.

REAL ESTATE BOARDS (continued)

National Association of Real Estate Boards. OFFICIAL ROSTER OF REALTORS.
Cedar Rapids, Iowa: Stamats Publishing Co.
> Published annually as a special issue of BUILDINGS mag-
> azine. Lists the constituent boards in a geographical
> arrangement, with names and addresses of all Realtor members.
> Includes a list of the state associations with addresses. Prior
> to 1959 the roster was printed in NATIONAL REAL ESTATE
> AND BUILDING JOURNAL.

National Association of Real Estate Boards. REAL ESTATE BOARDS IN ACTION,
by Margaret E. M. McKinney. Chicago: 1948. 118p. illus. pap.
> The main services, programs and methods of various boards:
> Administration, public relations and publicity, advertising, in-
> formation sources, education and technical.

National Association of Real Estate Boards. WHAT REAL ESTATE BOARDS ARE
DOING, 2d ed.   Chicago: 1942. 218p. pap. processed.

National Association of Real Estate Boards. WHAT STATE ASSOCIATIONS
ARE DOING, prepared by Carrie Maude Jones. Chicago: 1937. 113p. pap.
processed.
> Structure and activities. Speeches included as well: Admin-
> istration of a State Real Estate Association by Glenn D. Willa-
> man; New Activities of State Associations by Carrie Maude
> Jones.

National Association of Real Estate Boards. Committee on Multiple Listing Policy.
MULTIPLE LISTING SERVICE. Chicago: 1959. 7p. pap. processed.
> Steps to take in setting up a multiple listing service, recom-
> mended policies, procedure for merging as MLS operation into
> a service of a real estate board, suggested by-law amendments,
> Model set of rules and regulations.

National Association of Real Estate Boards. Committee on Professional Standards.
INTERPRETATIONS OF THE CODE OF ETHICS. Washington, D.C. 1963. 206p.
> "Presented to member boards of the National Association of
> Real Estate Boards as a guide in reaching proper decisions
> when applying the Code of Ethics to situations that may arise
> within the respective boards." Relates to ethical standards of
> the Realtor as distinguished from requirements of the law.

National Association of Real Estate Boards. Department of Field Services.
HELPFUL INFORMATION FOR SMALLER BOARDS. Chicago: 1961. various
paging. pap. processed.

National Association of Real Estate Boards. Department of Public Relations.
PUBLIC RELATIONS OF THE REAL ESTATE BOARD. Washington, D.C.: no
date. 12p. pap.
> Outlines three major objectives and provides suggestions for
> furthering these programs.

REAL ESTATE BOARDS (continued)

National Association of Real Estate Boards. General Counsel. SUGESTED BY-LAWS FOR A BOARD OF REALTORS. Chicago: 1962. 11p. pap. processed.
Latest revision.

National Association of Real Estate Boards. State Associations Committee. BASIC OPERATING POLICIES OF STATE ASSOCIATIONS, 2 pts. Chicago: 1961-1962. pap. processed.
State association replies to Executive Officer's Council survey; Basic operating Policies of Real Estate Boards.

National Association of Real Estate Boards State Associations Committee. SUGGESTED MODEL STATE ASSOCIATION BY-LAWS. Chicago: 1961. 6p. pap. processed.

National Association of Real Estate Boards. State Associations Department. THE STATE ASSOCIATION PROGRAM - WHAT? WHY? HOW? by William H. Lippold, Jr. Chicago: 1961. 10p. pap. processed.

National Real Estate Association. PROCEEDINGS OF THE FIRST ANNUAL MEETING HELD AT NASHVILLE, TENN. FEBRUARY 17, 18 AND 19, 1892. no date. 196p. pap.
Officers, members, constitution and by laws included.

Nelson, Herbert U. THE ADMINISTRATION OF REAL ESTATE BOARDS. (Land Economics Series; Standard Course in Real Estate). New York: Macmillan, 1925. 255p.
A classic in the literature of organized real estate.

Phoenix Real Estate Board, Inc. MIRROR OF JUSTICE, by W.J.B. Schimfessel. Phoenix: 1958. 178p.
Enforcement of the NAREB Code of Ethics by the Court of Ethics of the Phoenix Board "Vested with the authority of determining questions and conduct of the Board's members related to the by-laws or ethical standards and in connection with a specific act or case." Bulk of the book devoted to the decisions of the court.

Phoenix Real Estate Board, Inc. YOU ASKED THE QUESTION, by W.J.B. Schimfessel. Phoenix: 1960. 69p. pap.
Answers to questions on arbitration matters and ethical practice submitted to the Phoenix Board following the publication of MIRROR OF JUSTICE.

Real Estate Boards—Periodicals
(See Appendix for complete information concerning these publications.)

MULTIPLE LISTING DIGESTAIRE, WHAT REAL ESTATE BOARDS ARE DOING, NOTES FROM THE IDEA LABORATORY, REALTOR'S HEADLINES.

EDUCATION

National Association of Real Estate Boards. Committee on Education. SUG-GESTED INDOCTRINATION COURSE FOR NEW AND/OR PROSPECTIVE MEM-BERS OF A REAL ESTATE BOARD. Chicago: 1959. folder. pap.
"To acquaint the new and/or prospective members with his obligations to the board and the board's obligation to him."

National Association of Real Estate Boards. Department of Ecucation. COURSES IN REAL ESTATE AVAILABLE THROUGH THE EXTENSION FACILITIES OF UNI-VERSITIES AND COLLEGES (NOT FOR COLLEGE CREDIT) — AS REPORTED ... MARCH–MAY 1962. Chicago, 1962. 11p. pap. processed.

National Association of Real Estate Boards. Department of Education. PLACE-MENT BULLETIN. Chicago: 1957-   . pap. processed.
On cover: Containing the names and qualifications of young persons graduating from universities and colleges throughout the country who have successfully completed courses in real estate and are now prepared to commence their life work in the real estate field. The students have not been interviewed by the NAREB Department of Education, but rather have been referred to the Department by the real estate instructors at the various universities and/or colleges. Issued annually in March.

National Association of Real Estate Boards. Department of Education. STUDY OF REAL ESTATE COURSES OFFERED FOR COLLEGE CREDIT AT UNIVERSITIES AND COLLEGES THROUGHOUT THE U.S. Chicago: 1961. 46p. pap. processed.
Geographic listing of universities with courses, credit hours, texts, instruction by faculty or guest lectures, major field leading to a bachelor degree, graduate study, scholarship funds available.

National Association of Real Estate Boards. Department of Education. UNI-VERSITIES AND COLLEGES OFFERING CORRESPONDENCE COURSES. Chicago: 1960. 1p. pap. processed.
From National University Extension Association GUIDE TO CORRESPONDENCE STUDY, 1960 ed.

National Association of Real Estate Boards. Department of Education. UNI-VERSITIES AND COLLEGES OFFERING REAL ESTATE COURSES FOR COLLEGE CREDIT (AS REPORTED TO THE NATIONAL ASSOCIATION OF REAL ESTATE

EDUCATION (continued)

BOARDS). Chicago. 6p. pap. processed.

National Home Study Council. THE HOME STUDY BLUE BOOK AND DIREC-
TORY OF APPROVED PRIVATE HOME STUDY SCHOOLS AND COURSES MEET-
ING STANDARDS OF THE NATIONAL HOME STUDY COUNCIL, Washington,
D.C..

National University Extension Association. Division of Correspondence Study.
A GUIDE TO CORRESPONDENCE STUDY IN COLLEGES AND UNIVERSITIES.
Minneapolis: 1960. 35p. pap.
> Lists colleges and universities offering approved credit and
> noncredit correspondence courses in real estate principles and
> law, appraisal, land economics, property insurance. Revised
> every two or three years.

Section 3

APPRAISAL

American Institute of Real Estate Appraisers. THE APPRAISAL OF REAL ESTATE, 3rd ed. Chicago: 1960. 475p.
> Basic text on appraisal.

American Institute of Real Estate Appraisers. THE APPRAISAL OF REAL ESTATE SYLLABUS FOR REAL ESTATE APPRAISAL 1, INCLUDING STUDY AIDS AND RELATED MATERIAL, Rev. ed. Chicago: 1953. 80p. pap.
> "Written for students as well as for teachers ... developed primarily for use in the Institute's Course, Real Estate Appraisal 1." Revision by Robert L. Free now in preparation.

American Institute of Real Estate Appraisers. APPRAISAL REPORTING TECHNIQUES, 4 vols. Chicago: 1947-1954.
> "Illustrative appraisal reports ... on types of property most commonly the subject of appraisal assignments." Actual reports with property identification deleted.

American Institute of Real Estate Appraisers. APPRAISAL TERMINOLOGY AND HANDBOOK, 4th ed. Chicago: 1962. 254p.

American Institute of Real Estate Appraisers. COMPARATIVE STUDY OF NEW AND OLD OFFICE BUILDINGS. Chicago: (in preparation).
> Cooperative study with the National Association of Building Owners and Managers.

American Institute of Real Estate Appraisers. DEMONSTRATION APPRAISAL REPORTS, 3 vols. in 1, prepared by Students in Case–Study Courses conducted by the American Institute of Real Estate Appraisers. Chicago: 1957. 368p.
> Section 1: Single-family dwellings; Section II: Apartment building properties; Section III: Retail store properties. With critical comments by M.A.I.s.

American Institute of Real Estate Appraisers. A DIGEST OF REAL ESTATE APPRAISAL STANDARDS AND PRACTICES OF GOVERNMENTAL AGENCIES. Chicago: 1954. 351. pap. processed.
> Federal, state and local.

American Institute of Real Estate Appraisers. ECONOMIC FACTORS AND CASE STUDIES IN HOTEL AND MOTEL VALUATION, by Fred W. Eckert. Chicago: 1962. 86p. tables, charts. pap.

Grant from the Research and Education Trust Fund of the Institute. The Hotel and Motel Industry; Significance of Business
Trends; Projecting Earnings Potentials; Rate of Capitalization of
Earnings and Estimating Economic Values; Useful Lives of Hotels
and Motels; Case Studies in Hotel and Motel Valuation.

American Institute of Real Estate Appraisers. 101 RURAL APPRAISAL PROB-
LEMS WITH SUGGESTED SOLUTIONS, comp. by Walter F. Wilmette. Chicago:
1958. 76p. pap. processed.
Problems for use in the Institute's Case Study Course.

American Institute of Real Estate Appraisers. PROBLEMS IN URBAN REAL ES-
TATE APPRAISAL WITH SUGGESTED SOLUTIONS, 3rd ed. Chicago: 1963.
194p. tables, diagrs.
Problems for use in the Institute's Case Study Course II. Previous editions 1954 and 1956.

American Institute of Real Estate Appraisers. REAL ESTATE APPRAISAL PRAC-
TICE. Chicago: 1958. 694p.
Papers from the Silver Anniversary Conference of the Institute,
"devoted to fundamental principles and their application in the
appraisal of specific types of real property."

American Institute of Real Estate Appraisers. TEN CASE STUDIES OF SALES
OF LARGE REAL ESTATE INVESTMENT PROPERTIES, Rev. ed. Chicago: 1960.
47p. pap.
Included: from Casey, William J. TAX SHELTER IN REAL
ESTATE. 2d ed. New York: Institute for Business Planning,
1959. Chapter XII: How to Handle Depreciation p. 25-41;
prepared by Mortgage Bankers Association of America, Tax
Treatment of Real Estate Investment Trusts, p. 42-7.

American Society of Appraisers. APPRAISAL AND VALUATION MANUAL.
Washington, D.C.: 1955--.
Annual compilation of technical articles as well as official
Society information. Includes personal and real property.

Appraisal Institute of Canada. APPRAISAL REFERENCE MANUAL, 3rd ed.
Winnipeg, Manitoba: 1962. processed. looseleaf.
The official text of the Institute, designed to accommodate
future publications and additional material. Includes problems
and answers.

Appraisal Institute of Canada. DEMONSTRATION APPRAISAL REPORT GUIDE
ON RURAL PROPERTY. Winnipeg, Manitoba: 1959. 31p. pap.
Outline. "Fairly board coverage of farm appraisal reporting
particularly in connection with grain farms."

Appraisal Institute of Canada. ELEMENTS OF LAW FOR APPRAISERS. Winnipeg, Manitoba: 1960. 60p. pap.
> Central Mortgage and Housing Corporation appraisal training
> program lectures and articles from the APPRAISAL INSTITUTE
> MAGAZINE.

Appraisal Institute of Canada. MANUAL OF APPRAISAL FORMS. Winnipeg, Manitoba: 1961. 50p. pap.

Appraisal Institute of Canada. RURAL APPRAISING IN CANADA, by Ted L. Townsend. Winnipeg, Manitoba: 1962. 41p. pap.

Appraising. Section 5 In PRENTICE-HALL REAL ESTATE GUIDE. Englewood Cliffs, N.J.: Prentice-Hall, 1953--.
> General appraisal principles and practices approached from the
> broker's viewpoint; emphasis on residential property. Subsections
> on appraisal of specific property types; subdivisions, apartment
> and office buildings, stores and shopping centers, hotels and
> motels, industrial property and parks, rural property, leaseholds
> and special purpose properties.

Arnold, Ray H. HOW TO ESTIMATE MARKET VALUE IN SELLING REAL ESTATE. Englewood Cliffs, N.J.: Prentice-Hall, 1962. 250p.

Babcock, Frederick M. THE APPRAISAL OF REAL ESTATE. (Land Economics Series: Standard Course in Real Estate). New York: Macmillan, 1924. 380p. illus., tables.

Babcock, Frederick M. THE VALUATION OF REAL ESTATE. New York: McGraw-Hill, 1932. 593p.
> "Commences with a survey of the economic background of real
> estate values, develops a valuation theory, and concludes by
> particularizing and applying the theory to the solution of prac-
> tical valuation problems."

Bloom, George Frederick. THE APPRAISAL DATA PLANT. Unpublished Ph.D. thesis, Indiana University, 1953.
> Appraisal data plants of five members of the American Institute
> of Real Estate Appraisers examined in detail. Need for research
> on the subject raised by the Institute. Developed from: question-
> aires returned by 40% of the M.A.I.s; interviews; reports, letters,
> forms and related information from appraisers; and published in-
> formation.

Boeckh, E.H., and Associates. BOECKH INDEX CALCULATOR, TABLES FOR COMPUTING BOECKH BUILDING COST LOCAL INDEX NUMBERS, Rev. ed. Washington, D.C.: 1951. 64p. pap.
> "Provides the means of determining local cost conversion factors
> or indexes for areas not published in BUILDING COSTS."

Boeckh, E.H., and Associates. BOECKH'S MANUAL OF APPRAISALS, 6th ed., enl. and rev. Washington, D.C.: 1963. 1056p. Illu illus., tables.
> "Designed to furnish the present sound value of buildings, that

is Reproduction cost run on the basis of building costs at local prices at the time the appraisal is made, less depreciation and obsolescence." Three hundred different types of buildings with almost seven hundred variations in specifications and thirteen hundred base price tables providing one hundred thousand individual square and cubic foot costs. A schedule of corrective factors follows each base price table for deviation. Inspection and Appraisal Report Work Sheets provided. New edition in preparation. Base numbers for Boeckh's construction cost index changed in sixth edition to conform to those used by Federal government.

Boeckh, E.H., and Associates. STUDIES IN RELATIVE CONSTRUCTION COSTS. Washington, D.C.
"A specific historical index series for the major pricing areas of the United States and Canada. These index series are essential for cost-trending known costs of some prior date to a reproduction cost in today's market."

Bonbright, James C. THE VALUATION OF PROPERTY; A TREATISE ON THE APPRAISAL OF PROPERTY FOR DIFFERENT LEGAL PURPOSES, 2 vols. New York: McGraw-Hill, 1937. 1271p.
Published under the auspices of the Columbia University Council for Research in the Social Sciences. Concepts of value, Valuation for tax insurance, Eminent domain, Public utility, Mortgage and stock purposes.

Building Costs of a Thirty-Family Brick Apartment House Built in St. Louis. REAL ESTATE ANALYST REAL ESTATE TRENDS BULLETIN.
Annual. Cites costs of material, labor and overhead, 1913-- date on a quarterly basis.

California. University. Real Estate Research Program. ADVANCED REAL ESTATE APPRAISAL--RURAL X489; A SYLLABUS, prepared for University Extension by J. Herbert Snyder, et al. Berkeley: 1958. 103p. pap. processed.

Chapman, Herman H. FOREST VALUATION; WITH SPECIAL EMPHASIS ON BASIC ECONOMIC PRINCIPLES. New York: McGraw-Hill, 1947. 521p. tables.
Successor to FOREST VALUATION, 1925, and FOREST FINANCE, 1935.

Cherney, Richard A. APPRAISAL AND ASSESSMENT DICTIONARY. Englewood Cliffs, N.J.: Prentice-Hall, 1960. 337p.

Cleminshaw, J.M., and Company. THE APPRAISERS MANUAL, 3rd ed. Cleveland: 1601 Brookpark Road, zone 9, 1956. 298p. illus., charts.
Handbook of building costs. Supplement with a national building cost index.

Collier, Ronald. VALUATION FOR WAR DAMAGE AND TOWN PLANNING COMPENSATION. London: Butterworth, 1945. 354p.
> Reprinted from BUTTERWORTHS' EMERGENCY LEGISLATION SERVICE.

Cost Survey for a Standard Six-Room Frame House. REAL ESTATE ANALYST APPRAISAL BULLETIN.
> Annual. Construction costs for 236 American and 9 Canadian cities including total labor cost, total material cost, overhead total cost, cost per square foot, and cubic foot; also prices per cubic foot of space for: six-room frame, five-room brick Veneer, six-room brick, six-room California bungalow, and brick ranch.

Crouse, Earl F. and Everett, Charles H. RURAL APPRAISALS. Englewood Cliffs, N.J.: Prentice-Hall, 1956. 531p. illus., tables.
> The "American Rural Appraisal System" of the American Society of Farm Managers and Rural Appraisers.

A Description of the Cost Indexes and How to Use them. ENGINEERING NEWS-RECORD, vol. 168, No. 12, March 22, 1962, p. 79-82,

F.W. Dodge Corp. DOW BUILDING COST CALCULATOR AND VALUATION GUIDE. New York: 1959. various paging. tables. looseleaf, quarterly supplements.
> Contains a photograph and brief descriptions of buildings citing a base cost which excluded costs involved in site problems, profit rates and builder competition with base costs then adjusted to specific areas. Includes local cost multipliers, one for general purpose appraising, another for estimating for fire insurance. Indexes of historical costs, 1947--date, indexes for public utitlities, and machinery and building depreciation tables.

Frenzell, E.H. PROBLEMS RELATING TO THE APPRAISAL OF FARM LANDS IN CALIFORNIA. Sacramento, Calif.: 1957. 73p. pap. processed.
> To illustrate techniques for appraisal for condemnation purposes in California.

Friedman, Edith J., ed. ENCYCLOPEDIA OF REAL ESTATE APPRAISING. Englewood Cliffs, N.J.: Prentice-Hall, 1959. 890p.
> Part I: Appraisal theory and process; Part II: Appraisal of specific types of property; Part III: Appraisal of specialized property; Part IV: Special branches of appraisal practice; Part V: Appraisal as a business or profession.

Grant, Eugene L. and Norton, Paul T. DEPRECIATION. New York: Ronald Press, 1949. 472p.

Gunning, Walter E. A COMPARISON OF REAL ESTATE VALUATION IN GREAT BRITAIN AND THE UNITED STATES. Unpublished Ph.D. thesis. New

York University, 1959.

How to Appraise Real Property. Part VIII, p. 855-938 In Friedman, Edith J., ed. REAL ESTATE ENCYCLOPEDIA. Englewood Cliffs, N.J.: Prentice-Hall, 1960.
> Chapter 33: The Appraisal Process, by R.M. Fleshman; Chapter 34: Employment of Appraiser, by Harry R. Fenton; Chapter 35: Testifying as an Expert Appraiser, by Carroll Wright; Chapter 36: Appraisal for Tax Assessments, by Ernest H. Johnson.

International Association of Assessing Officers. ASSESSMENT AND APPRAISAL OF SHOPPING CENTERS; A SELECTED SERIES ON THE SUBJECT, BY EIGHT LEADING ASSESSING OFFICERS. Chicago: 1957. 47p. pap. processed.

Joint Committee on Building Costs of the Chicago Chapter of the American Institute of Architects and Appraisers Division, Chicago Real Estate Board. BUILDING COST MANUAL. New York: John Wiley, 1957. 367p. illus., tables.
> Cites overall costs, cubic and square foot costs, direct expenses for materials, labor and equipment. Local cost index for 21 cities, section on how to cube a building, information for building types with photo and description and unit cost.

Kingsbury, Laura M. THE ECONOMICS OF HOUSING AS PRESENTED BY ECONOMISTS, APPRAISERS, AND OTHER EVALUATING GROUPS. Morningside Heights, New York: King's Crown Press, 1946. 177p. pap.
> "Economic theory, so the present writer believes, should 'come down to earth' and make connection with measurable data, if it is to be either practically useful or aesthetically valid." Valuation by representative economists and valuation by the practical groups: appraisers, accountants and other groups--tax assessors, architects, housing managers, and the governmental public housing agencies.

Knowles, Jerome, Jr. and Pervear, John E. REAL ESTATE APPRAISAL MANUAL. Northeast Harbor, Maine: Jerome Knowles, Jr. and Associates, 1957. 227p. illus., tables.
> Handbook and cost estimating system providing square foot costs with adjustment factors for four grades of quality. Includes unusual shape lot tables, unit in place costs, general and structural additions, residential, small commercial, camp, cottage and motel, and miscellaneous buildings.

Kuehnle, Walter R. VALUATION OF REAL ESTATE FOR AD VALOREM TAX PURPOSES. Chicago: 22 West Monroe Street, zone 3, 1954. 66p. pap.
> "Describes a scientific approach to a mass appraisal of value and indicates internal administrative controls which tend to keep the entire assessment machinery in satisfactory working condition." Reprinted from the APPRAISAL JOURNAL, vol. 21, no. 1, 2, 3, and 4, January, April, July, and October, 1953.

Louie, Charles. DEPRECIATION. Prepared for American Institute of Real
Estate Appraisers Research Committee. 1959. 49p. typewritten.
"Attempts to evaluate the validity and usefulness of the dep-
reciation concepts employed within the theoretical framework
of the three approaches to valuation."
Two articles based on the study appeared in the APPRAISAL
JOURNAL, vol. 29, no. 4, October, 1961, p. 40-7; vol. 30,
no. 1, January, 1962, p. 507-16.

Marshall and Stevens Company. MARSHALL VALUATION SERVICE; RAPID
METHOD OF COMPUTING APPROXIMATE BUILDING VALUES. Los Angeles:
1645 Beverly Boulevard, zone 36, 1951-   illus., tables. looseleaf, monthly supplements.
Has separate manuals for eastern, central and western areas.
Four classes of building based on exterior walls, interior finish,
floors, fittings. Has cubic and square foot costs which may be
adjusted for variation from standard types by use of segregated
cost section which includes costs of wide variety of items.
Indexes for each major city and updating in these cities from
1930. Includes depreciation tables, assessor's multipliers.

Marshall and Stevens Company. RESIDENTIAL COST HANDBOOK; RAPID
METHOD OF COMPUTING RESIDENCE COSTS. Los Angeles: 1645 Beverly
Boulevard, zone 6, 1961-   . illus. looseleaf, quarterly supplements.

Marshall and Stevens Company. STEVENS VALUATION QUARTERLY. Los
Angeles: 1645 Beverly Boulevard, zone 6, 1959-   . illus., tables. Quarterly supplements.
Gives total costs per square foot on basis of four classes of
construction, cites variation adjustments for exterior wall, heating and cooling, sprinklers and elevators. Additive cost section
buildings. A unit-in-place section gives costs which may be
used with either the spot cost or additive cost section. Has
annuity and depreciation tables, index for adjusting for locale
on basis of major cities.

Marston, Anson, et al. ENGINEERING VALUATION AND DEPRECIATION,
2d ed. New York: McGraw-Hill, 1953. 508p.
"Is a discussion of the art of the appraisal of industrial property."

May, Arthur A. THE VALUATION OF RESIDENTIAL REAL ESTATE, 2d ed.
Englewood Cliffs, N.J.: Prentice-Hall, 1953. 286p.

McMichael, Stanley L. McMICHAEL'S APPRAISING MANUAL; A REAL ESTATE
APPRAISING HANDBOOK FOR USE IN FIELD WORK AND ADVANCED STUDY
COURSES, 4th ed. New York: Prentice-Hall, 1951. 731p.
Appraisal of Specific property types and handbook information.

Means, Robert Snow. BUILDING CONSTRUCTION COSTS DATA. Duxbury,

Mass.: 1943. various paging. pap. processed.
Annual. "Aimed primarily at industrial and commercial buildings costing $50,000 and up, or large housing projects."

Medici, Guiseppe. PRINCIPLES OF APPRAISAL. Ames: Iowa State College
Press, 1953. 254p.
Author is Head, Department of Appraisal, University of Naples.
"English translation of portions of the widely-read Italian book,
PRINCIPII DI ESTIMO." Farm lands.

Murray, J.F.N. PRINCIPLES AND PRACTICES OF VALUATION 3rd ed.
Sydney, Australia: Commonwealth Institute of Valuers, 1954. 475p.

Murray, William G. FARM APPRAISAL AND VALUATION, 4th ed. Ames:
Iowa State University Press, 1961. 433p.

NATIONAL APPRAISAL FORUM. WASHINGTON, D.C., NOVEMBER, 1937.
PROCEEDINGS OF THE GENERAL SESSIONS AND URBAN GROUP MEETINGS,
HELD UNDER THE AUSPICES OF THE JOINT COMMITTEE ON APPRAISAL AND
MORTGAGE ANALYSIS. Washington, D.C.: Central Housing Committee, 1937.
117p. pap. processed.
Appraisal data and its use. The DuBois, Hasse and Porter cat-
alogs were developed for the Forum. The Agricultural Economics
Bibliography, no. 60, was distributed as well to those attending
the Forum.
The Joint Committee was launched in 1937 by the Central Housing Coordinator. Their main purpose was the assembling, classifying and dissemination of information with respect to sources of
data.

NATIONAL APPRAISAL FORUM. WASHINGTON, D.C., NOVEMBER, 1937.
PROCEEDINGS OF THE RURAL GROUP SESSIONS HELD UNDER THE AUSPICES
OF THE JOINT COMMITTEE ON APPRAISAL AND MORTGAGE ANALYSIS.
Washington, D.C.: Central Housing Committee, 1938. 84p. pap. processed.
Compiled by L.G. Porter.

National Association of Real Estate Boards. INTRODUCTION TO REAL ESTATE
APPRAISALS, IN PREPARATION FOR THE CASE-STUDY COURSES OF THE AMER-
ICAN INSTITUTE OF REAL ESTATE APPRAISERS; LECTURE OUTLINES. Chicago:
1961. 76p. pap. processed.
On Cover: Set of Sixteen Lecture Outlines Distributed by the
Department of Education.

National Institute of Real Estate Brokers. ESTIMATING MARKET PRICE. (Brokers Institute Bulletin Service). Chicago: 1959. 62p. illus. pap.

Paine, Paul. OIL PROPERTY VALUATION. New York: John Wiley, 1942.
204p.

PAN PACIFIC VALUATION AND APPRAISAL CONVENTION. MARCH, 1959.
SYDNEY, AUSTRALIA. PAPERS. Sponsored by Commonwealth Institute of Valuers

and American Institute of Real Estate Appraisers. Sydney: Commonwealth Institute of Valuers, 1959. 108p. pap.

Parks, Roland D. EXAMINATION AND VALUATION OF MINERAL PROPERTY, 3rd ed. Cambridge, Mass.: Addison-Wesley Press, 1949. 504p.
>Oil Property Valuation, by Walter L. Whitehead and The Michigan Mine Appraisal System, by Franklin G. Pardee.
First and second editions: MINE EXAMINATION AND VALUATION, by Charles H. Baxter and Roland D. Parks.

Prouty, W.L., et al. APPRAISERS AND ASSESSORS MANUAL. New York: McGraw-Hill, 1930. 500p.
>"The building appraisal systems present classifications and costs per cubic foot which the assessor may use as a guide in his own local work." For major cities.

Ring, Alfred A. THE VALUATION OF REAL ESTATE. Englewood Cliffs, N.J.: Prentice-Hall, 1963. 430p. illus., tables, charts, diagrs.
>Intended as a nontechnical text for students and as a reference and guide for those professionally charged with estimating real estate values. Appendices: demonstration appraisal report of a single-family home; problems, questions, and solutions; tables.

Schmutz, George L. THE APPRAISAL PROCESS, 2d ed., rev. Manhattan Beach, Calif.: 1959. 335p. tables.
>1959 edition revised by George Theodore Schmutz.

Simpson, Herbert D. and Burton, John E. THE VALUATION OF VACANT LAND IN SUBURBAN AREAS; CHICAGO AREA. (Studies in Public Finance. Research Monograph no. 2. Richard T. Ely, editor). Chicago: The Institute for Economic Research, Northwestern University, 1931. 56p. tables, charts, maps. pap.

Society of Industrial Realtors. APPRAISING INDUSTRIAL PROPERTIES. Washington, D.C.: 1962. 20p. pap. processed.
>"A case-study discussion by eight S.I.R.'s of the Portland (Ore.) Woolen Mills, a property containing all types of appraisal problems which confront members of the Society of Industrial Realtors in their day-to-day business." Third annual workshop, May 11, 1961, Portland.

Society of Industrial Realtors. EVALUATING INDUSTRIAL REAL ESTATE, ed. by Lester W. Porter and Carl Lloyd. Washington, D.C.: 1953. 136. illus., tables. pap.

>Society of Industrial Realtors, Industrial Real Estate Seminar, Chicago, September, 1952.

Society of Residential Appraisers. APPRAISAL CLASSICS, AN ANTHOLOGY OF THE PROFESSIONAL JOURNAL OF THE INTERNATIONAL SOCIETY OF RESIDENTIAL APPRAISERS, 1935-1960. ed. by Jerry C. Davis. Chicago: 1961. 639p. illus.
>Articles from the Journal entitled, THE RESIDENTIAL APPRAISER, formerly THE REVIEW.

Society of Residential Appraisers. APPRAISAL GUIDE, Rev. ed. Chicago: 1956. 56p. pap. processed.

Society of Residential Appraisers. Appraisal Service Committee. APPRAISAL ADMINISTRATION UNDER EMINENT DOMAIN, 2d ed. Chicago: 1957. 29p. pap.
First edition entitled, SUGGESTED PROCEDURES--ACQUISITION OF PRIVATE PROPERTY FOR PUBLIC USE.
This booklet not for sale, but is made available to public agencies at the request of individual members as a public service.

Society of Residential Appraisers. REAL ESTATE APPRAISAL PRINCIPLES AND TERMINOLOGY. Chicago: 1960. 166p.

Teckemeyer, Earl B. HOW TO VALUE REAL ESTATE; THE FOREMOST FACTOR IN SELLING. Englewood Cliffs, N.J.: Prentice-Hall, 1956. 196p.

Thorson, Ivan A. SIMPLIFIED APPRAISAL SYSTEM: LAND ECONOMICS, 2d ed. Los Angeles: Realty Research Bureau, 1951. 228p.
Replaces the author's LAND ECONOMICS AND SIMPLIFIED APPRAISAL SYSTEM.

U.S. Army. Corps of Engineers. REAL PROPERTY APPRAISER'S HANDBOOK. Washington, D.C.: Government Printing Office, 1955. 131p. tables. looseleaf.

U.S. Department of the Interior. REPORT OF THE COMMITTEE ON LAND APPRAISAL PRACTICES IN THE DEPARTMENT OF THE INTERIOR. Washington, D.C.: 1956. 36p. pap. processed.

U.S. General Services Administration. APPRAISAL OF REAL PROPERTY; A G.S.A. HANDBOOK, Rev. ed. (Public Building Service. PBS P1005, 2A). Washington, D.C.: 1962. various paging. looseleaf. pap. processed.
"Provides guidance and technical instructions."

U.S. Urban Renewal Administration. REUSE AND VALUE APPRAISALS IN URBAN RENEWAL. (AB-8-58). Washington, D.C.: 1958. 9p. pap. processed.

U.S. Urban Renewal Administration. VALUATION PROBLEMS INVOLVING REUSE OF URBAN LAND. (AB-6-58). Washington, D.C.: 1958. 7p. pap. processed.

Wendt, Paul F. REAL ESTATE APPRAISAL; A CRITICAL ANALYSIS OF THEORY AND PRACTICE. New York: Holt, 1956. 320p.
"The pioneering work of Hurd, Dorau, Babcock, Bonbright, Schmutz, May and others has provided the basic theoretical framework which the author examines."

(Roy) Wenzlick Research Corporation. RESIDENTIAL APPRAISAL MANUAL. St. Louis: 706 Chestnut Street, 1959. 120p. processed. looseleaf.

"Is essentially a building cost manual." Includes a Residential Appraisal Report form. (Additional material issued annually). Provides detailed cost data for many types of buildings with local cost modifiers. About one-third of the manual is basic appraisal information, the balance devoted to building costs. Analyzes appraisal form in detail, presents sample appraisals. Has market price calculator for use where selling price is known for previous sales. Includes depth and depreciation tables.

Appraisal—Bibliographies

De Witt, Mary B. BIBLIOGRAPHY ON URBAN REAL ESTATE APPRAISAL. Compiled for the Joint Committee on Appraisal and Mortgage Analysis. Washington, D.C.: Central Mortgage Committee, 1942. 59p. pap. processed.
    Supplement to BIBLIOGRAPHY ON URBAN REAL ESTATE AP-PRAISAL, by Adelaide R. Hasse, 1937.

Du Bois, Ayers J. CATALOG OF URBAN REAL ESTATE APPRAISAL DATA SOURCES. Compiled for the Joint Committee on Appraisal and Mortgage Analysis. Washington, D.C.: Central Housing Committee, 1937. 242p. pap. processed.
    Chief of Valuation Section, Underwriting Division, Federal Housing Administration.

Hasse, Adelaide R. BIBLIOGRAPHY OF URBAN REAL ESTATE APPRAISAL. Compiled for the Joint Committee on Appraisal and Mortgage Analysis. Washington, D.C : Central Housing Committee, 1937. 328p. pap. processed.
    Research Consultant, Works Progress Administration. "The completeness and quality of the bibliography is an outstanding achievement." Classified, partially annotated. Supplement by Mary B. DeWitt issued April 1, 1942.

New York State Society of Real Estate Appraisers of the Real Estate Association of the State of New York. REAL ESTATE APPRAISAL BIBLIOGRAPHY, 3rd ed. Albany: 1945. 86p. pap.
    1946 supplement issued.

Porter, Lewis G. CATALOG OF RURAL APPRAISAL DATA SOURCES. Prepared for the Joint Committee on Appraisal and Mortgage Analysis. Washington, D.C.: Central Housing Committee, 1937. 22p. pap. processed.
    I: Land; Natural Forces, Characteristics; II: Population; III: Farm Land Utilization; IV: Markets and Outlets; V: Economic Conditions; VI: Legislative Acts and Policies.
    Classification, government agencies, libraries and bibliographies and a catalog of some data sources of use to appraisers of rural property.

Appraisal—Bibliographies (continued)

U.S. Department of Agriculture. Bureau of Agricultural Economics. VALUATION
OF REAL ESTATE WITH SPECIAL REFERENCE TO FARM REAL ESTATE. (Agricultural
Economics Bibliography no. 60). Washington, D.C.: 1935. 350p. pap. processed.
> Classified by subject with the exception of foreign. Compiled
> by Margaret T. Olcott and Helen E. Hennefrund under the direc-
> tion of Mary G. Lacy, Librarian, Bureau of Agricultural Eco-
> nomics.
> Supersedes a bibliography issued as Agricultural Economics Biblio-
> graphy no. 29, of the same title, compiled by Emily Day.

Appraisal—Periodicals
(See Appendix for complete information concerning these publications).

APPRAISAL DIGEST. APPRAISAL INSTITUTE MAGAZINE. APPRAISAL JOURNAL.
THE APPRAISER. BUILDING COSTS. CLIENTS SERVICE BULLETIN. IN THE
FIELD. JOURNAL OF THE AMERICAN SOCIETY OF FARM MANAGERS AND
RURAL APPRAISERS. NEW ZEALAND VALUER. REAL ESTATE ANALYST APPRAIS-
AL BULLETIN. RESIDENTIAL APPRAISER. RIGHT OF WAY. TECHNICAL VAL-
UATION. THE VALUER.

Section 4

BROKERAGE

GENERAL

Arnold, Ray H. HOW TO CLOSE IN SELLING HOMES. Englewood Cliffs, N.J.: Prentice-Hall, 1953. 210p.
> A systematic presentation of tested principles and methods involved in the closing stage of the sales process. Examples used to show the principles in action.

Arnold, Ray H. HOW TO ESTIMATE MARKET VALUE IN SELLING REAL ESTATE. Englewood Cliffs, N.J.: Prentice-Hall, 1962. 250p. tables.
> Presentation of cost estimating, property analysis, capitalization rates, etc. for the salesman. Residential, income-producing, and commercial property covered.

Arnold, Ray H. HOW TO OVERCOME OBJECTIONS IN SELLING REAL ESTATE. New York: Prentice-Hall, 1955. 211p.
> Discusses objections commonly encountered in selling real estate and outlines definite methods for dealing with them.

Bennett, Charles. HOW BIG IDEAS MAKE BIG MONEY SELLING REAL ESTATE. Englewood Cliffs, N.J.: Prentice-Hall, 1961. 274p.
> Suggested strategy, illustrated with examples, of recognizing possible sales and making the most of them.

Berge, A. John. CLOSING REAL ESTATE SALES; A SUMMARY OF TESTED METHODS IN SELLING REAL ESTATE. Chicago: Real Estate Press, 1928. 215p.
> Fifteen articles originally published in the NATIONAL REAL ESTATE JOURNAL.

Bohon, Davis T. HOW TO GET SALABLE REAL ESTATE LISTINGS. Englewood Cliffs, N.J.: Prentice-Hall, 1961. 205p.
> Discusses ways to get listings that will move with the minimum outlay of time and effort on the part of the broker and, therefore, with maximum profit. Includes chapters on listing forms, contracts, and price determination.

Brede, William J. SKYLINE BUILDERS: THE STORY OF NEW YORK'S CLEVER LAND DETECTIVES. New York: Early Brothers, 9 Rockefeller Plaza, zone 20, 1948. 94p. pap.

GENERAL (continued)

The assembling of land for some of the city's important buildings
and developments, the historical phases of these activities, and
the men behind them.

Brokerage. Section 57.700 In Casey, William J. REAL ESTATE INVESTMENT
DEALS, IDEAS, FORMS. New York: Institute for Business Planning, 1959--.
Includes subsections: Functions and Qualifications of the Broker;
Protection of the Broker's Position; Licensing.

California Real Estate Association. BLUEPRINT FOR SELLING REAL ESTATE.
Los Angeles: 117 West Ninth Street, zone 15, 1958. 64p. illus. pap.
Includes papers on merchandising of Investment properties and
exchanges.

California Real Estate Association. THE FUNDAMENTALS OF LISTING, AD-
VERTISING AND SELLING REAL ESTATE. Los Angeles: 117 West Ninth Street,
zone 15, 1961. 79p. pap.
Step-by-step from prospecting for listings to closing sales.

California Real Estate Association. KNOWLEDGE MAKES THE DIFFERENCE.
Los Angeles: 117 West Ninth Street, zone 15, 1959. 47p. forms. pap.
Papers by twelve Realtors. Practical suggestions on selling,
financing, etc.

California Real Estate Association. THIS IS YOUR LIFE...REAL ESTATE SALES-
MAN. Los Angeles: 117 West Ninth Street, zone 15, 1962. 76p. illus.,
forms. pap.
What makes a successful salesman, financing, setting correct
listing price, showing the property, and service after the sale.
Five papers presented at the Association's 1962 Education and
Sales Conferences.

Cook, G. Hall. HOW TO SELL REAL ESTATE BY THE SELL-AN-IDEA TECH-
NIQUE. Englewood Cliffs, N.J.: Prentice-Hall, 1957. 218p.
A presentation of the author's experience as a real estate broker
and the sales method he worked out for himself.

Curran, G. C. and Hardison, L. M. SELLING FARMS: FARM SALESMEN'S
MANUAL. Ft. Wayne, Ind.: Anthony Press, 1941. 129p. illus. pap.
processed.

Geer, Mary Warren. SELLING HOME PROPERTY. New York: Prentice-Hall,
1951. 267p.
The author's attempt to "cull out the facts of our business that
are most commonly overlooked, both in print and in practice...
to link the things we ordinarily do with the personal attitudes
that make their execution most effective."

Gross, Alfred. SELLING HOUSES SUCCESSFULLY; BUILDER'S SALES GUIDE.
New York: Simmons-Boardman, 1958. 160p. illus., charts.
Merchandising methods for the residential contractor.

GENERAL (continued)

Hinman, Albert G. and Dorau, Herbert B. REAL ESTATE MERCHANDISING.
Chicago: A. W. Shaw Co., 1926. 363p. illus., forms.
>A compilation and analysis of the factors and problems involved
>in effecting the transfer of land ownership. Includes chapters on
>real estate business administration, multiple listing, and measur-
>ing the success of merchandising methods. An outgrowth of work
>done by the authors in the Institute for Research in Land Eco-
>nomics and Public Utilities.

How to Obtain and Handle Real Estate Listings. Part II, p. 77-127 In
Friedman, Edith J., ed. REAL ESTATE ENCYCLOPEDIA. Englewood Cliffs,
N.J.: Prentice-Hall, 1960.
>Chapter 4: Listing of Property and Employment of Broker, by
>Clive Graham; Chapter 5: Aids to Increase Listings, by William
>C. Wilson; Chapter 6: Office Records of Listings, by Roger B.
>Conant.

How to Sell or Exchange Real Estate. Part III, p. 129-316 In Friedman,
Edith J., ed. REAL ESTATE ENCYCLOPEDIA. Englewood Cliffs, N.J.: Prentice-Hall, 1960.
>Chapter 7: Selling a House, by Walter J. Nolte; Chapter 8:
>Selling Commercial Property, by Barney A. Karbank; Chapter 9:
>Selling Industrial Property, by Howell H. Watson; Chapter 10:
>Selling Farm Property, by Robert J. Bradshaw; Chapter 11:
>Motel Sales and Operations, by Stephen W. Brener; Chapter 12:
>The Real Estate Salesman, by Clinton B. Snyder; Chapter 13:
>Exchanges of Real Estate, by Stanley Sotcher; Chapter 14: Auc-
>tion Sales of Real Estate, by R. C. Foland.

Kent, Robert Warren and Corb, Donald A. PRACTICAL REAL ESTATE BROKER-
AGE; A TEXTBOOK, TRAINING PROGRAM, GUIDE AND MANUAL FOR THE
SUCCESSFUL PRACTICE OF BROKERAGE IN REAL ESTATE. Englewood Cliffs,
N.J.: Prentice-Hall, 1961. 246p. charts, forms.
>The fundamentals of real estate selling, written primarily for
>salesmen's orientation.

King, A. Rowden. REAL ESTATE SELLING AIDS. Englewood Cliffs, N.J.:
Prentice-Hall, 1957. 271p. illus., forms.
>Techniques and signs, forms, displays, etc. for real estate ad-
>vertising and sales promotion. Appendix includes syllabus for
>training salesmen in the real estate business.

King, A. Rowden. REALTOR'S GUIDE TO ARCHITECTURE: HOW TO IDENTIFY
AND SELL EVERY KIND OF HOUSE. New York: Prentice-Hall, 1954. 234p.
illus.
>"Sales features, descriptions, comparisons, and pictures of all
>common types of homes existing in America today." Written for
>the salesman.

Krueger, Cliff W. SALESORAMA, A NEW, SPARKLING, PROFITABLE HOME
STUDY COURSE. Northfield, Ill.: Salesorama, 455 Sunset Ridge Road, 1958.

444p. illus. processed. looseleaf.
Thirteen units.

Krueger, Cliff W. SUCCESSFUL REAL ESTATE SELLING. New York: McGraw-
Hill Book Co., 1960. 279p.
"The fundamentals of salesmanship and their specific application
in real estate."

Marketing, Merchandising, and Research, Inc. THE MARKETING OF NEW
HOMES; A LIFE MARKETING LABORATORY STUDY. New York: 1960. 63p.
tables. pap. processed.
Report on home buyers preferences and reactions.

McMichael, Stanley L. SELLING REAL ESTATE, 3d ed. New York: Prentice-
Hall, 1950. 527p. tables, forms.
The techniques of real estate brokerage illustrated by the story
of a young salesman and his development in the business. Over
fifty pages of appended materials: forms, tables, etc.

Michigan. University. School of Business Administration. LECTURES AND PA-
PERS OF THE ANNUAL REAL ESTATE CLINIC. Ann Arbor: 1949--. pap.
processed.
Conducted in co-operation with the Michigan Real Estate Associ-
ation, the Ann Arbor Board of Realtors, and the State Office of
Vocational Education.

National Association of Real Estate Boards. REAL ESTATE SELLING. Chicago:
1927. 12 pts. pap. processed.
A brief course designed for use by individual Realtors and by
study groups of local real estate boards.

National Association of Real Estate Boards. Brokerage Management Committee.
THE SELECTION OF SALESMEN FOR REAL ESTATE BROKERAGE. Chicago:
1940? 38p. pap.
Generalizations and differences of opinion.

National Association of Real Estate Boards. Committee on Education. A COURSE
IN REAL ESTATE SALESMANSHIP, by James J. Spatz. Chicago: 1956. 47p.
pap. processed.
A set of sixteen lecture outlines.

National Institute of Farm Brokers. FARM AND RANCH BROKERS MANUAL.
Chicago: 1959. 100p. tables, charts, forms.
An aid and guide to those engaged in selling rural property.

National Institute of Real Estate Brokers. THE BROKERS INSTITUTE DIGEST;
40TH ANNIVERSARY REVIEW. Chicago: 1962. 160p. illus. pap.
A collection of condensed articles from Institute bulletins and
reports.

GENERAL (continued)

National Institute of Real Estate Brokers. BROKERS INSTITUTE BULLETIN
Service. Chicago: 1935--Quarterly.

> NOTE: Each bulletin, devoted to a specific subject, contains
> practical ideas that have been proven successful by Institute
> members in the operation of their businesses.

National Institute of Real Estate Brokers. BIBLIOGRAPHY OF
BROKERS INSTITUTE BULLETIN SERVICE, 1935-1945. Chicago:
November, 1945. 46p. pap.

Ackley, Leroy. REAL ESTATE SALES TECHNIQUES. Chicago:
August 1945. 90p. illus. pap.
> "Material...as originally compiled, was used as a
> text for a lecture course given at the University of
> Southern California."

Laronge, Joseph and Cooper, W. L. THE WORLD OF TOMOR-
ROW AND THE NEW HOUSE MARKET. Chicago: November
1945. 18p. pap.

LISTINGS; HOW TO SECURE THEM AND RESULT PRODUCING
LETTERS. Chicago: March 1946. 58p. illus. pap.

Driscoll, T. Loren, et al. SHOWING PROPERTY AND TYPES
OF HOMES; SALE AND SUBDIVISION. Chicago: May, 1946.
40p. illus. pap.
> "Types of Homes," by Victor D. Abel includes "Sale
> and Subdivision of Large Estates," by Edmund D. Cook
> and "Lakeview Subdivision--Its Restrictions," by
> Stewart B. Matthews.

National Institute of Real Estate Brokers. BEST LETTERS OF
REALTORS' ADVERTISING AND SALES IDEAS. Chicago:
August, 1946. 45p. illus. pap.

BROKERS INSTITUTE REALTOR CORPORATION AND COM-
MERCIAL PROPERTY CLINIC, Atlantic City, 1946. PRO-
CEEDINGS. Chicago: January 1947. 49p. pap.

National Institute of Real Estate Brokers. HOW BROKERS CAN
MAKE MONEY FROM NEW RENTAL HOUSING: SALES, MAN-
AGEMENT, MORTGAGES AND INSURANCE (INCLUDING SUG-
GESTED FHA FLOOR PLANS FOR PROJECTS). Chicago: Jan-
uary, 1947. 16p. illus. pap.

GENERAL (continued)
Brokers Institute Bulletins (continued)

Matthews, Stewart B. ARE YOU A REALTOR-BROKER, A
REALTOR-SPECULATOR OR BOTH? Chicago: July, 1947.
38p. pap.
>   Opinions of Realtors and State Real Estate Commis-
>   sion. Real estate license provisions and examina-
>   tions -- California, Iowa, Missouri, Washington,
>   D.C., and Nebraska.

THE ROUND TABLE; ANSWERS TO THE QUESTIONS EMANAT-
ING FROM THE TWO CLINICS SPONSORED BY THE BROKERS
INSTITUTE IN ATLANTIC CITY, NOVEMBER 14-15, 1946.
Chicago: September, 1947. 40p. pap.

HELLS' APOPPIN!...WITH PLENTY TO SELL, SAN FRANCISCO
BROKERAGE PANEL, AND THE ROUND TABLE. Chicago:
March, 1948. 57p. illus. pap.
>   1948 convention sessions on brokerage.

SALES IDEAS FOR REALTOR BROKER; BEST ENTRIES FROM THE
INSTITUTE'S LATEST CONTEST ON UP-TO-THE-MINUTE SEL-
LING AND PROMOTION METHODS AND PLANS. Chicago:
June, 1948. 44p. illus. pap.

Thorsen, Joseph A. OPERATING PROCEDURES OF A SMALL
REAL ESTATE OFFICE. Chicago: August, 1948. 57p. Illus.
pap.

Laronge, Louis S. PROBLEM PROPERTIES AND PROPERTY
PROBLEMS AND YOUR BUSINESS AND MINE. Chicago:
December, 1948. 61p. illus. pap.
>   Your Business and Mine. Brokerage Panel, New
>   York Convention, 1948. Transcription. p.37-59.
>   "Problem Properties..are the idle--misplaced--decay-
>   ing or improperly used buildings so often seen and
>   overlooked."

Reynolds, Welden. THIS BUSINESS OF REAL ESTATE, 2 vols.
Chicago: 1949--1950. illus. pap.
>   Book One: SALES METHODS, December 1949.
>   Book Two: OFFICE IDEAS AND PROCEDURES, May 1950.

Kirk, Arthur S., et al. SALES IDEAS THAT CLICK. Chicago:
September 1949. 57p. illus. pap.
>   How to get, display and sell listings; build good will
>   and improve office techniques; residential and commer-
>   cial property sales pointers, mottoes and sayings.

GENERAL (continued)

Brokers Institute Bulletins (continued)

Moore, Donald F. et al. BETTER WAYS TO OBTAIN PROFIT-
ABLE LISTINGS: A PRACTICAL AND PROFITABLE COLLECTION
OF PROVEN METHODS AND IDEAS FOR OBTAINING AND
HANDLING LISTINGS IN EVERY FIELD OF REALTY OPERA-
TION. Chicago: September 1950. 59p. illus. pap.

Bureau of Analyses. TAX SAVINGS IN REAL ESTATE TRANS-
ACTIONS. Chicago: January 1951. 98p. pap.
    Prepared by Bureau of Analyses, Davenport, Iowa.
    "This is not a compendium of all the tax aspects of
    real estate transactions...concerned only with tax
    savings. Thus we are dealing not with principles
    but with procedures."

Matthews, Stewart B. et al. SALES MEETINGS. Chicago:
April 1951. 46p. pap.
    Miami Beach sales meeting panel; sales contests,
    bonus plans, panel meeting procedures.

Wilbur, Albert A. et al. I AM A SALESMAN. Chicago:
July 1951. 62p. illus. pap.
    "Sales techniques for self-improvement."

Tucker, Fred C., Jr., and Knowles, Jerome, Jr. SUCCESS-
FUL SALES METHODS FOR TODAY'S MARKET. Chicago:
December 1951. 63p. pap.
    The impact of government regulations in the abnor-
    mal conditions of a forced economy on selling--
    solutions.

Todd, Harrison, L., et al. TODAY'S HOME...KNOW IT,
SHOW IT, SELL IT. Chicago: December 1952. 63p. illus.
pap.

Payne, Charles L., et al. THE RIGHT INVESTMENT IS EQUAL
TO A LIFETIME OF TOIL. Chicago: June 1953. 62p. photos.
pap.
    Investment real estate brokerage.

Morris, L. Allen, et al. NEGOTIATING THE SALE. Chicago:
September 1953. 63p. illus. pap.

Laronge, Joseph. FIFTY YEARS OF REAL ESTATE. Chicago:
December 1953. 63p. illus. pap.
    Ideas, ideals and interesting real estate transactions
    of Joseph Laronge upon completion of fifty years in
    the real estate business.

GENERAL (continued)
Brokers Institute Bulletins (continued)

Mayer, George E., Jr. THE MODERN BROKER'S OFFICE;
INSIDE STORY. Chicago: March 1954. 63p. illus. pap.
    Practices and procedures.

Dayton, Walter S., et al. AIR CONDITIONING; KEY TO
MORE HOME SALES. Chicago: September 1954. 63p.
illus. pap.

Bashaw, Frederick J. SELLING THE HIDDEN VALUES OF THE
AMERICAN HOME. Chicago: December 1954. 61p. illus.
pap.
    Some of his most popular lectures.

Commerce Clearing House, Inc. REAL ESTATE TRANSACTIONS
UNDER 1954 CODE. Chicago; Commerce Clearing House, Inc.,
1955. 96p. pap.
    Special printing for the Institute.

Johnstone, W. Gordon, et al. HIRING, TRAINING AND
FINANCING SALESMEN. Chicago: June 1955. 63p. pap.

Thorsen, Joseph A., et al. THE PACE OF PROGRESS; REAL
ESTATE TRENDS AND OPPORTUNITIES IN THESE CHANGING
TIMES. Chicago: December 1955. 63p. illus. pap.

Williamson, Gordon, et al. REALTOR AND BUILDER COOPER-
ATION. Chicago: June 1956. 63p. illus. pap.

Snyder, Clinton B., et al. THE SUCCESSFUL SALESMAN.
Chicago: September 1956. 62p. pap.
    How to be a successful salesman.

Peacock, Wallace A., et al. NEW BUSINESS FROM OLD.
Chicago: December 1956. 63p. illus. pap.
    Client relations tips, follow up. "Winning and
    holding clients."

Sheehan, Daniel F., et al. TESTED TALKS FOR SALES MEET-
INGS. Chicago: March 1957. 63p. photos. pap.

Jones, Richard L., et al. REAL ESTATE SYNDICATES AND HOW
THEY WORK. Chicago: March 1957. 63p. photos. pap.

Anderson, George F. PITFALLS; TRUE STORIES FROM THE
EXPERIENCE OF REAL ESTATE BROKERS WITH HELPFUL COM-
MENTS. Chicago: September 1957. 63p. pap.
    Legal comments.

GENERAL (continued)

Brokers Institute Bulletins (continued)

Morris, L. Allen, et al. DIRECT MAIL; HOW REALTORS SELL
BY MAIL. Chicago: December 1957. 63p. illus. pap.

Brown, Sam E., et al. REAL ESTATE ADVERTISING FEATURING
THE REALTOR'S AD WRITER, 5th ed. rev. Chicago: March
1958. 63p. illus. pap.

McBride, Frank, Jr., et al. SALES IDEAS THAT CLICK.
Chicago: June 1958. 63p. illus. pap.
     Same title as September, 1949 bulletin.
     "True stories of ideas that have led to actual sales."

Piplar, Charles L., et al. DOUBLE YOUR DOLLARS BY KNOW-
ING THE ANSWERS. Chicago: September 1958. 63p. illus.
pap.
     Overcoming objections in selling.

Herd, John J., et al. PUBLIC TRANSPORTATION AND YOUR
COMMUNITY. Chicago: December 1958. 63p. photos. pap.
     Statements from city planners, public officials, transit
     executives, highway engineers, traffic consultants,
     newspaper editors, merchants, industrialist, real estate
     brokers and many others.

Chain Store Guide. DIRECTORY OF LEADING CHAIN STORES
IN THE UNITED STATES. New York: Chain Store Business
Guide, 1959-- .
     Editions 1--7, 1936--1949, published by National In-
     stitute of Real Estate Brokers, CHAIN STORE DIREC-
     TORY. Headquarters, addresses and key executives,
     stores in operation, states in which chains operate.

Mayer, George E., et al. OFFICE POLICIES AND PROCE-
DURES. Chicago: March 1959. 63p. pap.
     "Selected examples of rules covering speeches, prob-
     lems and situations as well as the daily routine of the
     real estate profession." Reprinted from policy books
     of real estate brokers.

Snyder, Clinton B., et al. LEARN TO TRADE. Chicago: June
1959. 63p. illus. pap.
     Earlier bulletins; REAL ESTATE EXCHANGES; COM-
     MENTS AND PRACTICAL PROCEDURES, September
     1944. REAL ESTATE EXCHANGES; A FERTILE FIELD
     OF REAL ESTATE SELLING, October 1951. 63p.

GENERAL (continued)

Brokers Institute Bulletins (continued)

Waguespack, F. Poche, Jr., et al. ESTIMATING MARKET
PRICE. Chicago: September 1959. 62p. illus. pap.
    Earlier Bulletin: ESTIMATING SALES PRICE by
    Joseph Laronge, March 1940.

Mendenhall, Ed., et al. EVERYDAY REAL ESTATE; OFFICE
FACILITIES, POLICIES, PROCEDURES AND PAPERWORK ARE
IMPORTANT IN EFFICIENT OPERATION OF BRANCH OFFICES,
NEIGHBORHOOD AND SMALLER-TOWN OFFICES. Chicago:
December 1959. 63p. illus. pap.

Burns, Ron J., et al. HIGHER EARNINGS THROUGH BETTER
SALESMANSHIP. Chicago: June 1960. 63p. illus. pap.

Wanless, Gail M., et al. PRACTICAL ANSWERS TO YOUR
BROKERAGE QUESTIONS. Chicago: September 1960. 63p.
pap.
    The questions on numerous topics were presented dur-
    ing sales clinics and convention round tables.

Woodbury, Wallace R., et al. CREATING COMMERCIAL DEALS.
Chicago: December 1960. 63p. illus. pap.

Schuyler, Harold J., et al. BUSINESS BUILDING LETTERS
AND FORMS. Chicago: March 1961. 63p. illus. pap.

Jackson, Herbert T., et al. REAL ESTATE ADVERTISING FEATURING
THE BROKER'S AD WRITER. 6th rev. ed. Chicago: June
1961. 63p. illus. pap.

REAL ESTATE ADVERTISING AND THE AUTOMATIC CLASSIFIED
AD WRITER. 6th ed. Chicago: June 1961. 50p. illus. pap.

Waguespack, F. Poche, Jr., et al. SELECTION AND TRAIN-
ING OF SALESMEN. Chicago: September 1961. 63p.
illus. pap.

Hickman, Robert E., et al. THE DYNAMICS OF COMMERCIAL
PROPERTY. Chicago: December 1961. 63p. illus. pap.

Port, Rich. SELLING SELLERS SUCCESSFULLY. Chicago:
March 1962. 63p. illus. pap.

Mitchell, Winfred O., et al. REAL ESTATE SPECIALIZATIONS.
Chicago: June 1962. 63p. pap.
    Industrial and rural; counseling, appraising, management,
    insurance, mortgage banking, home building and urban
    renewal.

GENERAL (continued)
Brokers Institute Bulletins (continued)

Johnstone, W. Gordon. TOUCHDOWN PLAYS IN REAL ESTATE. Chicago: September 1962. 63p. illus. pap.

National Institute of Real Estate Brokers. REAL ESTATE SALESMAN'S HAND-BOOK, 3rd rev. ed. Chicago: 1959. 192p. tables, chart, forms.
A ready-reference manual. Covers real estate selling as a career, salesman-broker relationships, the salesman's contract, and various techniques of real estate salesmanship. Includes amortization and capitalization tables.

National Real Estate and Building Journal. SELL MORE! SELL BETTER! Cedar Rapids, Iowa: no date. 62p. illus. pap.
A collection of thirty-six articles on real estate sales techniques, reprinted from the JOURNAL.

Ohio State University. College of Business and Administration. PROCEEDINGS OF THE...ANNUAL CONFERENCE ON REAL ESTATE BROKERAGE. Columbus: 1950-- . pap. processed.
Conducted in co-operation with the Ohio Association of Real Estate Boards and the State Board of Real Estate Examiners.

REALTY MERCHANDISING SERVICE. Pelham, N.Y.: H. K. Simon Co., 1962-- . looseleaf.
A monthly looseleaf service of bulletins issued in several series. AD NOTES, CLOSING BULLETIN, REALTY RESEARCH REPORT, LISTING, IDEAS, ETC.

Russell, Sam G. HOW TO BE CONSISTENTLY SUCCESSFUL IN REAL ESTATE. Englewood Cliffs, N.J.: Prentice-Hall, 1958. 203p.
Suggestions for developing positive mental attitudes and sales techniques.

Sandford, William P. REAL ESTATE SALESMAN'S COMPLETE IDEAS HAND-BOOK. Englewood Cliffs, N.J.: Prentice-Hall, 1958. 210p.
Suggested techniques on all phases of brokerage: listing, clos-ing, building a strong sales personality, etc. Many points illustrated with typical situations.

Selling. Section 1 In PRENTICE-HALL REAL ESTATE GUIDE. Englewood Cliffs, N.J.: Prentice-Hall, 1953-- . illus. looseleaf.
Explains techniques of salesmanship and sales management and discusses in detail specialized activities: listing, filing systems and forms for listing, prospects, trade-ins, closing, and the sale of specific property types. Includes section on commission rates.

Sherman, Arthur Brown. HOW TO EXPLOIT AMENITIES AND HIDDEN VALUES IN SELLING REAL ESTATE. Englewood Cliffs, N.J.: Prentice-Hall, 1959. 214p.

GENERAL (continued)

An analysis of buying habits and the intangible desire that
motivate home buyers, with emphasis on methods brokers can
employ to emphasize considerations of beauty, comfort, luxury,
etc.

Sherman, Arthur Brown. SELLING BUSINESS REAL ESTATE; HOW TO INCREASE
YOUR EARNING POWER BY SELLING COMMERCIAL AND INDUSTRIAL PROP-
ERTY. New York: Prentice-Hall, 1955. 277p. illus., tables, forms.
Written to inform the residential broker of the possibilities of
selling non-residential properties. Discusses the basis factors in
selling non-residential property--appraising, law, insurance,
banking, etc.

Smith, Eytyle V. BRASS TACKS OF REAL ESTATE SELLING. Oakland, Calif.:
Ray Smith and Co., 6464 Moraga Avenue, zone 11, no date. 355p.
A practical text designed especially for use in sales training
courses.

Smith, Ray. REAL ESTATE SALESMAN'S TRAINING MANUAL. Dayton, Ohio:
Real Estate Broker's Digest Service, 3114 East 3rd Street, zone 3, 1958. 427p.
illus.
A systematic presentation of the fundamentals of selling real
estate, covering listings, showing property, closing, advertising,
etc.

Teckemeyer, Earl B. THE HOW OF SELLING REAL ESTATE: HOW TO LIST
IT, HOW TO SHOW IT, HOW TO CLOSE THE DEAL. Englewood Cliffs, N.J.:
Prentice-Hall, 1954. 202p.
Outlines the processes that make real estate selling different
from other sales jobs.

Teckemeyer, Earl B. TECKEMEYER ON SELLING REAL ESTATE. Englewood
Cliffs, N.J.: Prentice-Hall, 1962. 246p.
An expansion of the author's THE HOW OF SELLING REAL
ESTATE.

Vogel, Lois T. HOW TO HELP YOUR REAL ESTATE SALESMEN PRODUCE
MORE BUSINESS. Englewood Cliffs, N.J.: Prentice-Hall, 1957. 240p. forms.
A book on the training of salesmen, based on the author's twenty
years of experience in selling real estate. Includes material on
multiple listing service, exchanges, and office policy books.

Brokerage—Periodicals
(See Appendix for complete information concerning these publications.)

BROKERS ROUND TABLE. BUILDINGS, June 1958-- . CALIFORNIA REAL

GENERAL (continued)

ESTATE MAGAZINE. CANADIAN REALTOR. MONEY MAKING IDEAS FOR FELLOW REALTORS. NATIONAL REAL ESTATE AND BUILDING JOURNAL, 1910--May 1958.

ADVERTISING

Advertising. Section 3 in PRENTICE-HALL REAL ESTATE GUIDE. Engle-wood Cliffs, N.J.: Prentice-Hall, 1953- . Illus. looseleaf.
> Discussion and numerous examples of classified advertisements, direct mail, signs, billboards, window displays; subsections on copy preparation and advertising of specific property types.

Gifford, Ward C. REAL ESTATE ADVERTISING; A DISCUSSION OF THE PRACTICAL APPLICATION OF ADVERTISING TO THE REAL ESTATE BUSINESS. (Land Economics Series; Standard Course in Real Estate). New York: Macmillan, 1955. 194p. illus., diagrams.

Herrold, Lloyd D. ADVERTISING REAL ESTATE. New York: McGraw-Hill, 1931. 325p. illus.
> A general text for the student and a practical presentation of advertising as a sales force for the broker.

McDonald, Morton, J.A. HOW TO USE CLASSIFIED ADVERTISING TO SELL MORE REAL ESTATE. Englewood Cliffs, N.J.: Prentice-Hall, 1958. 248p. illus.
> How to prepare and use newspaper classified advertising to maxi-mum advantage. Actual advertisements shown.

McDonald, Morton, J.A. MASTER GUIDE TO SUCCESSFUL REAL ESTATE ADVERTISING. Englewood Cliffs, N.J.: Prentice-Hall, 1962. 267p. illus.
> The planning and use of all advertising media: newspaper, out-door signs, radio, novelty, etc. Advantages and disadvantages of each type discussed. Step-by-step procedures. Profusely illustrated.

McDonald, Morton, J.A. SUCCESSFUL REAL ESTATE ADVERTISING. Engle-wood Cliffs, N.J.: Prentice-Hall, 1958. 215p. illus.
> Discusses newspaper and other forms of advertising, describing successful practices by real estate brokers and others.

McKay, William H. REAL ESTATE ADVERTISING THAT CLICKS NOW. Culver City, Calif.: Murray and Gee, Inc., 1955. 100p. pap.
> "This handbook is intended to stimulate the thinking of the real estate broker and salesman and to aid him in writing better and more productive ads." Headings, lead lines, and descriptive

ADVERTISING (continued)

material for residential and commercial property, unimproved lots, etc.

National Association of Real Estate Boards. REAL ESTATE ADVERTISING. Chicago: 1929. 264p. Appendix. illus.

National Institute of Real Estate Brokers. PICTORIAL ADVERTISING AT WORK. (Brokers Institute Bulletin Service). Chicago: 1962. 64p. illus. pap.
Contributions from Realtors throughout the country on the imaginative use of pictures and the preparation of brochures for institutional, residential, commercial, and industrial properties.

National Institute of Real Estate Brokers. DIRECT MAIL; HOW REALTORS SELL BY MAIL. (Brokers Institute Bulletin Service). Chicago: 1957. 63p. illus. pap.

National Institute of Real Estate Brokers. ADVERTISING AND SALES IDEAS. (Brokers Institute Bulletin Service). Chicago: 1946. 48p. illus. pap.
Descriptions and illustrations. Successful promotion plans and materials selected from entries in an Institute contest.

National Institute of Real Estate Brokers. REAL ESTATE ADVERTISING; FEATURING THE BROKER'S AD WRITER, 6th rev. ed. (Brokers Institute Bulletin Service). Chicago: 1961. 63p. illus. pap.
Advertising budget and controls, classified and institutional advertising, and the Broker's Ad Writer, a special tool for the preparation of effective advertisements with speed and ease.

Parish, Chester. ADVERTISING REAL ESTATE. New York: Prentice-Hall, 1930. 380p. illus.
"Intended to record faithfully practices in real estate advertising up to this time."

Secretaries Council of the National Association of Real Estate Boards. A SURVEY OF LOCAL BOARD AND COMMUNITY RULINGS ON "FOR SALE" SIGNS. Chicago: 1954. 22p. pap. processed.

Stark, Jack. SUCCESSFUL PUBLICITY AND PUBLIC RELATIONS IN REAL ESTATE. Englewood Cliffs, N.J.: Prentice-Hall, 1958. 227p.
Techniques of direct mail, window display, press relations and other advertising and sales tools.

U.S. Federal Trade Commission. GUIDE FOR ADVERTISING SHELL HOMES. Washington, D.C.: 1962. 4p. pap.
Adopted April 25, 1962.

Woessner, Charles. HOW TO GET PROFITABLE REAL ESTATE LISTINGS THROUGH NEWSPAPER ADVERTISING. New York: Prentice-Hall, 1952. 191p. illus.

ADVERTISING (continued)

"New Ideas" for newspaper advertisements. Illustrated profusely
with examples used successfully by one firm.

Wyckoff, Bradford. SALES AND PROFIT APPROACH TO REAL ESTATE AD-
VERTISING, ed. by Howard Parish. Miami, Fla: Howard Parish Associates,
1959. 267p. illus.
Based on background material collected from a survey of real
estate brokers in the United States and Canada. Includes a
chapter on budgeting for advertising. Appendix of check lists
for testing advertisement quality.

EXCHANGING AND TRADE-INS

Minneapolis Honeywell Regulator Company. SERIES OF SIX BOOKLETS ON
TRADE-IN HOUSING, 6 vols. Minneapolis, Minn.: 1956. pap.
No. 1: A FUTURE FOR YOU--TRADING HOMES; No. 2:
THEY'RE TRADING HOMES IN DETROIT; No. 3: OREGON'S
REAL TALL REALTOR HAS TRADED HOMES FOR YEARS; No. 4:
THIRTY YEARS OF TRADING HOMES IN FORT WAYNE, INDI-
ANA; No. 5: A TRAIL-BLAZING HOME TRADER FROM DALLAS,
TEXAS; No. 6: THE BALTIMORE PLAN MAKES HOME TRAD-
ING BIG BUSINESS.

National Institute of Real Estate Brokers. LEARN TO TRADE. (Brokers Institute Bulletin Service). Chicago: 1959. 63p. illus. pap.
Reported experiences of Realtors; a collection of original contributions and selections reprinted from various issues of the
MONTHLY TRADER.

National Institute of Real Estate Brokers. REAL ESTATE EXCHANGES; A
FERTILE FIELD OF REAL ESTATE SELLING. (Brokers Institute Bulletin Service).
Chicago: 1951. 63p. illus., forms. pap.
Exchange techniques presented and discussed by Realtors. In-
cludes sections on tax aspects, preparation of agreements and
commission letters, and case studies.

National Institute of Real Estate Brokers. REAL ESTATE TRADER'S HANDBOOK,
1st rev. ed. Chicago: 1956. 152p. illus., tables, forms.
Principles and technical aspects of exchanges, including a section on the establishment of an exchange department in a real
estate office, discussion of tax considerations, and contracts.

EXCHANGING AND TRADE-INS (continued)

National Institute of Real Estate Brokers. International Traders Club. MUL-
TIPLE EXCHANGE PROCEDURE: PROPERTY AND TAX ANALYSIS. Chicago:
1962. 47p. illus., tables, forms.

National Institute of Real Estate Brokers. International Traders Club. SPRING
CLINIC ON ADVANCED EXCHANGING; 1962 PROCEEDINGS.. MAY 3...
CHICAGO, ILLINOIS. Chicago: 1962. 32p. illus. pap.
    Papers and discussions on the development of an exchange and
    on multiple exchanging.

Peter, John. PLAIN FACTS ABOUT TRADE-IN HOUSING, 2d ed. Buffalo:
National Gypsum Company, 1958. 35p. illus., forms. pap.

Reno, Richard R. PROFITABLE REAL ESTATE EXCHANGING. Englewood
Cliffs, N.J.: Prentice-Hall, 1956. 265p. illus., forms.
    "The what, why, how and when of real estate exchanging."
    Written for the broker.

Sotcher, Stanley. Exchanges of Real Estate. p. 270-97 In Friedman, Edith J.,
ed. REAL ESTATE ENCYCLOPEDIA. Englewood Cliffs, N.J.: Prentice-Hall,
1960.

Sotcher, Stanley. EXTRA DOLLARS TO YOU FROM REAL ESTATE EXCHANGES.
Los Angeles: 1955. various paging. pap.

Stanford University. Graduate School of Business. TRADE-IN HOUSING
MANAGEMENT, by John M. Hess. (Business Research Series, no. 11).
Stanford, Calif.: 1959. 106p. pap.
    Discusses basic principles and offers practical guidance on the
    management techniques of trading; treats trading as a marketing
    tool. Based on a doctoral dissertation. Bibliography included.

Stone, David. HOW TO OPERATE A REAL ESTATE TRADE-IN PROGRAM.
Englewood Cliffs, N.J.: Prentice-Hall, 1962. 189p. forms.
    Includes steps in starting a program, rules for negotiating success-
    ful trades, basic methods of trading residential properties, case
    histories. Reproduces thirty-four forms.

Exchanging—Periodicals
(See Appendix for complete information concerning these publications.)

MONTHLY TRADER.

Section 5

BUILDING, MODERNIZATION, AND
LAND DEVELOPMENT

BUILDING AND MODERNIZATION

The cost estimating literature is designed to equip the cost estimator with the knowledge of how to estimate the costs for each component of building from the materials through the construction schedule. The building cost services which give a base square foot and/or cubic foot cost, kept up to date with local cost modifiers, provide a tool for cost estimators in comparing types of design schemes. The building cost services are included in the APPRAISAL section, for the appraisers use the base costs in estimating reproduction cost, new, in one of the three approaches to value.

Bolton, Reginald Pelham. BUILDING FOR PROFIT; PRINCIPLES GOVERNING THE ECONOMIC IMPROVEMENT OF REAL ESTATE, 3rd. ed. New York: DeVinne Press, 1922, 133p.

Bouwcentrum and Technical University. HABITATION; PROGRAMME, DESIGN, PRODUCTION; ed. by J.H. Van Den Broek. (International Documentation Series 2). Amsterdam: Elsevier, 1959. 284p. illus., diagrs. (Distr. for U.S., Van Nostrand)
> At the request of the International Union of Architects. Belgium, Denmark, France, United Kingdom, Sweden, Switzerland, and Czechoslavakia. The function of the Bouwcentrum is to provide a center for the collection and dissemination of information on building research and documentation for the International Council for Building Research, Studies and Documentation.

Buckley, Ernest L. RESIDENTIAL CONSTRUCTION MANAGEMENT. New York: Wiley, 1959. 193p. illus.
> "To aid the home builder, who recognizes the trend toward industrialization and the tremendous potential of the housing market."

Building Research Institute, BUILDING SCIENCE DIRECTORY. Washington, D.C.: 1725 DeSales Street, Northwest, zone 6, 1956-
> Associations and societies; private research and testing facilities; college and university engineering research; and public agencies engaged in building research. "Individual data sheets are provided to give detailed information on structure, programs, and

BUILDING AND MODERNIZATION (continued)

publications of the 947 research organizations included." Completely indexed, kept up to date by means of annual supplements.

Burke, Arthur E., et al. ARCHITECTURAL AND BUILDING TRADES DICTIONARY. Chicago: American Technical Society, 1955. 377p. illus.
> Includes a 32 page supplement of "terms which have come into recent wide usage on the rapidly changing building trades scene."

Cal Pacific Estimators, ed. NATIONAL CONSTRUCTION ESTIMATOR. Los Angeles: Craftsman Book Company, 1952- .
> 9th edition-1960. Annual. Light and heavy construction costs.
> Formerly NATIONAL HOME ESTIMATOR.

California. University. Real Estate Research Program. MANAGEMENT IN THE LIGHT CONSTRUCTION INDUSTRY--A STUDY OF CONTRACTORS IN SOUTHERN CALIFORNIA, by James Gillies and Frank G. Mittelbach. Los Angeles: 1962. 109p. tables, charts. pap.

Carson, Eileen R. Sources of Information on Building. CANADIAN BUILDING DIGEST, no. 27, March 1962 (entire issue).
> An annotated guide to printed literature in English includes references to filing systems, index and abstract services, bibliographies, and digests.

Clough, Richard H. CONSTRUCTION CONTRACTING. New York: Wiley, 1960. 382p. tables, charts, forms.
> The management problems of small to medium-sized construction firms. "This book has been written specifically for the man who now occupies or would like to prepare himself to occupy, a supervisory position within a contractor's organization."

Colean, Miles L. and Newcomb, Robinson. STABILIZING CONSTRUCTION: THE RECORD AND POTENTIAL. New York: McGraw-Hill, 1952. 340p.

Coombs, William E. CONSTRUCTION ACCOUNTING AND FINANCIAL MANAGEMENT. New York: F.W. Dodge, 1958. 481p.

Cooper, George H. BUILDING CONSTRUCTION ESTIMATING, 2d ed. New York: McGraw-Hill, 1959. 398p. tables, diagrs.

Cowgill, Clinton H. BUILDING FOR INVESTMENT. New York: Reinhold, 1951. 482p. tables, charts, plans.
> Contents: The Owner; What May be Expected from the Architect; Investment in Real estate; Commercial Buildings; Housing; Cooperative Housing Organizations; Public Buildings; Industrial Buildings; Building Design, Construction and Equipment; Site Selection; Management and Modernization; Appraisal; Law and Ethics; Building for Investment; Appendices; Bibliography: p. 467-71.
> Appendix A: Form for Analyses of Charts Indicating Financial Set-up; B&C: Trends and Approximate Range of Rents for Stores and offices; D: Maintenance Costs for Office Buildings (graph);

BUILDING AND MODERNIZATION (continued)

E: Representative Percentages of Gross Sales Properly Assignable to Rent for Various Types of Retail Merchandising Establishments; F: Unit Costs of Buildings for Use in Preliminary Estimetes (based on data from Boeckh's MANUAL OF APPRAISALS).

Dallavia, Louis. ESTIMATING GENERAL CONSTRUCTION COSTS, 2nd ed. New York: F.W. Dodge, 1957. 197p.
> Method using a productivity factor with labor costs to deduce the actual cost of performing types of work.

Evers, Cecil C. THE COMMERCIAL PROBLEM IN BUILDINGS; A DISCUSSION OF THE ECONOMIC AND STRUCTURAL ESSENTIALS OF PROFITABLE BUILDING, AND THE BASIS FOR VALUATION OF IMPROVED REAL ESTATE. New York: Record and Guide, 1914. 274p. illus., plans.
> Principles of successful buildings "to call attention to and to endeavor to classify the different elements which are beneficial or detrimental to buildings from the utilitarian or financial standpoint; and to show the relation which exists between a building and the land it stands on, the earning power of which can be impaired or destroyed if the building is unsuitable."

Foster, Norman. CONSTRUCTION COSTS FROM TAKE-OFF TO BID. New York: F.W. Dodge, 1961. 246p. set of drawings in pocket.
> "The chapters on alterations, overhead and sub-bids--usually given scant attention in estimating books--have been treated rather fully ... Also included is the entire take off and estimate for a school building of almost $1,000,000. including all the pricing down to the final bid figure."

Geer, Mary Warren. HOW TO PROFIT BY REHABILITATING REAL ESTATE. Englewood Cliffs, N.J.: Prentice-Hall, 1957. 207p.

Grebler, Leo. PRODUCTION OF HOUSING: A RESEARCH MONOGRAPH ON EFFICIENCY IN PRODUCTION. New York: Social Science Research Council, 1950. 186p.
> Committee on Housing Research of the Social Science Research Council. Not only the efficiency of the productive factors going into the provision of new housing, but also the influences upon efficiency of the institutional framework in which new housing is produced, and the relationships between efficiency, breadth of the market and output flucuations.
> Selected bibliography.

Haas, John H. 3 R'S OF HOUSING; A GUIDE TO HOUSING REHABILITATION, RELOCATION HOUSING, REFINANCING. Washington, D.C.: General Improvement Contractors, 1962. 104p. pap. processed.
> Guide for professionals in the business of rehabilitation.

Home Improvement Council. HOW TO OPERATE A PROFITABLE REMODELING BUSINESS, by Don Moore, 2 vols. New York: no date. pap. processed.
> Past Executive Director of the Home Improvement Council. Operation Home Improvement and How's Your Home Contest results discussed.

BUILDING AND MODERNIZATION (continued)

How to Build and Modernize. Part X, p. 1065-252 In Friedman, Edith J.,
ed. REAL ESTATE ENCYCLOPEDIA. Englewood Cliffs, N.J.: Prentice-Hall,
1960.
> Chapter 14: Home Building, by John F. Rowlson; Chapter 15:
> Prefabricated Building, by George H. Frederking; Chapter 16:
> Apartment House Construction, by William E.P. Doelger; Chap-
> ter 44: Luxury Cooperative Apartment Housing, by Edward G.
> McLaughlin; Chapter 45: Low and Middle Income Cooperative
> Apartment Housing, by Eugene J. Morris; Chapter 46: Economic
> Design of Office Buildings, by George R. Bailey; Chapter 47:
> Modernization of Real Estate, by Alan M. Purling.

International Council for Building Research, Studies and Documentation. A-
BRIDGED BUILDING CLASSIFICATION (ABC) FOR ARCHITECTS, CIVIL ENGI-
NEERS AND BUILDERS. Rotterdam: 700 Weena.

International Council for Building Research, Studies and Documentation. BUILD-
ING RESEARCH AND DOCUMENTATION; CONTRIBUTIONS AND DISCUSSIONS
AT THE FIRST C.I.B. CONGRESS, ROTTERDAM, 1959. Amsterdam: Elsevier,
1961. 500p. (Distr. for U.S., Van Nostrand).
> Contents: Sociological and Functional Aspects of Housing De-
> sign; Design and Calculation of Constructions: Safety Factors;
> Dimensioning on the Building Site, Tolerances and Dimension
> Control; Research Problems Concerning Large Concrete Elements
> in Housing; Mass Housing in Rapidly Developing Tropical and
> Subtropical Areas; Flat Roofs; Fundamental Aspects of Trans-
> mission of Knowledge; Heat Insulation and Moisture Effects;
> Industrialization of Buildings; Operations Research.

International Council for Building Research, Studies and Documentation. DIREC-
TORY OF BUILDING RESEARCH AND DEVELOPMENT ORGANIZATIONS; OR-
GANIZATIONS IN EUROPEAN COUNTRIES, MEMBERS OF C.I.B. IN NON-
EUROPEAN COUNTRIES, INTERNATIONAL ORGANIZATIONS. Rotterdam:
Bouwcentrum, 1959. 163p. pap. (Distr. for U.S., Van Nostrand).
> Revised edition of DIRECTORY OF BUILDING RESEARCH AND
> DEVELOPMENT ORGANIZATIONS IN EUROPE.

International Council for Building Research, Studies and Documentation. INNO-
VATION IN BUILDING; CONTRIBUTIONS AT THE SECOND C.I.B. CONGRESS,
CAMBRIDGE, 1962. Amsterdam: Elsevier, 1962. 232p. illus., tables. (Distr.
for U.S., Van Nostrand).
> The influence of changing requirements and developments in ma-
> terials and components on design and construction.

Johnstone, B. Kenneth and Joern, Charles E., eds. THE BUSINESS OF HOME
BUILDING; A MANUAL FOR CONTRACTORS. New York: McGraw-Hill, 1950.
289p.
> For small builders.

Kay, N.W., ed. THE MODERN BUILDING ENCYCLOPEDIA; AN AUTHORITA-
TIVE REFERENCE TO ALL ASPECTS OF THE BUILDING AND ALLIED TRADES.

BUILDING AND MODERNIZATION (continued)

New York: Philosophical Library, 1955. 768p. illus.

Kelly, Burnham, et al. DESIGN AND PRODUCTION OF HOUSES. (ACTION Series in Housing and Community Development). New York: McGraw-Hill, 1959. 399p. illus., tables, charts.
"Explores the roles of the builder, the labor union, the manufacturer of building materials, the architect and the public official and points out ways in which their combined efforts can introduce many forms of improved design and technological innovation into future home building operations."

Kelly, Burnham. THE PREFABRICATION OF HOUSES. Cambridge, Mass.: Technology Press of the Massachusetts Institute of Technology and John Wiley, 1951. 466p. illus., tables, diagrs.

Long, Clarence D., Jr. BUILDING CYCLES AND THE THEORY OF INVESTMENT. Princeton, N.J.: Princeton University Press and London: Humphrey, Milford, Oxford University Press, 1940. 239p. charts, tables.

Lynch, Kevin. SITE PLANNING. Cambridge: Massachusetts Institute of Technology Press, 1962. 248p. illus.
"An introduction to the art of site planning, an exposition of its principles and a condensed technical reference."

Maisel, Sherman J. HOMEBUILDING IN TRANSITION; BASED ON STUDIES IN THE SAN FRANCISCO BAY AREA. Berkeley and Los Angeles: University of California Press, 1953. 390p. tables, charts, diagrs.
"Accurate, composite picture of who house builders are and how they operate."

Merritt, Frederick S. ed. BUILDING CONSTRUCTION HANDBOOK. New York: McGraw-Hill, 1958. various paging.
Composed of 29 sections by 25 authorities on building design and construction, written for the non-specialist. Comprehensive, but each topic is treated as briefly as clarity permits."

Nash, William W. RESIDENTIAL REHABILITATION: PRIVATE PROFITS AND PUBLIC PURPOSES. (ACTION Series in Housing and Community Development). New York: McGraw-Hill, 1959. 272p.

National Association of Home Builders. Builders' Economic Council. BUILDERS' OUTLOOK ... Survey Reports. Washington, D.C.: 1956-   tables. pap. processed.
A semiannual report based on information collected from builders throughout the country. Covers general market conditions, sales markets, builders' plans, and predicted housing characteristics.

National Association of Home Builders. Economics Department. (ESTIMATES OF NON-FARM HOUSING STARTS, 1940-1960), Revised. Washington, D.C.: 1961. 3p. tables. pap. processed.

National Association of Real Estate Boards. Build America Better Council. RE-HABILITATION AS A BUSINESS. Chicago: published jointly by the Council and the Institute of Real Estate Management, 1952. 99p. pap.

National Research Council. Building Research Institute. DOCUMENTATION OF BUILDING SCIENCE LITERATURE. (Publication 791). Washington, D.C.: 1960. 46p. pap. processed.
> Proceedings of a program conducted as a part of the 1959 Fall Conferences of the Building Research Institute, Division of Engineering and Industrial Research.

National Research Council. Building Research Institute. PERFORMANCE OF BUILDINGS; PROCEEDINGS OF A CONFERENCE HELD AS PART OF THE 1960 SPRING CONFERENCES OF THE BUILDING RESEARCH INSTITUTE DIVISION OF ENGINEERING AND INDUSTRIAL RESEARCH. Washington D.C.: 1961. 90p.
> Performance information needed by the architect, contractor and product manufacturer for commercial, industrial, residential and institutional buildings.

Peurifoy, R.L. ESTIMATING CONSTRUCTION COSTS, 2d ed. NEW YORK: McGraw-Hill, 1958. 446p. tables, diagrs.

Pulver, H.E. CONSTRUCTION ESTIMATES AND COSTS, 3d ed. New York: McGraw-Hill, 1960. 617p.

The Remodeling Story. JOURNAL OF HOMEBUILDING, vol. 15, no.8, August, 1961, p. 45-86.
> Includes selected bibliography, p. 86.

U.S. Bureau of the Budget. Central Statistical Board. HOUSING AND REAL PROPERTY; A SURVEY OF CONSTRUCTION AVAILABLE BASIC STATISTICAL DATA, by Jean H. Williams. Washington D.C.: Government Printing Office, 1940. 169p. tables.
> 246 series and special surveys of 21 Federal and 20 private sources. "Part I presents a brief summary description of existing data with an indication of the major gaps and of the principle improvements needed ... Part II contains a detailed description of each series ... Part III consists of two sections. The first is a list of the series in numerical order by agency, showing the frequency of each series and the major subject or subjects covered. The second section consists of an alphabetical subject index to the series descriptions."

U.S. Bureau of the Census. BUILDING PERMITS: NEW HOUSING UNITS AUTHORIZED BY LOCAL BUILDING PERMITS. (C-40 Series). Washington, D.C.: Government Printing Office. Monthly.
> Gives number of new housing units authorized by locally-issued building permits, by place. Approximately three thousand places listed (cities, towns, countries, etc.). Also public housing units for which construction contracts have been awarded.

BUILDING AND MODERNIZATION (continued)

U.S. Bureau of the Census. BUILDING PERMITS: NEW RESIDENTIAL CON-
STRUCTION AUTHORIZED IN PERMIT-ISSUING PLACES. (C-42 Series).
Washington, D.C.: Government Printing Office. Monthly.
> Number of housing units and valuations of new housekeeping
> residential construction authorized in permit-issuing places.
> Type of construction shown. Over three thousand places in-
> cluded. Also contracts awarded for public housing.

U.S. Bureau of the Census. CENSUS OF BUSINESS, 1935: CONSTRUCTION IN-
DUSTRY. Washington, D.C.: Government Printing Office, 1937. 3 vols. tables.
> Vol. I: WORK PERFORMED, PERSONNEL, PAYROLL AND
> COST OF MATERIAL, BY STATES AND CITIES AND BY KINDS
> OF BUSINESS; Vol. II: EMPLOYMENT BY MONTHS, AND
> BY OCCUPATIONAL GROUPS, BY STATES AND CITIES, AND
> BY KINDS OF BUSINESS; Vol. III: TYPES OF CONSTRUC-
> TION, COMPARISONS BETWEEN 1930 and 1935 AND MIS-
> CELLANEOUS DATA.

U.S. Bureau of the Census. CENSUS OF BUSINESS, 1939; VOLUME IV:
CONSTRUCTION. Washington, D.C.: Government Printing Office, 1943.
397p. tables.

U.S. Bureau of the Census. CENSUS OF DISTRIBUTION, 1930: CONSTRUC-
TION INDUSTRY. Washington, D.C.: Government Printing Office, 1933. 1362p.
> Reports by states with statistics for counties, and for cities of
> 100,000 population and over, a summary for the United States,
> and a study of the location and agencies of the construction
> industry. Chap. 1: Inauguration and Scope; Chap. 2: Organ-
> ization of the Construction Industry; Chap. 3: General Survey
> of the Construction Industry (including the value of the busi-
> nesses in 92 cities over 100,000 population); Chap. 4: Statis-
> tics by States; Chap. 5: Explanation of Tables. United States
> Summary.

U.S. Bureau of the Census. CONSTRUCTION ACTIVITY: VALUE OF NEW
CONSTRUCTION PUT IN PLACE. (C-30 Series). Washington, D.C.: Government Printing Office. Monthly.
> Estimates of value of new construction put in place, by type of
> construction. Current month compared with two preceding months
> and with same month one year previous. Current year-to-date
> compared with preceding year-to-date period.

U.S. Bureau of the Census. HOUSING STARTS. (C-20 Series). Washington,
D.C.: Government Printing Office. Monthly.
> Estimates of total and non-farm housing starts by ownership, by
> structure type, by metropolitan and non-metropolitan area, and
> by region. current and preceding calendar years and each
> month for the last 13-15 months given.

U.S. Department of Commerce and U.S. Department of Labor. CONSTRUC-
TION VOLUME AND COSTS, 1915-56; A STATISTICAL SUPPLEMENT TO
VOLUME 1 OF CONSTRUCTION REVIEW. Washington, D.C.: Government
Printing Office, 1955, 78p.

BUILDING AND MODERNIZATION (continued)

U.S. Department of Labor. Bureau of Labor Statistics. CONSTRUCTION DUR-
ING FIVE DECADES; HISTORICAL STATISTICS, 1907-52. (Bulletin 1146).
Washington, D.C.: Government Printing Office, 1953. 75p. tables, charts.
pap. processed.

U.S. Department of Labor. Bureau of Labor Statistics. NEW HOUSING AND
ITS MATERIALS, 1940-1956. (Bulletin 1231). Washington, D.C.: Government
Printing Office, August, 1958. 58p. tables. pap.
> "Analysis of trends, characteristics, facilities and prices of one-
> family and multi-family housing. Extensive tabulations on types,
> sizes, facilities, construction materials, plumbing, heating and
> other characteristics."

U.S. Department of Labor. Bureau of Labor Statistics. NONFARM HOUSING
STARTS 1889-1958. (Bulletin 1260). Washington, D.C.: Government Printing
Office, 1959. 37p. tables. pap. processed.

U.S. Department of Labor. Bureau of Labor Statistics. STRUCTURE OF THE
RESIDENTIAL BUILDING INDUSTRY IN 1949. (Bulletin 1170). Washington,
D.C.: Government Printing Office, 1954. 38p. pap.

U.S. Department of Labor. Bureau of Labor Statistics. TRENDS IN BUILDING
PERMIT ACTIVITY. (Bulletin no. 1243). Washington, D.C.: Government
Printing Office, 1959. 123p. tables, charts. pap.
> On Cover: Indexes of Volume, 1929-1956, Monthly Statistics,
> 1954-1956, Scope of Series, Types of Buildings, Volume in
> Principle Cities, Metropolitan Dispersion, Selected References.

U.S. Department of Labor. Information and Education Service. ECONOMICS
OF THE CONSTRUCTION INDUSTRY. Washington, D.C.: Government Printing Office, 1919. 263p. tables, diagrs.
> Contents: Summary; the Decreases in the Purchasing Power of
> Money; Cost and Supply of Construction Materials; Labor and
> Wages in the Construction Industry; Sources and Supply of Capi-
> tal for the Construction Industry; Rents and Land Values; De-
> ferred Construction; Bibliography; Lists of Charts.

U.S. Federal Housing Administration. LIST OF TECHNICAL STUDIES BY THE
FEDERAL HOUSING ADMINISTRATION, IN COOPERATION WITH TECHNICAL
STUDIES ADVISORY COMMITTEE AND BUILDING RESEARCH ADVISORY BOARD
OF THE NATIONAL ACADEMY OF SCIENCES--NATIONAL RESEARCH COUN-
CIL, Rev. (FHA No. 470). Washington, D.C.: 1960. 46p. pap. processed.
> Periodic revisions. Studies under contract, studies under con-
> sideration, subjects of potential interest and completed studies
> and reports.

U.S. Federal Housing Administration. MINIMUM PROPERTY REQUIREMENTS
FOR PROPERTIES OF THREE OR MORE LIVING UNITS. (FHA 160). Washington, D.C.: Government Printing Office, 1961. various paging. charts,

diagrs. looseleaf.
A new edition to be released April 1963. FHA's EXPLORATION, EXCAVATION AND FOUNDATION DESIGN CRITERIA FOR MULTI-FAMILY HOUSING PROJECTS, issued in 1962 as an expansion of the MINIMUM REQUIREMENTS FOR THREE OR MORE LIVING UNITS.

U.S. Federal Housing Administration. MINIMUM PROPERTY STANDARDS FOR LOW COST HOUSING. (FHA no. 18). Washington, D.C.: 1961. 31p. pap. processed.

U.S. Federal Housing Administration. MINIMUM PROPERTY STANDARDS FOR ONE AND TWO LIVING UNITS. (FHA no. 300). Washington, D.C.: Government Printing Office, 1958. 315p. charts, diagrs. looseleaf.
Index. Revised pages issued periodically.

United States Gypsum Company. A BLUEPRINT FOR PROFIT; A STUDY OF THE PROBLEMS OF BUSINESS MANAGEMENT AMONG RESIDENTIAL BUILDERS. Chicago: no date. 152p. illus. pap.
United States Gypsum, at the suggestion of the National Association of Home Builders, retained Cresap, McCormick and Paget, Management Consultants to analyze the problems of business management of residential builders. Documentary film entitled "A Blueprint for Profit Outlines the General Problems and Presents Recommendations for the Improvement of the Builder's Business." "Booklet expands upon these recommendations and includes a detailed discussion and explanation of selected phases of business management together with a specific program of action for the residential builder."

United States Gypsum Company. OPERATIVE REMODELING; THE NEW PROFIT FRONTIER FOR BUILDERS. Chicago: 1956. 126p. illus.
With the cooperation of the National Association of Home Builders. Prepared by the editors of the BUSINESS OF BUILDING and POPULAR HOME magazines.

U.S. Housing and Home Finance Agency. Division of Housing Research. CONSTRUCTION FINANCING FOR HOME BUILDERS, by Neal MacGiehan. Washington, D.C.: 1953. 123p. illus. pap.

Walker, Frank R. THE BUILDING ESTIMATOR'S REFERENCE BOOK; A PRACTICAL AND THROUGHLY RELIABLE REFERENCE BOOK FOR CONTRACTORS AND ESTIMATORS ENGAGED IN ESTIMATING THE COST OF CONSTRUCTION ON CLASSES OF MODERN BUILDING, 14th ed. Chicago: 1957. 1780p.

Warren, George F. and Pearson, Frank A. WORLD PRICES AND THE BUILDING INDUSTRY; INDEX NUMBERS OF PRICES OF 40 BASIC COMMODITIES FOR 14 COUNTRIES IN CURRENCY AND IN GOLD AND MATERIAL ON THE BUILDING INDUSTRY. New York: John Wiley, 1937. 240p. tables, charts.
"The most important single business indicator is the index of prices of basic commodities. The second most important is the

BUILDING AND MODERNIZATION (continued)

building cycle. Construction is important because of the large
amount of basic materials that is uses, and the large amount of
labor employed."

Waugh, Herbert R. and Burbank, Nelson L. HANDBOOK OF BUILDING TERMS
AND DEFINITIONS. New York: Simmons-Boardman, 1954. 421p. illus.

Building, Modernization and Land Development—Bibliographies

Great Britain, Department of Scientific and Industrial Research. BUILDING
SCIENCE ABSTRACTS. (Sold by Her Majesty's Stationery Office, York House,
London WC 2, England.)

National Housing Center. Library. BUILDING CODES; A LIST OF SELECTED
REFERENCES, Rev. ed. (Bibliography Series no. 5). Washington, D.C.:
National Association of Home Builders, 1960. 178p. pap. processed.
    784 citations. Section 1 lists the standard building codes.
    Includes sections on standards, research and court decisions.
    References annotated. Supplemented by National Housing Cen-
    ter Library Reference List no. 48, April, 1962.

NATIONAL HOUSING CENTER LIBRARY BULLETIN. National Association of
Home Builders, 1625 L Street N.W., Washington 6, D.C. Monthly.
    An index of periodical articles of interest to builders.

National Research Council. Building Research Institute. ABSTRACTS OF BUILD-
ING SCIENCE PUBLICATIONS. Washington D.C.: 1957-60. pap. processed.

National Research Council. Division of Building Research. ANNOTATED
BIBLIOGRAPHY; PERFORMANCE STANDARDS FOR SPACE AND SITE PLAN-
NING FOR RESIDENTIAL DEVELOPMENT, prepared by H.P. Oberlander and F.
Lasserre. (Bibliography no. 19). Ottawa, Canada: August, 1961. 33p.
pap. processed.
    Great Britain, United States and Canada.

National Research Council. Division of Building Research. CANADIAN BUILD-
ING ABSTRACTS. Ottawa, Canada:
    To provide a survey of articles pertaining to building research
    from Canadian technical journals. Printed in English and French.

National Research Council. Division of Building Research. SOURCES OF IN-
FORMATION ON BUILDING, by Eileen R. Carson. (Canadian Building Digest
27). Ottawa, Canada: 1962. 12p. pap.

U.S. National Bureau of Standards. SELECTED BIBLIOGRAPHY ON BUILDING

Building, Modernization and Land Development—Bibliographies

CONSTRUCTION AND MAINTENANCE, 3d ed., comp. by Edith R. Meggers. (Building Materials and Structures Report 140). Washington, D.C.: Government Printing Office, 1959. 30p. pap. processed.

Building, Modernization and Land Development—Periodicals
(See Appendix for complete information concerning these publications).

AMERICAN BUILDER. BUILDING COSTS. BUILDING PERMITS. BUILDING SCIENCE ABSTRACTS. BUSINESS TREND NEWS. COMMUNITY FACILITIES ADMINISTRATION NEWS. CONSTRUCTION ACTIVITY. CONSTRUCTION REVIEW. DODGE REPORTS. ENGINEERING NEWS RECORD. EXPENDITURES ON RESIDENTIAL ADDITIONS, ALTERATIONS, MAINTENANCE AND REPAIRS, AND REPLACEMENTS. FEDERAL RESERVE BULLETIN. HOMEBUILDING NEWS. HOUSE AND HOME. HOUSING REFERENCES. HOUSING STARTS. HOUSING TRENDS. JOURNAL OF HOMEBUILDING. NAHB LEGISLATIVE BULLETIN. NAHB WASHINGTON LETTER. PRACTICAL BUILDER. REAL ESTATE ANALYST CONSTRUCTION BULLETIN. SURVEY OF CURRENT RENT BUSINESS.

LAND DEVELOPMENT

Adams, Thomas. THE DESIGN OF RESIDENTIAL AREAS; BASIC CONSIDERATIONS, PRINCIPLES AND METHODS. (Harvard City Planning Studies, vol.6). Cambridge: Harvard University Press, 1934. 296p. illus., tables, diagrs.

American Public Health Association. Committee on the Hygiene of Housing. PLANNING THE NEIGHBORHOOD. (Standards for Healthful Housing, vol. 1). Chicago: Public Administration Service, 1948. 108p. pap.
    Reprinted in 1960 with a supplemental annotated bibliography. 1. Basic requirements for site selection; 2. Development of land, utilities and services; 3. Planning for residential facilities; 4 Provision of neighborhood community facilities; 5. Layouts for vehicular and pedestrian circulation; 6. Neighborhood density, coordination of housing elements.

American Society of Planning Officials. CLUSTER SUBDIVISIONS. (Planning Advisory Service Information Report no. 135). Chicago: 1960. 35p. pap. processed.

American Society of Planning Officials. MUNICIPAL WATERFRONTS: PLANNING FOR INDUSTRIAL AND COMMERCIAL USES. (Planning Advisory Service Information Report no. 45). Chicago: 1952. 21p. pap. processed.
    Selected bibliography: p. 19-21.

LAND DEVELOPMENT (continued)

American Society of Planning Officials. PERFORMANCE BONDS FOR THE IN-
STALLATION OF SUBDIVISION IMPROVEMENTS. (Planning Advisory Service
Information Report no. 48). Chicago: 1953. 26p. pap. processed.
"Requirements made by financial institutions upon private develop-
ers in the financing of improvements."

American Society of Planning Officials. PLANNING FOR APARTMENTS.
(Planning Advisory Service Information Report no. 139). Chicago: 1960. 44p.
pap. processed.

American Society of Planning Officials. RECORDING AND REPORTING STATIS-
TICS ON SUBDIVISION ACTIVITY. (Planning Advisory Service Information
Report no. 87). Chicago: 1956. 24p. pap. processed.
"Methods that can be used to compile, summarize and report statis-
tics on subdivision activity" for use as an important tool of plan-
ning.

American Society of Planning Officials. SUBDIVISION DESIGN--SOME NEW
DEVELOPMENTS. (Planning Advisory Service Information Report no. 102).
Chicago: 1957. 15p. pap. processed.

American Society of Planning Officials. WATERFRONTS: PLANNING FOR
RESORT AND RESIDENTIAL USES. (Planning Advisory Service Information Report
no. 118). Chicago: 1959. 40p. pap. processed.

Civil Engineers and Land Surveyors Association of California. A DRAFT OF A
SUBDIVISION ORDINANCE RECOMMENDED TO CITIES FOR CONSIDERATION,
4th ed., by Harold A. Barnett. Los Angeles: 608 South Hill Street, zone
14, 1961. 31p. pap. processed.

How to Develop Real Estate. Part 9, p. 939-1064 In Friedman, Edith J.,
ed. REAL ESTATE ENCYCLOPEDIA. Englewood Cliffs, N.J.: Prentice-Hall,
1960.
Chapter 37: Residential Subdivision Development, by Rodney M.
Lockwood and Robert C. Ledermann; Chapter 38: Development of
Shopping Centers, by Williard G. Rouse; Chapter 39: Industrial
Land Development, by Stuart P. Walsh; Chapter 40: City Planning
and Urban Renewal, by James Felt.

Iowa. State University of Iowa. Institute of Public Affairs and the League of Iowa.
Municipalities. A GUIDE TO SUBDIVISION ANNEXATION AND CONTROL.
Iowa City: 1959. 52p. pap.
Prepared by Robert L. Stoyles, Jr.

Isard, Walter and Coughlin, Robert E. MUNICIPAL COSTS AND REVENUES
RESULTING FROM COMMUNITY GROWTH. West Trenton, N.J.: Chandler-
Davis, 1957. 111p.
"Our approach is not to study individual communities, but to
study the individual activities and functions which generate
costs and revenues." A "building-block" approach with pro-

LAND DEVELOPMENT (continued)

cedures and materials provided with instructions to help the
reader ascertain costs and revenues, in a particular town.

James, Harlean. LAND PLANNING IN THE UNITED STATES FOR THE CITY,
STATE AND NATION. (Land Economics Series; Standard Course in Real Estate).
New York: Macmillan, 1926. 427p. illus.

Kostka, V. Joseph. NEIGHBORHOOD PLANNING. Winnipeg, Manitoba: School
of Architecture, University of Manitoba, 1957. 160p. diagrs.
　　　A companion volume to PLANNING RESIDENTIAL SUBDIVISIONS.
　　　Organized around numerous plan illustrations, the neighborhood
　　　unit is planned for the population of a school district. Sponsored
　　　by Appraisal Institute of Canada.

Lautner, Harold W. SUBDIVISION REGULATIONS; AN ANALYSIS OF LAND
SUBDIVISION CONTROL PRACTICES. Chicago: Public Administration Service,
1941. 346p.
　　　A standard reference.

Mandelker, Daniel R. GREEN BELTS AND URBAN GROWTH; ENGLISH TOWN
AND COUNTRY PLANNING IN ACTION. Madison: University of
Wisconsin Press, 1962. 176p.
　　　Bibliography: p. 161-72.
　　　Examination of the development control process, the actual
　　　mechanism through which these general aims are implemented.

McMichael, Stanley L. REAL ESTATE SUBDIVISIONS. New York: Prentice-
Hall, 1949. 393p.
　　　"This volume deals largely with the problems associated with the
　　　acquisition, development and sale of subdivision land; relatively
　　　little attention is paid to the techniques..."

Monchow, Helen C. SEVENTY YEARS OF REAL ESTATE SUBDIVIDING IN THE
REGION OF CHICAGO. (Northwestern University Studies in the Social
Sciences no. 3). Evanston, Ill.: Northwestern University, 1939. 200p.
tables, charts.
　　　"The objective of the study is the discovery of the underlying
　　　forces that have caused or been associated with subdividing
　　　activity as it has taken place in the Chicago metropolitan area."
　　　Index of residential land needs. Institutional background of
　　　the subdividing business.

Monchow, Helen C. THE USE OF DEED RESTRICTIONS IN SUBDIVISION
DEVELOPMENT. (Studies in Land Economics, Research Monograph no. 1).
Chicago: Institute for Research in Land Economics and Public Utilities, 1928.
84p. tables. pap.

National Association of Home Builders. LEGAL PROBLEMS OF LAND SUB-
DIVISION; AN ANALYSIS OF LEADING CASES IN THE FIELDS OF ZONING,
LOT AND HOUSE RESTRICTIONS, FEES, LICENSING AND PROBLEMS OF

LAND DEVELOPMENT (continued)

WATER MAIN EXTENSION, by Philip A. Ryan and Eugene J. McDonald.
Washington, D.C.: 1960. 60p. pap.
>   25 pages of footnotes citing cases.
>   1st ed., 1958, entitled, THE LEGALITY OF GOVERNMENTAL
>   RESTRICTIONS UPON LAND USE AND HOME BUILDERS.

National Association of Home Builders. RESIDENTIAL DEVELOPMENT--A
FINANCIAL ASSET TO THE COMMUNITY, by Robert C. Ledermann. Washington,
D.C.: 1960. 12p. pap. processed.
>   "An evaluation of surveys and reports on the impact of new homes
>   on a community cost-revenue structure."

National Association of Home Builders. Community Facilities and Urban
Renewal Department. KEEPING THE LID ON LAND COSTS, prepared by
Robert C. Ledermann and David S. Clark. Washington, D.C.: 1961. 1 vol. plus
supplemental material in folder.

National Association of Home Builders. Rental Housing Department. WHAT
BUILDERS SHOULD KNOW ABOUT GARDEN-TYPE APARTMENTS, by
Arnold M. Kronstadt and James F. Neville. (Rental TB-11). Washington,
D.C.: 1960. 86p. illus., charts, diagrs. pap. processed.

National Institute of Municipal Law Officers. NIMLO MODEL SUBDIVISION
ORDINANCE. Washington, D.C.: 1953. 21p. pap.

Nelson, Richard L. and Aschman, Frederick T. REAL ESTATE AND CITY PLAN-
NING. Englewood Cliffs, N.J.: Prentice-Hall, 1957. 507p.
>   "Both real estate values and the transfer of property are affected
>   by planning decisions."

Nolen, John and Hubbard, Henry V. PARKWAYS AND LAND VALUES.
(Harvard City Planning Studies no. 9). Cambridge: Harvard University Press,
1937. 135p.

North Carolina. University. Institute of Government. MUNICIPAL COST-
REVENUE RESEARCH IN THE UNITED STATES; A CRITICAL SURVEY OF RESEARCH
TO MEASURE MUNICIPAL COSTS AND REVENUES IN RELATION TO LAND
USES AND AREAS; 1933-1960, by Ruth L. Mace. Chapel Hill: 1961. 201p.
tables, charts. pap.
>   Contents: Background and Previews; Slum Losses and Redevelop-
>   ment Gains; Balancing Land Uses in the Suburbs; Cost Revenue
>   Analysis in Connection with Annexation; the Missing "By Picture;"
>   Summary and Forecast.

Regional Plan of New York and Its Environs. NEIGHBORHOOD AND COMMUNITY
PLANNING. (Regional Survey volume 7). New York: 1929. 363p. illus.
>   Comprising 3 monographs: THE NEIGHBORHOOD UNIT, by
>   Clarence Arthur Perry; SUNLIGHT AND DAYLIGHT FOR URBAN
>   AREAS, by Wayne D. Heydecker and Ernest P. Goodrich;
>   PROBLEMS OF PLANNING UNBUILT AREAS, by Thomas Adams,

LAND DEVELOPMENT (continued)

et al. "Presents the results of studies made regarding the principles, methods and laws of planning subdivisions, neighborhoods and communities."

Spence-Sales, Harold. HOW TO SUBDIVIDE; A HANDBOOK ON THE LAYOUT OF HOUSING DEVELOPMENTS. Ottawa, Canada: Community Planning Association of Canada, 1950. 36p. pap.

Subdivisions. Section 57,000 In Casey, William J. REAL ESTATE INVESTMENT DEALS, IDEAS, FORMS. New York: Institute for Business Planning, 1959-
> Includes subsections: How Does a Developer Compute His Income; How to Get Capital Gains on Subdivision Sales.

U. S. Federal Housing Administration. HOW TO TEST FINANCIAL SOUNDNESS OF RENTAL HOUSING PROPERTIES. (Form 2484). Washington, D.C.: Government Printing Office, 1951. 22p. Charts, forms. pap. processed.

U.S. Federal Housing Administration. NEIGHBORHOOD STANDARDS. (Land Planning Bulletin no. 3). Washington, D.C.: 1960. illus., diagrs. pap. processed.
> Bulletin issued to reflect local conditions and practices in various regions. Acceptable methods of complying with local standards for land development. National requirements and detailed technical data included.

U. S. Housing and Home Finance Agency. THE COST OF MUNICIPAL SERVICES IN RESIDENTIAL AREAS, by William L. C. Wheaton and Morton J. Schussheim. (PB 111652). Washington, D.C.: Government Printing Office, 1955. 55p. pap.

U. S. Housing and Home Finance Agency. PLANNING LAWS; HOUSING, URBAN PLANNING ASSISTANCE, COMMUNITY FACILITIES, URBAN RENEWAL....A COMPARATIVE DIGEST OF STATE STATUTES FOR COMMUNITY, COUNTY, REGION AND STATE PLANNING THROUGH DECEMBER, 1957, 2d ed. Washington, D.C.: 1958. 77p. pap.

U. S. Housing and Home Finance Agency. SUGGESTED LAND SUBDIVISION REGULATIONS, 3rd rev. ed. Washington, D.C.: 1962. 68p. illus., diagrs. pap. (Sold by Government Printing Office).
> Original edition, 1952. Revised in 1957 and 1960. Appendices; FHA Data Sheets on Subdivision Exhibits; Federal Housing Administration Data Sheet on Protective Covenants; Bibliography; and HHFA Office Offering Assistance Including Local FHA Insuring Offices. "To help guide the preparation of the regulations which a locality may wish to adopt. It covers the technical elements of land subdivision control designed to assure the maximum return on the local government's investment, and at the same time to assure the subdivider full consideration of his interests and responsibilities." Control for developments financed pursuant to federal regulations.

LAND DEVELOPMENT (continued)

U. S. Housing and Home Finance Agency. VIEWS ON REDUCTION OF
HOUSING COSTS; SYMPOSIUM OF LETTERS WRITTEN AT THE REQUEST OF
NORMAN P. MASON, U. S. HOUSING ADMINISTRATOR. Washington,
D.C.: 1961. 72p. pap. processed.
> Academicians; architects; builders, prefabricators, and mobile
> home manufacturers; producers of building products; other pro-
> fessions.

United States Savings and Loan League. WHAT THE SAVINGS AND LOAN
ASSOCIATION NEEDS TO KNOW ABOUT LAND PLANNING; YOUR GUIDE
TO THE BEST PRACTICE FOR DEVELOPING SUBDIVISIONS THAT WILL HOLD
THEIR VALUE. Chicago: 1956. 32p. pap.

Urban Land Institute. THE EFFECTS OF LARGE LOT SIZE ON RESIDENTIAL
DEVELOPMENT, by Massachusetts Department of Commerce and Massachusetts
Institute of Technology. (Technical Bulletin no. 32). Washington, D.C.:
1958. 52p. diagrs., maps. pap.

Urban Land Institute. HOME BUILDERS MANUAL FOR LAND DEVELOPMENT,
2d rev. ed. Washington, D.C.: National Association of Home Builders, 1958.
264p. illus. pap.
> "This manual presents general principles and criteria for good
> land planning practice based upon practical experience and
> demonstration." Includes some information on shopping centers,
> marinas and garden apartments.

Urban Land Institute. MISTAKES WE HAVE MADE IN COMMUNITY DEVELOP-
MENT, by J. C. Nichols. (Technical Bulletin no. 1). Washington, D.C.:
1945. 8p. pap.

Urban Land Institute. PLANNING COMMUNITY FACILITIES FOR BASIC
EMPLOYMENT EXPANSION, by Max S. Wehrly. (Technical Bulletin no. 16).
Washington, D.C.: 1951. 27p. illus., tables. pap.

Urban Land Institute. UTILITIES AND FACILITIES FOR NEW RESIDENTIAL
DEVELOPMENT; A SURVEY OF MUNICIPAL POLICY, by J. Ross McKeever.
(Technical Bulletin no. 27). Washington, D.C.: 1955. 100p. tables. pap.

Urban Land Institute. WHO PAYS FOR STREET AND UTILITY INSTALLATIONS
IN NEW RESIDENTIAL AREAS; A SURVEY OF MUNICIPAL POLICY, by
Seward H. Mott and Max S. Wehrly. (Technical Bulletin no. 13). Washington,
D.C.: 1950. 7p. tables. pap.

Urban Land Institute. Community Builders Council. THE COMMUNITY BUILDERS
HANDBOOK, 3d ed. Washington, D.C.: 1960. 476p. illus., tables, charts,
diagrs.
> Section 1 -- Residential Communities. Section 2 -- Planning
> and Operation of Shopping Centers.
> Section 1 -- Residential Communities: Part 1. Preliminary Steps
> in Community Development: Market Analysis, Technical Planning

LAND DEVELOPMENT (continued)

Service, Selection of the Site; Part 2. Planning the Development:
Protective Convenants, Maintenance and Homes Association, Main-
tenance in Apartment Development, Selling the Project; Part 3.
Protecting the Future of the Development: Protective Convenants,
Maintenance and Homes Associations, Maintenance in Apartment
Development, Selling the Project.
Appendices: Protective Convenants, FHA; Protective Covenants,
Sample Form; Declaration of Incorporation, Homes Association,
Sample Form; By-Laws of Homes Association, Sample Form.

Urban Land Institute and National Association of Home Builders. NEW
APPROACHES TO RESIDENTIAL LAND DEVELOPMENT; A STUDY OF
CONCEPTS AND INNOVATIONS. (Technical Bulletin no. 40). Washington,
D.C.: Urban Land Institute, 1961. 151p. illus., diagrs. pap.
Harman, O'Donnell & Henninger Associates, Inc., Technical
Advisors.

Warner, Sam B., Jr. STREETCAR SUBURBS, THE PROCESS OF GROWTH IN
BOSTON, 1870-1900. (Publication of the Joint Center for Urban Studies).
Cambridge, Mass.: Harvard University Press and the M.I.T. Press, 1962.
208p. illus., tables, charts, diagrs.
"The book's unique method is analysis of the building permits
issued for 23,000 new houses that went up in the three towns
from 1870 to 1900. These records tell a good deal not only
about the houses but also about the society that built them."

Land Development—Bibliographies

Bestor, George C. and Jones, Holway R. CITY PLANNING; A BASIC BIBLIO-
GRAPHY OF SOURCES AND TRENDS, 2d ed. Sacramento, Calif.: California
Council of Civil Engineers and Land Surveyors, 1962. 195p. pap. processed.
Detailed subject index--classified listing of over 1,000 citations. Includes precise reference to a number of foreign language
city planning periodicals; publishers' addresses, organization services
and periodicals; separate author, title and subject indexes; American
city planning collections.

National Housing Center. Library. COMMUNITY FACILITIES; A LIST OF
SELECTED REFERENCES, Rev. ed. (Bibliography Series no. 4). Washington,
D.C.: National Association of Home Builders, 1959. 170p. pap. processed.

National Housing Center, Library. LAND PLANNING AND SUBDIVISION; a
CHECKLIST OF BOOKS AND RECENT ARTICLES, Rev. (Reference List no. 50).
Washington, D.C.: National Association of Home Builders, 1962. 9p. pap.
processed.

National Research Council, Division of Building Research. ANNOTATED
BIBLIOGRAPHY, PERFORMANCE STANDARDS FOR SPACE AND SITE PLANNING

Land Development—Bibliographies

FOR RESIDENTIAL DEVELOPMENT, by H. P. Oberlander and F. Lasserre. (Bibliography no. 19). Ottawa: 1961. 33p. pap.

Urban Land Institute. A PRACTICABLE CITY PLANNING BIBLIOGRAPHY, by Harold W. Lautner. (Technical Bulletin no. 5). Washington, D.C.: 1946. 8p. pap. processed.

Section 6

COUNSELING

American Society of Real Estate Counselors. THE AMERICAN SOCIETY OF REAL ESTATE COUNSELORS. Chicago: 1960. 10p. pap.

American Society of Real Estate Counselors. THE REAL ESTATE COUNSELOR: WHAT MANNER OF MAN IS HE? THE SECOND IN A SERIES OF STUDIES ON REAL ESTATE COUNSELING, PREPARED FROM INFORMATION SUPPLIED BY MEMBERS OF THE AMERICAN SOCIETY OF REAL ESTATE COUNSELORS. Chicago: (in preparation).

American Society of Real Estate Counselors. THE REALTOR'S ROLE IN REAL ESTATE COUNSELING. Chicago: 1961. 11p. pap.
> Describes the profession of counseling, its requirements, compensations, etc.

American Society of Real Estate Counselors. WHAT IS REAL ESTATE COUNSELING? THE FIRST IN A SERIES OF STUDIES OF REAL ESTATE COUNSELING, PREPARED FROM INFORMATION SUPPLIED BY MEMBERS OF THE AMERICAN SOCIETY OF REAL ESTATE COUNSELORS. Chicago: (in preparation).

Askew, C. D. and Curtiss, Robert S. Counseling. p. 20-4 In National Institute of Real Estate Brokers. REAL ESTATE SPECIALIZATIONS. Chicago: 1962.

Landauer, James D. How Does a Counselor Counsel Himself? Here's the Answer. REALTOR'S HEADLINES, vol. 29, no. 41, section 2, October 8, 1962, p. 4.

Landauer, James D. What is Counseling? REALTOR'S HEADLINES, vol. 27, no. 47, November 21, 1960, p. 2.

Shattuck, Charles R. The Realtor and Real Estate Counseling. APPRAISAL JOURNAL, vol. 30, no. 1, January 1962, p. 32-9.

Section 7

FINANCE

GENERAL

Financing. Section 6 In PRENTICE-HALL REAL ESTATE GUIDE. Englewood
Cliffs, N.J.: Prentice-Hall, 1953-   illus. looseleaf.
> Describes types of properties requiring financing, types of financ-
> ing used in real estate transactions, sources of funds, instruments,
> and costs.

Financing. Section 55,300 In Casey, William J. REAL ESTATE INVEST-
MENT DEALS, IDEAS, FORMS. New York: Institute for Business Planning,
1959-
> Contents: Types of Mortgages; How to Get Financing in a Tight
> Money Market; How Mortgages Figure in Buying and Selling Real
> Estate; What to Consider in Foreclosing Mortgages; Mortgages as
> a Form of Real Estate Investment.

Grebler, Leo, et. al. CAPITAL FORMATION IN RESIDENTIAL REAL ESTATE,
TRENDS, AND PROSPECTS. (National Bureau of Economic Research. Studies
in Capital Formation and Financing, no. 1). Princeton, N. J.: Princeton
University Press, 1956. 519p. tables, charts.

Hoagland, Henry Elmer and Stone, Leo D. REAL ESTATE FINANCE, Rev. ed.
Homewood, Ill.: Richard D. Irwin, 1961. 587p.
> Written for the student and the professional reader. Treats the
> "form and operation of the significant financial institutions under-
> lying the American real estate market." Questions and answers
> at chapter ends.

How to Finance Real Estate Transactions. Friedman, Edith J., ed. REAL
ESTATE ENCYCLOPEDIA. Englewood Cliffs, N.J.: Prentice-Hall, 1960.
> Chapter 15: Broker's Role in Financing Real Estate Transactions,
> by James Andrews; Chapter 16: Home Financing, by Norman
> Strunk; Chapter 17: Apartment House Financing, by Thomas L.
> Lowe; Chapter 18: Commercial Property Financing, by J. F.
> Hott; Chapter 19: Farm Financing, by Beach Craigmyle.

Hoyt, Homer. Financing the Future Commercial and Industrial Requirements
in Metropolitan Growth of the United States. JOURNAL OF FINANCE, vol.
15, no.2, May, 1960, p. 263-73.
> Commercial, industrial and housing space projections.

GENERAL (continued)

Mao, James C. T. CASES IN REAL ESTATE FINANCE. (Michigan Business Reports, no. 31). Ann Arbor: University of Michigan, Bureau of Business Research, 1959. 115p. tables, charts, diagrs.
    A case book designed for use in an introductory course on real estate finance. A series of ten cases.

Maryland. University. Bureau of Business and Economic Research. RESIDEN-TIAL MORTGAGE AND CONSTRUCTION FINANCING, HAGERSTOWN, MARYLAND. College Park: University of Maryland, 1951. 35p. pap.

McMichael, Stanley L. and O'Keefe, Paul T. HOW TO FINANCE REAL ESTATE, 2d ed. New York: Prentice-Hall, 1953. 366p. tables, diagrs., forms, plans.
    Describes all sources of real estate credit and explains policies, methods, and terms of each.

Mortgage Bankers Association of America. A STATEMENT OF PUBLIC POLICY ON LEGISLATION AFFECTING REAL ESTATE FINANCE. Chicago: 1962. 12p.
    Title varies. 1953: A STATEMENT OF THE FEDERAL GOVERN-MENT'S HOUSING AGENCIES AND PROGRAMS. Statements also issued in 1956, 1958, and 1960. Formal presentations of the Associations's attitude on important issues affecting mortgage finance.

Pinnell, W. George. Residential Real Estate Finance in the 1960's. JOURNAL OF FINANCE, vol. 15, no. 2, May, 1960. p. 250-62.
    Projections of housing starts and financing.

President's Conference on Home Building and Home Ownership, Washington, D.C., 1931. HOME FINANCE AND TAXATION; REPORTS OF THE COMMIT-TEE ON FINANCE AND TAXATION, ed. by John M. Gries and James Ford. Washington, D.C.: 1932. 278p. charts.
    On Cover: LOANS, ASSESSMENTS, AND TAXES ON RESI-DENTIAL PROPERTY.

Sherman, Malcolm C. MORTGAGE AND REAL ESTATE INVESTMENT GUIDE. Boston: 1952- . processed. looseleaf.
    "The summary which follows the laws and statutes of 50 states, D.C., British Columbia, Ontario, Puerto Rico and Quebec answers the salient legal questions concerning mortgage loans (conventional, F. H. A. and V. A.) and real estate investments in such jurisdictions or furnishes a starting point."

U. S. Housing and Home Finance Agency. CAPITAL FUNDS FOR HOUSING IN THE UNITED STATES. Washington, D.C.: Government Printing Office, 1960. 32p. tables. pap.
    "Describes the operation of the private financing system for housing in the United States."

GENERAL (continued)

U. S. Housing and Home Finance Agency. Office of International Housing.
HOUSING FINANCE IN THE UNITED STATES. Washington, D.C.: 1962.
51p. pap.

Finance—Periodicals

(See Appendix for complete information concerning these publications.)

CONVENTIONAL LOANS MADE TO FINANCE ACQUISITION AND DEVELOP-
MENT OF LAND. ESTIMATED HOME MORTGAGE DEBT AND FINANCING
ACTIVITY. FHA MONTHLY REPORT OF OPERATIONS. FSLIC INSURED
SAVINGS AND LOAN ASSOCIATIONS. FARM MORTGAGE LENDING
EXPERIENCE. FEDERAL HOME LOAN BANK BOARD DIGEST. FEDERAL
RESERVE BULLETIN. LEGAL BULLETIN; THE LAW AFFECTING SAVINGS
ASSOCIATIONS. MORTGAGE BANKER. MORTGAGE BULLETIN FOR
BANKS OF DEPOSIT. MORTGAGE INTEREST RATES ON CONVENTIONAL
LOANS. MORTGAGE MARKET. MORTGAGE RECORDING LETTER.
NATIONAL DELINQUENCY SURVEY. NON-FARM REAL ESTATE FORECLOSURE
REPORT. QUARTERLY ECONOMIC REPORT OF TRENDS IN THE MORTGAGE
INDUSTRY. REAL ESTATE ANALYST MORTGAGE BULLETIN. SAVINGS AND
LOAN JOURNAL. SAVINGS AND LOAN NEWS. SURVEY OF CURRENT
BUSINESS.

FEDERAL PROGRAMS

NOTE: A list of Federal government agencies involved in housing and finance
programs appears in Appendix C.

The annual and special reports, administrative regulations, and
miscellaneous publications of these agencies, as well as Congressional
hearings and documents relating to the programs are primary sources. The
MONTHLY CATALOG OF U. S. GOVERNMENT PUBLICATIONS lists
such items.

Break, George F. THE ECONOMIC IMPACT OF FEDERAL LOAN INSURANCE;
A SPECIAL PROJECT REPORT. Washington, D.C.: National Planning Associ-
tion, 1961. 271p. tables.
Includes mortgage insurance, direct loan, public housing, and
urban renewal programs.

FEDERAL PROGRAMS (continued)

Colean, Miles L. IMPACT OF GOVERNMENT ON REAL ESTATE FINANCE IN THE UNITED STATES. (NBER, Financial Research Program, Studies in Urban Mortgage Financing, no. 2). New York: National Bureau of Economic Research, 1950. 171p. (Dist. by Princeton University Press, Princeton, N.J.)

Colean, Miles and Newcomb, Robinson. STABILIZING CONSTRUCTION: THE RECORD AND POTENTIAL (Committee for Economic Development Research Study). New York: McGraw-Hill, 1952. 340p.
As a factor in the business cycle.

Eastburn, David P. REAL ESTATE CREDIT CONTROLS AS A SELECTIVE INSTRU-MENT OF FEDERAL RESERVE POLICY. Unpublished Ph. D. thesis, University of Pennsylvania, 1957.

Federal Aids to Financing. Section 12 In PRENTICE-HALL REAL ESTATE GUIDE. Englewood Cliffs, N. J.: Prentice-Hall, 1953-   . illus. looseleaf.
A concise digest of the National Housing Act and the Servicemen's Readjustment Act.

Federal National Mortgage Association. BACKGROUND AND HISTORY OF THE FEDERAL NATIONAL MORTGAGE ASSOCIATION. Washington, D.C.: 1958. 44p. tables. pap. processed.

Federal National Mortgage Association. REPORT AND FINANCIAL STATEMENT OF THE SECONDARY MARKET OPERATIONS. Washington, D.C.: Government Printing Office, 1954-   . pap.
Balance sheet and income and expense statements. Issued quarterly.

Federal National Mortgage Association. SEMIANNUAL REPORTS, June 30, 1949-   pap.

Federal Regulation. Section 10 In PRENTICE-HALL REAL ESTATE GUIDE. Englewood Cliffs, N. J.: Prentice-Hall, 1953-
"Explains the organizations and functions of the Federal agencies that promulgate (or enforce) the rules and regulations set forth in the Federal Aids to Financing section."

Fisher, Ernest M. and Rapkin, Chester. THE MUTUAL MORTGAGE INSURANCE FUND. New York: Columbia University Press, 1956. 162p.
Institute for Urban Land Use and Housing Studies.

Grebler, Leo. Criteria for Appraising Governmental Housing Programs. AMERICAN ECONOMIC REVIEW, vol. 50, no. 2, May, 1960, p. 321-32.

Grebler, Leo. THE ROLE OF FEDERAL CREDIT AIDS IN RESIDENTIAL CON-STRUCTION. (NBER Occasional Paper 39). New York: National Bureau of Economic Research, 1953. 76p. pap.

Haar, Charles M. FEDERAL CREDIT AND PRIVATE HOUSING; THE MASS
FINANCING DILEMMA. (ACTION Series in Housing and Community Develop-
ment). New York: McGraw-Hill, 1960. 408p. tables, charts.
   Describes and evaluates the residential financing programs of the
   Federal government.

Harriss, C. Lowell. HISTORY AND POLICIES OF THE HOME OWNERS'
LOAN CORPORATION. (NBER Financial Research Program. Studies in
Urban Mortgage Financing, no. 4). New York: National Bureau of Economic
Research, 1931. 204p. tables, charts.

McDonnell, Timothy L. THE WAGNER HOUSING ACT; A CASE STUDY OF
THE LEGISLATIVE PROCESS. Chicago: Loyola University Press, 1957. 470p.

President's Advisory Committee on Government Housing Policies and Programs.
RECOMMENDATIONS ON GOVERNMENT HOUSING POLICIES AND PRO-
GRAMS; A REPORT. Washington, D.C.: Government Printing Office, 1953.
377p.
   "Action is recommended in five areas: First, a vigorous
   attack on slums and a broad effort to prevent the spread of
   slums; second, the effective maintenance and utilization of
   existing houses; third, a steady increase in the volume of building new houses; fourth, special assistance for families of low
   income; fifth, reorganization of the Housing Agency itself for
   greater efficiency and economy."

The Question of Extending Federal Housing Aid, Pro and Con. CONGRESSION-
AL DIGEST, vol. 38, no. 3, March 1959, p. 67-96.

Roles of FNMA and FHLBS in the Mortgage Market. MONTHLY REVIEW,
FEDERAL RESERVE BANK OF SAN FRANCISCO, May, 1960, p. 76-83.

Saulnier, R. J., et al. FEDERAL LENDING AND LOAN INSURANCE.
(National Bureau of Economic Research, Financial Research Program, Other
Studies no. 2). Princeton, N. J.: Princeton University Press, 1958. 566p.
illus.
   Describes the credit programs of Federal agencies and government-
   sponsored organizations, their history, operations and impact.

Skilton, Robert H. Government and the Mortgage Debtor, 1940-1946. UNI-
VERSITY OF PENNSYLVANIA LAW REVIEW, vol. 95, no. 2, December 1946,
p. 119-43.
   Discusses Federal legislation and programs and their effects on
   the mortgage market; includes material on moratorium and deficiency judgment action.

U. S. Department of Agriculture. Bureau of Agricultural Economics. FARM-
MORTGAGE CREDIT FACILITIES IN THE UNITED STATES, by Donald C. Horton, et al. (Miscellaneous Publication, no. 478). Washington, D.C.: Government Printing Office, 1942. 262p. illus., maps.

FEDERAL PROGRAMS (continued)

U. S. Federal Housing Administration. ANNUAL REPORT. Washington, D.C.: Government Printing Office, 1934-   . pap.
   From 1947 to date, issued as part of the Housing and Home Finance Agency ANNUAL REPORT and separately.

U. S. Federal Housing Administration. THE FHA STORY IN SUMMARY, 1934-1959. Washington, D.C.: Government Printing Office, 1959. 22p. illus. pap.

U. S. Federal Housing Administration. UNDERWRITING MANUAL, 8th revision. Washington, D.C.: 1959.
   Also available in looseleaf form.

U. S. Housing and Home Finance Agency. ANNUAL REPORT. Washington, D.C.: Government Printing Office, 1947-   . pap.
   Includes annual reports of the Federal Housing Administration, Public Housing Administration, Federal National Mortgage Association, Community Facilities Administration, and Urban Renewal Administration.

U. S. Housing and Home Finance Agency. STUDY OF HOUSING PROGRAMS AND POLICIES, prepared for the U. S. Housing Administrator...by Ernest M. Fisher. Washington, D.C.: 1960. 61p. pap. processed.

U. S. Housing and Home Finance Agency. URBAN AFFAIRS AND HOUSING; THE COORDINATED PROGRAMS OF THE HOUSING AND HOME FINANCE AGENCY. Washington, D.C.: 1962. 32p. pap.
   Lists regional offices: H.F.A., P.H.A., F.H.A., F.N.M.A. and V.H.M.C.P. Where information about programs can be obtained. Programs administered by the Office of the Administrator, Community Facilities Administration, Urban Renewal Administration.

U. S. Housing and Home Finance Agency. Office of the Administrator. BASIC STATUTES, PUBLIC REGULATIONS AND FORMAL ORDERS OF THE ADMINISTRATOR, 2 vols. Washington, D.C.: Government Printing Office. looseleaf.

U. S. Housing and Home Finance Agency. Office of the Administrator. A SUMMARY OF THE EVOLUTION OF HOUSING ACTIVITIES IN THE FEDERAL GOVERNMENT. Washington, D.C.: Government Printing Office, 1951. 24p. pap.
   Covers period from 1930 to 1950. Narrative.

U. S. Library of Congress. Legislative Reference Service. YOUR CONGRESS AND AMERICAN HOUSING: THE ACTIONS OF CONGRESS ON HOUSING FROM 1892 to 1951..., by Jack Levin. (82d Cong., 2d Sess., House Document no. 532). Washington, D.C.: Government Printing Office, 1952. 37p. pap.
   Concise history of legislation; topical arrangement.

FEDERAL PROGRAMS (continued)

Vidger, Leonard Perry. FEDERAL NATIONAL MORTGAGE ASSOCIATION,
1938-1957. Unpublished Ph. D. thesis, University of Washington, 1960.
"The past of this institution ... and the impact of its operations
upon the real estate industry and mortgage banking." Bibliography:
p. 370-90.

Voluntary Home Mortgage Credit Program. ANNUAL REPORT BY THE ADMINI-
STRATOR, HOUSING AND HOME FINANCE AGENCY. Washington, D.C.:
1955-   . pap. processed.
Issued as part of the Housing and Home Finance Agency ANNUAL
REPORT and separately.

Wendt, Paul F. THE ROLE OF THE FEDERAL GOVERNMENT IN HOUSING.
(National Economic Problems Series no. 460). Washington, D.C.: American
Enterprise Association, 1956. 48p. charts. pap.
"Traces the evolution of Federal housing policies and programs
and evaluates specific programs in terms of their contribution
to the solution of the nation's housing problems." , References:
p. 39-45.

Wood, Ramsay. Government-Backed Mortgage Loan Programs; What They
Were in the Beginning and What They Are Now. MORTGAGE BANKER, vol.
16, no. 6, March 1956, p. 35-40, 59.

INVESTMENT

Boyd, Osborne T. A New Overseas Frontier for the Real Estate Investor.
p. 88-90 In National Real Estate Investor. NATIONAL REAL ESTATE
HANDBOOK AND DIRECTORY. New York: 1962.

Burkhard, Paul L. Some Pitfalls of Real Estate Investment Overseas.
p. 91-5 In National Real Estate Investor. NATIONAL REAL ESTATE
HANDBOOK AND DIRECTORY. New York: 1962.

Cadwallader, Clyde T. HOW TO BUY REAL ESTATE FOR PROFIT. Englewood
Cliffs, N. J.: Prentice-Hall, 1958. 308p. tables, diagrs.
Written for the new investor. Presents the investment potentials
of real estate and describes the possibilities of three areas:
Chicago, San Francisco, and Los Angeles.

Cadwallader, Clyde T. HOW TO DEAL IN REAL ESTATE. New York:
Prentice-Hall, 1955. 362p.
How real estate should be bought and sold with profit to the
seller and the buyer, written for the investor with limited capital and the investor with more ample resources.

INVESTMENT (continued)

Cadwallader, Clyde T. HOW TO MAKE MONEY SPECULATING IN REAL
ESTATE. Englewood Cliffs, N. J.: Prentice-Hall, 1960. 239p.
Describes three elements of profitable speculation, (buying the
right kind of property, proper promotion, and renting or selling
advantageously), and presents principles for each.

California Real Estate Association. CREATIVE REAL ESTATE INVESTMENT.
Los Angeles: 117 West Ninth Street, zone 15, 1962. 120p. pap.
Seven papers presented at the Association's 1962 Creative Real
Estate Investment Conference.

California. University. Real Estate Research Program. LOS ANGELES REAL
ESTATE; A STUDY OF INVESTMENT EXPERIENCE, by Fred E. Case. Los
Angeles: 1960. 103p. tables, charts. pap.
Long term investment performance of 108 Los Angeles investment
properties: apartment houses, office buildings and commercial
property. Bibliography.

Casey, William J. HOW TO BUY AND SELL LAND. New York: Institute
for Business Planning, 1962. 203p. tables. processed.
Describes the forces that create land values and demands for
land and relates them to commercial interests; discusses financing,
improving, and disposing of land and the tax aspect of land transactions.

Casey, William J. REAL ESTATE INVESTMENT DEALS, IDEAS, FORMS,
2 vols. New York: Institute for Business Planning, 1955-   processed.
looseleaf.
A looseleaf service, supplemental monthly. "Recommended for
the reader who wants to keep up with the new forms of transaction which develop regularly and with changes dictated by
new decisions and rulings." Includes sections on transfers, mortgages, forms of ownership, leases, depreciation, subdividing,
financing, cooperative buildings, brokerage. Includes REAL
ESTATE INVESTMENT LETTER.

Casey, William J. REAL ESTATE INVESTMENT TABLES. New York: Institute
for Business Planning, 1961. 60p.
This set of tables also an appendix in the author's REAL ESTATE
DESK BOOK.

Casey, William J. REAL ESTATE INVESTMENTS AND HOW TO MAKE THEM.
New York: Institute for Business Planning, 1958. 210p.

First Research Corporation. HOW TO MAKE MONEY IN FLORIDA REAL
ESTATE. Englewood Cliffs, N. J.: Prentice-Hall, 1960. 214p. tables,
charts, maps.

Grebler, Leo. EXPERIENCE IN URBAN REAL ESTATE INVESTMENT; AN
INTERIM REPORT BASED ON NEW YORK CITY PROPERTIES. (Publication of

INVESTMENT (continued)

the Institute for Urban Land Use and Housing Studies, Columbia University).
New York: Columbia University Press, 1955. 277p. tables, charts.
> Long term investment performance of 312 properties: apartments,
> single family houses, rooming houses, office buildings, lofts and
> taxpayers.

Institute of Real Estate Management. APARTMENT BUILDING EXPERIENCE
EXCHANGE. (Special issue of the JOURNAL OF PROPERTY MANAGEMENT).
Chicago: 1957-   tables, charts. pap.

Institutional Investments. LAW AND CONTEMPORARY PROBLEMS, vol. 17,
no. 1, Winter 1952 (entire issue).
> The changing importance of institutional investors in the American
> capital market, trends of yields on the investments of financial
> institutions; legal framework, trends and developments in invest-
> ment practices of life insurance companies; mutual savings banks;
> lending and investment practices of commercial banks; legal back-
> ground, trends and recent developments in the investment of trust
> funds; current trends and developments in the investment practices
> of endowments and pension funds; institutional investment and the
> problem of equity financing; Federal debt management and the
> institutional investor; institutional size--life insurance; corporate
> financing in Great Britain.

Kent, Robert W. HOW TO GET RICH IN REAL ESTATE. Englewood Cliffs,
N. J.: Prentice-Hall, 1961. 208p.
> A popular guide on the investment potential of multiple dwellings
> and how to exploit it.

Long, Clarence D., Jr. BUILDING CYCLES AND THE THEORY OF INVEST-
MENT. Princeton, N. J.: Princeton University Press, 1940. 239p. tables,
diagrs.

New York State. Division of Housing. REPORT ON PENSION FUNDS AND
HOUSING INVESTMENT, by Joseph P. McMurray. Albany: 1956. 31p.
pap.
> A report to the Governor.

Nickerson, William. HOW I TURNED $1,000 INTO A MILLION IN REAL
ESTATE--IN MY SPARE TIME. New York: Simon and Schuster, 1959. 497p.
> Describes a method of "pyramiding" real estate investments.

Rubel, S. M. SBIC'S --- a New Source of Real Estate Capital. p. 120-5
In National Real Estate Investor. NATIONAL REAL ESTATE HANDBOOK AND
DIRECTORY. New York: 1962.

Schmutz, Robert E. LIFE INSURANCE HOUSING PROJECTS. (S. S. Huebner
Foundation for Insurance Education, University of Pennsylvania). Homewood,
Ill.: Richard D. Irwin, 1956. 154p. tables.

INVESTMENT (continued)

Life insurance funds invested in the equity ownership of housing developments, covering the experience of all major housing projects together with an examination of the legal, economic and social implications.

Sherman, Malcolm C. MORTGAGE AND REAL ESTATE INVESTMENT GUIDE. Boston: The Author, 1952-   . processed. looseleaf.
"The summary which follows of the laws and statutes of 50 states, D. C., British Columbia, Ontario, Puerto Rico, and Quebec answers the salient legal questions concerning mortgage loans, (conventional, F. H. A. and V. A.) and real estate investments in such jurisdictions or furnishes a starting point."

Snider, Harold Wayne. LIFE INSURANCE INVESTMENT IN COMMERCIAL REAL ESTATE. Homewood, Ill.: Richard D. Irwin, 1956. 136p.

U. S. Federal Housing Administration. FOUR DECADES OF HOUSING WITH A LIMITED DIVIDEND CORPORATION. Washington, D.C.: 1939. 108p.
A report on investment experience.

U. S. Federal Housing Administration. Division of Research and Statistics. A SURVEY OF APARTMENT DWELLING OPERATING EXPERIENCE IN LARGE AMERICAN CITIES. Washington, D.C.: 1940. 138p. tables, charts. pap.

U. S. Housing and Home Finance Agency. Office of the Administrator. Division of Law. EQUITY INVESTMENT IN HOUSING BY INSURANCE COMPANIES, BUILDING AND LOAN ASSOCIATIONS, AND SAVINGS BANKS, Rev. ed. Washington, D.C.: 1957. 18p. chart. pap.
"Comparative study of the principle provisions of state statutes which authorize insurance companies, building and loan associations and savings banks to make direct or equity investments in the ownership and operation, or construction and sale, of housing accommodations."

Urban Land Institute. INVESTORS AND DOWNTOWN REAL ESTATE--OPINION AND COMMENT, by Arthur M. Weimer. (Technical Bulletin no. 39). Washington, D.C.: 1960. 24p. pap.

Winnick, Louis. RENTAL HOUSING: OPPORTUNITIES FOR PRIVATE INVESTMENT. (ACTION Series in Housing and Community Development). New York: McGraw-Hill, 1958. 295p.

Finance—Periodicals

HOUSE AND HOME. NATIONAL REAL ESTATE INVESTOR. NEWS DIGEST;

A BRIEF SUMMARY OF FINANCIAL PROPOSALS FILED WITH AND ACTIONS BY THE S. E. C. REAL ESTATE INVESTMENT. REAL ESTATE INVESTMENT LETTER.

MORTGAGES

American Bankers Association. MORTGAGE OFFICE HANDBOOK. New York: (in preparation).
> Latest practices and procedures in mortgage lending, government laws and regulations.

American Bankers Association. NEW OPPORTUNITIES IN THE MORTGAGE MARKET, A JOINT STUDY BY THE ECONOMIC POLICY COMMISSION AND THE SAVINGS AND MORTGAGE DIVISION. New York: 1959. 39p. pap.

Behrens, Carl F. COMMERCIAL BANK ACTIVITIES IN URBAN MORTGAGE FINANCING. (NBER Financial Research Program, Studies in Urban Mortgage Financing, no. 5). New York: National Bureau of Economic Research, 1952. 131p.

Bogue, Allan G. MONEY AT INTEREST; THE FARM MORTGAGE ON THE MIDDLE BORDER. Ithaca, N.Y.: Cornell University Press, 1955. 293p. tables.
> Bibliography: p. 277-88.

Brimmer, Andrew F. LIFE INSURANCE COMPANIES IN THE CAPITAL MARKET. (MSU Business Studies). East Lansing,: Michigan State University, Bureau of Business and Economic Research, 1962. 394p. tables, charts.
> Chapter 7: Investment Behavior in the Mortgage Market, p. 217-86.

Bryant, Willis R. MORTGAGE LENDING FUNDAMENTALS AND PRACTICES, 2d ed. New York: McGraw-Hill 1962. 423p. charts, forms.
> A textbook sponsored by the Mortgage Bankers Association of America.

California. University. Real Estate Research Program. INSTITUTIONAL RESIDENTIAL MORTGAGE LENDING IN LOS ANGELES COUNTY, 1946--1951; SIX SIGNIFICANT YEARS OF MORTGAGE LENDING, by James Gillies and Clayton Curtis. Los Angeles: 1956. 202p. tables. pap.
> Lending activity of commercial banks, savings and loan associations and life insurance companies; the effect of government programs on the supply of mortgage funds; and a comparison of the Los Angeles market with other local markets throughout the nation.

MORTGAGES (continued)

California. University. Real Estate Research Program. THE SUPPLY OF
RESIDENTIAL MORTGAGE. FUNDS IN THE SAN FRANCISCO BAY AREA,
1950--1960, by Albert Heeley Schaaf. (Research Report no. 19). Berkeley:
1961. 73p. tables. pap. processed.

Clark, Horace F. and Chase, Frank A. ELEMENTS OF THE MODERN BUILDING
AND LOAN ASSOCIATION. (Land Economics Series; Standard Course in Real
Estate). New York: Macmillan, 1925. 540p. tables.
    Text for the American Savings, Building and Loan Institute.

Colean, Miles L. MORTGAGE COMPANIES; THEIR PLACE IN THE FINANCIAL
STRUCTURE, by Miles L. Colean for the Mortgage Bankers Association of
America. (Monograph prepared for the Commission on Money and Credit).
Englewood Cliffs, N. J.: Prentice-Hill, 1962. 51p.
    Characteristics of mortgage companies, their development and
    growth, methods of operation, etc. A comprehensive study.

Conference for Senior Executives in Mortgage Banking. PROCEEDINGS OF
THE....ANNUAL CONFERENCE. New York: New York University, 1946--
    Sponsored jointly by the Mortgage Bankers Association of America
    and the Graduate School of Business Administration of New York
    University.

Conference on Savings and Residential Financing. PROCEEDINGS. Chicago:
United States Savings and Loan League, 1958--

Conway, Lawrence V. MORTGAGE LENDING. Chicago: American Savings
and Loan Institute Press, 1960. 744p. tables, charts, forms.
    "Principles and fundamental procedures embodied in the mortgage
    lending function of savings associations."

Cornell Home Buying Study. HOME BUYING AND FINANCING PRACTICES
IN UPSTATE NEW YORK; FIVE-YEAR SUMMARY, 1957-1961, by Marilyn
Langford and Sylvia G. Wahl. (Cornell Home Buying Study, Fifth Annual
Report--1961). Ithaca, N.Y.: Cornell University, 1962. 38p. pap.
    A publication of the New York State College of Home Economics
    and the Center for Housing and Environmental Studies, Cornell
    University. "This study, although limited in geographical coverage,
    is unique in that it brings together in a single report selected
    data which relate the characteristics of the mortgage to those of
    the family and the house. Other series of available data, such
    as those FHA--insured and VA--guaranteed mortgages, those covering
    the loan activities of savings and loan associations and mutual
    savings banks, and those relating to family income patterns, pro-
    vide nationwide data. Most of the data from these sources,
    however, cover individual aspects of the total home buying and
    financing situation." Summarizes mortgage activity covered by
    this study from 1957 through 1961.

DeHuszar, William I. MORTGAGE SERVICING. Chicago: Mortgage Bankers

MORTGAGES (continued)

Association of America, 1954. 201p. tables. forms.
First published in 1949 under the title: HANDBOOK OF MORT-
GAGE LOAN SERVICING PRACTICES.
Procedures required for handling the accounting and reporting
of mortgage operations.

Federal Home Loan Bank Board. MORTGAGED HOMES IN THE U. S. (IN-
CLUDING FORECLOSURE RATES). Washington, D.C. tables. pap. processed.
Issued annually.

Federal Home Loan Bank Board. NONFARM MORTGAGE INVESTMENTS OF
LIFE INSURANCE COMPANIES . Washington, D.C.: 1934- . tables.
pap. prc essed.
Issued annually. A summary of all nonfarm real estate loans
and mortgages of U. S. legal reserve life insurance companies.

Federal Home Loan Bank Board. SAVINGS AND HOME FINANCING CHART
BOOK. Washington, D.C.: 1957- . charts. pap. processed.
"Graphic presentations of data...which with few exceptions are
currently published in the SOURCE BOOK." Issued annually.

Federal Home Loan Bank Board. SAVINGS AND HOME FINANCING SOURCE
BOOK. Washington, D.C.: 1953- . tables, charts. pap. processed.
An annual continuation of various periodic reports issued by the
Board. Contains, with few exceptions, data published previously.
Statistics on FHA and VA mortgage activities included.

Federal Home Loan Bank Board. TRENDS IN THE SAVINGS AND LOAN
FIELD. Washington, D.C.: 1952- . tables. pap. processed.
Presents asset and liability items for all operating savings and
loan associations. Figures for the U.S. and the eleven FHLB
districts. Issued annually.

Grebler, Leo and Gillies, James. JUNIOR MORTGAGE FINANCING IN
LOS ANGELES COUNTY, 1958--1959. (Research Report, no. 2). Los
Angeles: University of California, Real Estate Research Program, 1960. 71p.
processed.

Home Financing. LAW AND CONTEMPORARY PROBLEMS, vol. 5, no. 4.
Autumn, 1938 (entire issue).
Survey of Federal legislation affecting private home financing
since 1932, shifts in the sources of funds for home financing
since 1932, state legislative relief for the mortgage debtor
during the Depression, the effects of defective mortgage laws
on home financing, the new proposal for a uniform real estate
mortgage act, the need for special, simplified mechanics' lien
acts applicable to home construction, large scale rental developments as an alternative to home ownership, the financing of
large-scale rental housing, adjusting the mortgagors' obligation
to economic cycles.

MORTGAGES (continued)

Jones, Lawrence A. and Durand, David. MORTGAGE LENDING EXPERIENCE IN AGRICULTURE. (National Bureau of Economic Research. Financial Research Program, Studies in Agricultural Finance, no. 1). Princeton, N. J.: Princeton University Press, 1954. 226p.
> Main emphasis on two decades between the world wars; main purpose: "to determine some of the important causes of farm mortgage distress."

Jones, Oliver and Grebler, Leo. SECONDARY MORTGAGE MARKET, ITS PUR-POSE, PERFORMANCE, AND POTENTIAL. Los Angeles: University of California, Real Estate Research Program, 1961. 281p. tables. pap.
> Detailed study of the market, the evolution of market facilities, and proposals for reform--principally the central mortgage bank. Analysis of situation in California and its metropolitan areas, primarily Los Angeles.

Kendall, Leon T. THE SAVINGS AND LOAN BUSINESS; ITS PURPOSES, FUNCTIONS, AND ECONOMIC JUSTIFICATION, by Leon T. Kendall for the United States Savings and Loan League. (Monograph prepared for the Commission on Money and Credit). Englewood Cliffs, N. J.: Prentice-Hall, 1962. 173p. tables, charts, maps.
> A detailed analysis of the business, its adequacy as an economic tool, the effect of money flow, etc.

Klaman, Saul B. POSTWAR RESIDENTIAL MORTGAGE MARKET. (National Bureau of Economic Research. Studies in Capital Formation and Financing, no. 8). Princeton, N. J.: Princeton University Press, 1961. 301p. tables, graphs.
> A detailed, statistical analysis of a segment of the capital market, a comprehensive study of market holdings and flow, on a quarterly basis.

Klaman, Saul B. THE POSTWAR RISE OF MORTGAGE COMPANIES. (NBER Occasional Paper no. 60). New York: National Bureau of Economic Research, 1959. 102p. tables, charts. pap.
> A detailed study, covering nature and characteristics of mortgage companies, their size, financial structure, and operations.

Lintner, John Virgil. MUTUAL SAVINGS BANKS IN THE SAVINGS AND MORTGAGE MARKETS. Boston: Harvard University, Graduate School of Business Administration, Divison of Research, 1948. 559p.

Mao, James C. T. RESIDENTIAL MORTGAGE FINANCING, A LONG RANGE PROJECTION. (Michigan Business Reports no. 34). Ann Arbor: University of Michigan, Bureau of Business Research, 1960. 39p. tables, charts. pap.
> Housing and credit demands projected to 1970.

Mitiguy, Harry R. APPRAISING AND MORTGAGE LENDING: NEW ENGLAND FARM PROPERTIES. New Brunswick, N. J.: 1960. 104p. tables, charts.

Mortgage Bankers Association of America. A PLACE FOR YOU IN THE

MORTGAGES (continued)

MORTGAGE BANKING PROFESSION. Chicago: no date. 30p. pap.
    Vocational literature.

Mortgage Bankers Association of America. THE FEDERAL LAND BANK SYSTEM,
by Miles L. Colean and Raymond J. Saulnier. Chicago: 1963. 60p. tables.
pap.

Mortgage Bankers Association of America. THE REAL ESTATE LENDING ACTI-
VITIES OF THE FARMERS HOME ADMINISTRATION, by Miles L. Colean and
Raymond J. Saulnier. Chicago: 1963. 19p. pap.

Mortgage Bankers Association of America. TRUSTEED FUNDS DISCOVER HIGHER
YIELD IN FAMILIAR FIELD. Chicago: 1962. 19p. pap.
    A tool developed to reach the growing pension and deferred
    profit sharing market, emphasizing the role of the mortgage banker
    in the investment field, as well as the advantages of mortgages
    as an investment medium.

MORTGAGE FINANCING SYMPOSIUM, 19 -- . Montclair, N.J.: Consolidated Reporting Company, 94 Valley Road, 19 -- . pap. processed.
    Collections of papers on all aspects of mortgage financing,
    delivered at meetings of banking and savings and loan groups
    throughout the country or reprinted from journals.

Mortgages. Section 50, 200 In Casey, William J. REAL ESTATE INVEST-
MENT DEALS, IDEAS, FORMS. New York: Institute for Business Planning,
1959-   .
    Includes a checklist of points to be considered in drawing
    mortgages and specimen forms.

Morton, Joseph E. URBAN MORTGAGE LENDING: COMPARATIVE MARKETS
AND EXPERIENCE. (National Bureau of Economic Research, Financial
Research Program, Studies in Urban Mortgage Financing, no. 6). Princeton,
N.J.: Princeton University Press, 1956. 187p. tables, charts.

National Association of Mutual Savings Banks. FACTS AND FIGURES, MUTUAL
SAVINGS BANKING, 3rd ed. New York: 1962. 42p.
    Included with annual report. Section 3, Capital Market Investments,
    Section 5, Mutual Savings Banks in the Mortgage and Securities
    Markets.

National Association of Real Estate Boards. REAL ESTATE MORTGAGES AS
INVESTMENTS FOR INSURANCE COMPANIES, prepared by Institute for
Research in Land Economics and Public Utilities. Chicago: 1923. 16p.
tables, charts.

MORTGAGES (continued)

New York University. Graduate School of Business Administration. INVEST-MENT STATUS OF FHA AND VA MORTGAGES, by G. Rowland Collins and Jules I. Bogen. New York: 1959. 32p. tables, charts.

Pease, Robert H. and Cherrington, Homer V. MORTGAGE BANKING. New York: McGraw-Hill, 1953. 458p. tables, forms.
Sponsored by the Mortgage Bankers Association of America.
"Fundamentals and techniques." (1963 revision in preparation).

Perring, Katherine. Private Secondary Market Prices for FHA--Insured Home Mortgages, 1949-1960. CONSTRUCTION REVIEW, vol. 7, no. 8, August 1961, p. 6-11.
"National data analyzed with respect to the trends and character istics of national averages and the response of secondary market prices and general money market conditions."

Perring, Katherine. Regional Trends in Secondary Market Prices for FHA-Insured Home Mortgages, 1949-1960. CONSTRUCTION REVIEW, vol. 8, no. 1, January 1962, p. 5-8.
"Examines the characteristics and movement of regional averages."

Reep, Samuel N. SECOND MORTGAGES AND LAND CONTRACTS IN REAL ESTATE FINANCING. New York: Prentice-Hall, 1928. 225p. forms.
References at end of each chapter.

Russell, Horace and Prather, William. The Flexible Mortgage Contract. LEGAL BULLETIN; THE LAW AFFECTING SAVINGS ASSOCIATIONS, vol. 19, no. 5, September 1953 (entire issue).
Cover note: A Consideration of the Legal and Practical Aspects of the Flexible Mortgage Contract in the Various Jurisdictions, Including: 1. The Package Mortgage; 2. The Open-End Mort-gage; 3. Other Flexible Features; 4. Illustrative Forms.

Sauer, Donald H. THE DEMAND FOR AND THE SUPPLY OF NONFARM RESIDENTIAL MORTGAGE FUNDS, 1960 to 1970. Unpublished Ph.D. thesis, Indiana University, 1959.

Saulnier, R. J. COSTS AND RETURNS ON FARM MORTGAGE LENDING BY LIFE INSURANCE COMPANIES, 1945-1947. (NBER Occasional Paper, no. 30). New York: National Bureau of Economic Research, 1949. 55p. tables, pap.

Saulnier, R. J. URBAN MORTGAGE LENDING BY LIFE INSURANCE COMPA-NIES. (NBER Financial Research Program. Studies in Urban Mortgage Financing, no. 1). New York: National Bureau of Economic Research, 1950. 180p. charts. (Distr. by Prineton University Press, Princeton, N. J.).

Schaaf, Albert Heeley. FEDERAL INTEREST RATE POLICY ON INSURED AND GUARANTEED MORTGAGES. Unpublished Ph.D. thesis, University of Califor-nia, 1955.

MORTGAGES (continued)

Schecther, Henry B. and Davis, Milton B. Residential Mortgage Capital,
CONSTRUCTION REVIEW, vol. 6, no. 8, August 1960, p. 5–10; vol. 6,
no. 10, October 1960, p. 5–10.
> Part 1: Mortgage Funds and Housing Construction. Part 2: In-
> vestment Practices of Lenders.

U. S. Congress. House. Committee on Banking and Currency. SECOND
MORTGAGE PRACTICES; STAFF REPORT TO THE SUBCOMMITTEE ON HOUS-
ING .....
85th CONGRESS, 1st SESSION, DECEMBER 21, 1957. Washington, D.C.:
Government Printing Office, 1957. 117p. pap.
> Reports obtained from a survey of the field offices of FHA, VA,
> and other Federal agencies. Including Federal Reserve System
> and Federal Home Loan Bank Board, FDIC, and Treasury Depart-
> ment.

U. S. Congress. House. Committee on Banking and Currency. SECOND
MORTGAGES, LAND SALE CONTRACTS, AND OTHER FINANCING DEVICES
EMPLOYED IN CONVENTIONAL MORTGAGE LENDING; STAFF REPORT TO
REPRESENTATIVE ALBERT RAINS, CHAIRMAN, SUBCOMMITTEE ON HOUSING
....86th Congress, 2d Session, January 22, 1960. Washington, D.C.: Govern-
ment Printing Office, 1960. 94p. pap.
> Responses to a survey made by FHA and VA field offices.

U. S. Congress. Senate. Committee on Banking and Currency. STUDY OF
MORTGAGE CREDIT; HEARINGS BEFORE A SUBCOMMITTEE ... ON A STUDY
OF THE QUESTION: DOES THE DECADE 1961-70 POSE PROBLEMS IN PRIVATE
HOUSING AND MORTGAGE MARKETS WHICH REQUIRE FEDERAL LEGISLATION
BY 1960? (86th Congress, 1st session). Washington, D.C.: Government
Printing Office, 1959. 451p. Appendix of 397p.

U. S. Congress. Senate. Committee on Banking and Currency. STUDY OF
MORTGAGE CREDIT; REPORT OF SUBCOMMITTEE ON HOUSING (UNDER S.
RES. 221)...APRIL 15,1960. Washington, D.C.: Government Printing Office,
1960. 75p. tables, charts. pap.
> Discusses demand, need, and supply factors in farm and nonfarm
> mortgage financing; also basic Federal programs.

U. S. Department of Agriculture. Agricultural Research Service. FARM
INVESTMENTS OF LIFE INSURANCE COMPANIES. (ARS 43). Washington,
D.C.: 1956-1960. tables, charts. pap. processed.

U. S. Department of Agriculture. Economic Research Service. FARM REAL
ESTATE DEBT. Washington, D.C.:
> Issued annually.
> Total amount of farm mortgage debt outstanding and amounts
> held by major lender groups. U.S. figures given for several
> years, state figures for most recent year. (Was ARS-43 Series).

MORTGAGES (continued)

U. S. Department of Agriculture. Economic Research Service. Farm
Economics Division. FARM MORTGAGES RECORDED IN 1959; INTEREST
RATES, TERMS, AND SITES WITH HISTORICAL DATA, 1949--1959, by
Van E. Eitel. (ERS--61). Washington, D.C.: 1962. 33p. tables,
charts. pap. processed.

U. S. Federal Housing Administration. HOMES IN METROPOLITAN DIS-
TRICTS; CHARACTERISTICS OF MORTGAGES, HOMES, BORROWERS, UNDER
THE FHA PLAN, 1934-1940. (FHA Form no. 2387). Washington, D.C.:
Government Printing Office, 1942. 238p.

U. S. Housing and Home Finance Agency. RESIDENTIAL MORTGAGE
FINANCING, JACKSONVILLE, FLORIDA, FIRST SIX MONTHS OF 1950,
by George B. Heviff. (Housing Research Paper no. 23). Washington, D.C.:
Government Printing Office, 1953. 97p.

U.S. Housing and Home Finance Agency. Office of the Administrator. Division
of Housing Research. THE SAN FRANCISCO BAY-AREA RESIDENTIAL MORT-
GAGE MARKET, by Paul F. Wendt and Daniel B. Rathbun, (Housing research
paper no. 20). Washington, D.C.: 1962. 48p. pap.

United States Savings and Loan League. GUIDE TO FEDERAL LAWS AND
REGULATIONS AFFECTING SAVINGS AND LOAN ASSOCIATIONS AND
CO-OPERATING BANKS. Chicago: 1953-   . looseleaf.
        Cover title: FEDERAL GUIDE.

United States Savings and Loan League. SAVINGS AND LOAN ANNALS.
Chicago: 1930-   .
        Proceedings of the annual convention of the League. Title
        1930-1938: BUILDING AND LOAN ANNALS.

United States Savings and Loan League. SAVINGS AND LOAN FACT BOOK.
Chicago: 1954-   .
        "Continues as only reference source for date encompassing all
        aspects of thrift and home financing in America....includes a
        wide range of statistics about personal income and savings, home
        building, home financing, home ownership, savings and loan
        operation, and government activity as it relates to thrift, home
        financing and home construction." Issued annually.

Wright, Ivan. FARM MORTGAGE FINANCING. New York: McGraw-Hill,
1923. 343p. illus.
        Discusses the many aspects of farm mortgages. Appendices in-
        clude data on land title registration laws, state loans, the
        Federal Farm Loan Act of 1923. Bibliography: 249-61.

MORTGAGES (continued)

Mortgage Bankers Association of America. CURRENT PUBLICATIONS RELATED
TO THE MORTGAGE BANKING INDUSTRY. Chicago: 1962. 18p. pap.
processed.
> "A selected list of daily, weekly, semi-monthly, monthly, bi-
> monthly, quarterly, and annual publications that deal with
> housing, mortgage finance, general business and economics."

PROPERTY TAXATION AND ASSESSMENT

In addition to the publications cited below, the manuals for tax assessors
issued by most states should be mentioned. REAL PROPERTY ASSESSMENT
MANUAL, Illinois Department of Revenue, Property Tax Division, and
KENTUCKY REAL PROPERTY APPRAISAL MANUAL, Kentucky Department of
Revenue, are examples. A discussion of manuals appears in the APPRAISAL
JOURNAL, vol. 27, no. 4, October 1959, p. 491-6: Essential Contents
for Assessment Manuals, by Wallace B. Appelson.

Another group of publications on assessment is the proceedings of special
courses conducted for assessing officers at state universities, such as
PROCEEDINGS OF THE ... ANNUAL SHORT COURSE FOR ASSESSING
OFFICERS, University of Michigan; PROCEEDINGS OF THE ...ANNUAL
SCHOOL FOR MASSACHUSETTS ASSESSORS, University of Massachusetts;
PROGRAM AND PROCEEDINGS OF THE ANNUAL SCHOOL FOR SOUTH
DAKOTA ASSESSING OFFICERS, University of South Dakota.

Bird, Frederick L. THE GENERAL PROPERTY TAX: FINDINGS OF THE
1957 CENSUS OF GOVERNMENTS. Chicago: Public Administration Service,
1960. 83p. pap.

Brown, Harry Gunnison, et al., eds. LAND VALUE TAXATION AROUND THE
WORLD. New York: Robert Schalkenbach Foundation, 1955. 216p.

Clemson University. Agricultural College. ALTERNATIVE METHODS AND
TECHNIQUES FOR THE ASSESSMENT OF FARM REAL ESTATE, by J. Robert
Cooper. Clemson, S.C.: 1957. 64p. tables, charts. pap. processed.

The Collection of Real Property Taxes. LAW AND CONTEMPORARY PROBLEMS,
vol. 3, no. 3, June 1936 (entire issue).
> Thirteen papers on the ad valorem property tax, delinquency, tax
> foreclosures and sales, etc.

Commerce Clearing House. STATE TAX GUIDE. Chicago: 1937-
> A looseleaf service.

Federation of Tax Administrators. FEDERAL PROPERTY, FEDERAL RESERVA-

PROPERTY TAXATION AND ASSESSMENT (continued)

TIONS AND STATE AND LOCAL PROPERTY TAXES. Chicago: 1960. 5p. pap. processed.

Goode, Richard. Imputed Rent of Owner-Occupied Dwellings under the Income Tax. JOURNAL OF FINANCE, vol. 15, no. 4, December 1960, p. 503-30.

International Association of Assessing Officers. ASSESSMENT ADMINISTRATION; PAPER PRESENTED AT THE ... INTERNATIONAL CONFERENCE ON ASSESS-MENT ADMINISTRATION. Chicago: 1935-   . pap. processed.

International Association of Assessing Officers. CONSTRUCTION AND USE OF TAX MAPS. Chicago: 1937. 51p.

Kindahl, James K. Housing and the Federal Income Tax. NATIONAL TAX JOURNAL, vol. 13, no. 4, December 1960, p. 376-82.

Morton, Walter A. HOUSING TAXATION. Madison: University of Wisconsin Press, 1955. 262p.

National Municipal League. Committee on a Program of Model Fiscal Legislation. MODEL REAL PROPERTY TAX COLLECTION LAW, 2d ed. New York: The League, 1954. 40p. pap.

National Tax Association. PROCEEDINGS OF THE ..... ANNUAL CONFER-ENCE ON TAXATION. Harrisburg, Pa.: 1907-   .
    Includes papers on property taxes. Index in each volume.
    Proceedings for 1907 through 1912 issued under title: STATE AND
    LOCAL TAXATION. Place of publication varies.

New York State College of Agriculture. THE ASSESSMENT OF REAL ESTATE; RECENT CHANGES IN THE PROVISIONS OF 43 STATES, by M. Slade Kendrick. (Cornell Extension Bulletin 1041). Ithaca, N.Y.: 1960. 31p. tables. pap.

New York State. Tax Commission. FULL VALUE REAL ESTATE ASSESSMENT AS A PREREQUISITE TO STATE AID IN NEW YORK, by Chester Baldwin Pond. (Special Report no. 3). Albany: 1931. 189p. tables. pap.

Rowlands, David T. THE PROPERTY TAX IN ATLANTA AND OTHER LARGE CITIES. Atlanta, Ga.: The City, 1957. 87p. pap.

U. S. Bureau of the Census. 1962 CENSUS OF GOVERNMENTS; PRELIMINARY REPORT NO. 4: PROPERTY TAX ASSESSMENTS IN THE UNITED STATES. Washington, D.C.: 1962. 15p. tables. pap. processed.
    Statistics on the value of assessed property by state and type,
    number of properties, etc.

PROPERTY TAXATION AND ASSESSMENT (continued)

U. S. Department of Agriculture. Economic Research Service. STATE ACTION RELATING TO TAXATION OF FARMLAND ON THE RURAL-URBAN FRINGE, by Peter House. (ERS--13). Washington, D.C.: 1961. 23p. table. pap. processed.

Urban Land Institute. CHANGING URBAN LAND USES AS AFFECTED BY TAXATION; A CONFERENCE SUMMARY REPORT, by Jerome P. Pickard. (Research Monograph no. 6). Washington, D.C.: 1962. 105p. illus., charts, tables. pap.
> Bibliography included. First publication of the new Urban Land Institute Research-Conference Program, summarizing the results of four conferences on the impact of taxation on urban land use and change. In addition, extensive analytical material is included, prepared by Jerome Pickard, Research Director of U.L.I.

Urban Land Institute. PROPERTY TAXATION AND URBAN DEVELOPMENT: EFFECTS OF THE PROPERTY TAX ON CITY GROWTH AND CHANGE, by Mary Rawson. (Research Monograph no. 4). Washington, D. C.: 1961. 54p. tables, charts, maps. pap.
> "Documented case study of what would happen in terms of land use and development in a municipality if the local ad valorem tax were shifted from land and improvements toward a land value tax." Bibliography and References: p. 51-4.

Urban Land Institute. URBAN LAND USE AND PROPERTY TAXATION, by Max S. Wehrly and J. Ross McKeever. (Technical Bulletin no. 18). Washington, D.C.: 1952. 27p. tables. pap.

Utah Foundation. EQUALIZATION OF PROPERTY TAX ASSESSMENTS. (Research Report no. 134). Salt Lake City: 1956. 4p. pap.
> The revaluation programs of forty-four states examined, five in detail.

Walker, Mabel. Unsettled Questions in Real Estate Taxation. TAX POLICY, vol. 27, no. 6, June 1960, p. 1-4.

Property Taxation and Assessment—Bibliography

International Association of Assessing Officers. ASSESSMENT STUDY GUIDE. Chicago; 1955, 52p.
> "Bibliography of generally available material covering important phases of the assessment function."

Property Taxation and Assessment—Periodicals
(See Appendix for complete. information concerning these publications.)

ASSESSORS NEWS LETTER; FROM THE STATE CAPITALS - REAL PROPERTY TAX TRENDS SUMMARIZED; REAL ESTATE ANALYST TAX BULLETIN; TAX INSTITUTE BOOKSHELF.

SYNDICATES, INVESTMENT TRUSTS, AND PUBLIC CORPORATIONS

Berman, Daniel S.   HOW TO PUT TOGETHER A REAL ESTATE SYNDICATE, 2 vols. New York: Syndicate Books, 350 Broadway, zone 13, 1961. processed. Format and tax aspects of syndicates, with analyses of specific operations.   Volume 2: a compilation of forms.

Commerce Clearing House.   REAL ESTATE INVESTMENT TRUSTS: NEW INCOME TAX TREATMENT; EXPLANATION, LAW, COMMITTEE REPORT. Chicago: 1961. 32p. pap.

Kronfeld, Edwin. Real Estate Investment Trusts and Form S--11. JOURNAL OF PROPERTY MANAGEMENT, vol. 27, no. 2, Winter 1961, p. 80-4.

Lewis, Bertram.   PROFITS IN REAL ESTATE SYNDICATIONS; A GUIDE FOR THE INVESTOR. New York: Harper, 1962. 181p.

Lifton, Robert K. How to Organize a Syndication. p. 121-25. In National Real Estate Investor. DIRECTORY. New York: 1961.

Markeim, J. William.   Real Estate Syndicates. p. 1255-81 In Friedman, Edith J., ed. REAL ESTATE ENCYCLOPEDIA. Englewood Cliffs, N. J.: Prentice-Hall, 1960.

MOODY'S BANK AND FINANCE MANUAL: BANKS, INSURANCE, REAL ESTATE, INVESTMENT TRUSTS; AMERICAN AND FOREIGN. New York: Moody's Investors Service.
Data on real estate securities, listed by firm.

National Association of Real Estate Investment Funds. Real Estate Investment Trusts. p. 82-3 In National Real Estate Investor. NATIONAL REAL ESTATE HANDBOOK AND DIRECTORY. New York: 1962.
Firm names and addresses in an alphabetical arrangement.

National Institute of Real Estate Brokers. REAL ESTATE SYNDICATES AND HOW THEY WORK. (Brokers Institute Bulletin Service). Chicago: 1957. 63p. illus. pap.

Phillips, R. M. and Eisenberg, M.   Impact of Securities Laws on Syndicates,

SYNDICATES, INVESTMENT TRUSTS, AND PUBLIC CORPORATIONS (continued)

Corporations, and Trusts.   p. 104-9 In National Real Estate Investor.
NATIONAL REAL ESTATE HANDBOOK AND DIRECTORY.   New York: 1962.

Poole, Horace I.   Should Your Company Have a Public Stock Offering?
p. 110-4 In National Real Estate Investor.   NATIONAL REAL ESTATE HAND-
BOOK AND DIRECTORY.   New York: 1962.

Publicly Held Real Estate Companies.   p. 65-71 In National Real Estate
Investor.   NATIONAL REAL ESTATE HANDBOOK AND DIRECTORY.   New
York: 1962.
        Firm names and addresses in a geographical arrangement.

Real Estate Investment Trusts Symposium.   VIRGINIA LAW REVIEW, vol. 48,
no. 6, October 1962, p. 1007-148.
        Articles: Taxation of Real Estate Investment Trusts, by Marvin
        S. Kahn; Real Estate Investment Trust Trustees and the "Inde-
        pendent Contractor," by J. B. Riggs Parker; State Securities
        Regulation of Real Estate Investment Trusts, The Midwest
        Position, by John G. Sobieski; and An Attorney's Viewpoint,
        by Arthur O. Armstrong, Jr.
        NOTES: Liability of Shareholders in a Business Trust and the
        Real Estate Investment Trust in Multistate Activity.

Realty Stocks.   NATIONAL REAL ESTATE INVESTOR, a section appearing in
each issue.
        Articles plus quotations on real estate securities under several
        classifications (real estate stocks, real estate investment trusts,
        and real estate bonds).

Robbins, Charles E.   How to Go Public.   p. 126-8 In National Real Estate
Investor.   DIRECTORY.   New York: 1961.

Rothschild, Hugo.   HOW TO MAKE MONEY IN REAL ESTATE SYNDICATES.
New York: Syndicate Books, 350 Broadway, 1961. 127p.
        A practical guide to this investment medium, written for the
        potential investor.

Stock Market.   HOUSE & HOME, a feature in the News section of each
issue.
        Reports figures for HOUSE & HOME'S index of housing issues and
        quotations on specific issues under several classifications (building,
        shell homes, savings and loan associations, realty investment,
        mortgage banking, real estate investment trusts, land development,
        and prefabrication).   Also lists new issues.

Swesnik,   Richard H.   Making Money via the Syndicate Route.   JOURNAL
OF PROPERTY MANAGEMENT, vol. 27, no. 2, Winter 1961. p. 85-7.

Syndicates.   Section 56, 800 In Casey, William J.   REAL ESTATE INVESTMENT
DEALS, IDEA, FORMS.   New York: Institute for Business Planning, 1959-   .

SYNDICATES, INVESTMENT TRUSTS, AND PUBLIC CORPORATIONS (continued)

Syndicates and real estate investment trusts, examples of typical syndicates, the real estate corporation as a syndicate, and how to sell a syndicate share.

Syndicators. p. 47-6 In National Real Estate Investor. NATIONAL REAL ESTATE HANDBOOK AND DIRECTORY. New York: 1962.
Firm names and addresses in a geographical arrangement.

U. S. Securities and Exchange Commission. Division of Corporation Finance. REAL ESTATE INVESTMENT TRUSTS FILING UNDER THE SECURITIES ACT OF 1933. Washington, D.C.: June 30, 1962. 11p. pap. processed.
To be issued periodically.

Williamson, John C. The Real Estate Investment Trust Act; the Catalyst Which is Making Real Estate 'Go Public.' JOURNAL OF PROPERTY MANAGEMENT, vol. 27, no. 2, Winter 1961, p. 68-79.
The law, taxing formula and proposed regulation. Six categories of real estate investment trusts described.

Syndicates, Investment Trusts, and Public Corporations—Periodicals

See list of periodicals under INVESTMENTS.

TAX ASPECTS OF REAL ESTATE TRANSACTIONS

Anderson, Paul E. TAX FACTORS IN REAL ESTATE OPERATIONS. Englewood Cliffs, N.J.: Prentice-Hall, 1960. 345p.
"A comprehensive introduction." For the investor and the broker or land developer. Emphasis on Federal income tax; some data on Federal gift and estate taxes included. Table of Cases: p. 315-33. Includes sections on mortgage financing and foreclosure.

Atlas, Martin. TAX ASPECTS OF REAL ESTATE TRANSACTIONS, 2d ed. Washington, D.C.: Bureau of National Affairs, 1956. 224p.

Atlas, Martin. TAX PLANNING FOR THE CONSTRUCTION INDUSTRY, ANNOTATED. Washington, D.C.: Bureau of National Affairs, 1962. 276p. tables. processed.
Tax problems of the owner-builder, the contractor, and the sub-contractor. Designed for use by the lawyer and the accountant

TAX ASPECTS OF REAL ESTATE TRANSACTIONS (continued)

as well as the businessman engaged in the real estate construction industry.

Baylor University. School of Business. SOME IMPLICATIONS OF FEDERAL INCOME TAX LAWS FOR INDIVIDUAL INVESTORS IN REAL ESTATE, by James F. Goodman. (Baylor Business Studies, vol. 54, no 13). Waco, Texas: 1951. 38p. pap.

Casey, William J. REAL ESTATE INVESTMENT DEALS, IDEAS, FORMS, 2 vols. New York: Institute for Business Planning 1959-   . processed. looseleaf.
A looseleaf service, supplemented monthly, "Recommended for the reader who wants to keep up with the new forms of trans- action which develop regularly and with changes dictated by new decisions and rulings."

Casey, William J. TAX CONTROL, 2 vols. New York: Institute for Busi- ness Planning, 1957-   . processed. looseleaf.
A looseleaf service, supplemented monthly. Section cited by cross reference in Casey's REAL ESTATE INVESTMENT DEALS, IDEAS, FORMS.

Casey, William J. TAX SHELTER IN REAL ESTATE, 2d ed. New York: Institute for Business Planning, 1959. 220p. tables. processed.
Reviews various techniques of real estate operations -- sale- lease-back, cooperatives, syndicates, etc. -- and analyzes the tax situations for each. Chapter 1: How the 1958 Tax Law Affects Real Estate Transactions.

Casey, William J. TAX TESTED FORMS OF AGREEMENTS, RESOLUTIONS AND PLANS, 2 vols. New York: Institute for Business Planning, 1956- processed. looseleaf.
A looseleaf service, supplemented monthly. Contains cross reference to Casey's TAX CONTROL.

Dean, Stephen T. Tax Aspects of Real Estate Development. p. 137-60 In New York University. PROCEEDINGS OF THE EIGHTEENTH ANNUAL INSTITUTE ON FEDERAL TAXATION. Albany: Matthew Bender, 1960.

Depreciation and Amortization. Section 55,900 In Casey, William J. Real Estate Investment Deals, Ideas, Forms. New York: Institute for Business Planning, 1959-
Includes subsections: How to Determine the Useful Life of an Asset; How to get the Maximum Write-Off on the Cost of Leased Property; Accounting for Depreciation. Tables.

Federal Taxation. Section 11 In PRENTICE-HALL REAL ESTATE GUIDE. Englewood Cliffs, N.J.: Prentice-Hall, 1953-   .
Treats those sections of the Internal Revenue Code that affect real estate transactions.

TAX ASPECTS OF REAL ESTATE TRANSACTIONS (continued)

Haber, Paul and Kotkin, Bernard. TAX OPPORTUNITIES IN REAL ESTATE.
Los Angeles: Tax Publishers, 1955. 206p. pap.
> Uses "a chronological framework and (follows) the typical career
> line of a real estate investor as he acquires, uses and disposes
> of the property."

Herzberg, Arno. SAVING TAXES THROUGH CAPITAL GAINS. Englewood
Cliffs, N.J.: Prentice-Hall, 1957. 430p.
> Real estate operations one of the businesses discussed.

J. K. Lasser Tax Institute. LASSER'S ENCYCLOPEDIA OF TAX PROCEDURES,
2d ed. Englewood Cliffs, N.J.: Prentice-Hall, 1960. 1210p.
> Part I: Investments, includes How to Buy, Sell, and Hold Real
> Estate, by Irving Schrieber and Yale H. Gellman; Financing
> and Investment Aspects of Sale-Leasebacks, by John D. Cunnion;
> Causes and Effects of a Negative Basis in Mortgage Transactions,
> by Alvin D. Lurie; Purchases and Sales of Residences , by Charles
> R. Ringo.

J. K. Lasser Tax Institute. SUCCESSFUL TAX PLANNING FOR REAL ESTATE,
ed. by Sydney Prerau and Bernard Greisman. Larchmont, New York:
American Research Council, 1961. 218p. tables.
> "Designed to show the many tax strategies available to ownership,
> leasing, management, construction, buying and selling of improved
> and unimproved real estate." Syndicate, trust, corporation and
> other forms of ownership treated.

Maddrea, T. Grayson and Butler, F. Elmore. Tax Considerations in Real
Estate Transactions. p. 1282-329 In Friedman, Edith J., ed. REAL ESTATE
ENCYCLOPEDIA. Englewood Cliffs, N.J.: Prentice-Hall, 1960.

Roberts, S. I. Developments in Federal Income Taxation of Real Estate.
p. 97-103 In National Real Estate Investor. NATIONAL REAL ESTATE
HANDBOOK AND DIRECTORY. New York: 1962.

U. S. Bureau of Internal Revenue. INCOME TAX DEPRECIATION AND OB-
SOLESCENCE, ESTIMATED USEFUL LIVES AND DEPRECIATION RATES.
(Bulletin F, rev. January 1942). Washington, D.C.: Government Printing
Office, 1942. 93p. tables. pap.

U. S. Internal Revenue Service. DEPRECIATION GUIDELINES AND RULES.
(Publication no. 456; 7-62). Washington, D.C.: Government Printing Office,
1962. 56p. tables. pap.

U. S. Internal Revenue Service. HOW THE FEDERAL INCOME TAX APPLIES
TO CONDEMNATIONS OF PRIVATE PROPERTY FOR PUBLIC USE. (Document
no. 5383; 10-61). Washington, D.C.: 1961. 17p. pap.
> Prepared in co-operation with the Bureau of Public Roads.

TAX ASPECTS OF REAL ESTATE TRANSACTIONS (continued)

U. S. Internal Revenue Service. TABLES FOR APPLYING REVENUE PROCEDURE 62-21. (Publication no. 457; 8-62). Washington, D.C.: Government Printing Office, 1962. 20p. tables. pap.

Weir, Robert H. ADVANTAGES IN TAXES. Chicago: National Institute of Farm Brokers, 1960. various paging.
> A practical manual covering the "broad principles of taxation as they apply to real estate" and certain tax advantages of real estate investments. Supplements issued periodically. (Extensive revision scheduled for 1963.)

Section 8

INSURANCE

Building Managers' Association of Chicago. Insurance Committee. INSURANCE MANUAL FOR OWNERS AND MANAGERS OF OFFICE AND LOFT BUILDINGS, Rev. Chicago: 1958. 68p. pap. processed.
> Divided into sections by type of loss, presenting kinds of insurance policies to cover each. Chicago and Illinois laws as basis. 1st issue in 1949.

Butwin, Stanley. A Checklist of Real Estate Insurance. p. 156-9 In National Real Estate Investor. NATIONAL REAL ESTATE HANDBOOK AND DIRECTORY. New York: 1962.

Elliott, Curtis M. PROPERTY AND CASUALTY INSURANCE. (National Association of Insurance Agents - McGraw-Hill Insurance Bookshelf). New York: McGraw-Hill, 1960. 200p.
> An introductory text, designed for use in college courses, firm and trade association educational programs, and employee orientation.

Gordis, Philip. PROPERTY AND CASUALTY INSURANCE; A GUIDE BOOK FOR AGENTS AND BROKERS, 9th ed. Indianapolis, Ind.: Rough Notes Co., 1142 North Meridian Street, zone 6, 1962. 604p.
> A text for use by applicants for license examination of New York State. Practical rather than academic approach.

Hedges, J. Edward and Williams, Walter. PRACTICAL FIRE AND CASUALTY INSURANCE, 7th ed. Cincinnati, Ohio: National Underwriter Co., 1961. 311p.
> A textbook. 1st ed. 1943.

Huebner, S.S. and Black, Kenneth, Jr. PROPERTY INSURANCE, 4th ed. New York: Appleton-Century-Crofts, 1957. 568p. tables, forms.
> Real property treated extensively. Facts, principles, and practices in compact, classified form. Prepared primarily as a textbook. Will present nature of property insurance to owners and managers. Earlier editions 1911, 1922, 1938.

Insurance. p. 471-87 In Downs, James C., Jr. PRINCIPLES OF REAL ESTATE MANAGEMENT. Chicago: Institute of Real Estate Management, 1959.

Insurance Information Institute. PROPERTY INSURANCE FACT BOOK. New York, N.Y.: 1959- . pap.

Annual compilation of statistics on fire and catastrophe losses, taken mainly from records of the National Board of Fire Underwriters.

McCormick, Roy C. COVERAGES APPLICABLE, 8th ed. Indianapolis: Rough Notes Co., 1142 North Meridian Street, zone 6, 1956. 111p. illus. pap. processed.
Keyed to ROUGH NOTES POLICY, FORM AND MANUAL ANALYSIS SERVICE. "Policies are listed for each business category under Building Property Damage, Contents and Personal Property Damage and Business Operations."

Magee, John H. PROPERTY INSURANCE, 3d ed. (Irwin Series in Risk and Insurance). Homewood, Ill.: Richard D. Irwin, 1955. 767p.
A textbook with references and review questions at chapter ends. Typical contracts analyzed.

PROPERTY AND CASUALTY INSURANCE COMPANIES; THEIR ROLE AS FINANCIAL INTERMEDIARIES, prepared by the American Mutual Insurance Alliance, Association of Casualty and Surety Companies, and National Board of Fire Underwriters. (Monograph prepared for the Commission on Money and Credit). Englewood Cliffs, N.J.: Prentice-Hall, 1962. 65p. tables.
Discusses insurance as an economic institution, forms of organization, capital stock and mutual companies, investment policies.

Reed, Prentiss B. ADJUSTMENT OF PROPERTY LOSSES, 2d ed. (McGraw-Hill Insurance Series). New York: McGraw-Hill, 1953. 667p. tables, forms.
A practical text for the adjuster. 1st ed. - 1929.

Rodda, William H. FIRE AND PROPERTY INSURANCE. Englewood Cliffs, N.J.: Prentice-Hall, 1956. 563p.
A textbook with review questions at chapter ends.

Ryan, W.J. Insurance in the Real Estate Office. p. 1330-64 In Friedman, Edith J., ed. REAL ESTATE ENCYCLOPEDIA. Englewood Cliffs, N.J.: Prentice-Hall, 1960.

Schultz, Robert E. and Bardwell, Edward C. PROPERTY INSURANCE. New York: Rinehart, 1959. 468p. tables, forms.
Technical and detailed analyses of coverages, rates, and underwriting used to illustrate basic principles. A college textbook.

Snider, H. Wayne, ed. READINGS IN PROPERTY AND CASUALTY INSURANCE. (Irwin Series in Insurance). Homewood, Ill.: Richard D. Irwin, 1959. 543p.
Fifty-four selections from the literature of insurance.

Insurance—Bibliography

INSURANCE LITERATURE. Special Libraries Association, Insurance Division. 10 issues per year.

Lists new publications and selected periodical articles in a classified arrangement.

Insurance—Periodicals
(See Appendix for complete information concerning these publications.)

ANNUALS OF THE SOCIETY OF CHARTERED PROPERTY AND CASUALTY UNDERWRITERS. BEST'S INSURANCE NEWS, FIRE AND CASUALTY EDITION. EASTERN UNDERWRITER. INSURANCE LITERATURE. JOURNAL OF INSURANCE. NATIONAL UNDERWRITER, FIRE AND CASUALTY EDITION. SPECTATOR.

PROPERTY MANAGEMENT

Agency Management: Job and Income Profile. BUILDINGS, vol. 56, no. 12, December 1962, p. 38-9.

American Society of Planning Officials. CONDOMINIUM. (Planning Advisory Service Information Report no. 159). Chicago: 1962. 24p. diagrs. pap.
    Includes a bibliography.

Associated Home Builders of the Greater Eastbay. CONDOMINIUM ABECEDARIUM; PREPARED AS A HANDBOOK FOR THE CONDOMINIUM CONFERENCE ON NOVEMBER 28, 1961, ed. by William T. Leonard. Berkeley, Calif.: 1961. n.p. illus., diagrs., forms. pap.
    A guide for organizing a condominium development, sample documents, and general background. 1962 handbook also issued.

Bliss, Howard L. and Sill, Charles H. REAL ESTATE MANAGEMENT. New York: Prentice-Hall, 1953. 353p. illus., charts, forms.
    A practical guide for the property manager; discusses business aspects of his job, physical care of buildings, tenant relations, etc.

Brett, Wyckoff, Potter, and Hamilton. THE COOPERATIVE APARTMENT HOUSE. New York: 1957. 40p. pap.
    Brochure developed for prospective buyers.

Building Managers' Association of Chicago. THE PERCENTAGE LEASE. Chicago: 38 South Dearborn Street, 1955. 20p. pap. processed.
    "Complete manual of principles and practices." Supplementary information issued annually on rates.

Building Managers' Association of Chicago. Insurance Committee. INSURANCE MANUAL FOR OWNERS AND MANAGERS OF OFFICE AND LOFT BUILDINGS. Rev. Chicago: 1958. 68p. pap. processed.

California. University. Real Estate Research Program. LOS ANGELES REAL ESTATE; A STUDY OF INVESTMENT EXPERIENCE, by Fred E. Case. Los Angeles: 1960. 103p. tables, charts. pap.

Cohen, Albert D. LONG TERM LEASES; PROBLEMS OF TAXATION, FINANCE AND ACCOUNTING. (Michigan Business Studies, vol. 11, no. 5). Ann Arbor: Bureau of Business Research, University of Michigan, 1954. 150p. tables. pap.
    Discusses fundamental theory and appraises the long term lease as a financing device. Tax considerations covered. Developed from a doctoral dissertation presented in 1953.

Condominiums--A Symposium. APPRAISAL JOURNAL, vol. 30, no. 4.
October 1962, p. 453-69.
> Schlitt, Carl D., History of Condominium; Lippman, William
> J., Legal Problems of Condominium; and O'Keefe, Raymond
> T., Financial Aspects of Condominiums.

Cooperatives. Section 57,400 In Casey, William J. REAL ESTATE INVEST-
MENT DEALS, IDEAS, FORMS. New York: Institute for Business Planning,
1959-   .
> Includes subsections: Selling Cooperative Apartments; The
> Cooperative Tenant.

Cowgill, Clinton H. BUILDING FOR INVESTMENT. New York: Reinhold,
1951. 482p. illus., tables, charts.
> Written for the owner of investment property. Deals with the
> design and construction of various types of buildings. Includes
> chapters on site selection, appraisal, and law. Appendix in-
> cludes unit costs for various types of structure.

Davidson, W. F. RENTING OFFICES. Chicago: National Association of
Building Owners and Managers, 1928. 277p.

Downs, James C., Jr. PRINCIPLES OF REAL ESTATE MANAGEMENT, 7th ed.
Chicago: Institute of Real Estate Management, 1961. 512p. illus., charts, forms.
> A textbook of techniques and practices with review questions
> and references at chapter ends.

Eckert, Fred W. THE HOTEL LEASE. Chicago: Hotel Monthly Press, 1947.
221p.

Grebler, Leo. EXPERIENCE IN URBAN REAL ESTATE INVESTMENT; AN
INTERIM REPORT BASED ON NEW YORK CITY PROPERTIES. (Publications of
the Institute for Urban Land Use and Housing Studies, Columbia University).
New York: Columbia University Press, 1955. 277p. tables, charts.

Greenfield, Harvey and Griesinger, Frank K. SALE-LEASEBACKS AND LEASING
IN REAL ESTATE AND EQUIPMENT TRANSACTIONS. (McGraw-Hill Consultant
Reports on Current Business Problems). New York: McGraw-Hill Book Company,
1958. 107p. processed.
> Describes this financing technique and its use, with advantages
> and disadvantages. Bibliography: p. 103-7

Handbook of Building Operations. BUILDINGS, the November issue each year.
> Building and equipment maintenance information, operating costs,
> and Reference Roundup, a complete guide to useful information
> for owners, managers and operators of commercial buildings. Refer-
> ences are classified under operational phases of real estate manage-
> ment.

How to Lease Real Property. Part VII, p. 773-853 In Friedman, Edith J.,
ed. REAL ESTATE ENCYCLOPEDIA. Englewood Cliffs, N.J.: Prentice-Hall,
1960.

Chapter 31: Lease Contracts, by J. Benton Tulley; Chapter 32: Broker's Role in Leasing Commercial Property, by Robert P. Boblett.

How to Manage Real Property. p. 583-772 In Friedman, Edith J., ed. REAL ESTATE ENCYCLOPEDIA. Englewood Cliffs, N.J.: Prentice-Hall, 1960.
    Chapter 25: Management of Small Properties, by J. Maximilian Martin; Chapter 26: Apartment House Management, by William S. Everett; Chapter 27: Management of Office and Commercial Buildings, by Maynard Hokanson; Chapter 28: Management of an Industrial Park, by W. C. Windsor, Jr.; Chapter 29: Farm Management, by Bruce Russell; Chapter 30: Hotel Ownership, Operation and Management, by Roger P. Sonnabend.

Institute of Real Estate Management. APARTMENT BUILDING EXPERIENCE EXCHANGE. (Special Issue of the JOURNAL OF PROPERTY MANAGEMENT). Chicago: 1957-   . tables, charts. pap.
    Annual.

Institute of Real Estate Management. BUILDING MAXIMUM PROFITS INTO INCOME PROPERTY. Chicago: 1961. various paging. processed.
    Suggestions from Certified Property Managers, contractors and architects on building design and materials. Pt. 1: APARTMENT BUILDINGS; Pt. 2: OFFICE, COMMERCIAL AND INDUSTRIAL BUILDINGS; Pt. 3: EXHIBITS.

Institute of Real Estate Management. COOPERATIVE APARTMENTS: THEIR ORGANIZATION AND PROFITABLE OPERATION; ALL TYPES, INCLUDING CONDOMINIUMS, CONVENTIONAL, FHA INSURED; FEATURING ASPECTS OF ORGANIZING, FINANCING, BUDGETING, MANAGING. 2d. ed. Chicago: 1961. 96p. illus., tables, plans. pap.
    An assembly of source materials by six authors.

Institute of Real Estate Management. FUNDAMENTALS AND STANDARDS BULLETIN. Chicago: 1945--
    Numbers 1 to 4 issued as MANUALS. Each BULLETIN on a specific subject: practical aspects of materials, maintenance, personnel, equipment, etc.

Institute of Real Estate Management. PRACTICAL REAL ESTATE MANAGEMENT, 2 vols. Chicago: 1958. charts.
    A ready reference manual of articles from the JOURNAL OF PROPERTY MANAGEMENT. Includes data on specific types of property, tax, and legal considerations.

Institute of Real Estate Management.: THE REAL ESTATE MANAGEMENT DEPARTMENT: HOW TO ESTABLISH AND OPERATE IT. Chicago: 1958. 135p. forms.
    "Authoritative information on the implementation and operation of a management department within the framework of the general real estate organization." Sample forms: p. 96-135.

Leases. Section 6800 In Casey, William J. TAX TESTED FORMS OF AGREEMENTS, RESOLUTIONS AND PLANS; ANNOTATED. New York: Institute for Business Planning, 1956-   .

Includes specimen forms for several specific property types.

Leases. Section 55,500 In Casey, William J. REAL ESTATE INVESTMENT
DEALS, IDEAS, FORMS. New York: Institute for Business Planning, 1959-
Includes checklist of points to be considered in drafting leases;
specimen forms and alternative clauses.

Leasing. Section 55,600 In Casey, William J. REAL ESTATE INVESTMENT
DEALS, IDEAS, FORMS. New York: Institute for Business Planning, 1959-
Considerations of the landlord's and the tenant's position.

Lieberman, Milton N. EFFECTIVE DRAFTING OF LEASES FOR REAL PROPERTY,
WITH CHECK LISTS AND SUGGESTED FORMS. Newark, N.J.: Gann Law
Books, 1956. 974p.
Written for the attorney, to serve as a convenient reference and
reminder of the prime and fine points to be considered in drafting
of leases. Thoroughly indexed.

Management. Section 4 In PRENTICE-HALL REAL ESTATE GUIDE. Englewood
Cliffs, N.J.: Prentice-Hall, 1953-
Contents: Getting Management Business; Leasing and Renting
Ideas; Percentage Leases; Collecting Rents; Building and Site
Maintenance; Management Accounting Methods; Tenant Relation-
ships.

Mandel, H. Robert. REAL ESTATE MANAGEMENT; A MANUAL FOR PROFIT-
ABLE PROPERTY OPERATION. New York: Ronald Press, 1939. 218p.
"Handy reference guide to the basic principles and practices
which govern property management."

March, C.A. BUILDING OPERATION AND MANAGEMENT. New York:
McGraw-Hill, 1950. 384p. illus., forms.
"A compendium of facts for use in dealing with the questions
that come up in (the owner's or manager's) everyday work."

McCaleb, C.A. and Hannon, J.R. SUCCESSFUL RENTING METHODS, 2d ed.
Chicago: Real Estate Press, 1939. 128p. illus. pap.

McGonagle, James R. APARTMENT HOUSE RENTAL, INVESTMENT, AND
MANAGEMENT. New York: Prentice-Hall, 1937. 420p. illus., tables,
forms.
Includes chapters on bookkeeping, rent collection, cooperative
apartments.

McMichael, Stanley L. and O'Keefe, Paul T. LEASES: PERCENTAGE, SHORT
AND LONG TERM, 5th ed. Englewood Cliffs, N.J.: Prentice-Hall, 1959.
511p. forms.
The theory, construction, and use of leases for various types of
property, including shopping centers and chain stores   First
edition title: LONG TERM LAND LEASEHOLDS. Second and
third editions: LONG AND SHORT TERM LEASEHOLDS.

National Association of Building Owners and Managers. APARTMENT HOUSE

EXCHANGE. Chicago: 1924-1930.

National Association of Building Owners and Managers. OFFICE BUILDING
EXPERIENCE EXCHANGE REPORT; ANALYSIS OF RENTAL INCOME AND
OPERATING EXPENSES. Chicago: 1919-
> An annual analysis of costs per square foot for country, regions,
> and selected cities. Special sections on specific operations.
> 1960--41st annual.

National Association of Building Owners and Managers. OPERATING HAND-
BOOK. Chicago: 1954-   . illus., diagrs., charts. pap. processed.
> Sections issued in pamphlet form as completed: 1. PAINTING,
> 1954; 2. INTERIOR MAINTENANCE, 1956; 12. OFFICE LAYOUT,
> 1956; 6. ELECTRICAL, 1957; 7. ELEVATORS, 1959; 3. AIR
> CONDITIONING, 1962.

National Association of Building Owners and Managers. PROCEEDINGS OF
THE ANNUAL CONVENTION, 1908-   Chicago: 1908-

National Association of Building Owners and Managers. STANDARD METHOD
OF FLOOR MEASUREMENT FOR OFFICE BUILDINGS, 3rd rev. ed. Chicago:
1956. 5p. plans. pap.
> 1915 NABOM National Standard revised to conform to American
> Standards Association, American Standard of which the association
> is co-sponsor. "Recommended in order that any measurement ex-
> pressed in square feet of rentable area (whether 'net' or 'full
> floor') may have an exact and well understood meaning."

National District Heating Association. PRINCIPLES OF ECONOMICAL HEATING,
6th ed. Pittsburgh: 827 North Euclid Avenue, 1962. 46p. tables, charts,
diagrs.
> Published by National District Heating Association in collabora-
> tion with the National Association of Building Owners and Man-
> agers.

National Institute of Real Estate Brokers. PERCENTAGE LEASES, 10th ed..
(Brokers Institute Bulletin Service). Chicago: 1961. 95p. pap.
> Specific information selected from more than one thousand actual
> percentage leases negotiated during the period from 1957 through
> 1961. Type of operation, location, percentage rental rate,
> length of lease, and actual minimum rental given for sixty-three
> types of business.

Operating the Property. Section 56,200 In Casey, William J. REAL
ESTATE INVESTMENT DEALS, IDEAS, FORMS. New York: Institute for
Business Planning, 1959-
> Costs in operating real estate: repairs, taxes, casualty losses,
> demolition losses, miscellaneous costs; year-end tax tips.

Rent levels in various cities. REAL ESTATE ANALYST, vol. 31, no. 25,
June 30, 1962 (entire issue).
> Rental figures for cities, on unfurnished houses, duplexes, and
> apartments, according to number of rooms, for months of May

and November, 1955 to 1962. (only May for 1962). Result
of analysis of newspaper advertisements.

Rosahn, Beatrice Greenfield and Goldfield, Abraham. HOUSING MANAGE-
MENT PRINCIPLES AND PRACTICES. New York: Covici, Friede, 1937.
414p.
"Describes in detail the practices of model large-scale developments, and tends to emphasize certain desirable principles in
public housing management."

Rowles, Rosemary J., ed. HOUSING MANAGEMENT, ed. for the Society
of Housing Managers. London: Isaac Pitman and Sons, 1959. 330p.
Management of existing housing estates in the United Kingdom.

Schultz, Robert E. LIFE INSURANCE HOUSING PROJECTS. (S. S. Huebner
Foundation for Insurance Education, University of Pennsylvania). Homewood,
Ill.: Richard D. Irwin, 1956. 154p. tables.

Sheridan, Donald T. Professional Management for Investment Protection.
pages 148-51 In National Real Estate Investor. NATIONAL REAL ESTATE
HANDBOOK AND DIRECTORY. New York: 1962.

Sheridan, Leo J. and Karkow, Waldemar. Sheridan-Karkow Formula for
Determining Rental Value of Office Space, Prepared to Reflect the Relative
Value of Space in a Given Building to the Base Rate of that Building.
BUILDINGS, vol. 54, no. 13, December 1960, p. 49.
Formula originally compiled and copyrighted in 1934. Revision of
this formula discussed in SKYSCRAPER MANAGEMENT, vol. 44,
no. 9, September, 1959, page 7: Modern Developments Suggest
Revision of Formula for Rental Values.

Shopping Center Leases. SHOPPING CENTER AGE, a feature appearing in
each issue from June to November 1962.
A different business type covered each month. Data obtained
from the International Council of Shopping Centers and other
sources.

State Laws: Digest of State Lease Laws. Section 15 In PRENTICE-HALL
REAL ESTATE GUIDE. Englewood Cliffs, N.J.: Prentice-Hall, 1953-

SUCESSFUL RENTING AND LEASING. Cedar Rapids, Iowa: Stamats Publishing
Co., no date. 44p. illus., tables. pap. processed.
Articles on office building management from BUILDINGS, THE
MAGAZINE OF BUILDING MANAGEMENT.

U. S. Federal Housing Administration. CONDOMINIUMS; MODEL STATUTE
FOR CREATION OF APARTMENT OWNERSHIP AND COMMENTARY. Wash-
ington, D.C.: 1962. 22p. pap. processed.
State enabling legislation.

U. S. Federal Housing Administration. FOUR DECADES OF HOUSING WITH
A LIMITED DIVIDEND CORPORATION. Washington, D.C.: 1939. 108p.
Investment experience.

U. S. Federal Housing Administration. Division of Research and Statistics.
A SURVEY OF APARTMENT DWELLING OPERATING EXPERIENCE IN LARGE
AMERICAN CITIES. Washington, D.C.: 1940. 138p. tables, charts. pap.

Vogel, Harold N. THE CO-OP APARTMENT; A GUIDE FOR CO-OP BUYERS
AND OWNERS. New York: Libra Publishers, Inc., 445 West 23rd Street,
1960. 119p. pap.
> "Aims to present enough facts to help a family make a well-
> considered decision concerning the investment in a co-operative
> apartment." Question and answer format. Includes model by-
> laws, proprietary lease, etc.

Wolff, Lewis N. The Application of Corporate Investment Techniques to
Real Estate Expenditure Analyses. REAL ESTATE ANALYST APPRAISAL
BULLETIN, vol. 30, no. 16, p. 147-52.
> "Two systems of developing rates of return for contemplated
> capital expenditures."

Property Management—Periodicals
(See Appendix for complete information concerning these publications.)

APARTMENT AND OWNER. APARTMENT JOURNAL. APARTMENT MAN-
AGEMENT IN NEW ENGLAND. BUILDINGS. FUNDAMENTALS AND
STANDARDS BULLETIN. HOTEL AND APARTMENT MANAGER. HOUSING
VACANCIES. JOURNAL OF PROPERTY MANAGEMENT. REAL ESTATE
ANALYST. RENTAL HOUSING. SKYSCRAPER MANAGEMENT.

Section 10

URBAN RENEWAL

ACTION, Inc. ORGANIZATIONS IN RENEWAL, 2d ed. New York: 1959.
32p. pap.
>"Statements prepared by national organizations actively interested
in urban renewal describing their objectives, materials, functions
and services."

ACTION, Inc. A PROGRAM OF RESEARCH IN URBAN RENEWAL, 2 vols. New
York: 1954. pap. processed.
>Vol. 1: SUMMARY OF URBAN RENEWAL RESEARCH PROGRAM, Vol.2:
URBAN RENEWAL BIBLIOGRAPHY, comp. by Katherine McNamara.

ACTION, Inc. URBAN RENEWAL OUTLINE; AN OUTLINE DESCRIPTION OF
URBAN RENEWAL ACTIVITIES AND HOW THEY ARE UNDERTAKEN. New York:
no date. 20p. pap. processed.

Bloom, Max Robert. ECONOMIC CRITERIA AND THE USE OF LAND IN SUB-
SIDIZED URBAN REDEVELOPMENT AREAS. Unpublished Ph.D. thesis, American
University, 1959.

Building Industry Congress on Urban Renewal, National Housing Center, March
1958. SUMMARY REPORT. SPONSORED BY NATIONAL HOUSING CENTER
AND AMERICAN COUNCIL TO RENEW OUR NEIGHBORHOODS. Washington
D.C.: National Housing Center, 1958. 26p. pap. processed.
>Theme: How the Building Industry Tackles Urban Renewal.

California. University. Bureau of Public Administration. THE NEW RENEWAL;
PROCEEDINGS OF A CIVIC SEMINAR: THE NEXT BIG TASKS IN URBAN RE-
NEWAL. Berkeley: 1961. 158p.

California. University. Real Estate Research Program. COST-BENEFIT ANALYSIS
IN URBAN REDEVELOPMENT, by Nathaniel Lichfield. (Research Report
no. 20). Berkeley: 1962. 52p. tables, diagrs. pap. processed.

California. University. Real Estate Research Program. ECONOMIC ASPECTS OF
URBAN RENEWAL: THEORY, POLICY AND AREA ANALYSIS, by A.H. Schaaf.
(Research Report 14). Berkeley: 1960. 51p. charts. pap.

California. University. Real Estate Research Program. PRIVATE INVESTMENT IN
URBAN REDEVELOPMENT, by Richard U. Ratcliff. (Research Report no. 17).
Berkeley: 1961. 69p.

Colean, Miles L. RENEWING OUR CITIES. New York: Twentieth Century

Fund, 1953. 181p. illus.

> Results used for a film by Encyclopedia Britannica Films, as well. Describes the "process and effects of urban growth and decay and suggests ways in which we can prune out the decay and nourish the growth toward consciously planned objectives of better living. This study embodies an attempt to take a broad view of the problems cities encounter in maintaining their vitality amid the onrush of population increase and technological changes and to review some of the efforts that are being made to cope with these problems."

Conference on Problems in Urban Renewal. PROCEEDINGS OF THE ... WORKING CONFERENCE ... Washington, D.C.: National Association of Housing and Redevelopment Officials, 1956-   . pap. processed.

> Title of proceedings, report of sixth conference: PRIVATE FINANCING CONSIDERATIONS IN URBAN RENEWAL.

Conferences on the Manufacturer's Stake in Urban Renewal and Remodeling, National Housing Center, July 1961. A REPORT. Washington D.C.: National Association of Home Builders, 1625 L Street, N.W., zone 6, 1961. 32p. pap. processed.

Detroit. City Plan Commission. RENEWAL AND REVENUE; AN EVALUATION OF THE URBAN RENEWAL PROGRAM IN DETROIT: A DEMONSTRATION GRANT STUDY BY THE DETROIT CITY PLAN COMMISSION IN COOPERATION WITH THE HOUSING AND HOME FINANCE AGENCY. Detroit: 1962. 128p. illus., tables, charts. pap.

> "Measures the affect of blight on the city's revenue system by relating degrees of blight with variations in assessed value; estimates future blight by measurement of the useful life remaining in the stock of structures: and evaluates the problems encountered in implementing urban renewal projects in the city."

Dyckman, John W. and Isaacs, Reginald R. CAPITAL REQUIREMENTS FOR URBAN DEVELOPMENT AND RENEWAL. (ACTION Series in Housing and Community Development). New York: McGraw-Hill, 1961. 334p. tables.

> "The authors explore the questions of our ability to pay for required investment in cities and the organization of our economy necessary to realize urban goals... They translate national expenditure totals into specific changes in the urban environment and convert specific local programs into a national bill of goods."

Everett, Robinson O., ed. Urban Renewal. LAW AND CONTEMPORARY PROBLEMS. vol. 25, no. 4, Autumn 1960 (entire issue); vol 26, no. 1, Winter 1961 (entire issue).

> Part I: A New Pattern for Urban Renewal; Federal Urban Renewal Legislation; The Workable Program - A Challenge for community Improvement; Rehabilitation and Conservation; The Disposition Problem in Urban Renewal; The Federal Urban Renewal Program: a Ten Year Critique; State and Local Incentives and Techniques for Urban Renewal. Part II: Problems and Opportunities of Relocations; Leasing in the Disposition of Urban Renewal Land; The Relation of Local Government Structure to Urban Renewal; Property, et al. v. Nuisance, et al; Current Problems Affect-

ing Costs of Condemnation; Economics of Urban Renewal; Urban
Redevelopment - the Viewpoint of Counsel for a Private Re-
developer.

Groberg, Robert P. The Impact of Urban Renewal on Downtown Areas. DOWN-
TOWN IDEA EXCHANGE. SPECIAL STUDY. Part 1: Oct 1961, 2p. Part 2:
Dec. 15, 1961, 4p. Part 3: Feb. 1962, 4p. Part 4: Mar., 1962, 2p. pap.

Haas, John H. 3R'S OF HOUSING; A GUIDE TO HOUSING REHABILITATION,
RELOCATION HOUSING, REFINANCING. Washington D.C.: General Improve-
ment Contractors, 1962. 104p. pap.
Guide for professionals in the business of rehabilitation.

Hemdahl, Reuel. URBAN RENEWAL. New York: Scarecrow Press, 1959. 367p.
Methods. "Analytical survey of local administration of urban
renewal."

International Seminar on Urban Renewal, The Hague, August 22-29, 1958.
PROCEEDINGS, PAPERS AND CONCLUSIONS, ed. by P.T. Van Der Hoff
and George S. Duggar. The Hague: International Federation for Housing and
Planning, no date. 120p. illus., maps. pap.
Sponsored by the International Federation for Housing and Planning and the Netherlands Housing and Town Planning Institute.
"Focused on what urban renewal experience indicated should
occur in physical planning." Renewal and Urbanism; Land Use
and Circulation; Area Appraisal and Selection; Developing Proposals and Effectuation of Renewal Programs, with a Critique
of Selected Programs.

Jacobs, Jane. THE DEATH AND LIFE OF GREAT AMERICAN CITIES. New
York and Toronto: Random House, 1961. 458p.
"This book is an attack on current city planning and rebuilding.
It is also, and mostly, an attempt to introduce new principles..."

Kinnard, William N., Jr. and Malinowski, Zenon S. THE IMPACT OF DIS-
LOCATION FROM URBAN RENEWAL AREAS ON SMALL BUSINESS. Storrs:
University of Connecticut, 1960. 89p. tables. pap. processed.
Prepared by the University of Connecticut under the Small Busi-
ness Administration Research Grant Program.

Lange, John D. Private Investment in Urban Renewal Real Estate. p. 136-9
In National Real Estate Investor. NATIONAL REAL ESTATE HANDBOOK
AND DIRECTORY. New York: 1962.

Low Cost Housing and Slum Clearance. LAW AND CONTEMPORARY PROB-
LEMS, Vol. 1, no. 2, March 1934 (entire issue).
A Century of the Housing Problems; Housing the Poor: Mirage
or Reality; Urban Housing and Land Use; the Regional Approach
to the Housing Problem; Housing as a Political Problem; the Drafting of Housing Legislation; Financing Slum Clearance; The Relation of Housing to Taxation; Housing Projects and City Planning;
Land Assembly for Housing Developments; A Note on the Power
of the Federal Government to Condemn for Housing; Control of
Housing Administration; The Housing Authority and the Housed.

NAHB Eastern Regional Builders Urban Renewal Conference, Baltimore, March
1961. SUMMARY REPORT: PROGRESS AND PROFIT THROUGH URBAN RE-
NEWAL. Washington D.C.: 1961. 54p. pap. processed.
    Co-sponsored by Home Builders Association of Maryland with the
    cooperation of the National Association of Housing and Redevel-
    opment Officials.

National Association of Home Builders. Community Facilities and Urban Renewal
Department. HOME BUILDERS GUIDE TO URBAN RENEWAL. Washington,
D.C.: 1961. 38p. pap.

National Association of Housing and Redevelopment Officials. SAVING CITIES
THROUGH CONSERVATION AND REHABILITATION; SELECTED ARTICLES FROM
THE JOURNAL OF HOUSING. Chicago: 1956. 37p. pap. processed.

National Association of Real Estate Boards. Build America Better Committee.
ADVISORY TEAM REPORTS. Washington D.C.: 1957-   .
    Prepared for the cities as a blueprint for action for urban renewal.
    Controlled distribution: Alburquerque, N.M.; Belleville, Ill.;
    Bellflower, Calif.; Charleston, W. Va.; Columbus, Ohio; Dallas,
    Tex.; Des Moines, Iowa; El Paso, Tex.; Honolulu, Hawaii;
    Huntington, W. Va.; Jersey City, N.J.; Nashville, Tenn.;
    Philadelphia, Pa.; Pittsburgh, Pa.; San Francisco, Calif.; Waco,
    Tex.; Waterloo, Iowa.

National Association of Real Estate Boards. Build America Better Committee.
BLUEPRINT FOR NEIGHBORHOOD CONSERVATION; A PROGRAM FOR LARGE-
SCALE ELIMINATION OF SLUM, BLIGHT AND UNFIT HOUSING CONDITIONS.
Washington D.C.: 1953. 48p. illus. pap.
    1953 edition revised by BAB Committee and Henry J. Kaiser Com-
    pany and distributed by Henry J. Kaiser Company. Case histories
    of progress in seven cities including a draft of a state act for em-
    bodying the neighborhood conservation proposal in state legisla-
    tion. New edition in preparation.

National Association of Real Estate Boards. Build America Better Committee.
BUILD AMERICA BETTER KIT. Washington D.C.: 1962. various paging.
    Includes a variety of materials to assist Realtors in undertaking
    conservation-centered urban renewal activities: BAB Committee,
    Housing and Home Finance Agency, Urban Renewal Administration
    and Federal Housing Administration publications.

National Association of Real Estate Boards. Build America Better Committee.
HOW TO MODERNIZE YOUR COMMUNITY; GUIDES TO REHABILITATION IN
SMALLER CITIES. Washington D.C.: 1962. 16p. pap.

Rapkin, Chester. THE REAL ESTATE MARKET IN AN URBAN RENEWAL AREA;
TENURE, OWNERSHIP AND PRICES OF RESIDENTIAL REAL PROPERTY IN A
TWENTY-BLOCK AREA OF MANHATTAN'S WEST SIDE. New York: City Plan-
ning Commission, 1959. 139p. tables, charts. pap.

Rapkin, Chester and Grigsby, William G. THE DEMAND FOR HOUSING IN
EASTWICK; A PRESENTATION OF ESTIMATES AND FORECASTS, INCLUDING
METHODS AND TECHNIQUES FOR ANALYZING THE HOUSING MARKET IN

A LARGE SCALE OPEN OCCUPANCY REDEVELOPMENT AREA. Philadelphia: Institute for Urban Studies, University of Pennsylvania, 1960. 83p. charts, tables. pap.
>Prepared under contract for the Redevelopment Authority of the City of Philadelphia.

Rapkin, Chester and Grigsby, William G. THE DEMAND FOR HOUSING IN RACIALLY MIXED AREAS; A STUDY OF THE NATURE OF NEIGHBORHOOD CHANGE. (Publications of the Commission on Race and Housing). Berkeley and Los Angeles: University of California Press, 1960. 170p. illus., maps, tables.

Rapkin, Chester and Grigsby, William G. RESIDENTIAL RENEWAL IN THE UR-BAN CORE; AN ANALYSIS OF THE DEMAND FOR HOUSING IN CENTER CITY, PHILADELPHIA, 1957 TO 1970, WITH REFERENCE TO WASHINGTON SQUARE EAST REDEVELOPMENT AREA. Philadelphia: Institute for Urban Studies, University of Pennsylvania, 1960. 131p.

Rossi, Peter H. and Dentler, Robert A. THE POLITICS OF URBAN RENEWAL; THE CHICAGO FINDINGS. New York: Free Press of Glencoe, 1961. 308p.
>Demonstration Urban Renewal Administration grant project. "... how citizens in a deteriorating community on the south side of Chicago developed ways to halt blight by helping to create a workable plan for the conservation and renewal of the physical plant of this community." (Hyde Park-Kenwood.)

Steiner, Oscar H. OUR HOUSING JUNGLE - AND YOUR POCKETBOOK; HOW TO TURN OUR GROWING SLUMS INTO ASSETS. New York: University Publishers, 1960. 180p. illus. pap.
>"... Steiner is now president of the building corporation that has shown its home town that private enterprise with an eye to the general welfare can reach the lower income market and make it pay."

Tax Responsibility for the Slum. TAX POLICY. vol. 26, no. 10, October 1959 (entire issue)
>Address before the 26th Annual Conference of National Association of Housing and Redevelopment Officials, Cincinnati, 1959.

Tennessee. State Planning Commission. CITIZEN PARTICIPATION IN URBAN RE-NEWAL, by William Bishop Nixon and Joseph M. Boyd, Jr. (Publication no. 279). Nashville: 1957. 245p. illus., diagrs. pap.
>Report of a Housing and Home Finance Agency demonstration project conducted in Dyersburg, Tennessee to explore methods of creating understanding and enlisting support and participation on the part of citizens for launching an urban renewal program in a small community.

U.S. Congress. Senate. Committee on Banking and Currency. HEARINGS BE-FORE A SUBCOMMITTEE, 85TH CONGRESS, FIRST SESSION, ON URBAN RE-NEWAL AND OTHER HOUSING PROBLEMS IN SELECTED CITIES. Washington, D.C.: 1957. 1491p. tables. pap.
>Hearings in Chicago, Illinois; Portland, Maine; Pittsburgh, Philadelphia; Huntsville, Alabama; and Mobile, Alabama.

U.S. Federal Housing Administration. A STUDY AND REPORT OF THE DISPOSI-TION AND FINANCING PROCESSES FOR RESIDENTIAL REDEVELOPMENT IN URBAN RENEWAL, submitted by Seymour Baskin. New York: ACTION, 1962.

43p.

> Reprinted with permission. "The study was undertaken for the
> FHA by Seymour Baskin, assisted by an advisory committee re-
> cruited by ACTION and representatives of local urban renewal
> agencies, private redevelopers, and other specialists in the rede-
> velopment process."

U.S. Housing and Home Finance Agency. FEDERAL LAWS, URBAN RENEWAL;
EXCERPTS FROM HOUSING ACT OF 1949 AND RELATED LAWS AS AMENDED
THROUGH JUNE 30, 1961. Washington, D.C.: 1961. 62p. pap. processed.
(Sold by Government Printing Office).

U.S. Housing and Home Finance Agency. HOW LOCALITIES CAN DEVELOP A
WORKABLE PROGRAM FOR URBAN RENEWAL, Rev. Washington D.C.: Government Printing Office. 1956. 12p. pap.

U.S. Housing and Home Finance Agency. WORKABLE PROGRAM FOR COMMU-
NITY IMPROVEMENT, Rev. ed. Washington D.C.: Government Printing Office,
1962. 43p. illus. pap.

> "is a plan of action for better living - a practical plan through
> which people work together to banish slums and blight and block
> their return."

U.S. Urban Renewal Administration. ADVISORY BULLETINS. Washington, D.C.:
1958.

> For Local Public Agency Guidance. No. 1: CODES AND ORDI-
> NANCES; No. 2: WARNING URBAN RENEWAL AREA PROPERTY
> OWNERS AGAINST PREMATURE IMPROVEMENTS; No. 3: EARTH
> FILLING ... FOR SITE IMPROVEMENTS; No. 4: LOCAL STAND-
> ARDS FOR DETERMINING ACCEPTABILITY OF REHOUSING RE-
> SOURCES. No. 5: (Replaced by Technical Guide no. 2), QUES-
> TIONS AND ANSWERS ON RELOCATION PAYMENTS; No. 6:
> VALUATION PROBLEMS INVOLVING REUSE OF URBAN LAND;
> No. 7: ADVERTISING AND MERCHANDISING URBAN RENEWAL
> PROJECT LAND; No. 8: REUSE AND VALUE APPRAISALS IN
> URBAN RENEWAL; No. 9: ESTIMATING CAPITAL GRANT RES-
> ERVATIONS.

U.S. Urban Renewal Administration. A LIST OF URBAN RENEWAL PROJECTS,
CLASSIFIED BY TYPE OF REDEVELOPMENT USE, 1949-1960. Washington, D.C.:
1961. 58p. pap. processed.

U.S. Urban Renewal Administration. LISTING OF LAND AVAILABLE FOR PRI-
VATE REDEVELOPMENT. Washington D.C.: 1962. 31p. pap. processed.

U.S. Urban Renewal Administration. TECHNICAL GUIDES. Washington D.C.:
1960-   . (Sold by Government Printing Office).

> No. 1: SELECTING CONSULTANTS FOR PROJECT PLANNING,
> July 1960; No. 2: QUESTIONS AND ANSWERS ON RELOCA-
> TION PAYMENTS, September 1960; No. 3: SELECTING AREAS
> FOR CONSERVATION, September 1960; No. 4: IMPLEMENT-
> ING CONSERVATION, October 1960; No. 5: FAMILY SURVEYS
> IN CONSERVATION AREAS, November 1960; No. 6: RESI-
> DENTIAL PROPERTY CONSERVATION STANDARDS, March 1961;
> No. 7: RESIDENTIAL PROPERTY SURVEYS IN CONSERVATION
> AREAS, March 1961; No. 8: NEIGHBORHOOD ORGANIZATION
> CONSERVATION AREAS, March 1961; No. 9: DETERMINING
> LOCAL RELOCATION STANDARDS, August 1961; No. 10:

COST ESTIMATES FOR PROJECT IMPROVEMENTS AND SITE PREP-
ARATION, May 1962; No. 11: USING CENSUS DATA FOR
URBAN RENEWAL PURPOSES, Rev., August 1962.

U.S. Urban Renewal Administration. URBAN RENEWAL MANUAL; POLICIES
AND REQUIREMENTS FOR LOCAL PUBLIC AGENCIES, 3 Vols. Washington D.C.:
1960. various paging. looseleaf. (Sold by Government Printing Office).
Subscription includes periodic supplements.

U.S. Urban Renewal Administration. URBAN RENEWAL SERVICE BULLETINS.
Washington: 1960- . illus. (Sold by Government Printing Office).
Informational, for the nonprofessional. No. 1: OAKLAND
MOBILIZES FOR URBAN RENEWAL, September 1960. Includes
as exhibits: Oakland Renewal Foundation, Selection and Train-
ing of Urban Renewal Representatives, Urban Renewal Representa-
tives Field and Office Manual, Residential Building Improvement
Checklist. Bulletin 2: HOME IMPROVEMENT ... LESSONS
FROM EXPERIENCE, October 1960; Bulletin 3: CLEVELAND'S
NEIGHBORHOOD IMPROVEMENT PROGRAM, June 1961.

Urban Land Institute. THE CHALLENGE OF URBAN RENEWAL, by M. Carter
McFarland. (Technical Bulletin no. 34). Washington D.C.: 1958. 44p. tables.
pap.
"Based on a series of lectures delivered in Ottawa, Canada under
the auspices of the Central Housing and Mortgage Corporation."

Urban Land Institute. DISCUSSION OF PRINCIPLES TO BE INCORPORATED IN
STATE URBAN REDEVELOPMENT ENABLING ACTS. (Technical Bulletin no. 2).
Washington D.C.: 1945. 4p. pap.
Revision issued March, 1946. 7p. pap. processed.

Urban Land Institute. EUROPE'S REBORN CITIES, by Leo Grebler. (Technical
Bulletin no. 28). Washington D.C.: 1956. 104p. illus. pap.

Urban Land Institute. PREPARING YOUR CITY FOR THE FUTURE; HOW TO
MAKE AN ECONOMIC STUDY OF YOUR COMMUNITY, by Robert B. Garrabrant. (Technical Bulletin no. 29). Washington D.C.: 1956. 27p. diagrs.
pap.

Urban Land Institute. WHAT IS THE MARKET VALUE OF 'IMPROVED' LAND IN
SLUMS? by Clarence W. Beatty, Jr. (Technical Bulletin no. 7). Washington
D.C.: 1947. 16p. pap. processed.

Urban Land Institute. Central Business District Council. THE CITY FIGHTS
BACK; A NATION-WIDE SURVEY OF WHAT CITIES ARE DOING TO KEEP
PACE WITH TRAFFIC, ZONING, SHIFTING POPULATION, SMOKE, SMOG
AND OTHER PROBLEMS, Narrated and ed. by Hal Burton. New York: 1954.
318p. illus., tables. (Distr. by Citadel Press).

Vernon, Raymond. THE CHANGING ECONOMIC FUNCTION OF THE CENTRAL
CITY. New York: Committee for Economic Development, 1959. 92p. pap.
Much of the material was developed for the New York Metropol-
itan Region Study.

Vernon, Raymond. METROPOLIS 1985; AN INTERPRETATION OF THE FINDINGS OF THE NEW YORK METROPOLITAN REGION STUDY. Cambridge: Harvard University Press, 1960. 252p. tables, charts.

> "The Regional Plan Association requested the Graduate School of Public Administration of Harvard University to undertake a three year study of the region. The challenging task was to analyze the key economic and demographic features of the region and project them to 1965, 1975, and 1985. Its end product as presented in this volume is an analysis of the region's probable devlopment..."

Vigman, Fred K. CRISIS OF THE CITIES. Washington D.C.: Public Affairs Press, 1955. 155p.

> "Part I: a study of the three principle elements of urban decline and the preposessions and social hopes that lie in city planning; Part II: A study of a selected group of cities in the throes of urban crisis, a brief chapter on Los Angeles and a forecast of the future of American cities."

Woodbury, Coleman, ed. THE FUTURE OF CITIES AND URBAN REDEVELOPMENT. Chicago: University of Chicago Press, 1953. 764p.

> This volume and its companion, URBAN REDEVELOPMENT: PROBLEMS AND PRACTICES, are the chief products of the Urban Redevelopment Study 1948-51, made possible by a grant by the Spelman Fund of New York to Public Administration Clearing House. "Underlying factors in urban growth and development that, more or less directly, have helped to produce the problems ... and certain questions of objectives and values that underlie many of the actual program and policy issues."

Woodbury, Coleman, ed. URBAN REDEVELOPMENT: PROBLEMS AND PRACTICES. Chicago: University of Chicago Press, 1953. 525p.

> "Major operating problems and practices in local redevelopment programs." Measures the quality of housing; urban densities and their costs; private covenants; urban redevelopment short of clearance; relocation; eminent domain in acquiring subdivision and open land.

Urban Renewal—Bibliography

ACTION. URBAN RENEWAL BIBLIOGRAPHY, comp. by Katherine McNamara. New York: 1954. 313p. pap. processed.

> Appendices: Urban renewal check list and 3 special subject bibliographies: Twenty-Five City Planning References to Serve as an Introduction to Urban Renewal; Techniques for Population Forecasting; and an Annotated List of References on Housing Codes.

American Society of Planning Officials. SELECTED BIBLIOGRAPHY ON URBAN REDEVELOPMENT. Chicago: 1951. 31p. pap. processed.

District of Columbia. Public Library. PUBLICATIONS RELATING TO URBAN RE-
NEWAL. Washington, D.C.: 1956-   . pap. processed.
     Continuation of ACTION'S URBAN RENEWAL BIBLIOGRAPHY, 1954.

National Association of Housing and Redevelopment Officials. SELECTED REFER-
ENCES ON FAMILY AND BUSINESS RELOCATION CAUSED BY URBAN RENEWAL
AND OTHER PUBLIC IMPROVEMENTS. (Publication no. N428). Chicago: 1960.
6p. pap.

National Housing Center. Library. URBAN RENEWAL; A NON-SELECTIVE LIST OF
HOLDINGS, 1959-1961. (Reference List no. 43). Washington D.C.: National
Association of Home Builders, 1961. 14p. pap. processed.

Tenant Relocation in Urban Renewal: A Bibliography. MUNICIPAL REFERENCE
LIBRARY NOTES. vol. 24, no.20, December 1959, p. 221-36.

U.S. Housing and Home Finance Agency. Library. RELOCATION IN URBAN
AREAS; A SELECTED LIST OF BOOKS AND ARTICLES, 1951-1961. Washington,
D.C.: 1961. 29p. pap. processed.

Urban Renewal—Periodicals
(See Appendix for complete information concerning these publications.)

BUILD AMERICA BETTER BULLETIN. FROM THE STATE CAPITALS. HOUSING REF-
ERENCES. NAHB STATE LEGISLATIVE BULLETIN. RENEWAL INFORMATION SERV-
ICE NEWSLETTER. SEARS URBAN OBSERVER. URBAN RENEWAL NOTES.

Section 11

LAND ECONOMICS

Barlowe, Raleigh. LAND RESOURCE ECONOMICS. Englewood Cliffs: Prentice-Hall, 1958. 585p.

Bye, Carl Rollinson. DEVELOPMENTS AND ISSUES IN THE THEORY OF RENT. New York: Columbia University Press, 1940. 133p.
    Bibliography included.

Ely, Richard T. and Morehouse, Edward W. ELEMENTS OF LAND ECONOMICS. (Land Economics Series; Standard Course in Real Estate). New York: Macmillan, 1924. 363p. tables.

George, Henry. PROGRESS AND PROPERTY; AN INQUIRY INTO THE CAUSE OF INDUSTRIAL DEPRESSIONS AND OF INCREASE OF WANT WITH INCREASE OF WEALTH; THE REMEDY, 50th anniversary edition. New York: Random House, 1929. 571p.
    "The Appletons in New York brought out the first regular market edition in January, 1880." The Single Tax.

Illinois. University. Land Economics Institute. MODERN LAND POLICY. Urbana: 1960. 449p. tables, charts, maps. processed.
    Papers from the program, June 17-July11, and July 14-Aug. 8, 1958.

Isard, Walter. LOCATION AND SPACE-ECONOMY; A GENERAL THEORY RELATING TO INDUSTRIAL LOCATION, MARKET AREAS, LAND USE, TRADE AND URBAN STRUCTURE. New York: John Wiley, 1956. 330p.

Isard, Walter, et al. METHODS OF REGIONAL ANALYSIS; AN INTRODUCTION TO REGIONAL SCIENCE. New York: Technology Press, Massachusetts Institute of Technology and Wiley, 1960. 784p.
    Supplementary to LOCATION AND SPACE ECONOMY.

Johnson, V. Webster and Barlowe, Raleigh. LAND PROBLEMS AND POLICIES. New York: McGraw-Hill, 1954. 422p. illus.

Keiper, Joseph S., et al. THEORY AND MEASUREMENT OF RENT. Philadelphia: Chilton, 1961. 194p. tables, charts.
    Lincoln Foundation grant. "Part 1. Historical development of rent theory and its relevance to contemporary economic problems. Part 2. Contains an analysis of the real property values on which estimates for 1956 are based. Separate estimates for the various classes of real property, broken down by states are presented ..."

LAND ECONOMICS SERIES. New York: Macmillan, 1922-1940.
In addition to six titles listed below, the series includes the eight volumes comprising the STANDARD COURSE IN REAL ESTATE, the titles of which are cited in the Real Estate Business - Principles and Practices section.

Bennett, J. M. ROADSIDE DEVELOPMENT. 1929.

Dorau, Herbert B. and Hinman, Albert G. URBAN LAND ECONOMICS. 1928.

Ely, Richard T. and Wehrwein, George S. LAND ECONOMICS. 1940.

Fisher, Ernest McKinley. ADVANCED PRINCIPLES OF REAL ESTATE PRACTICE. 1930.

Hibbard, Benjamin Horace. A HISTORY OF THE PUBLIC LAND POLICIES. 1924.

Williams, Frank Backus. THE LAW OF CITY PLANNING AND ZONING. 1922.

Lincoln, John C. GROUND RENT, NOT TAXES: THE NATURAL SOURCE OF REVENUE FOR THE GOVERNMENT, AN ECONOMIC STUDY. New York: Exposition Press, 1957. 72p.
"The Lincoln Foundation was founded to get people to see that ground rent belongs to the community and that it will be possible to abolish the taxation of wealth if it was collected by the community for community expenses."

Ratcliff, Richard U. URBAN LAND ECONOMICS. New York: McGraw-Hill, 1949. 533p.

Renne, Roland R. LAND ECONOMICS; PRINCIPLES, PROBLEMS, AND POLICIES IN UTILIZING LAND RESOURCES. New York: Harper, 1947. 736p. illus., tables, charts, maps.
References at chapter ends.

Land Economics—Periodicals
(See Appendix for complete information concerning these publications.)

LAND ECONOMICS.

Section 12

LAND USE

Bartholomew, Harland. LAND USES IN AMERICAN CITIES. (Harvard City Planning Studies No. 15). Cambridge: Harvard University Press, 1955. 196p. illus., diagrs., maps, plans.

Bertrand, Alvin L. and Corty, Floyd L., eds. RURAL LAND TENURE IN THE UNITED STATES; A SOCIO-ECONOMIC APPROACH TO PROBLEMS, PROGRAMS, AND TRENDS. Baton Rouge: Louisiana State University Press, 1962. 313p. tables, charts.

Beuscher, J. H., comp. LAND USE CONTROLS — CASES AND MATERIALS. Madison, Wis.: College Printing and Typing Company, various paging. pap. processed.

Chapin, F. Stuart, Jr. URBAN LAND USE PLANNING. New York: Harper, 1957. 397p. tables, diagrs., maps.
"An attempt is made to bring together in one book the theoretical background for land use planning and to summarize techniques the city planner employs in diagnosing the ills and needs of land development."

Clawson, Marion, et al. LAND FOR THE FUTURE. Baltimore: Johns Hopkins Press, 1960. 570p.

El Paso Texas. Department of Planning. A DATA STORAGE SYSTEM FOR LAND USE ANALYSES, A DESCRIPTION. (Technical Report 62-1). El Paso: 1962. 53p. diagrs. pap. processed.
(Technical Report 62-1).

Firey, Walter. LAND USE IN CENTRAL BOSTON. Cambridge: Harvard University Press, 1947. 367p.
Originally submitted as a doctoral dissertation to the Dept. of Sociology, Harvard. Central problem "concerns the scope of cultural values and community sentiments on conditioning land use patterns of central Boston."

Green, Raymond Joseph. THE IMPACT OF THE CENTRAL BUSINESS DISTRICT ON THE MUNICIPAL BUDGET. (J. C. Nichols Foundation Research Study). Washington D.C.: Urban Land Institute, 1962. 198p. tables. maps. pap. processed.
Grant from the J. C. Nichols Foundation of the Urban Land Institute to the University of North Carolina, 1959-1960. The Central Business District, its legacy and problems; cost revenue

analyses - theoretical considerations , general methodology for
making a cost-revenue analysis of the CBD; a case study (Char-
lotte, North Carolina.)

Haar, Charles M.   LAND PLANNING IN A FREE SOCIETY; A STUDY OF
THE BRITISH TOWN AND COUNTRY PLANNING ACT.   (Harvard Legal
Studies Series).   Cambridge: Harvard University Press, 1951.   213p.   illus.

Haar, Charles M.   LAND USE PLANNING; A CASEBOOK ON THE USE,
MISUSE AND RE-USE OF URBAN LAND.   Boston: Little, Brown, 1959.   790p.
tables, charts, maps.
Materials to enable analysis of the "legal and administrative problems of allocating and developing that increasingly scarce resource-
urban land in metropolitan areas."

Herr, Philip B.   THE REGIONAL IMPACT OF HIGHWAYS.   Cambridge:
School of Architecture, Massachusetts Institute of Technology, 1959.   58p.

Horwood, Edgar M., et al.   STUDIES OF THE CENTRAL BUSINESS DISTRICT
AND URBAN FREEWAY DEVELOPMENT.   Seattle: University of Washington Press.   1959.   184p.   pap.

Jacobs, Jane.   THE DEATH AND LIFE OF GREAT AMERICAN CITIES.   New
York and Toronto: Random House, 1961.   458p.

LAND UTILIZATION IN THE UNITED STATES.   Des Moines, Iowa: Soil Conservation Society of America, 838 Fifth Avenue, 1957.   31p.   illus., charts.
pap.
Papers presented at symposium held at the 1956 annual meeting of
the Society; reprinted from various issues of the JOURNAL OF
SOIL AND WATER CONSERVATION.

Meyerson, Martin., et al, eds.   Metropolis in Ferment.   ANNUALS OF THE
AMERICAN ACADEMY OF POLITICAL AND SOCIAL SCIENCE, vol. 314,
November 1957 (entire issue).

Mitchell, Robert B. and Rapkin, Chester.   URBAN TRAFFIC; A FUNCTION OF
LAND USE.   (Publications of the Institute for Urban Land Use and Housing
Studies).   New York: Columbia University Press, 1954.   226p.   tables,
charts, diagrs.
"Traffic has been analyzed in terms of its underlying causes--the
necessity for people to move and goods to be transported, from
one place to another ... These activities are land based."

National Institute of Real Estate Brokers.   PUBLIC TRANSPORTATION AND
YOUR COMMUNITY.   (Brokers Institute Bulletin Service), Chicago: 1958.
63p.   illus.   pap.
Statements from city planners, public officials, transit executives,
highway engineers, traffic consultants, newspaper editors, merchants, industrialists, real estate brokers and many others.

National Research Council. Highway Research Board. ACQUISITION OF LAND FOR FUTURE HIGHWAY USE; A LEGAL ANALYSIS. (Special Report 27). Washington D.C.: 1957. 80p. illus., tables. pap.

National Research Council. Highway Research Board. HIGHWAY RESEARCH REVIEW. Jan. 1962, (Number 5). Washington, D.C.: 1962. 389p.
"An annotated census of highway research projects as reported by state highway departments, federal agencies, colleges, universities and other sources."

National Research Council. Highway Research Board. HIGHWAYS AND ECONOMIC DEVELOPMENT. (Bulletin no. 227). Washington, D.C.: 1959. 88p. pap.

National Research Council. Highway Research Board. LAND ACQUISITION. Washington D.C.: 1947-   .
Annual Committee on Land Acquisition and Control of Highway Access and Adjacent Areas report.

National Research Council. Highway Research Board. SOME EVALUATIONS OF HIGHWAY IMPROVEMENT IMPACTS. (Bulletin 268). Washington D.C.: 1960. 119p. pap.
Presented at the annual meeting.

Nelson, Richard L. SELECTION OF RETAIL LOCATIONS. New York: F. W. Dodge, 1958. 422p. tables, diagrs.
"This book is the first major exposition of comprehensive scientific procedures for locating retail facilities. It is not only a compilation of existing techniques but also sets forth new techniques for research, market analysis, and statistical consideration of locational problems."

Owen, Wilfred. CITIES IN THE MOTOR AGE. New York: Viking Press, 1959. 176p.

Spengler, Edwin H. LAND VALUES IN NEW YORK IN RELATION TO TRANSIT FACILITIES. New York: Columbia University Press, 1930. 179p. tables, charts.
Study of value of property adjacent to transit facilities.

Taylor, Gerald Kirkbridge, Jr. RELATIONSHIP BETWEEN LAND VALUE AND LAND USE IN A CENTRAL BUSINESS DISTRICT. (J.C. Nichols Foundation Research Study). Washington D.C.: Urban Land Institute, 1957. 77p. tables, charts. pap. processed.
Grant from the J. C. Nichols Foundation of the Urban Land Institute to Georgia Institute of Technology, 1955-56. "Study of the effects of land values on the forms of development of land and on the character of the uses to which it is put." Atlanta central business district.

U.S. Department of Agriculture. LAND USE AND ITS PATTERNS IN THE UNITED STATES, by F. J. Marschner. (Agricultural Handbook no. 153).

Washington, D.C.: Government Printing Office, 1959. 277p. illus., charts, maps. pap.

U.S. Department of Agriculture. Agricultural Research Service. MAJOR USES OF LAND IN THE UNITED STATES - SUMMARY FOR 1954. (Agriculture Information Bulletin no. 168).

Urban Land Institute. METROPOLITANIZATION OF THE UNITED STATES, by Jerome P. Pickard. (Research Monograph no. 2). Washington D.C.: 1959. 96p. tables, charts. pap.
"...This study develops projections of population growth, based upon the dynamic regional trends of our economy, rather than predicitons of this growth..."

Urban Land Institute. TECHNICAL BULLETIN SERIES. Washington, D.C.: 1945--   . pap.
No. 1. MISTAKES WE HAVE MADE IN COMMUNITY DEVELOPMENT, by J. C. Nichols. March 1945, 8p. pap.

No. 2. DISCUSSION OF PRINCIPLES TO BE INCORPORATED IN STATE URBAN REDEVELOPMENT ENABLING ACTS. June, 1945. 4p. pap.
Revised March 1946.

No. 3. OPINION SURVEY OF TRENDS ON URBAN DEVELOPMENT AND REDEVELOPMENT. June 1945. 8p. diagrs. pap. processed.

No. 4. MISTAKES WE HAVE MADE IN DEVELOPING SHOPPING CENTERS, by J. C. Nichols. August 1945. 15p. pap.
Reprinted April 1960.

No. 5. A PRACTICABLE CITY PLANNING BIBLIOGRAPHY. 8p. processed.

No. 6. AUTOMOBILE PARKING IN CENTRAL BUSINESS DISTRICTS, by Seward H. Mott and Max S. Wehrly. July 1946. 15p. tables, diagrs. pap.

No. 7. WHAT IS THE MARKET VALUE OF 'IMPROVED' LAND IN SLUMS?, by Clarence W. Beatty, Jr. January 1947. 16p. pap. processed.

No. 8. SUBDIVISION REGULATIONS AND PROTECTIVE COVENANTS, THEIR APPLICATION TO LAND DEVELOPMENT, by Seward H. Mott and Max S. Wehrly. June 1947. 8p. pap.

No. 9. COMMERCIAL PARKING IN RESIDENTIAL AREAS, by Seward H. Mott and Max S. Wehrly. June 1948. 8p. pap. table. pap.

No. 10. THE PROHIBITION OF RESIDENTIAL DEVELOPMENT INDUSTRIAL DISTRICTS, by Seward H. Mott and Max S. Wehrly.

November 1948. 7p. illus. pap.

No. 11. SHOPPING CENTERS, AN ANALYSIS, by Seward H. Mott and Max Wehrly. July 1949. 46p. illus., tables, diagrs. pap.

No. 12. MARKET ANALYSIS OF SHOPPING CENTERS, by Homer Hoyt. October 1949. 7p. pap.

No. 13. WHO PAYS FOR STREET AND UTILITY INSTALLATIONS IN NEW RESIDENTIAL AREAS?, by Seward H. Mott and Max S. Wehrly. April 1950. 8p. illus., tables. pap.

No. 14. MARINAS--THEIR PLANNING AND DEVELOPMENT, by C. A. Chaney. October 1950. 24p. illus., tables. pap.

No. 15. SPECIAL OR BENEFIT ASSESSMENTS FOR PARKING FACILITIES, by David R. Levin and Conya Hardy. April 1951. 28p. tables, diagrs.

No. 17. WATER FOR INDUSTRY, A REVIEW OF WATER RE-SOURCES AFFECTING INDUSTRIAL LOCATION, by Max S. Wehrly and Milburn L. Forth. November 1951. 31p. diagrs. pap.

No. 18. URBAN LAND USE AND PROPERTY TAXATION, by Max S. Wehrly and J. Ross McKeever. May 1952. 27p. tables. pap.

No. 19. PLANNED INDUSTRIAL DISTRICTS, THEIR ORGANI-ZATION AND DEVELOPMENT, by Milburn L. Forth and J. Ross McKeever. October 1952. 55p. illus., diagrs. pap.

No. 20. SHOPPING CENTERS, PRINCIPLES AND POLICIES, by J. Ross McKeever. July 1953. 91p. illus., diagrs. pap.

No. 21. THE COMMUNITY AND INDUSTRIAL DEVELOPMENT, by Robert B. Garrabrant. September 1953. 16p. pap.

No. 22. CONSERVATION AND REHABILITATION OF MAJOR SHOPPING DISTRICTS, by Richard L. Nelson and Frederick T. Aschman. February 1954. 44p. pap.

No. 23. SPACE FOR INDUSTRY, AN ANALYSIS OF SITE AND LOCATION REQUIREMENTS, by Dorothy A. Muncy. July 1954. 44p. tables, charts. pap.

No. 24. SHOPPING HABITS AND TRAVEL PATTERNS, by Alan M. Voorhees, Gordon B. Sharpe, and J. T. Stegmaier. March 1955. 24p. tables, charts. pap.

No. 25. REDEVELOPMENT FOR INDUSTRIAL USE, by Robert B. Garrabrant. May 1955. 32p. illus., diagrs. pap.

No. 26. CROWDED STREETS--A SYMPOSIUM ON PUBLIC TRANS-
PORTATION. June 1955. 76p. illus., tables, diagrs.

No. 27. UTILITIES AND FACILITIES FOR NEW RESIDENTIAL
DEVELOPMENT; A SURVEY OF MUNICIPAL POLICY, by J.
Ross McKeever. December 1955. 100p. tables. pap.

No. 28. EUROPE'S REBORN CITIES, by Leo Grebler. March
1956. 104p. illus., diagrs. pap.

No. 29. PREPARING YOUR CITY FOR THE FUTURE, HOW TO
MAKE AN ECONOMIC STUDY OF YOUR COMMUNITY, by
Robert B. Garrabrant. May 1956. pap.

No. 30. SHOPPING CENTERS RE-STUDIED, by J. Ross McKeever.
February 1957, PART ONE--EMERGING PATTERNS. 78p.; PART
TWO--PRACTICAL EXPERIENCES. 166p. illus., tables. diagrs.
pap.

No. 31. THE NEW HIGHWAYS: CHALLENGE TO THE METRO-
POLITAN REGION, September 1957. 92p. pap.

No. 32. THE EFFECTS OF LARGE LOT SIZE ON RESIDENTIAL
DEVELOPMENT, by Massachusetts Department of Commerce and
Urban Studies Section, Massachusetts Institute of Technology.
July 1958. 52p. tables, charts, maps. pap.

No. 33. A RE-EXAMINATION OF THE SHOPPING CENTER
MARKET, by Homer Hoyt. September 1958. 12p. pap.

No. 34. THE CHALLENGE OF URBAN RENEWAL, by M. Carter
McFarland. December 1958. 44p. tables. pap.

No. 35. BANKING EXPANSION--NEW FRONTIERS AHEAD,
by Robert H. Armstrong. May 1959. 22p. illus., tables.

No. 36. SECURING OPEN SPACE FOR URBAN AMERICA: CON-
SERVATION EASEMENTS, by William H. Whyte, Jr. December
1959. 67p. diagr. pap.

No. 37. DYNAMIC FACTORS IN LAND VALUES, by Homer
Hoyt. March 1960. 15p. charts. pap.

No. 38. THE URBAN REAL ESTATE CYCLE--PERFORMANCES AND
PROSPECTS, by Homer Hoyt. June 1960. 16p. charts. pap.

No. 39. INVESTORS AND DOWNTOWN REAL ESTATE--OPIN-
ION AND COMMENT, by Arthur M. Weimer. 24p. pap.

No. 40. NEW APPROACHES TO RESIDENTIAL LAND DEVELOP-
MENT, A STUDY OF CONCEPTS AND INNOVATIONS, by
Harman, O'Donnell & Henninger Associates, Inc. January
1961. 151p. illus., diagrs. pap.

No. 41. INDUSTRIAL DISTRICTS RESTUDIED, AN ANALYSIS
OF CHARACTERISTICS, by Robert E. Boley. April 1961.
77p. illus., tables, maps. pap.
    Includes selective bibliography.

No. 42. DENSITY ZONING--ORGANIC ZONING FOR PLANNED
RESIDENTIAL DEVELOPMENTS, by Eldridge Lovelace and
William L. Weismentel. July 1961. 40p. diagrs. pap.

No. 43. WORLD URBANIZATION, by Homer Hoyt. April 1962.
50p. tables, charts. pap.

Wingo, Lowdon, Jr. TRANSPORTATION AND URBAN LAND. Washington,
D.C.: Resources for the Future, 1961. 132p.

Land Use—Bibliography

Bestor, George C. and Jones, Holway R. CITY PLANNING; A BASIC BIBLIO-
GRAPHY OF SOURCES AND TRENDS, 2nd ed. Sacramento: California
Council of Civil Engineers and Land Surveyors, 1962. 195p. pap. processed.
    A classified listing of over 1,000 citations with a detailed subject
    index. Includes prices, foreign language city planning periodicals,
    publishers' addressed, organization services and periodicals, sepa-
    rate author, title and subject indexes, and American city planning
    collections.

California. University. Bureau of Public Administration. LAND UTILIZATION;
A BIBLIOGRAPHY, comp. by Dorothy Campbell Culver. Berkeley: 1935.
222p. pap. processed.
    Reissued with typographical corrections, 1937. Supplement
    issued 1937. 139p. pap. processed. Materials in English
    on land utilization in the United States.

U. S. Department of Agriculture. BIBLIOGRAPHY ON LAND UTILIZATION,
1918-36, comp. by Louise O. Bercaw and Annie M. Hannay in cooperation
with the Land Utilization Division, Resettlement Administration. (Miscellaneous
Publication no. 284). Washington D. C.: Government Printing Office, 1938.
1508p. pap.
    Economic aspects of land utilization and land policy in the
    United States and in foreign countries.

U. S. Department of Agriculture. URBANIZATION AND CHANGING LAND
USE; A BIBLIOGRAPHY OF SELECTED REFERENCES, 1950-1958, compiled
by Elizabeth Gould Davis, et al. (Miscellaneous Publication no. 825).
Washington, D.C.: 1960. 212p. pap. processed.

Virginia Council of Highway Investigation and Research. THE ECONOMIC AND SOCIAL EFFECTS OF HIGHWAY IMPROVEMENT: AN ANNOTATED BIBLIOGRAPHY, comp. by Warren A. Pillsbury. Charlottesville: May 1961. 106p. pap.
> In cooperation with the U.S. Bureau of Public Roads. Bibliographies, general references and economic impact studies.

Section 13

LAND USE CONTROLS

American Society of Planning Officials. SHOPPING CENTER ZONING, 2 pts. (Planning Advisory Service Information Report no. 128 and 129). Chicago: 1959. pap.

American Society of Planning Officials. ZONING FOR GROUP HOUSING DEVELOPMENTS. (Planning Advisory Service Information Report No. 27). Chicago: 1951. 30p. pap.

Delafons, John. LAND-USE CONTROLS IN THE UNITED STATES. Cambridge; Joint Center for Urban Studies of the Massachusetts Institute of Technology and Harvard University, 1962. 100p. tables. processed. (Distr. by Harvard University Press, Cambridge 38, Mass.)

    A treatise on the history, objectives, and methods of land-use controls in the United States, prepared for British readers. Appendix of extracts from various municipal and county zoning ordinances.

Detroit Land Classification Advisory Committee. LAND USE CLASSIFICATION MANUAL. Chicago: Public Administration Service, 1962. 53p. pap.

    A numerical coding system for use in collecting and presenting land use data.

Horack, Frank E., Jr. and Nolan, Val, Jr. LAND USE CONTROLS. St. Paul, Minn.: West Publishing Co., 1955. 240p.

Institute on Planning and Zoning. PROCEEDINGS, 1960- . Albany: Matthew Bender, 1961- .

    Sponsored by the Southwestern Legal Foundation. "Significant articles on planning for municipal development and rehabilitation, including the problems of city-county relations, thoroughfares, flood control, residential and industrial districts, practical administration of zoning ordinances, and legal aspects of aesthetics."

Kramer, Robert, ed. Land Planning in a Democracy. LAW AND CONTEMPORARY PROBLEMS, vol. 20, no. 2, Spring 1955 (entire issue).

    Constitutional Law and Community Planning; Zoning for Aesthetic Objectives: A Reappraisal; the Relationship of Zoning to Traffic-generators; Large Scale Developments and One House Zoning Controls; Zoning for Amenities; Discretionary Powers of the Board of Zoning Appeals; Regulating the Timing of Urban Development; Elimination of Incompatible Uses and Structures; Planning Law and Democratic Living.

Metzenbaum, James. THE LAW OF ZONING, 2d ed, 3 vols. New York: Baker, Voorhis and Co., 1955.
　　Cumulative supplemental pocket parts issued periodically.

National Industrial Zoning Committee. PRINCIPLES OF INDUSTRIAL ZONING. Columbus, Ohio: 1951. n.p. illus. pap.
　　One of a series of pamphlets issued by the Committee.

Rathkopf, Charles A. and Rathkopf, Arden H. THE LAW OF ZONING AND PLANNING, 3rd ed. rev., 2 vols. New York: Clark Boardman and Matthew Bender. 1960.
　　Revision and text material by Arden H. Rathkopf. "Reference has been made to law review notes and articles." Cumulative supplements issued.

Regional Plan of New York and Its Environs. BUILDINGS: THEIR USES AND THE SPACES ABOUT THEM. (Regional Survey, Vol. 6). New York: 1931. 465p. illus.
　　Comprising three monographs: THE CHARACTER, BULK AND SURROUNDINGS OF BUILDINGS, by Thomas Adams; HOUSING CONDITIONS IN THE NEW YORK REGION, by Thomas Adams and Wayne L. Heydicker; CONTROL OF BUILDING HEIGHTS, DENSITIES AND USES BY ZONING, by Edward M. Bassett.

U.S. Department of Agriculture. THE WHY AND HOW OF RURAL ZONING. (Agriculture Information Bulletin no. 196). Washington, D.C.: Government Printing Office, 1959. 58p. illus. pap.

Urban Land Institute. A MODEL PROCEDURE FOR THE ADMINISTRATION OF ZONING REGULATIONS, by Robert M. Leary. (J.C. Nichols Foundation Research Studies). Washington, D.C.: 1958. 95p. illus. pap. processed.

Urban Land Institute. SUBDIVISION REGULATIONS AND PROTECTIVE COV-ENANTS; THEIR APPLICATION TO LAND DEVELOPMENT, by Seward H. Mott and Max S. Wehrly. (Technical Bulletin no. 8). Washington, D.C.: 1947. 8p. pap.

Williams, Frank Backus. THE LAW OF CITY PLANNING AND ZONING. (Land Economics Series). New York: Macmillan, 1922. 738p.

Yokley, E. C. ZONING LAW AND PRACTICE, 2nd ed., 2 vols. Charlottes-ville, Va.: Michie Company, 1953. 474p.
　　Cumulative supplements issued.

Section 14

CONDEMNATION AND
EMINENT DOMAIN

American Association of State Highway Officials. Committee on Right-of-Way.
ACQUISITION FOR RIGHT-OF-WAY. Washington, D.C.: 1962. 747p.
illus., tables, diagrs.
> A collection of forty-six papers, presented as a concise text for
> use in a training program for state right-of-way personnel.
> Glossary, capitalization and conversion tables included in appen-
> dix section.

American Institute of Real Estate Appraisers. CONDEMNATION APPRAISAL
PRACTICE. Chicago: 1961. 586p.
> Articles and case references by judges, attorneys and appraisers
> selected from the APPRAISAL JOURNAL, the quarterly publica-
> tion of the Institute, to serve as a reference guide.

American Right of Way Association. NATIONAL SEMINAR PROCEEDINGS.
Los Angeles: 1955-   .
> Annual. Highway, pipeline, railroad and utility right of way
> acquisition including appraisal, negotiation, legal and title
> aspects and administration.

California. Division of Highways. RIGHT OF WAY MANUAL, 3rd ed.
Sacramento: State Printing Office, 1959. 430p. charts. pap.
> Published for the information and guidance of the officers and
> employees of the Division of Highways and its Right of Way
> Department. A companion volume of forms is available.

California. Law Revision Commission. RECOMMENDATION AND STUDY RE-
LATING TO THE REIMBURSEMENT FOR MOVING EXPENSES WHEN PROPERTY
IS ACQUIRED FOR PUBLIC USE. Sacramento: State Printing Office, 1960.
36p. pap.

Institute on Eminent Domain, Southwestern Legal Center, Dallas, Texas.
PROCEEDINGS, ed. by Robert A. Wilson. Albany: Matthew Border. 1959-
> Annual institute of lawyers, judges and appraisers; discussions of
> law and practice.

Jahr, Alfred D. LAW OF EMINENT DOMAIN VALUATION AND PROCEDURE.
New York: Clark-Boardman, 1953. 736p.
> Forms, table of cases. Written by the former assistant Corporation
> Counsel, Condemnation Division, City of New York.

Kaltenbach, Henry J. JUST COMPENSATION; A PRACTICAL LEGAL SERVICE FOR THE RIGHT OF WAY ENGINEER, APPRAISER, ATTORNEY AND LAND ACQUISITION AGENT. Warrenton, Va., 1956– . looseleaf.
>State Summaries and U.S. Summary including case lists; monthly supplements with cumulative indexes. Constitutional and statutory decisions are limited to those of a general nature or those handed down by the highest state court since 1916. Revision in preparation.

Luedders, William R. CONDEMNATION JURORS DICTIONARY. Detroit: Detroit Real Estate Board, (1962). 28p. pap.
>Real estate and appraisal terms.

Montana State University. Bureau of Business and Economic Research. AN ANALYSIS OF PROPERTY VALUATION SYSTEMS UNDER EMINENT DOMAIN, by Willis P. Rokes. Missoula: 1961. 65p. pap.
>Analysis of condemnation systems in operation and a proposed solution by adoption of a system capable of uniform application – a valuation tribunal.

National Research Council. Highway Research Board. CONDEMNATION OF PROPERTY FOR HIGHWAY PURPOSES; A LEGAL ANALYSIS, 2 pts. (Special Reports no. 32 and 33). Washington, D.C.: 1958. pap.

Orgel, Louis, VALUATION UNDER THE LAW OF EMINENT DOMAIN, 2nd ed., 2 vols. Charlottesville, Va.: Michie Co., 1953.
>Analyses of legal rules underlying the meaning of value under the law of eminent domain including a discussion of the significant cases. forms. table of cases.

Pittsburgh. University. Bureau of Business Research in Cooperation with the Law School. THE APPRAISER'S JOB IN EMINENT DOMAIN PROCEEDINGS. Pittsburgh: University of Pittsburgh, 1957. 57p. pap. processed.
>Originally delivered as speeches before a special seminar in condemnation appraising at the University of Pittsburgh.

Right of Way Acquisition Conference. SELECTED PAPERS. Sponsored by Alabama State Highway Department, Alabama Chapter, American Institute of Real Estate Appraisers. University, Ala.: University of Alabama, 1956–1960. pap.

Sachman, Julius L. and Van Brunt, Russell D. NICHOLS' THE LAW OF EMINENT DOMAIN, 3d ed., 6 vols. Albany: Matthew Binder, 1950.
>Vol. 1: Part 1: INTRODUCTION AND JURISDICTION; Part 2: CONSTITUTIONAL RIGHTS AND LIMITATIONS; Vol. 2: PROPERTY AND OWNERSHIP, TAKING AND DAMAGE, THE PUBLIC USE; Vol. 3: COMPENSATION, TITLE ACQUIRED AND SERVITUDES THEREON; Vol. 4: VALUATION AND DAMAGES; Vol. 5: EVIDENCE; Vol. 6: ADMINISTRATIVE AND JUDICIAL PROCEDURE, FEDERAL PRACTICES; REMEDIES OF OWNER, FEDERAL, STATE AND CORPORATE LIABILITY. Supplemented by pocket parts.

Schmutz, George L. CONDEMNATION APPRAISAL HANDBOOK; PROPERTY VALUATION, CONDEMNATION PROCEDURE, COURT TESTIMONY, Rev. ed. New York: Prentice-Hall, 1949. 361p.

U.S. Internal Revenue Service. HOW THE FEDERAL INCOME TAX APPLIES TO CONDEMNATION OF PRIVATE PROPERTY FOR PUBLIC USE. (Document no. 5383; 10-61). Washington, D.C.: Government Printing Office, 1961. 17p. pap.
        Prepared in co-operation with the Bureau of Public Roads.

Watson, Jairus H. CONDEMNATION APPRAISAL TEXT AND REFERENCE. Washington, D.C.: American Society of Appraisers, 1028 Connecticut Avenue, N.W., 1959. 148p. looseleaf.
        Several papers presented by guest authors included. Text in appraisal for condemnation purposes.

Condemnation and Eminent Domain—Periodicals
(See Appendix for complete information concerning these publications.)

APPRAISAL DIGEST; APPRAISAL INSTITUTE MAGAZINE; APPRAISAL JOURNAL; JOURNAL OF THE AMERICAN SOCIETY OF FARM MANAGERS AND RURAL APPRAISERS; RESIDENTIAL APPRAISER; RIGHT OF WAY; TECHNICAL VALUATION.

Section 15

LAW

American Bar Association. Section of Real Property, Probate, and Trust Law. PROCEEDINGS. Chicago: 1934-   .
> Reports significant developments, decisions, Federal and state legislation, and literature. Addresses, panel discussions, and committee reports presented at the annual meetings. Section Name 1934-1936: Section of Real Property.

AMERICAN LAW REPORTS ANNOTATED: SECOND SERIES. Rochester, N.Y.: Lawyers Cooperative Publishing and San Francisco: Bancroft-Whitney, 1957. vol. 53, p. 788-811.
> "Drafting or filling in blanks in printed forms, of instruments re-lating to land by real estate agents, brokers, or managers as constituting practice of law." (See ALR Digests, Attorneys 1.7 (4). Consult ALR 2d. Supplement Service for subsequent cases.)

Anderson, George F. AM I ENTITLED TO A COMMISSION? Chicago: University Printing Co., 1410 East 62nd Street, zone 37, 1952. 52p. pap.
> Questions and answers in sections devoted to such topics as aban-donment, liability of broker, misappropriation. Largely reprinted from the author's column in REALTY AND BUILDING.

Anderson, George F. ANECDOTES OF A COMMON LAWYER (BEHIND THE IRON CURTAIN - OF A LAW OFFICE). Chicago: University Printing Co., 1410 East 62nd Street, zone 37, no date. 64p. pap.
> Occurrences in the career of an outstanding authority on real estate law.

Anderson, George F. CLOSING THE DEAL. Chicago: University Printing Co., 1410 East 62nd Street, zone 37, no date. 50p. pap.
> Excerpts from the author's column in REALTOR'S HEADLINES.

Anderson, George F. Legal Lines. REALTOR'S HEADLINES. Weekly column.

Anderson, George F. LEGAL LINES. Chicago: University Printing Co., 1410 East 62nd Street, zone 37, no date. 77p. pap.
> Reprinted from the author's "Legal Lines" column in REALTOR'S HEADLINES. Excerpts arranged in sections on the broker and his commission, contracts, and real estate law.

Anderson, George F. Points of Property Law. BUILDINGS. Monthly Column.

GENERAL (continued)

Anderson, George F. REAL ESTATE LAW IN ACTION. Chicago : University Printing Co., 1410 East 62nd Street, zone 37, 1956. 112p. pap.
Traces all steps in the progress of a real estate transaction, the responsibilities of the parties involved, and points out pitfalls to be avoided. Based on a series of lectures sponsored by the Chicago Bar Association.

Anderson, George F. REAL ESTATE SALES CONTRACTS. Chicago: University Printing Co., 1410 East 62nd Street, zone 37, no date. 60p. pap.
What should and should not go into a sales contract, how to draft such a contract, and how to observe the provisions of a signed contract.

Bentley, Byron R. REAL ESTATE LAW, WITH CASES, TEXT, AND FORMS, 2d ed. Chicago: Callaghan and Co., 1940. 502p.
"Designed to present the major principles of the law of real estate and property management as those principles have been developed and enunciated by our courts."

Beurhaus, George H. KNOW YOUR REAL ESTATE. San Francisco: Mercury Press, 1946. 196p.
A discussion of legal forms relating to real property for the layman.

Beurhaus, George H. WHO HANDLES YOUR REAL ESTATE?, 4th ed. San Francisco: Mercury Press, 1947. 182p.
Discusses legal forms used in selling real estate. Based on laws of the State of Washington.

Bigelow, Harry A. INTRODUCTION TO THE LAW OF REAL PROPERTY, 3d ed. St. Paul, Minn.: West Publishing Co., 1945. 96p. pap.
A section of the author's CASES ON RIGHTS IN LAND. History of property law.

Callahan, Parnell. THE LAW OF REAL ESTATE; A GUIDE TO THE PURCHASE AND SALE OF PROPERTY, 2d ed. (Legal Almanac Series No. 4). New York: Oceana Publications, 1951. 95p.
Written for the layman. Covers ownership of real property, deeds and conveyances, buying and selling, mortgages, contracts, title closing, and special situations involving servicemen.

Casner, A. James, ed. AMERICAN LAW OF PROPERTY; A TREATISE ON THE LAW OF PROPERTY IN THE UNITED STATES, 8 vols. Boston: Little, Brown, 1952-1954.
Supplemented by pocket parts.

Casner, A. James and Leach, W. Barton. CASES AND TEXT ON PROPERTY. (Law School Casebook Series). Boston: Little, Brown, 1959. 1439p.
Designed for the first-year law student. The edition of 1951 with a 1959 supplement. Part 4: Estates in Land; Part 7:

Landlord and Tenant; Part 8: The Modern Land Transaction; Part 9: Controlling the Use of Land; Part 10: Easements and Licenses.

Cribbet, John E. PRINCIPLES OF THE LAW OF PROPERTY. (University Textbook Series). Brooklyn, N.Y.: Foundation Press, 1962. 354p.
A textbook tailored to new concept of the subject as being taught today that aims to present the basic picture of property law, both in depth and scope, and to make the reader aware of the changing nature of the subject. To bridge the gap between multi-volume treatises and concise outlines.

Dunham, Allison. MODERN REAL ESTATE TRANSACTIONS; CASES AND MATERIALS, 2d. ed. (University Casebook Series). Brooklyn, N.Y.: Foundation Press, 1958. 872p.
"To bring together for teaching purposes the legal concepts and institutions of the marketing of land."

Dykstra, Gerald O. and Dykstra, Lillian G. THE BUSINESS LAW OF REAL ESTATE. New York: Macmillan, 1956. 852p.
Designed as a textbook and as a reference book for laymen. Part 6: "Real Estate Brokers."

Friedman, Milton R. CONTRACTS AND CONVEYANCES OF REAL PROPERTY. Chicago: Callaghan and Co., 1954. 425p.
Cumulative supplemental pocket parts issued annually. Table of cases.

Grange, William J. REAL ESTATE; A PRACTICAL GUIDE TO OWNERSHIP, TRANSFER, MORTGAGING, AND LEASING OF REAL PROPERTY, Rev. New York: Ronald Press, 1940. 541p.
Part 1: Real Estate and Its Ownership; Part 2: Sales; Part 3: Mortgages and Mortgage Transactions; Part 4: Leases; Part 5: Miscellaneous Matters of Law and Practice; List of 93 forms: Pages 397-514. Part 6: Forms.

Greenberg, Henry. MANUAL OF REAL ESTATE PRACTICE AND FORMS. New York: Central Book Co., 1936. 717p.
Analyzes sale and mortgage clauses, title registration, selling, etc.

Hannah, Harold W. LAW ON THE FARM; A DISCUSSION OF LEGAL PROBLEMS WHICH ARISE IN THE BUSINESS OF FARMING. New York: Macmillan, 1948. 399p.
Chapter 5: Farm Land and Real Estate; Chapter 6: Rights in Land; Chapter 7: Family Interest in the Ownership of Farm Land; Chapter 8: Landlord and Tenant.

Harvey, David C. B. REAL ESTATE LAW AND TITLE CLOSING; DEEDS, CONTRACTS, MORTGAGES, WITH FORMS, 3rd ed. New York: Clark Boardman Co.,

1956. 895p.
>Title and mortgage closing and real estate laws generally as
they bear on conveyances. Supplemental pocket parts issued
periodically.

Kirkwood, Marion R. CASES AND MATERIALS ON THE LAW OF CONVEY-
ANCES, 2d ed. (University Casebook Series). Chicago: Foundation Press,
1941. 765p.
>"A casebook presenting problems growing out of conveyances of
land other than those relating to estates and future interests."

Kratovil, Robert. REAL ESTATE LAW, 3d ed. Englewood Cliffs, N.J.:
Prentice-Hall, 1958. 504p.
>An exposition of fundamental principles, intended for readers
without legal training. Include chapters on sources of real
estate law, easements, legal descriptions, titles, deeds, sales
contracts, subdivisions, and waters.

Kuchler, Frances W. H. LANDLORD, TENANT, AND CO-OP HOUSING.
(Legal Almanac Series no. 11). New York: Oceana Publications, 1960. 93p.
pap.
>Non-technical treatment of the rights of landlords and tenants,
leases, rent control, and cooperative housing.

Lawler, J. John and Lawler, Gail Gates. A SHORT HISTORICAL INTRODUC-
TION TO THE LAW OF REAL PROPERTY. Chicago: Foundation Press, 1940.
204p.
>Text for use in an introductory course. References at chapter
ends.

Lawson, F. H. INTRODUCTION TO THE LAW OF PROPERTY. Oxford:
Clarendon Press, 1958. 200p.
>A survey of real and personal property, private and public, for
the beginning student and general reader. No case notes or
references.

Lesar, Hiram H. LANDLORD AND TENANT. Boston: Little, Brown, 1957.
563p.
>The legal relations of lessees and lessors. Largely reprinted
from American Law of Property, part 3. Index of cases, table
of statutes, appendix of forms.

Lewis, Clarence M. THE LAW OF LEASES OF REAL PROPERTY, 2d ed.
New York: Baker, Voorhis and Co., 1930. 941p.
>"A guide to the preparation, construction, and litigation of
leases." Forms of leases clauses, with citations of pertinent
decisions and literature.

Lieberman, Milton N. EFFECTIVE DRAFTING OF CONTRACTS FOR THE SALE
OF REAL PROPERTY, WITH CHECK LIST AND SUGGESTED FORMS. Newark:

GENERAL (continued)

Gann Law Books, 1954. 365p. forms.

Lieberman, Milton N. EFFECTIVE DRAFTING OF LEASES WITH CHECK LISTS
AND FORMS. Newark: Gann Law Books, 1956. 974p. forms.
> Appendix A: Sample leases for apartments, stores. Percentage
> and long-term leases. Bibliography and sources for forms: p. 832-4.

Lusk, Harold F. LAW OF THE REAL ESTATE BUSINESS. Homewood, Ill.:
Richard D. Irwin, 1958. 377p.
> Written for the real estate business man, the attorney, and the
> student. Devoted primarily to ownership, conveyancing, and
> leasing. Supplemented by CASES IN LAW OF THE REAL ESTATE
> BUSINESS, 1961. 118p. pap.

MacChesney, Nathan William. THE PRINCIPLES OF REAL ESTATE LAW;
REAL PROPERTY, REAL ESTATE DOCUMENTS AND TRANSACTIONS. (Land
Economics Series; Standard Course in Real Estate). New York: Macmillan,
1927. 891p.
> "It is believed that the present volume is a real contribution
> to the actual knowledge of how things are done in this field ...
> It is believed also that the book is unique in bringing together,
> as has not been done elsewhere the parts of the several fields
> of law which are concerned in the handling of real estate trans-
> actions." Detailed discussion of legal forms.

MacChesney, Nathan William. THE LAW OF REAL ESTATE BROKERAGE.
Chicago: Foundation Press, 1938. 172p.
> Developed from a series of lectures prepared for a course given
> at the University of Chicago in 1936, under the auspices of the
> National Association of Real Estate Boards. "Brings together the
> particular law and practical effects having to do with a particular
> type of real estate transaction, however much the legal questions
> involved may differ as to their legal classification, as does the
> author's PRINCIPLES OF REAL ESTATE LAW, 1927.

Martz, Clyde O. RIGHTS INCIDENT TO POSSESSION OF LAND. Boston:
Little, Brown, 1954. 258p.
> Reprinted from AMERICAN LAW OF PROPERTY. Freedom from
> trespass, freedom from nuisance, the right to support and water
> rights. Tables of cases and statutes.

National Association of Real Estate Boards. REAL ESTATE BROKERS AND
UNAUTHORIZED PRACTICE OF LAW, prepared by Thomas F. Scully. Chicago:
1961. 29p. pap. processed.

National Association of Real Estate Boards. State Associations Committee.
PROVISIONS IN STATE LICENSE LAWS RE: PRACTICE OF LAW AND USE OF
STANDARD FORMS. Chicago: 1962. 5p. pap. processed.

National Institute of Real Estate Brokers. PITFALLS; TRUE STORIES FROM THE

GENERAL (continued)

EXPERIENCE OF REAL ESTATE BROKERS WITH HELPFUL COMMENTS, by
George F. Anderson. (Brokers Institute Bulletin Service). Chicago: 1957.
63p. pap.
    A collection of the author's columns.

Nussbaum, Louis M. LAW FOR THE HOMEOWNER, REAL ESTATE OPERATOR
AND BROKER. (Legal Almanac Series, no. 43). New York: Oceana Publications, 1956. 96p. pap.
    A guide for the layman, dealing with property rights and the buy-
    ing and selling of real property.

Osborne, G. E. CASES AND MATERIALS ON PROPERTY SECURITY. St.
Paul, Minn.: West Publishing Co., 1954. 725p.

Osborne, G. E. HANDBOOK OF THE LAW OF MORTGAGES. St. Paul,
Minn.: West Publishing Co., 1951. 1117p.

Pachter, Adrian. HOW TO CLOSE REAL ESTATE DEALS. St. Louis: Thomas
Law Book Co., 1929. 124p.
    A concise guide, emphasizing the chain of title. Contains infor-
    mation pertaining to the law and matters of accounting directly
    affecting real estate transactions.

Powell, Richard R. THE LAW OF REAL PROPERTY, 7 vols. Albany: Matthew
Bender, 1949.
    Cumulative supplements issued.

Real and Personal Property. NEW YORK UNIVERSITY LAW REVIEW. Annually
in the February issue.
    "Discusses reported cases and cites pertinent new books and legal
    periodical material without attempting any general survey of pro-
    perty legislation."

Sadler, Walter C. LEGAL ASPECTS OF CONSTUCTION. New York,: McGraw-
Hill, 1959. 387p. diagrs.
    "Written for practical use in the construction industry." Sections:
    This Business of Contracting; Construction Liabilities of the Owner,
    Architect, Engineer, and Contractors; Boundaries, Foundations,
    and Damages.

Semenow, Robert W. QUESTIONS AND ANSWERS ON REAL ESTATE, 4th ed.
Englewood Cliffs, N.J., Prentice-Hall, 1961. 602p. charts, forms.
    "Intended to assist the applicant in preparing for real estate licen-
    sure and as an aid to the practitioner." True-false and multiple-
    choice. Includes glossary, table of cases. Samples.

State Laws: Digest of State Lease Laws. Section 15 In PRENTICE-HALL
REAL ESTATE GUIDE. Englewood Cliffs, N.J.: Prentice-Hall, 1953-   .

Stone, Robert E. BUSINESS AND PROPERTY LAW. (University Business Book

Series). **Chicago:** Foundation Press, 1941. 1033p.
    Includes chapters on real property.

Stumpf, Felix F., et al, eds. LEGAL ASPECTS OF REAL ESTATE TRANSACTIONS.
Berkeley: Extension Division, University of California, 1956. 736p.
    Covers contracts, leases, taxation, title insurance, escrow, mort-
    gages.

Thompson, George W. COMMENTARIES ON THE MODERN LAW OF REAL
PROPERTY; BEING A COMPREHENSIVE TREATMENT OF EVERY PHASE OF THE
SUBJECT WITH SPECIAL REFERENCE TO THE ACQUISITION. ENCUMBRANCE
AND ALIENATION OF REAL PROPERTY WITH COMPLETE FORMS ... ADAPTING
SPECIAL TOPICS FROM THE WORKS OF LEONARD A. JONES, Permanent
ed., rev. and enl., 12 vols. Indianapolis, Bobbs-Merrill Co., 1939.
    Comprehensive Treatment of the entire field of real property law.
    Volume 11: Forms. Volume 12: Index and Table of Cases.
    Supplemental pocket parts issued periodically.

Tiedman, Christoper G. CASES ON REAL PROPERTY, rev. by Guy M.
Wood. St. Louis: Thomas Law Book Co., 1925. 820p.
    To be used with the author's TREATISE ON REAL PROPERTY.

Tiffany, Herbert Thorndike. THE LAW OF REAL PROPERTY, 3rd ed., 6 vols.,
by Basil Jones. Chicago: Calaghan and Co., 1939.
    Supplemented by pocket parts.

Tomson, Bernard. IT'S THE LAW; RECOGNIZING AND HANDLING THE LEGAL
PROBLEMS OF PRIVATE AND PUBLIC CONSTRUCTION, ed. by Norman A.
Coplan. Great Neck, N.Y.: Channel Press, 1960. 436p. forms.
    Contents: Part 1: Statutes regulating the practice of architecture,
    engineering and construction; Part 2: Organization and business
    problems of architectural, engineering and construction firms;
    Part 3: Architect, engineer, contractor and owner--the employment
    relation; Part 4: Rights and liabilities of architects, engineers
    and contractors; Part 5: Restrictions upon the use of property;
    Index of cases; appendix of contract and miscellaneous forms,
    p. 373-436.

The Unauthorized Practice of Law Controversy. LAW AND CONTEMPORARY
PROBLEMS, vol. 5, no. 1, Winter 1938 (entire issue).
    Drafting of Real Estate Instruments: The Problem from the Stand-
    point of Realtors, by Herbert U. Nelson; Drafting of Real Estate
    Instruments: The Problem from the Standpoint of the Bar, by
    Stanley B. Houck; Real Estate Brokers and the Courts, by Harry
    Weller Hill.

Van Buren, DeWitt. REAL ESTATE BROKERAGE AND COMMISSIONS - LAW
AND PRACTICE. New York: Prentice-Hall, 1948. 349p. forms.
    The fundamental principles of land ownership and of agency.
    Written as a text for real estate license applicants, real estate
    attorneys, and practicing real estate men.

GENERAL (continued)

Vogel, Joshua, et al. SURVEYS, SUBDIVISION AND PLOTTING AND
BOUNDARIES; WASHINGTON STATE LAWS AND JUDICIAL DECISIONS, Rev.
ed. (Bureau of Governmental Research and Services Report no. 137). Seattle:
University of Washington Press, 1958.
>Revision of Report no. 96, June 1949. Location of tracts in rela-
>tionship to water and riparian rights in connection therewith under
>state and federal jurisdiction included.

Walsh, W.F. and Niles, R.D. CASES ON THE LAW OF PROPERTY, 2d ed.
3 vols. Indianapolis: Bobbs-Merrill, 1951-1957.

RENT CONTROL

Friedlander, Bernard and Curreri, Anthony. RENT CONTROL: FEDERAL, STATE
AND MUNICIPAL; WITH AN APPENDIX CONTAINING STATUTES, REGULA-
TIONS, LOCAL LAWS, INTERPRETATIONS AND FORMS, ed. by Arthur I.
Winard. New York: Central Book Co., 1948. 845p.
>Supplement issued in 1950.

Grebler, Leo. Implications of Rent Control Experience in the United States.
INTERNATIONAL LABOUR REVIEW, April 1952, p. 1-24.

Rent Control, Federal and State. Section 13 In PRENTICE-HALL REAL ESTATE
GUIDE. Englewood Cliffs, N.J.: Prentice-Hall, 1953-   . illus. looseleaf.
>History of the Housing and Rent Act of 1947; state rent control
>laws.

Wendt, Paul F. Effects of Federal Rent Control. APPRAISAL JOURNAL,
vol. 18, no. 1, January 1950, p. 3-14.

Law—Bibliography

American Bar Foundation. INDEX TO LEGAL THESES AND RESEARCH
PROJECTS. Chicago: 1954-   . pap.
>Theses presented for graduate law degrees listed by subject;
>current research by law schools, bar associations, professional
>organizations, and individuals. Real Estate Agents, Real Property,
>Titles, etc., among subjects. Author index.

INDEX TO LEGAL PERIODICALS. New York: H.W. Wilson Co., 1910–
Published in co-operation with the American Association of Law
Libraries.

TITLES AND ABSTRACTS

Basye, Paul E. CLEARING LAND TITLES. St. Paul, Minn.: West Publishing
Co., 1953. 729p.
> Supplemented by pocket parts. Part I: Marketable Title and
> Statutes Relating to Evidence Thereof; Part II: Marketable Title
> and Statutes of Limitation; Part III: Marketable Titles and
> Curative Statutes; Part IV: Marketable Title Redefined.

Chandler, Alfred N. LAND TITLE ORIGINS; A TALE OF FORCE AND FRAUD.
New York, N.Y.: Robert Schalkenbach Foundation, 1945. 550p.

Fitch, Logan D. ABSTRACTS AND TITLES TO REAL PROPERTY, 2 vols.
Chicago: Callaghan and Co., 1954.
> Author states that basic material in the fourth edition of WARVELLE
> ON ABSTRACTS was used.

Flick, C. I. ABSTRACT AND TITLE PRACTICE, WITH FORMS, 2d ed., 3 vols.
St. Paul, Minn.: West Publishing Co., 1958.

Harvey, David C. B. REAL ESTATE LAW AND TITLE CLOSING; DEEDS,
CONTRACTS, MORTGAGES WITH FORMS, 3d ed. New York: Clark Boardman Co., 1956. 895p.

How to Convey Title and Transfer Real Estate. Part V, p. 463-582 In
Friedman, Edith J., ed. REAL ESTATE ENCYCLOPEDIA. Englewood Cliffs,
N.J.: Prentice-Hall, 1960.
> Chapter 20: Real Property Interests, Ownership, and Use, by
> Edith J. Friedman; Chapter 21: Broker's Role in Transfer of
> Title to Real Estate, by Milton Krieger; Chapter 22: Abstracts
> of Title, by Lowell J. Burger; Chapter 23: Title Insurance, by
> Charles F. Grimes; Chapter 24: Closing of Title, by T. J.
> Bomar.

McDermott, T. J. DESKBOOK ON LAND TITLES AND LAND LAW. Cincinnati: Anderson, 1954. 711p.

Patton, Rufford G. and Patton, Carroll G. PATTON ON LAND TITLES, 2d
ed., 3 vols. St. Paul, Minn.: West Publishing Co., 1957.

Roberts, Ernest F., Jr., et al, eds. PUBLIC REGULATION OF TITLE INSUR-
ANCE COMPANIES AND ABSTRACTERS. Philadelphia: Villanova University
Press, 1961. 346p.

Traces growth of title insurance since 1876 and analyzes laws of
states, territories, and possessions. Case and statute citations
complete to January 1, 1961.

Sackman, Julius L. THE LAW OF TITLES, 1st ed. Albany: Matthew Bender,
1959. 1155p. tables. looseleaf.
National in scope, exhaustively annotated; full documentation
illustrates each principle. Sections on sources, transfers, ad-
judication.

Simes, Lewis M. and Taylor, Clarence B. THE IMPROVEMENT OF CONVEY-
ANCING BY LEGISLATION. Ann Arbor: University of Michigan Law School,
1960.
Published under the auspices of the Law School and the Ameri-
can Bar Association Section on Real Property, Probate, and
Trust Law.

Simes, Lewis M. and Taylor, Clarence B. MODEL TITLE STANDARDS. Ann
Arbor: University of Michigan Law School, 1960. 99p. pap.
Published under the auspices of the Law School and the American Bar Association Section on Real Property, Probate, and
Trust Law. Comment, citation of similar state standards, and
authorities listed under each standard. List of twenty-three
state title standards included.

U.S. Department of Justice. Lands Division. STANDARDS FOR THE PREPARA-
TION OF TITLE EVIDENCE IN LAND ACQUISITION BY THE UNITED STATES.
Washington D.C.: Government Printing Office, 1962. 24p. pap.

Section 17

COMMERCIAL PROPERTY

The operation of particular types of property is covered in the PROPERTY MAN-AGEMENT section. Investment experience is included in the INVESTMENT section as well.

A discussion of the usefulness of operating ratios and a list of some of those most used appears in the APPRAISAL JOURNAL, vol. 30, no. 4, October 1962, p.535-7. THE ACCOUNTANT'S INDEX includes citations to information of this type.

Applebaum, William, et al. STORE LOCATION AND DEVELOPMENT STUDIES. Worcestor, Mass.: Clark University, 1961. 95p. illus., tables, maps. pap.
    Seven reprints from ECONOMIC GEOGRAPHY.

Architectural Record. COMMERCIAL BUILDINGS. New York: F.W. Dodge, 1953. 406p. illus., maps. plans.
    All material reprinted from ARCHITECTURAL RECORD. Office buildings, banks, transportation buildings, radio and television buildings, and theatres treated in separate sections. Bibliography: p. 183-5, 354.

Architectural Record. DESIGN FOR MODERN MERCHANDISING; STORES, SHOPS, SHOWROOMS. New York: F.W. Dodge, 1954. 247p. illus., plans.

Architectural Record. OFFICE BUILDINGS. New York: F.W Dodge, 1961. 248p. illus., plans.

Bailey, George R. Economic Design of Office Buildings. p. 1227-35. In Friedman, Edith J., ed. REAL ESTATE ENCYCLOPEDIA. Englewood Cliffs, N.J.: Prentice-Hall, 1960.

California. University. Bureau of Governmental Research. BUSINESS DECEN-TRALIZATION IN METROPOLITAN LOS ANGELES, by Edward F. Staniford. Los Angeles: 1960. 57p. pap.
    Suburban versus downtown department stores, banks and public utilities.

California. University. Real Estate Research Program. COMMERCIAL AND IN-VESTMENT PROPERTIES; A SERIES OF LECTURES, ed. by Paul F. Wendt. (Hand-book no. 1). Berkeley: 1955. 290p. pap.
    Outgrowth of a course. Twelve lectures on various property types, sale-leaseback plans, and income tax consideration.

California. University. Real Estate Research Program. DETERMINATION OF
INTRA-URBAN RETAIL TRADE AREAS, by David L. Huff and John W. Haggerty.
Los Angeles: 1962. 47p. tables, charts. pap.
Consumer behavior and shopping center selection.

California. University. Real Estate Research Program. GROWTH OF THE SAN
FRANCISCO BAY AREA URBAN CORE, by Mary Branaman. (Research
Report no. 8). Berkeley: 1956. 57p. tables, maps, charts. pap.

California. University. Real Estate Research Program. LOS ANGELES REAL
ESTATE; A STUDY OF INVESTMENT EXPERIENCE, by Fred E. Case. Los Angeles:
1960. 103p. tables, charts. pap.
Long term investment performance of 108 Los Angeles investment
properties -- apartment houses, office buildings, and commercial
property. Includes bibliography.

California. University. Real Estate Research Program. THE SUBURBANIZATION
OF ADMINISTRATIVE OFFICES IN THE SAN FRANCISCO BAY AREA, by Donald
L. Foley. (Research Report no 10). Berkeley: 1957. 48p. pap.

California. University. Real Estate Research Program. VENTURA BOULEVARD:
A STRING-TYPE SHOPPING STREET. Los Angeles: 1958. 63p. tables, maps.
pap.
"Will provide basic data from which, at a later date, analyses
can be made of the effect of paralleling freeways."

CENTRAL BUSINESS DISTRICT STUDIES, by Raymond E. Murphy, Jr., et al.
Worcestor, Mass.: Clark University, 1955. various paging. pap.
Reprints from ECONOMIC GEOGRAPHY, with additions.

Chain Store Guide. DIRECTORY OF DISCOUNT CENTERS; A LISTING OF
NAMES AND ADDRESSES OF THE DISCOUNT STORES AND ONE-STOP SHOP-
PING CENTERS CURRENTLY IN OPERATION THROUGHOUT THE UNITED STATES.
New York: Business Guides, Inc., 1961- .
On cover: "An authoritative list of discount stores, one-stop
shopping centers, open-and-closed-door consumer organizations
in the United States, headquarters addresses, individual store
locations, buying offices, size of stores, operating executives,
trade names."

Chain Store Guide. DIRECTORY OF LEADING CHAIN STORES IN THE UNITED
STATES; A CATEGORICAL LISTING OF ... LEADING CHAIN STORE COM-
PANIES, THEIR HEADQUARTERS, THE STATES IN WHICH THEY OPERATE AND
THE NAMES OF THEIR MANAGING EXECUTIVES. New York: 1959- .
Issued bienially.

Current Downtown Mall Strategies. DOWNTOWN IDEA EXCHANGE. SPECIAL
STUDY. New York: Downtown Idea Exchange, 125 East 23rd Street, zone 10,
1960. 2p. pap.

Cuzzort, Raymond P. SUBURBANIZATION OF SERVICE INDUSTRIES WITHIN
STANDARD METROPOLITAN AREAS. (Studies in Population Distribution no.
10). Oxford, Ohio: Scripps Foundation for Research in Population Problems,

Miami University and Population Research and Training Center, University of Chicago, 1955. 71p. tables, charts.

De Baer, S.R. SHOPPING DISTRICTS. (Studies in City Planning). Washington, D.C.: American Planning and Civic Association, 1937. 112p.
"In the plan of a city each type of business house has a certain location which is most advantageous to it, as well as to the city at large. This small volume tries in a general way to indicate which is the best location and the best treatment of buildings for each one of these groups."

Downtown's Position in Metropolitan Problems. DOWNTOWN IDEA EXCHANGE. SPECIAL STUDY. New York: Downtown Idea Exchange, 125 East 23rd Street, zone 10, 1957. 4p. pop.

Grebler, Leo. EXPERIENCE IN URBAN REAL ESTATE INVESTMENT; AN INTERIM REPORT BASED ON NEW YORK CITY. (Publication of the Institute for Urban Land Use and Housing Studies, Columbia University). New York: Columbia University Press, 1955. 277p. tables, charts.
Long term investment performance of 313 properties; apartments, single family houses, rooming houses, office buildings, lofts, and taxpayers.

Hattrell, W.S., et al. HOTELS, RESTAURANTS, BARS. New York: Reinhold, 1962. 146p. illus., tables, diagrs., plans.
"Hotels, restaurants and bars have been analyzed and the pattern which emerges has been described and illustrated." An analysis of design principles, illustrated with examples of structures in many countries.

The Impact of the Mall on Downtown. DOWNTOWN IDEA EXCHANGE. SPECIAL STUDY. New York: Downtown Idea Exchange, 125 East 23rd Street, zone 10, 1959. 3 parts. 12p. pap.

Ketchum, Morris, Jr. SHOPS AND STORES, Rev. ed. New York: Reinhold, 1957. 263p. illus.

Manasseh, Leonard and Cunliffe, Roger. OFFICE BUILDINGS. New York: Reinhold, 1962. 208p. illus., charts, diagrs., plans.
Design, financing, and construction presented as a concept of combined operation; for architects, developers, tenant organizations.

National Institute of Real Estate Brokers. COMMERCIAL PROPERTY CLINIC. PROCEEDINGS. Chicago: 1949-   . pap.
Transcript made available to those who attend the annual Clinic, held each May in Chicago.

National Institute of Real Estate Brokers. CREATING COMMERCIAL DEALS. (Brokers Institute Bulletin Service). Chicago: 1960. 63p. illus. pap.

National Institute of Real Estate Brokers. THE DYNAMICS OF COMMERCIAL PROPERTY. (Brokers Institute Bulletin Service). Chicago: 1961. 63p. illus. pap.

National Institute of Real Estate Brokers. SELLING AND LEASING COMMER-
CIAL PROPERTY. (Brokers Institute Bulletin Service). Chicago: 1952. 64p.
illus. pap.

National Real Estate Investor. (LIST OF) CHAIN STORES. New York: 20
West 38th Street, zone 18.
> Approximately 10,000 chains in all categories with more than
> four stores. Names of managers of real estate departments given.

National Real Estate Investor. (LIST OF) INVESTMENT COMPANIES. New
York: 20 West 38th Street, zone 18.
> Approximately 1,000 publicly-held real estate companies, trusts,
> syndicates, and investment companies.

National Real Estate Investor. (LIST OF) OIL COMPANY GASOLINE STATION
CHAINS. New York: 20 West 38th Street, zone 18.
> Approximately 150 companies with ten or more stations. Names
> of real estate managers included.

National Research Bureau, Inc. DIRECTORY OF DISCOUNT HOUSES AND
SELF-SERVICE DEPARTMENT STORES. Chicago: 1961-   . pap. processed.
> Annual, with 1960 monthly supplements. 1960 edition covers
> 2,730 discount stores and self-service department stores currently
> in operation, planned, or under construction. Includes a list of
> discount chain headquarters.

National Research Council. Highway Research Board. ZONING FOR TRUCK-
LOADING FACILITIES, by David R. Levin. Washington, D.C.: 1952. 101p.

National Retail Merchants Association. Retail Research Institute. THE PLAN-
NING OF BRANCH STORES; CHOOSING A STORE SITE, by Perry Meyers.
New York: 1960. 56p. tables, diagrs.

Nelson, Richard L. SELECTION OF RETAIL LOCATIONS. New York: F.W.
Dodge, 1958. 422p.
> "This book is the first major exposition of comprehensive scientific
> procedures for locating retail facilities. It is not only a compi-
> lation of existing techniques, but also sets forth new techniques
> for research, market analysis, and statistical consideration of
> locational problems."

North Carolina. University. Department of City and Regional Planning. THE
CENTRAL BUSINESS DISTRICT IN TRANSITION, by Shirley F. Weiss. Chapel
Hill: 1957. 44p. pap.

Parnes, Louis, PLANNING STORES THAT PAY; ORGANIC DESIGN AND LAY-
OUT FOR EFFICIENT MERCHANDISING. (An Architectural Record Book). New
York: F.W. Dodge, 1948. 313p. illus., diagrs.

Pfouts, Ralph W., ed. THE TECHNIQUES OF URBAN ECONOMIC ANALYSIS.
West Trenton, N.J.: Chandler-Davis, 1960. 410p.

Ratcliff, Richard U. THE PROBLEM OF RETAIL SITE SELECTION. (Michigan
Business Studies, vol 9, no. 1). Ann Arbor: Bureau of Business Research

University of Michigan, 1939. 93p. tables, charts. pap.
Bibliography: p.89-93.

A Re-evaluation of the Downtown Mall. DOWNTOWN IDEA EXCHANGE. SPE-
CIAL STUDY. New York: Downtown Idea Exchange, 125 East 23rd Street,
zone 10, 1960. 2p. pap.

Reilly, William J. LAW OF RETAIL GRAVITATION, 2d ed. New York: 1953.
75p. tables.
Reprint of 1931 edition. "To establish the boundaries of the
retail trade territories of the various cities throughout the United
States."

Ripnen, Kenneth H. OFFICE BUILDING AND OFFICE LAYOUT PLANNING.
New York: McGraw-Hill, 1960. 182p. illus., diagrs.
"Techniques for solving office building and office space planning,
construction, equipping and maintenance problems."

Schultz, Earle and Simmons, Walter. OFFICES IN THE SKY. Chicago: National Association of Building Owners and Managers, 1959. 328p.
The story of the skyscraper "as a tool of commerce and a prime
factor in the growth of cities." In connection with the fiftieth
anniversary of the association.

Snibbe, Richard W. SMALL COMMERCIAL BUILDINGS. (Progressive Architecture Library). New York: Reinhold, 1956. 216p. illus., plans.
At head of title: A photographic record of 100 selected designs
for small commercial buildings executed within the last twenty
years with a challenging introduction, plans of each project and
critical text by Richard W. Snibbe.

Snider, Harold Wayne. LIFE INSURANCE INVESTMENT IN COMMERCIAL REAL
ESTATE. Homewood, Ill.: Richard D. Irwin, 1956. 136p.

Sternlieb, George. THE FUTURE OF THE DOWNTOWN DEPARTMENT STORE.
Cambridge, Mass.: Joint Center for Urban Studies of the Massachusetts Institute of Technology and Harvard University, 1962. 205p. tables, charts. processed. (Distr. by Harvard University Press, Cambridge 38, Mass.)
A study of the changing environment and clientele of the department store in the central business district, with special attention
to conditions in Philadelphia, Pittsburgh, and Boston, and management responses to meet the changes. Conclusions and suggestions
for management presented. Bibliography: p. 190-9.

Trends in Office Location. TAX POLICY, Sept.-Oct., 1957.
Part III: The Plant, the Office and the City.

Urban Land Institute. CONSERVATION AND REHABILITATION OF MAJOR
SHOPPING DISTRICTS, by Richard L. Nelson and Frederick T. Aschman.
(Technical Bulletin no. 22). Washington, D.C.: 1954. 44p. illus. pap.

Urban Land Institute. INVESTORS AND DOWNTOWN REAL ESTATE---OPINION
AND COMMENT, by Arthur M. Weimer. (Technical Bulletin no. 39). Washington, D.C.: 1960. 24p. pap.

Results of a personal investigation into the attitudes and opinions of the principle institutional leaders in the investment field.

Urban Land Institute. SHOPPING HABITS AND TRAVEL PATTERNS, by Alan M. Vorhees, et al. (Technical Bulletin no. 24). Washington, D.C.: 1955. 24p. illus. pap.

FINANCIAL INSTITUTIONS

United States Savings and Loan League. LOCATION FACTORS FOR SAVINGS AND LOAN ASSOCIATION OFFICES, adapted from a study made by Fred Kniffin for the Indiana University School of Business and the United States Savings and Loan League. Chicago: 1956. 64p. pap.

Urban Land Institute. BANKING EXPANSION--NEW FRONTIER AHEAD, by Robert H. Armstrong. (Technical Bulletin no. 35). Washington, D.C.: 1959. 22p. tables. pap.

HOTELS AND MOTELS

American Institute of Real Estate Appraisers. ECONOMIC FACTORS AND CASE STUDIES IN HOTEL AND MOTEL VALUATION, by Fred W. Eckert. Chicago: 1962. 86p. pap. processed.
> Contents: The Hotel and Motel Industry, - Significance of Business Trends, Projecting Earnings Potentials, Rate of Capitalization of Earnings in Estimating Economic Values, Useful Lives of Hotels and Motels, Case Studies in Hotel and Motel Valuation.

American Motel Magazine. READER'S SERVICE KIT, by Alice M. Patterson. Chicago: Patterson, 5 South Wabash Avenue, zone 3, 1958. various paging. illus., plans. pap. processed.
> From material published in AMERICAN MOTEL magazine. Contents: Things to Consider; Financing; Location; Planning; Furnishing and Decorating; the Motel Restaurant; General Information; Books for Profit.

American Society of Planning Officials. MOTELS AND MOTEL REGULATION. (Planning Advisory Service Information Report no. 51). Chicago: 1953. 40p. pap. processed.

Architectural Record. MOTELS, HOTELS, RESTAURANTS AND BARS, 2d ed. New York: F.W. Dodge, 1960. 327p. illus., plans.

Baker, Geoffrey and Funaro, Bruno. MOTELS. (Progressive Architecture Library). New York: Reinhold, 1955. 204p. illus., plans.

HOTELS AND MOTELS (continued)

Eckert, Fred William. THE HOTEL LEASE; A STUDY OF THE BUSINESS ELE-
MENTS AND PRINCIPLES INVOLVED IN MAKING LEASES THAT ARE EQUITA-
BLE TO BOTH LEASEE AND LESSOR. Chicago: Hotel Monthly Press, 1947. 221p.

Harris, Kerr, Forster and Company. TRENDS IN THE HOTEL BUSINESS: TRAN-
SIENT, RESIDENTIAL, RESORT, MOTOR HOTEL; ANNUAL REVIEW. New York:
1936-   . tables, charts. pap.

Horwath and Horwath. HOTEL OPERATIONS: OPERATING RATIOS OF 100 HOTELS
LOCATED IN 53 CITIES; ANNUAL STUDY. New York: 1932-   . tables,
charts. pap.

Kane, C. Vernon. MOTOR COURTS--FROM PLANNING TO PROFITS. New
York: Ahrens, 1954. 243p. illus., tables , diagrs.

PARKING

Baker, Geoffrey and Funaro, Bruno. PARKING. New York: Reinhold, 1958.
202p. illus., charts, diagrs.

Eno Foundation for Highway Traffic Control. PARKING, by Robert H. Burrage
and Edward G. Mogren. Saugatuck, Conn.: 1957. 401p. illus., tables, charts,
diagrs. pap.
     Complete coverage including surveying needs, design and operation
     of all types of facilities. Reports have been issued for each type
     of facility as well.

National Parking Association. PARKING INDUSTRY OPERATING COST SURVEY.
Washington, D.C.: 1958-   . tables. pap.
     A biennial report on all types of parking facilities, by regions.

U.S. Bureau of Public Roads. Division of Research. PARKING GUIDE FOR CITIES.
Washington, D.C.: 1956. 172p. illus., tables, charts. pap.
     Parking studies, travel habits and parking problems in the central
     business district and action for relief of parking congestion by
     private, public and cooperative approaches of providing parking
     facilities.

Urban Land Institute. AUTOMOBILE PARKING IN CENTRAL BUSINESS DISTRICTS;
SUGGESTED SOLUTIONS TO THIS VITAL PROBLEM BY THE CENTRAL BUSINESS
DISTRICT COUNCIL, by Seward H. Mott and Max S. Wehrly. (Technical
Bulletin no. 6). Washington, D.C.: 1946. 15p. tables, diagrs. pap.

Urban Land Institute. COMMERCIAL PARKING IN RESIDENTIAL AREAS; A TRAN-
SITIONAL USE UNDER ZONING by Seward H. Mott and Max S. Wehrly. (Technical Bulletin no. 9). Washington, D.C.: 1948. 8p. illus. pap.

PARKING (continued)

Urban Land Institute. SPECIAL OR BENEFIT ASSESSMENTS FOR PARKING FACIL-
ITIES, by David R. Levin and Conya Hardy. (Technical Bulletin no. 15). Washington, D.C.: 1951. 8p. pap.

SERVICE STATIONS

American Society of Planning Officials. GASOLINE STATION LOCATION AND
DESIGN. (Planning Advisory Service Information Report no. 140). Chicago:
November 1960. 24p. pap.

SHOPPING CENTERS

Baker, Geoffrey and Funaro, Bruno. SHOPPING CENTERS; DESIGN AND OPERA-
TION. New York: Reinhold, 1951. 288p. illus., diagrs.
    Includes plans, pictures and store list for 63 shopping centers,
    large and small.

California. University. Real Estate Research Program. A STUDY OF SHOPPING
CENTERS, by Richard Grant Thompson. Berkeley: 1961. 106p. tables. pap.
processed.
    MBA thesis. Report based on discussion with developers to determine
    their opinions of the methods and procedures of successful centers
    with an integration of published studies on procedure.

Davidson, Thomas Lea. SOME EFFECTS OF THE GROWTH OF PLANNED AND
CONTROLLED SHOPPING CENTERS ON SMALL RETAILERS. Storrs: School of
Business Administration, University of Connecticut, 1960. 178p. tables. pap.
    Small Business Administration Management Research Grant Program.
    Study originated from research under the auspices of the Interna-
    tional Council of Shopping Centers. Study of effects of the cen-
    ters' growth on small independent, local retail merchants... what
    opportunity does the small owner have to locate in a planned shop-
    ping center. Study of 81 centers--tenants, financing, mortality or
    expansion of the center and of individual stores, income and overage
    paid by AAA tenants or small businesses, to what extent are new
    retail businesses born in shopping centers and should efforts be
    made to provide better opportunities for location in shopping cen-
    ters of small business.

Gruen, Victor and Smith, Larry. SHOPPING TOWNS--U.S.A.; THE PLANNING
OF SHOPPING CENTERS. New York: Reinhold, 1960. 288p. illus., charts,
diagrs.

SHOPPING CENTERS (continued)

"Discussion is not limited to physical planning alone, but includes
the economic, financial, legal, engineering, sociological, traffic
and merchandising aspects of planning as they apply to shopping
center problems."

International Council of Shopping Centers. CONVENTION PROCEEDINGS. New
York: 1959- . pap.
Speeches on practical aspects. Particularly good on leasing,
financing and operating.

International Council of Shopping Centers. RECOMMENDED LEASE FORM. New
York: no date. pap.
Detailed guide lease. For members only.

International Council of Shopping Centers. SHOPPING CENTER MERCHANTS
ASSOCIATIONS, by Robert S. Nyburg. New York: 1959. 62p. pap.

Jonassen, C.T. THE SHOPPING CENTER VERSUS DOWNTOWN; A MOTIVATION
RESEARCH ON SHOPPING HABITS AND ATTITUDES IN THREE CITIES. Columbus:
Bureau of Business Research, Ohio State University, 1955. 170p.
Made possible by a grant from the Highway Research Board.
Consumer attitudes and practices for three metropolitan areas--
Columbus, Ohio; Seattle, Washington; and Houston, Texas.

Kelley, Eugene J. SHOPPING CENTERS; LOCATING CONTROLLED REGIONAL
CENTERS. Saugatuck, Conn.: Eno Foundation for Highway Traffic Control, 1956.
192p. illus., tables, diagrs. pap.
"Part I: Results of a review of published materials on the location
of economic institutions, providing a basis for comparison of location,
theory and business practice; Part II: Described the actual location
procedures used by some prominent developers; Part III: Includes
generalizations on regional center site selection and the significance
of the regional center movement to marketing theory."

National Institute of Real Estate Brokers, SHOPPING CENTER PANEL TRANSCRIPT.
Chicago: 1959- . pap. processed.
Annual convention session speeches and discussion.

National Research Bureau, Inc. DIRECTORY OF SHOPPING CENTERS IN THE
UNITED STATES AND CANADA. Chicago: 1956- . pap. processed.
Annual, with monthly supplements. Alphabetical listing by state,
giving owner-developer, center manager, promotion manager or agency, leasing agent, executive secretary of merchant association,
architect, number of stores and parking spaces, auditorium facilities,
sales volume, size and cost of center, date opened, availability
of rental space and names of tenant stores. Includes a listing of
centers with enclosed malls and leading national chains located in
shopping centers.

National Retail Merchants Association. SHOPPING CENTERS; PLANNING AND
MANAGEMENT, by Paul E. Smith. New York: 1956. 157p. illus., tables.
pap. processed.

SHOPPING CENTERS (continued)

"This study was approached with the objective of securing the answers to the questions that beset large stores which are planning to open branch stores in shopping centers."

U. S. Congress. Senate. Select Committee on Small Business. HEARING BEFORE A SUBCOMMITTEE ON ALLEGED DISCRIMINATORY PRACTICES AGAINST SMALL-BUSINESS CONCERNS IN SUBURBAN SHOPPING CENTERS, 86th CONGRESS, 1ST SESSION. Washington, D.C.: 1959. 242p. charts. pap. (Sold by Government Printing Office).

Urban Land Institute. MARKET ANALYSIS OF SHOPPING CENTERS, by Homer Hoyt. (Technical Bulletin no. 12). Washington, D.C.: 1949. 7p. pap.

Urban Land Institute. MISTAKES WE HAVE MADE IN DEVELOPING SHOPPING CENTERS, by J. C. Nichols. (Technical Bulletin no. 4). Washington, D.C.: 1945. 15p. pap.
    Reprinted in April 1960.

Urban Land Institute. A RE-EXAMINATION OF THE SHOPPING CENTER MARKET, by Homer Hoyt. (Technical Bulletin no. 33). Washington, D.C.: 1958. 12p. pap.

Urban Land Institute. SHOPPING CENTERS; AN ANALYSIS, by Seward H. Mott and Max S. Wehrly. (Technical Bulletin no. 11). Washington, D.C.: 1949. 46p. illus. pap.

Urban Land Institute. SHOPPING CENTERS; PLANNING, PRINCIPLES AND TESTED POLICIES, by J. Ross McKeever. (Technical Bulletin no. 20). Washington, D.C.: 1953. 91p. illus. pap.

Urban Land Institute. SHOPPING CENTERS RE-STUDIED; EMERGING PATTERNS AND PRACTICAL EXPERIENCES, 2 vols., by J. Ross McKeever. (Technical Bulletin no. 30). Washington, D.C.: 1957. illus., tables. pap.

Urban Land Institute. Community Builders Council. COMMUNITY BUILDERS HANDBOOK, 3rd ed. Washington, D.C.: 1960. 476p. illus., tables, charts, diagrs.
    Contents devoted to subdivisions and shopping centers. Complete information: Planning preliminaries, planning the site, architectural and structural design, management, maintenance and operation. Appendices: Retail Expenditure in Selected Kinds of Retail Stores in 1958; Per Capita and Family Retail Expenditures on Goods and Services in Selected Retail Stores in 1958; Consumer Expenditure on Selected Products and Services in 1958, Schedule of Average per Foot Gross Sales and Percent of Gross Sales for Rent Paid by Retail Types; List of Stores by Locations; a Shopping Center Lease Form and By-Laws of Merchants Association; Taxation and the Shopping Center, a Statement of Policy.

Urban Land Institute. Community Builders Council. THE DOLLARS AND CENTS OF SHOPPING CENTERS; A STUDY OF RECEIPTS AND EXPENSES, 2 vols. Washington, D.C.: 1961-1962. tables, charts. pap.

SHOPPING CENTERS (continued)

Part I , The Entire Center. Part II, Tenant Characteristics.
Elements that make a shopping center successful--comparative
costs for guidance. Neighborhood, community and regional centers.

Urban Land Institute. Community Builders Council. OPERATION SHOPPING
CENTERS: GUIDEBOOK TO EFFECTIVE MANAGEMENT AND PROMOTION,
by Donald L. Curtiss. Washington, D.C.: 1961. 188p. illus.
Operational practices: Merchants' associations, advertising policies, promotional events. Promotion budgets included.

Urban Land Institute. Community Builders Council. STANDARD MANUAL OF
EXPENSE ACCOUNTS FOR SHOPPING CENTERS. Washington, D.C.: 1961.
25p. pap.
Karney A. Brasfield of Touche, Ross, Bailey and Smart, Washington,
D.C., consultant.
"It is in the expense accounting area that the needs of the industry dictate a specialized system of accounts in order to supply
management with data of optimum usefulness and lay the foundation
for industry reporting on a consistent basis."

TELEVISION STATIONS

Duschinsky, Walter J. TV STATIONS; A GUIDE FOR ARCHITECTS, ENGINEERS
AND MANAGEMENT. (Progressive Architecture Library). New York: Reinhold,
1954. 136p. illus., diagrs.

THEATRES

Society of Motion Picture Engineers, Inc. THE MOTION PICTURE THEATER;
PLANNING, UPKEEP, ed. by Helen M. Stote. New York: 1948. 428p. illus.,
diagrs.
"Thirty-eight articles on the technical aspects of motion picture
theater planning, construction, maintenance. modernization, and
theater television prepared for presentation before the Society of
Motion Picture Engineers."

Commercial Property—Bibliographies

Council of Planning Librarians. CENTRAL BUSINESS DISTRICTS. (Exchange Bibliography no. 12). Oakland, Calif.: 6318 Thornhill Drive, zone 11, 1959. 56p. pap. processed.

Council of Planning Librarians. FURTHER REFERENCES ON CENTRAL BUSINESS DISTRICTS. (Exchange Bibliography no. 16). Oakland, Calif.: 6318 Thornhill Drive, zone 11, 1960. 26p. pap. processed.

Holmes, Jack D.L. A SELECTED AND ANNOTATED BIBLIOGRAPHY OF SHOP-PING CENTERS, Rev. ed. Austin; Bureau of Business Research, University of Texas, 1960. 59p. pap. processed.

International Council of Shopping Centers. SELECTED BIBLIOGRAPHY ON SHOP-PING CENTERS, New York: 1962. 9p. pap. processed.

Kroger Company. SELECTED, ANNOTATED BIBLIOGRAPHY ON SHOPPING CENTERS, comp. and annotated by Saul B. Cohen. Cincinnati: 35 East Seventh Street, 1957. 20p. pap. processed.

Regional Science Research Institute. CENTRAL PLACE STUDIES; A BIBLIOGRAPHY OF THEORY AND APPLICATIONS, by Brian J.L. Berry and Allen Pred. (Bibliography Series no. 1). Philadelphia: 1961. 153p. pap.
"A comprehensive coverage of geographic theory and empirical work relating to the size, spacing, and functions of cities; trading areas and urban spheres of influence; fairs and markets; consumer shopping and travel behavior."

Commercial Property—Periodicals
(See Appendix for complete information concerning these publications.)

ARCHITECTURAL FORUM. ARCHITECTURAL RECORD. BUILDINGS. CHAIN STORE AGE. EXECUTIVE EDITION. DISCOUNT STORE NEWS. DOWN-TOWN IDEA EXCHANGE. ECONOMIC GEOGRAPHY. HORWATH ACCOUNT-ANT. HOSPITALITY. NATIONAL MARKET LETTER. PROGRESSIVE ARCHI-TECTURE. REAL ESTATE ANALYST. SHOPPING CENTER AGE. SHOPPING CENTER IDEA LIBRARY. SKYSCRAPER MANAGEMENT. SUPERMARKET MERCHANDISING. TOURIST COURT JOURNAL. TRAFFIC QUARTERLY. URBAN LAND NEWS AND TRENDS IN CITY DEVELOPMENT.

Section 18

FARM PROPERTY

American Institute of Real Estate Appraisers. 101 RURAL APPRAISAL PROBLEMS WITH SUGGESTED SOLUTIONS, comp. by Walter F. Willmette. Chicago: 1958. 76p.

Beneke, Raymond R. MANAGING THE FARM BUSINESS. New York: John Wiley, 1955. 464p. illus., tables, charts, diagrs., maps.
  A text written principally for use in secondary schools and junior colleges. Principles emphasized.

Black, John D., et al. FARM MANAGEMENT. New York: Macmillan, 1947. 1073p. illus., tables, charts.
  A text prepared primarily for use in the junior and senior years in agricultural colleges.

Board of Governors of the Federal Reserve System. FARM LOANS AT COMMERCIAL BANKS; A SERIES OF ARTICLES REPORTING THE FINDINGS OF THE AGRICULTURAL LOAN SURVEY MADE AS OF JUNE 30, 1956...REPRINTED FROM FEDERAL RESERVE BULLETIN FOR NOVEMBER, 1956, JANUARY, FEBRUARY, AND MARCH, 1957; WITH A LISTING OF ARTICLES PUBLISHED BY THE FEDERAL RESERVE BANKS. Washington, D.C.: 1957. 54p. tables. pap.
  Includes section on loans to buy farm real estate.

Boss, Andrew and Pond, George A. MODERN FARM MANAGEMENT; PRINCIPLES AND PRACTICE. St. Paul, Minn.: Itasca Press, Webb Publishing Co., 1947. 494p. illus., tables, charts, diagrs., maps, forms.
  A textbook prepared for use in a general farm management course in colleges and in the senior year in vocational high schools. Develops the background of successful farming and discusses the problems and procedures of "acquiring, organizing, and operating a farm."

Bradford, Lawrence A. and Johnson, Glenn L. FARM MANAGEMENT ANALYSIS. New York: John Wiley, 1953. 438p. illus.

California. University. Agricultural Experiment Station. WHAT YOU SHOULD KNOW ABOUT FARM LEASES, by A. D. Reed and J. H. Snyder. (Circular 491). 1960. 10p. pap.
  Presents farm lease worksheet and demonstrates its use by landlords and tenants in devising mutually satisfactory leases. Includes checklist of points to include.

Case, Harold C. M. and Williams, D. B. FIFTY YEARS OF FARM MANAGEMENT. Urbana: University of Illinois Press, 1957. 386p. tables, charts.

"Historical review of farm management, with special reference to research, extension, and teaching as developed in the land-grant colleges and the United States Department of Agriculture."

Case, Harold C. M., et al. PRINCIPLES OF FARM MANAGEMENT, 2d ed. Philadelphia: J. B. Lippincott, 1960. 467p. illus.

Castle, Emery and Becker, Manning. FARM BUSINESS MANAGEMENT; THE DECISION-MAKING PROCESS. New York: Macmillan, 1962. 423p. tables, charts.
A textbook containing sections on farm management in general; tools and techniques such as record keeping and budgeting; capital and land acquisition; management of crops, livestock, labor, machinery; income taxation. Recommended readings at chapter ends.

Clemson Agricultural College. Department of Agricultural Economics. ALTERNATIVE METHODS AND TECHNIQUES FOR THE ASSESSMENT OF FARM REAL ESTATE, by J. Robert Cooper. (A. E. 124). Clemson, S.C.: 1957. 64p. tables, charts. pap. processed.

Cook, R. L. SOIL MANAGEMENT FOR CONSERVATION AND PRODUCTION. New York: John Wiley, 1962. 527p. illus., tables, charts, diagrs., maps.
A textbook of principles and practices.

Craigmyle, Beach. Farm Financing. p. 427-462 In Friedman, Edith J., ed. REAL ESTATE ENCYCLOPEDIA. Englewood Cliffs, N.J.: Prentice-Hall, 1960.

Crouse, Earl F. and Everett, Charles H. RURAL APPRAISALS. Englewood Cliffs, N.J.: Prentice-Hall, 1956. 531p. illus., tables, diagrs., maps, forms.

Curran, G. C. and Hardison, L. M. SELLING FARMS; FARM SALESMEN'S MANUAL. Fort Wayne, Ind.: Anthony Press, 1941. 129p. illus. pap. processed.

Doane Agricultural Service, Inc. DOANE AGRICULTURAL DIGEST. St. Louis: looseleaf.
A looseleaf service issued in several regional editions. Includes sections on leases, property taxes, farm management, soils, credit, land values, and appraising. Practical guides, statistics, reports of research, detailed farm operation information.

Donahue, Roy L. OUR SOILS AND THEIR MANAGEMENT (AN INTRODUCTION TO SOIL AND WATER CONSERVATION), 2d ed. Danville, Ill.: Interstate Printers and Publishers, 1961. 568p. illus., tables, charts, diagrs., maps.
A textbook of principles and practices. References at chapter ends.

Donahue, Roy L. SOILS; AN INTRODUCTION TO SOILS AND PLANT GROWTH. Englewood Cliffs, N.J.: Prentice-Hall, 1958. 349p. illus., tables, charts, diagrs., maps.
A textbook on the fundamentals and applications of soil science. References at chapter ends. Appendix A: Glossary of terms.

Efferson, J. Norman. PRINCIPLES OF FARM MANAGEMENT. New York: McGraw-Hill, 1953. 431p. tables, charts, maps, forms.
Designed primarily as a text for students of agriculture. Exercises and references at chapter ends.

Florida. University. Agricultural Experiment Station. FLORIDA FIELD LEASE GUIDE, by Daniel E. Alleger, et al. (Southeast Regional Land Tenure Committee Regional Publication no. 18; circular S-79). Gainesville: 1955. 8p. pap.
Illustrates use of a farm lease developed to be consistent with Florida law.

Forster, G. W. FARM ORGANIZATION AND MANAGEMENT, 3rd ed. New York: Prentice-Hall, 1953. 490p. illus., tables, charts.
Questions and references at chapter ends.

Frenzell, E. H. PROBLEMS (QUESTIONS AND ANSWERS) RELATING TO THE APPRAISAL OF FARM LANDS IN CALIFORNIA. Sacramento: 1957. 73p. pap. processed.
Seventy-five drill problems.

Hall, I. F. and Mortensen, W. P. FARM MANAGEMENT HANDBOOK. Danville, Ill.: Interstate Printers and Publishers, 1954. 576p. illus. tables, charts, diagrs., maps, forms.
"The principles of good farm organization, planning, management, and operation which are used by outstanding farmers." Marketing, soil conservation, and safety included. Appendices of general economic information, business law, legal matters, etc.

Hamilton, James E. and Bryant, W. R. PROFITABLE FARM MANAGEMENT. Englewood Cliffs, N.J.: Prentice-Hall, 1956. 394p. illus., tables, diagrs., forms.
Intended for the beginning farmer or farm manager as an aid in finding answers to specific management problems. Chapter 9: Renting or Buying a Farm. Questions and suggested activities at chapter ends.

Hannah, Harold W. LAW ON THE FARM; A DISCUSSION OF LEGAL PROBLEMS WHICH ARISE IN THE BUSINESS OF FARMING. New York: Macmillan, 1948. 399p.
Chapter V: Farm Land and Real Estate; Chapter VI: Rights in Land; Chapter VIII: Family Interest in the Ownership of Farm Land; Chapter XIII: Landlord and Tenant.

Heady, Earl O. and Jensen, Harold R. FARM MANAGEMENT ECONOMICS. New York: Prentice-Hall, 1954. 645p. tables, charts.
A textbook for use in college and adult education programs. Covers "all phases of crop production, soil management, livestock production and engineering applied to machinery and buildings." Discussion questions at chapter ends.

Heady, Earl O., et al, eds. RESOURCE PRODUCTIVITY, RETURNS TO SCALE, AND FARM SIZE. Ames: Iowa State University Press, 1956. 208p. charts. processed.

A collection of twenty-two papers, assemblied and published
under the sponsorship of the North Central Farm Management Research Committee.

Hedges, Trimble R. FARM MANAGEMENT DECISIONS. Englewood Cliffs,
N.J.: Prentice-Hall, 1963. 628p. illus., tables, charts.
A textbook on the application of specific economic principles
and analytical procedures to the usual problems encountered in
farm operation. References at chapter ends.

Hopkins, John A. and Turner, Deane A. RECORDS FOR FARM MANAGEMENT.
Englewood Cliffs, N.J.: Prentice-Hall, 1958. 218p. illus., tables, charts,
forms.
A simple system of keeping and analyzing farm records. Farm
accounting presented as a practical tool of farm management.

Horton, Donald C. PATTERNS OF FARM FINANCIAL STRUCTURE; A CROSS-
SECTION VIEW OF ECONOMIC AND PHYSICAL DETERMINANTS.
(National Bureau of Economic Research, Financial Research Program, Studies in
Agricultural Finance no. 2). Princeton, N.J.: Princeton University Press,
1957. 185p. tables, charts, map.
How the economic and physical characteristics of agriculture
affect its financing and descriptions of the roles of credit and
equity funds in the financing of agricultural production.

Illinois. University. Agricultural Experiment Station. FARM LEASE PRACTICES
IN EAST-CENTRAL ILLINOIS, by Franklin J. Reiss. (Bulletin 677). Urbana:
1961. 56p. tables, map. pap.
Report on a survey in twenty-two counties.

Illinois. University. Agricultural Extension Service. PARTNERSHIPS IN THE
FARM BUSINESS, by N. G. P. Krausz and Fred L. Mann. (Circular 786).
Urbana: 1958. 39p. illus., tables, forms. pap.
Defines a partnership, lists advantages and disadvantages of this
ownership form, indicates how a partnership is formed and
operated. Sample agreements included.

Illinois. University. College of Agriculture. Extension Service in Agriculture
and Home Economics. CORPORATIONS IN THE FARM BUSINESS, by N. G. P.
Krausz and Fred L. Mann. Rev. (Circular 797). Urbana: 1960. 46p. forms. pap.
Discusses advantages and disadvantages of incorporation and
methods for organizing, operating, and dissolving a farm corporation. Reproduces sample forms and agreements.

Illinois. University. College of Agriculture. Extension Service in Agriculture
and Home Economics. FARM PROPERTY AND TRUSTS, by N. G. P. Krausz.
(Circular 842). Urbana: 1962. folder. pap.
A brief explanation of the "nature of trusts and their application
to farm estates."

Illinois. University. College of Agriculture. Extension Service in Agriculture
and Home Economics. INSTALLMENT LAND CONTRACTS FOR FARMLAND,
by N. G. P. Krausz. (Circular 823). Urbana: 1960. 24p. tables. pap.

Illinois. University. College of Agriculture. Extension Service in Agriculture and Home Economics. INSURANCE FOR FARMERS: PROPERTY, LIABILITY, MEDICAL, by N. G. P. Krausz. (Circular 823). Urbana: 1961. 24p. tables. pap.
> A guide for the determination of insurance needs and selection of types for purchase.

Iowa State University. Cooperative Extension Service. THE FARM CORPORA- TION: WHAT IT IS, HOW IT WORKS, HOW IT IS TAXED, by John C. O'Byrne, et al. (Pamphlet 273; North Central Regional Extension Publication no. 11). Ames: 1960. 19p. pap.

Johnson, Sherman E., et al. MANAGING A FARM. New York: Van Nostrand, 1946. 365p. illus., tables, charts, maps.
> "Practical guidance in thinking through managerial problems" in full-time and part-time farming. A revision and expansion of material originally issued as Educational Manual 810 of the U.S. Armed Forces Institute.

Kansas State University. Agricultural Experiment Station. LEASING IRRI- GATED LAND, by Wilfred H. Pine and Warren L. Trock. (Circular 370). Manhattan: 1959. 15p. tables, charts. pap.
> "Describes a basis for developing equitable leases and suggests some leasing arrangements for irrigated land."

Kansas State University. Agricultural Experiment Station. WHAT ABOUT INCOR- PORATING FARMS IN KANSAS?, by N. D. French, et al. (Circular 376). Manhattan: 1960. 14p. tables. pap.
> Defines a corporation, lists advantages and disadvantages of this ownership form, and gives directions for forming and dissolving a corporation in the state of Kansas.

King, Frank P. and Hardin, L. S. BETTER FARM MANAGEMENT. Atlanta: Turner E. Smith and Co., 1956. 426p. illus., tables, charts.
> A textbook. Study suggestions and references at chapter ends.

Michigan State University. Agricultural Experiment Station. FAMILY FARM TRANSFERS AND SOME TAX CONSIDERATIONS, by Elton B. Hill and Marshall Harris. (North Central Regional Publication no. 127; Special Bulletin no. 436). East Lansing; 1961. 48p. illus., tables, chart. pap.
> "Intra-family farm-transfer arrangements...with the addition of information on state and federal taxes." Fourteen states covered.

Michigan State University. Agricultural Experiment Station. THE LAND CON- TRACT AS A FARM FINANCE PLAN; by Elton B. Hill and John W. Fitzgerald. (Special Bulletin no. 431). East Lansing: 1960. 39p. tables. pap.

Michigan State University. Cooperative Extension Service. FARM AND FIELD RENTAL AGREEMENTS, by E. B. Hill. (Extension Folder F-176). East Lansing: 1955. 15p. tables. pap.
> A brief discussion of the various types of farm leases and their provisions, with a table showing usual practices.

Michigan State University. Cooperative Extension Service. MANAGING THE
SMALL PART-TIME FARM, by H. S. Wilt. (Extension Bulletin no. 341). East
Lansing: 1957. 46p. illus., tables, map. pap.
> A report on part-time farms in Michigan and planning guidelines
> on amount of land, crop and livestock selection, equipment and
> building needs.

Michigan State University. Cooperative Extension Service. SHOULD WE INCOR-
PORATE THE FARM BUSINESS?, by E. B. Hill. (Extension Bulletin 371).
East Lansing: 1959. 15p. pap.

Montana State College. Extension Service. FARM AND RANCH LEASES, by
M. E. Quenemoen. (Circular 277). Bozeman: 1960. 12p. tables. pap.
> Presents methods for judging fairness of leases, the extent to
> which a given lease encourages efficient production and affords
> adequate legal protection.

Murray, William G. FARM APPRAISAL; CLASSIFICATION AND VALUATION
OF FARM LAND AND BUILDINGS, 4th ed. Ames: Iowa State University
Press, 1961. 433p.

National Institute of Farm Brokers. FARM AND RANCH BROKERS MANUAL.
Chicago: 1959. 100p. tables, diagrs., forms. pap.

Nebraska. University. College of Agriculture. Extension Service. IS YOUR
LEASE "FAIR"?, by Philip A. Henderson. (North Central Regional Publication
no. 9). Lincoln: 1960. 12p. tables. pap.
> Discusses the elements that serve as the bases for determining
> farm rents and outlines methods by which they may be judged.
> Prepared with the co-operation of the U.S. Department of
> Agriculture.

New York State College of Agriculture. INCORPORATION OF THE FARM
BUSINESS, Rev., by Robert S. Smith. (Cornell Extension Bulletin no. 1016).
Ithaca: 1959. 16p.
> Lists advantages and disadvantages of incorporation, provides a
> short checklist to help make the decision, and describes ex-
> perience of four farm corporations.

Oklahoma State University. Extension Service. FARM PARTNERSHIPS AND
FATHER-SON AGREEMENTS, by C. D. Maynard, et al. (Circular E-710).
Stillwater: 1960. 37p. pap.
> Includes a sample father-son income sharing agreement.

Organization for European Economic Co-operation. European Productivity Agency.
FARM MANAGEMENT IN THE UNITED STATES; REPORT BY A GROUP OF
EXPERTS. (No. 2193/10045; Project no. 395/B). Paris: 1958. 126p. illus.,
tables, charts. pap.
> Results of visits to North Carolina, Illinois, and Minnesota by
> a team of thirteen farm management advisory workers from six
> European countries.

Parks, W. Robert. SOIL CONSERVATION DISTRICTS IN ACTION. Ames: Iowa State College Press, 1952. 242p. illus., tables.
> A report on fifteen years' experience of the districts; intergovernmental relations examined. Described as an administrative device.

Robertson, Lynn S. FARM MANAGEMENT. Philadelphia: J. B. Lippincott, 1958. 445p. illus., tables, charts.
> Information on the farm as a business unit. Intended primarily for high-school students. Suggestions for further study and references at chapter ends.

Russell, Bruce. Farm Management. p. 732-55 In Friedman, Edith, J., ed. REAL ESTATE ENCYCLOPEDIA. Englewood Cliffs, N.J.: Prentice-Hall, 1960.

Russell, E. Walter. SOIL CONDITIONS AND PLANT GROWTH, 9th ed. London: Longmans, Green, 1961. 688p. illus., tables, charts.
> A comprehensive scientific treatise on soil as a medium for plant growth. Extensive references cited in footnotes. First edition, 1912, through seventh edition, 1937, by E. John Russell.

Stallings, J. H. SOIL CONSERVATION. Englewood Cliffs, N.J.: Prentice-Hall, 1957. 575p. illus., tables, charts, maps.
> Sections on the historical phases of soil erosion, fundamental conservation problems, practices, and planning. References at chapter ends.

Thompson, Louis M. SOILS AND SOIL FERTILITY, 2d ed. (McGraw-Hill Publications in the Agricultural Sciences). New York: McGraw-Hill, 1957. 451p. illus., tables, charts, diagrs., maps.
> Prepared as a text for introductory courses in soils for students of agriculture. References at chapter ends.

United Nations. Food and Agriculture Organization. METHODS OF FARM MANAGEMENT INVESTIGATIONS FOR IMPROVING FARM PRODUCTIVITY, by W. Y. Yang. (FAO Agricultural Development Paper No. 64). Rome: 1958. 228p. tables, charts. pap.
> Section 10: Land Tenure Problems--tenancy rent determination, land settlement. Introduces methods. Technical and non-technical discussions illustrating the nature and requirements of farm management research. Bibliography: p. 226-8.

NOTE: The first United States Census of Agriculture was taken in 1840. Thereafter, through 1950, each Decennial Census included a census of agriculture. Mid-Decennial Agricultural Census began in 1925. Agricultural Censuses are now conducted as of October for years ending in "4" and "9," the first such occurring in 1954. Censuses of Irrigation and Drainage occur in years ending in "9."

U.S. Bureau of the Census. 1954 CENSUS OF AGRICULTURE. Washington, D.C.: Government Printing Office, 1955-1957. 3 vols.

The 1957 CATALOG OF UNITED STATES CENSUS PUBLICA-
TIONS contains in the appendix a consolidated list of the
publications of the census.

Final Reports:
Vol. 1, COUNTIES AND STATE ECONOMIC AREAS.
33 pts. pap.
Vol. 2, GENERAL REPORT -- STATISTICS BY SUB-
JECTS. 1418 p. (also 13 separates. pap.)
Chap. 1: Farms and land in farms; Chap. 5:
Size of Farm; Chap. 11: Economic Class of
Farm; Chap. 12: Type of Farm;
Vol. 3, SPECIAL REPORTS. 12 pts. (Pt. 9 con-
sisting of 11 chapters).

Preliminary Reports AC54-1 and AC54-2 superseded by Vol. 1
(AC54-1: 3,075 multilithed repts.; AC54-2: 49
multilithed repts.; AC54-3: 5 multilithed repts.)

U.S. Bureau of the Census. 1954 CENSUS OF AGRICULTURE: FARM-MORT-
GAGE DEBT (A COOPERATIVE REPORT). (Special Reports, vol. III, pt. 5).
Washington, D.C.: Government Printing Office, 1956. 82p. tables. pap.
"Number of mortgaged farms, amount of debt, principal lending
agencies."

U.S. Bureau of the Census. 1954 CENSUS OF AGRICULTURE: FARM-MORT-
GAGE DEBT RISES WITH INCREASING FARM VALUE. (AC54-3 Series, no. 2).
Washington, D.C.: 1957. 8p. tables. pap. processed.
Cooperative report with the Agricultural Research Service, U.S.
Department of Agriculture. Amount of debt 1930-1956; amount
held by principal lenders, with average interest rates 1910-1956.

U.S. Bureau of the Census. 1959 CENSUS OF AGRICULTURE: Washington,
D.C.: Government Printing Office, 1960-2.
Vol. 1, COUNTIES. Consists of 54 separate reports. Data includes number and acreage of, farms, land use practices, farm
facilities. Supersedes PRELIMINARY REPORTS, series AC59-1
and AC59-2.

U.S. Bureau of the Census. IRRIGATION OF AGRICULTURAL LANDS (PRE-
LIMINARY). Washington, D.C.: 19 . 18 pts.
Data for seventeen states and a summary.

U.S. Department of Agriculture. AGRICULTURAL STATISTICS. Washington,
D.C.: Government Printing Office, 1936- . tables.
Taxes and values of farm real estate over a number of years.
Preceded by the Statistical Section of the YEARBOOK OF AGRI-
CULTURE. Issued biennially.

U.S. Department of Agriculture. THE FARM REAL ESTATE SITUATION.
(Circular Series). Washington, D.C.: Government Printing Office, 1926-
tables, charts, maps. pap.

Issued annually from 1926 to 1948-1949. Statistics on sales and
prices of farm lands. (1926-1927--Circular 13).

U.S. Department of Agriculture. FATHER-SON AGREEMENTS FOR OPERATING
FARMS. (Farmer's Bulletin no. 2179). Washington, D.C.: 1961. 18p. illus.
pap.
>Prepared by the Farm Economics Division, Economic Research
>Service, as a revision of Farmer's Bulletin no. 2026. Deals
>with farm-operating agreements only.

U.S. Department of Agriculture. FORM AD 564: ANNUAL SUPPLEMENT TO
THE FARM LEASE. Washington, D.C.: 1960.

U.S. Department of Agriculture. LAND; THE YEARBOOK OF AGRICULTURE,
1958. Washington, D.C.: Government Printing Office, 1958. 605p. Illus.,
tables, charts, maps.
>Sections written by various authors. A broad survey of the land
>of the United States, "its importance in our history and growth,
>the use and management of public and private lands, the income
>and valuation of land, resources and prospective needs, and
>emerging problems of ownership and control."

U.S. Department of Agriculture. SIZES OF FARMS IN THE UNITED STATES,
by Kenneth L. Bachman and Donald W. Jones. (Technical Bulletin no. 1019).
Washington, D.C.: Government Printing Office, 1950. 79p. tables, charts,
maps. pap. processed.
>Data on farm classification by economic units. Compiled with
>the co-operation of the U.S. Bureau of the Census. Bibliog-
>raphy: p. 78-9.

U.S. Department of Agriculture. SOIL; THE YEARBOOK OF AGRICULTURE,
1957. Washington, D.C.: Government Printing Office, 1957. 784p. illus.,
charts, diagrs., maps.
>Sections contributed by various authors. Soil management,
>classification, etc. Supplements the YEARBOOK OF AGRICUL-
>TURE, 1938. Glossary included.

U.S. Department of Agriculture. YOUR CASH FARM LEASE. (Miscellaneous
Publication no. 836). Washington, D.C.: 1961. 16p. forms. pap.

U.S. Department of Agriculture. YOUR CROP-SHARE-CASH FARM LEASE, by
Marshall Harris. (Miscellaneous Publication no. 838). Washington, D.C.:
1961. 16p. forms. pap.
>Gives a table for estimating rent and provides instructions for
>filling out U.S. Department of Agriculture form AD 561.

U.S. Department of Agriculture. YOUR FARM LEASE CHECKLIST, by Marie B.
Harmon and Marshall Harris. (Farmer's Bulletin no. 2163). Washington,
D.C.: Government Printing Office, 1961. 11p. pap.

U.S. Department of Agriculture. YOUR FARM LEASE CONTRACT, by Marshall
Harris and Howard L. Hill. (Farmer's Bulletin no. 2164). Washington, D.C.:
Government Printing Office, 1961. 20p. illus. pap.

Outlines functions of a good lease and discusses various provisions, such as property rights, improvements, shares.

U.S. Department of Agriculture. YOUR FARM RENT DETERMINATION PROBLEM, by Marshall Harris and Virgil Hurlburt. (Farmer's Bulletin no. 2162). Washington, D.C.: Government Printing Office, 1961. 23p. forms. pap.
Discusses the problems in and outlines procedures for determining a fair rental.

U.S. Department of Agriculture. YOUR LIVESTOCK-SHARE FARM LEASE, by Marshall Harris. (Miscellaneous Publication no. 837). Washington, D.C.: 1961. 16p. forms. pap.
Gives a table for estimating rent and provides instructions for filling out U.S. Department of Agriculture form AD 563.

U.S. Department of Agriculture. YOUR FARM RENTING PROBLEM, by Marshall Harris. (Farmer's Bulletin no. 2161). Washington, D.C.: Government Printing Office, 1961. 16p. pap.
Describes types of farm leases and their characteristics, other agreements, and stresses importance of good leasing practices.

U.S. Department of Agriculture. Agricultural Marketing Service. DIRECTORY OF STATE DEPARTMENTS OF AGRICULTURE, Rev. ed. Washington, D.C.: 1962. 50p. pap. processed.

U.S. Department of Agriculture. Agricultural Research Service. AGRICULTURAL FINANCE REVIEW. Washington, D.C.: Government Printing Office. tables. pap. processed.
Supplements to some volumes. Farm credit, farm insurance, farm taxation, farm real estate. Vol. 22, September, 1960--has Supplement dated July, 1961. Issued annually.

U.S. Department of Agriculture. Agricultural Research Service. THE TENURE STATUS OF FARMWORKERS IN THE UNITED STATES, by Frank H. Maier, et al. (USDA Technical Bulletin no. 1217). Washington, D.C.: 1960. 91p. tables, charts, maps. pap. (Sold by Government Printing Office).

U.S. Department of Agriculture. Conservation Needs Inventory Committee. BASIC STATISTICS OF THE NATIONAL INVENTORY OF SOIL AND WATER CONSERVATION NEEDS. (Statistical Bulletin 317). Washington, D.C.: Government Printing Office, 1962. 164p. tables, maps. pap. processed.

U.S. Department of Agriculture. Economic Research Service. FARM COSTS AND RETURNS: COMMERCIAL FARMS BY TYPE, SIZE, AND LOCATION. (Agriculture Information Bulletin no. 230). Washington, D.C.: tables, charts, maps. pap. processed.
Revised annually. Estimates on about thirty types of farms in major farming areas of the U.S. Size of farm and land use covered.

U.S. Department of Agriculture. Economic Research Service. FARM MORTGAGES RECORDED IN 1959; INTEREST RATES, TERMS, AND SIZES WITH HISTORICAL DATA, 1949-1959. (ERS--61). Washington, D.C.: 1962. 33p. tables. pap. processed.

U.S. Department of Agriculture. Economic Research Service. FARM REAL ESTATE TAXES. Washington, D.C.
>An annual report, giving amount of tax per acre and per $100.00 of full value, by years, by states and by geographical region.

U.S. Department of Agriculture. Economic Research Service. MAJOR USES OF LAND AND WATER IN THE UNITED STATES, WITH SPECIAL REFERENCE TO AGRICULTURE; SUMMARY FOR 1959. Washington, D.C.: 1962. 54p. tables, charts. pap. processed.
>Issued at five year intervals since 1910. "Brings together from the many available sources, Federal, state and private -- a summary account of the extent and distribution of the major agricultural land and water uses and a general analysis of the situation as of 1959 to 1961."

U.S. Farm Credit Administration. THE FEDERAL LAND BANK SYSTEM, HOW IT OPERATES. (Circular 35). Washington, D.C.: Government Printing Office, 1957. 18p. illus., map. pap.

U.S. Geological Survey. METHODS OF MEASURING SOIL MOISTURE IN THE FIELD, by A. I. Johnson. (Geological Survey Water-Supply Paper 1619-U). Washington, D.C.: Government Printing Office, 1962. 25p. illus. pap.
>Subtitle: EVALUATES METHODS FOR MEASURING SOIL MOIS-TURE AND DESCRIBES THE EQUIPMENT USED. Bibliography: p. 15-25.

U.S. Soil Conservation Service. ESTABLISHED AND TENTATIVE SOIL SERIES OF THE UNITED STATES. Washington, D.C.: 1961. 46p. pap.
>An alphabetical list of the series by place name, with one of five regions indicated for each.

U.S. Soil Conservation Service. LAND-CAPABILITY CLASSIFICATION, by A. A. Klingebiel and P. H. Montgomery. (Agriculture Handbook no. 210). Washington, D.C.: Government Printing Office, 1962. 21p. pap.
>Establishes relationship of soil mapping units and capability units. A grouping of soils and definitions of the classes and subclasses; an introduction to the soil map for farmers and other land users developing conservation plans.

Virginia Polytechnic Institute. Agricultural Extension Service. EQUITABLE FARM LEASES, by W. L. Gibson, Jr. and K. E. Loope. (Bulletin 254). Blacksburg, Va.: 1959. 18p. tables. pap.
>Prepared in co-operation with the U.S. Department of Agricul-ture. Suggests methods for determining the fairness of a given cash-rent or share-rent base. (Southeast Land Tenure Committee Publication no. 31).

Virginia Polytechnic Institute. Agricultural Experiment Station. FARMING AS A PART OWNER, by R. S. Crickenberger, and W. L. Gibson, Jr. (Bulletin 504). Blacksburg, Va.: 1959. 42p. tables. pap.
>Explores the possibility of part ownership of real property as a solution to an individual's limitation of capital. (Southeast Land Tenure Research Committee Publication no. 34).

Virginia Polytechnic Institute. Agricultural Experiment Station. VIRGINIA FARM LEASE GUIDE, by W. L. Gibson, Jr., et al. (Bulletin 491). Blacksburg, Va.: 1958. 23p. pap.
> Prepared in co-operation with the University of Virginia School of Law and the U.S. Department of Agriculture, Agricultural Research Service. Presented as an aid to formulating contracts in written form. (Southeast Land Tenure Committee Publication no. 30).

Wallace, James J. and Beneke, Raymond R. MANAGING THE TENANT-OPERATED FARM, 2d ed. Ames: Iowa State College Press, 1960. 280p. illus., tables, charts, forms.
> An approach to the technical problems of farming from the position of the farm manager. Includes chapters on leasing, record keeping, and planning. Written for teachers, students, investors, and any who serve in an advisory capacity to farm owners and tenants.

Washington State University. Agricultural Experiment Stations. FARM ADJUSTMENTS ON LEASED LAND...COLUMBIA BASIN PROJECT, by B. D. Parrish and Earl R. Franklin. (Bulletin 620). Pullman, Wash.: 1960. 22p. tables. pap.
> An analysis of leasing experience.

Weir, Robert H. ADVANTAGES IN TAXES. Chicago: National Institute of Farm Brokers, 1960. various paging.
> Supplements issued periodically. (Extension revision scheduled for 1963).

Wisconsin. University. Agricultural Experiment Station. A MODIFICATION OF LEASING ARRANGEMENTS TO EXPAND FARM OPPORTUNITIES, by Howard L. Hill and Sydney D. Staniforth. (Research Bulletin 213). Madison: 1959. 23p. tables. pap.
> Suggests the possibility of lowering capital requirement for tenant and adjusting basis of sharing.

Farm Property—Bibliographies

AGRICULTURAL INDEX. H. W. Wilson Co., 950 University Avenue, New York, zone 52. 1916- .
> Published monthly except September; cumulations issued. Includes periodicals, books, agricultural experiment station and extension service publications. Federal and state government documents, Food and Agriculture Organization reports.

BIBLIOGRAPHY OF AGRICULTURE. Washington, D.C.: U.S. National Agricultural Library, 1942- . (Sold by Government Printing Office).
> A monthly index of publications on agriculture and related sub-

jects received in the National Agricultural Library. Lists approximately 100,000 items annually. Subtitle: A LIST OF RECENT U.S.D.A. PUBLICATIONS, STATE AGRICULTURAL EXPERIMENT STATION PUBLICATIONS, AGRICULTURAL EXTENSION SERVICE PUBLICATIONS, F.A.O. PUBLICATIONS, AND AUTHOR INDEX.

Denman, D. R., et al. BIBLIOGRAPHY OF RURAL LAND ECONOMY AND LAND OWNERSHIP, 1900--1957. Cambridge, England: Department of Estate Management, Cambridge University, 1958. 412p.
      Coverage of the British Isles full; coverage of the United States
      selective.

U.S. Department of Agriculture. FARM TENANCY IN THE UNITED STATES, 1940-1945; A LIST OF REFERENCES, by A. M. Hannay. (Library List no. 2, rev.). Washington, D.C.: 1946. 84p. pap.

U.S. Department of Agriculture. LIST OF AVAILABLE PUBLICATIONS, comp. by Eleanor W. Clay and Ella J. Green. (List no. 11). Washington, D.C.: Government Printing Office, 1962. 104p.
      Department publications available as of September 1, 1961;
      classified arrangement, indexed.

U.S. Department of Agriculture. MAJOR STATISTICAL SERIES OF THE U.S. DEPARTMENT OF AGRICULTURE: HOW THEY ARE CONSTRUCTED AND USED; VOLUME 6--LAND VALUES AND FARM FINANCE. (Agriculture Handbook no. 118). Washington, D.C.: Government Printing Office, 1957. 56p. tables. pap.

U.S. Department of Agriculture. Agricultural Economics. PERIODIC REPORTS OF AGRICULTURAL ECONOMICS, ECONOMIC RESEARCH SERVICE, STATISTICAL REPORTING SERVICE. Washington, D.C.: 1962. 15p. pap. processed.

U.S. Department of Agriculture. Agricultural Research Service. ABSTRACTS OF RECENT PUBLISHED MATERIAL ON SOIL AND WATER CONSERVATION, by Charles B. Crook. Washington, D.C.: 1949- . tables, pap. processed.
      Issued at irregular intervals. No. 22 dated May, 1962. Soil
      and Water Conservation Research Division.

U.S. Department of Agriculture. Agricultural Research Service. FARM ECONOMICS PUBLICATIONS CURRENTLY AVAILABLE. Washington, D.C.: 1958. 44p. pap. processed.
      Includes list of charts and maps.

U.S. Department of Agriculture. Economic Research Service. Farm Economics Division. AGRICULTURAL RENTS IN THEORY AND PRACTICE; AN ANNOTATED BIBLIOGRAPHY, comp. by Carey B. Singleton, Jr. (Miscellaneous Publication 901). Washington, D.C.: Government Printing Office, 1960. 81p. pap. processed.
      Specific material on the United States and Great Britain. 368
      references; author index.

Farm Property—Periodicals
(See Appendix for complete information concerning these publications.)

Agricultural letters form the various Federal Reserve Banks. FARM COST SIT-
UATION. FARM INDEX. FARM MORTGAGE LENDING EXPERIENCE. FARM
REAL ESTATE DEBT. FARM REAL ESTATE MARKET DEVELOPMENTS. JOURNAL
OF FARM ECONOMICS. JOURNAL OF THE AMERICAN SOCIETY OF FARM
MANAGERS AND RURAL APPRAISERS. REAL ESTATE ANALYST AGRICULTURAL
BULLETIN. RURAL REALTOR. SOIL CONSERVATION.

Section 19

GOVERNMENT REAL ESTATE

National Institute of Real Estate Brokers. REALTORS' DIRECTORY OF FEDERAL
REAL ESTATE ACTIVITIES, prepared by Office of War Information at the
Request of Realtors' Washington Committee. Chicago: 1943. 61p. pap.
processed.
    On cover: Organization, Functions, Officers and Addresses.

U. S. Commission on Organization of the Executive Branch of the Government
(1955). REAL PROPERTY MANAGEMENT; A REPORT TO THE CONGRESS,
June 1955, Washington, D.C.: Government Printing Office, 1955. 53p. pap.

U. S. Congress. House. Committee on Government Operations. REAL
AND PERSONAL PROPERTY INVENTORY REPORT (CIVILIAN AND MILITARY)
OF THE UNITED STATES GOVERNMENT LOCATED IN THE CONTINENTAL
UNITED STATES, IN THE TERRITORIES, AND OVERSEAS, AS OF JUNE 30..
INTERMEDIATE REPORT OF THE....Washington, D. C.: Government Printing
Office. tables, pap.
    Issued annually.

U. S. Congress. House. Committee on Public Works. PUBLIC BUILDINGS
PROGRAM; HEARINGS BEFORE THE SUBCOMMITTEE ON PUBLIC BUILDINGS
AND GROUNDS, ON H. R. 4660, and H. R. 6993. Washington, D.C.:
Government Printing Office, 1957. 234p. tables, pap.
    The lease-purchase program.

U. S. Congress. Senate. Committee on Public Works. AMENDING THE
LEASE-PURCHASE ACTS REPORT. 85th CONGRESS, 1st SESSION, (Senate
Report no. 540), Washington, D. C.: Government Printing Office, 1957.
28p. tables. pap.
    To accompany S.2261.

U. S. General Services Administration. INVENTORY REPORT ON REAL
PROPERTY OWNED BY THE UNITED STATES THROUGHOUT THE WORLD, AS
OF JUNE 30... Washington, D. C.: Government Printing Office. tables,
pap.
    Issued annually.

U. S. Library of Congress. Legislative Reference Service. SURVEY OF NA-
TIONAL POLICIES ON FEDERAL LAND OWNERSHIP, WITH SPECIAL REFER-
ENCE TO STUDIES PRODUCED BY COMMITTEES OF THE CONGRESS OR
COMMISSIONS OF THE EXECUTIVE BRANCH OF THE FEDERAL GOVERNMENT,
85th CONG., 1st SESS., by John Kerr Rose. (Senate Document no. 56),
Washington, D.C.: Government Printing Office, 1957. 44p. pap.

U. S. Post Office Department. CONSTRUCTION REQUIREMENTS FOR LEASED POSTAL FACILITIES; BIDDERS' INSTRUCTIONS. Washington, D.C.: 1959. 27p. pap. processed.

U. S. Post Office Department. LEASE-PURCHASE PROCEDURES AND DOCUMENTS; TITLE 2, PUBLIC LAW 519, 83rd CONGRESS. (POD Publication No. 12). Washington, D.C.: 1956. 64p. pap. processed.

Wallace, Karl E. "Selling and Leasing Real Estate to the Government." p. 126-31 In National Real Estate Investor. NATIONAL REAL ESTATE HANDBOOK AND DIRECTORY. New York: 1962.

Section 20

INDUSTRIAL PROPERTY

American Standards Association. AMERICAN STANDARD METHODS OF DETER-
MINING AREAS IN INDUSTRIAL BUILDINGS. (Z 65.5--1962). New York:
1962. 4p. pap.
     Concerns the computation of floor space.

Architectural Record. BUILDINGS FOR INDUSTRY. New York: F. W. Dodge,
1957. 309p. illus., charts, diagr., plans.
     A successor to INDUSTRIAL BUILDING. All material reprinted
     from ARCHITECTURAL RECORD. Section 1: Design principles;
     Section 2: Warehousing.

Architectural Record. INDUSTRIAL BUILDINGS; THE ARCHITECTURAL RECORD
OF A DECADE, comp. by Kenneth Reid. New York: F. W. Dodge, 1951.
541p. illus., plans.
     A collection of articles that appeared in the ARCHITECTURAL
     RECORD from 1940 to 1949. Bibliography: p. 509.

Bredo, William. INDUSTRIAL ESTATES; TOOL FOR INDUSTRIALIZATION.
(Stanford Research Institute International Industrial Development Center
Publication). Glencoe, Ill.: Free Press, 1960. 240p. illus.
     Industrial districts in several countries described and compared.

Bryce, Murray D. INDUSTRIAL DEVELOPMENT; A GUIDE FOR ACCELERATING
ECONOMIC GROWTH. New York: McGraw-Hill, 1960. 282p. forms.

California. University. Extension Division. WORKBOOK AND SYLLABUS FOR
COMMERCIAL AND INVESTMENT PROPERTIES X 492 AB, PRESENTED BY THE
REAL ESTATE CERTIFICATE PROGRAM--BUSINESS ADMINSTRATION. Los
Angeles: 1959. 107p. tables. pap. processed.

Chamber of Commerce of the United States. THE COMMUNITY INDUSTRIAL
DEVELOPMENT SURVEY; THE FIRST STEP IN A COMMUNITY INDUSTRIAL
EXPANSION PROGRAM. Washington, D.C.: no date. 16p. pap.
     Topical outline for an industrial survey, sources of survey
     information, and some helpful references.

Chamber of Commerce of the United States. SOURCES OF STATE INFORMATION
AND STATE INDUSTRIAL DIRECTORIES. Washington, D.C.: 1958. 18p.
pap.

Chamber of Commerce of the United States. WHAT NEW INDUSTRIAL JOBS
MEAN TO A COMMUNITY. Washington, D.C.: 1954. 12p. pap.

Dunham, Clarence Whiting. PLANNING INDUSTRIAL STRUCTURES, lst ed. New York: McGraw-Hill, 1948. 481p. illus.

Florence, P. Sargant and Baldamus, W. INVESTMENT, LOCATION, AND SIZE OF PLANT; A REALISTIC INQUIRY INTO THE STRUCTURE OF BRITISH AND AMER-ICAN INDUSTRIES. (National Institute of Economic and Social Research Economic and Social Studies no. 7). Cambridge: Cambridge University Press, 1948. 211p. tables.

Garrabrant, Robert B. Performance Standards for Industrial Zoning; An Appraisal. URBAN LAND NEWS AND TRENDS, vol. 15, no. 6, June, 1956, p. 3-6.

Greenhut, Melvin L. PLANT LOCATION IN THEORY AND IN PRACTICE; THE ECONOMICS OF SPACE. Chapel Hill, N.C.: University of North Carolina Press, 1956. 338p. tables, diagrs.

Industrial Development. AREA DEVELOPMENT; A GUIDE FOR COMMUNITY LEADERS. Atlanta, Ga.: Conway Publishing Co., 1960.
Chapter 9: Sources of Information.

Industrial Firms with Real Estate Departments. p. 96 In National Real Estate Investor. DIRECTORY. New York: 1961.
Firm names and addresses in an alphabetical arrangement; names of official concerned with real estate included in most instances.

Kitagawa, Evelyn M. and Bogue, Donald M. SUBURBANIZATION OF MANU-FACTURING ACTIVITY WITHIN STANDARD METROPOLITAN AREAS. Oxford, Ohio: Scripps Foundation for Research in Population Problems, Miami University, and Population Research and Training Center, University of Chicago, 1955. 162p.

Liggett, Donald R. SMALL INDUSTRY DEVELOPMENT ORGANIZATIONS; A WORLDWIDE DIRECTORY. (Stanford Research Institute, International Industrial Development Center Publication). Glencoe, Ill.: Free Press, 1959. 137p.
List of organizations "engaged in development work or in research on small industry problems;" arranged by country. Governmental, private, financial, and educational agencies and institutions included.

(List of State Planning and Development Agencies, with addresses and names of chief official.) In BOOK OF THE STATES. Chicago: Council of State Governments.
Biennial. Shown in Supplement 2: Administrative Officials Classified by Functions.

Madigan, Jerome J. Manufactured Homes: The New Growth Industry. p. 140-2 In National Real Estate Investor. NATIONAL REAL ESTATE HANDBOOK AND DIRECTORY. New York: 1962.

McMannon, George M. FACTORS AND PROCESSES OF INDUSTRIAL SITE SELECTION. Unpublished Ph. D. thesis, Syracuse University, 1958.

Munce, James F. INDUSTRIAL ARCHITECTURE; AN ANALYSIS OF INTERNATIONAL BUILDING PRACTICE. New York: F. W. Dodge, 1960. 232p. illus., diagrs., plans.

> Analyzes the modern factory for four basic industry types: heavy, light, utility, and process. Practices in the United States, Great Britain, and Germany emphasized. Includes a chapter on industrial parks.

National Association of Real Estate Boards. Industrial Property Divison. IDEA SERVICES, 1927-1930. Chicago: 1927-1930. processed. looseleaf.

National Association of Real Estate Boards. Industrial Property Division. INDUSTRIAL REAL ESTATE; THE ADDRESSES AND DISCUSSIONS AT THE THIRD ANNUAL FALL CONFERENCE...OCTOBER 27-28, 1930. Chicago: 1930. 74p. pap. processed.

1961 Industrial Plant Design Survey. POWER, vol. 104, no. 10, October 1961, p. 85-108.

> Steam generation, electric distribution, and air conditioning features of newly completed or modernized industrial plants and commercial buildings.

Owen, LeRoy D. INDUSTRIAL REAL ESTATE. Los Angeles: State Real Estate Institute of the California Real Estate Association at University of Southern California, 1936. 25p. tables. pap.

Plant Engineering. PLANT ENGINEERING PRACTICE. New York: F. W. Dodge, 1958. 694p. illus., tables, charts, diagrs., forms, plans.

> Published in co-operation with the Technical Publishing Company. "A compilation of carefully selected articles that appeared in PLANT ENGINEERING magazine." Includes sections on sites and layouts and on construction.

The Plant, The Office, and The City. TAX POLICY. vol. 22, no. 8-9, August-September 1955; vol. 23, no. 2-3, February-March 1956; vol. 24, no. 9-10, September-October 1957.

> Part 1: Industrial Location Trends and Factors; Part 2: Industrial Location Impacts; Part 3: Trends in Office Location.

Protecting Future Industrial Sites; Industrial Council Studies Growth Problems in Alameda County, California. URBAN LAND NEWS AND TRENDS, vol. 16, April 1957, p. 1-5.

Sales Management. DIRECTORY OF KEY PLANTS, ACCOUNTING FOR HALF OF ALL VALUE ADDED IN U. S. MANUFACTURING; ALL PLANTS WITH 500 OR MORE EMPLOYEES. New York: 1960. various paging. pap. processed.

Shubin, John A. and Madeheim, Huxley. PLANT LAYOUT; DEVELOPING AND IMPROVING MANUFACTURING PLANTS. New York: Prentice-Hall, 1951. 433p. illus., tables, charts, diagrs., plans.

> Deals with principles, techniques, and procedures of selection and layout of industrial plant facilities.

Simmons-Boardman Publishing Corp. PLANT LOCATION. New York: 1959- .

illus., tables, maps.
> Annual. Data to assist industrialists in selecting locations.
> Marketing, transportation, tax and labor laws, finance informa-
> tion for each state. Community appraisal guide checklist. Lists
> state development agencies.

Society of Industrial Realtors. THE DEVELOPMENT OF INDUSTRIAL DISTRICTS;
A PANEL REPORT, ed. by Earle Palmer Brown. Washington, D.C.: 1949.
45p. illus. pap.
> A collection of six papers on land acquisition, financing, con-
> struction, promotion, and transportation considerations.

Society of Industrial Realtors. EVALUATING INDUSTRIAL REAL ESTATE.
Washington, D.C.: 1953. 136p. illus., tables. pap.
> Papers and discussions presented at a conference held in Chicago,
> September 1952. Three demonstration appraisals included.

Society of Industrial Realtors. HOW FEDERAL TAXES AFFECT INDUSTRIAL
REAL ESTATE: DEPRECIATION, CAPITAL GAINS AND LOSSES. Washington,
D.C.: 1952. 43p. pap.
> Developed from a one-day Federal Tax Study, held in Chicago,
> May 1952.

Society of Industrial Realtors. INDUSTRIAL REAL ESTATE LECTURES, PREPARED
FOR RE-11--A COURSE IN INDUSTRIAL REAL ESTATE SPONSORED BY BOSTON
UNIVERSITY AND THE NEW ENGLAND CHAPTER, SOCIETY OF INDUSTRIAL
REALTORS, 2 vols. Washington, D.C.: 1948. pap. processed.

Society of Industrial Realtors. MARKETING WAREHOUSE PROPERTIES; SELLING
INDUSTRIAL REAL ESTATE. Washington, D.C.: 1952. 31p. pap.
> Papers and discussion on air freight, rail, and truck terminals;
> listing, advertising, and financing of industrial property.
> Transcribed at meeting in Cincinnati, November 1951.

Society of Industrial Realtors. PRINCIPLES AND PRACTICES OF INDUSTRIAL
REAL ESTATE; A COURSE SYLLABUS, by William M. Shenkel. Washington,
D.C.: 1963. 139p. pap. processed.

Society of Industrial Realtors. THE 1959 STORY: FINANCING INDUSTRIAL
PROPERTY; A SPECIAL REPORT FOR MEMBERS, COMPILED BY THE SOCIETY'S
MORTGAGE AND FINANCE COMMITTEE. Washington, D.C.: 1959. 48p.
pap.
> Results of a survey of mortgage money sources, including insur-
> ance companies, pension funds, college and university endowment
> funds. Geographical arrangement.

Society of Industrial Realtors. (PAPERS PRESENTED AT THE NATIONAL CON-
FERENCE ON INDUSTRIAL REAL ESTATE, JULY 10-11, 1941.) Washington,
D.C.: 1941. 68p. pap. processed.

Society of Industrial Realtors. REPORT TO THE MEMBERSHIP. Washington,
D.C.: 1944, 1947. various paging. pap. processed.

Society of Industrial Realtors and National Association of Real Estate Boards.
Division of Research. INDUSTRIAL PROPERTY STUDY. Washington, D.C.:
1956. 10p. tables. pap. processed.
> Report on sales and leases of industrial buildings and sites
> throughout the United States for 1955 and first quarter of 1956.

Survey of State Industrial Directories. SALES MANAGEMENT, vol. 87, no.
11, November 10, 1961, p. 70-3.

Tennessee. University. Bureau of Public Administration. INDUSTRIAL SITES,
A COMMUNITY PROBLEM, by Charles M. Stephenson. Knoxville: 1961.
19p. pap.
> Describes programs in ten communities.

Thompson, Wilbur R. and Mattila, John M. AN ECONOMETRIC MODEL OF
POSTWAR STATE INDUSTRIAL DEVELOPMENT. Detroit: Wayne State University,
1959. 116p. tables, maps.
> Presents a method of forecasting industrial development at the
> state level.

U. S. Department of Commerce. Area Development Division. BASIC INDUS-
TRIAL LOCATION FACTORS; GUIDE FOR EVALUATING AN AREA'S RESOURCES
FOR INDUSTRIAL DEVELOPMENT, Rev. ed. Washington, D.C.: Government
Printing Office, 1947. 18p. charts. pap.

U. S. Department of Commerce. Office of Area Development. COMMUNITIES
WITH LOCALLY FINANCED INDUSTRIAL DEVELOPMENT ORGANIZATIONS.
Washington, D.C.: 1958. 45p. pap.

U. S. Department of Commerce. Office of Area Development. DATA SOURCES
FOR PLANT LOCATION ANALYSIS. Washington, D.C.: 1959. 42p. (Sold
by Government Printing Office).
> Appendices: state economic development agencies, state water
> agencies, state employment security agencies, state tax departments,
> railroad industrial departments and field offices of the U. S.
> Department of Commerce.

U. S. Department of Commerce. Office of Technical Services. ORGANIZED
INDUSTRIAL DISTRICTS; A TOOL FOR COMMUNITY DEVELOPMENT, by
Theodore K. Pasma. Washington, D.C.: Government Printing Office, 1954.
109p. illus.
> Deals with the establishment of planned industrial areas that are
> the counterpart of residential subdivisions. Includes case
> histories of successful districts. Bibliography: p. 108-9.

Urban Land Institute. THE COMMUNITY AND INDUSTRIAL DEVELOPMENT,
by Robert B. Garrabrant. (Technical Bulletin no. 21). Washington, D.C.:
1953. 16p. pap.

Urban Land Institute. INDUSTRIAL DISTRICTS RESTUDIED; AN ANALYSIS OF
CHARACTERISTICS, by Robert E. Boley. (Technical Bulletin no. 41). Washington, D.C.: 1961. 77p. illus. pap.
> Includes a selected bibliography.

Urban Land Institute. PLANNED INDUSTRIAL DISTRICTS; THEIR ORGANIZA-
TION AND DEVELOPMENT, ed. by Milburn L. Forth and J. Ross McKeever.
(Technical Bulletin no. 19). Washington, D.C.: 1952. 55p. illus. pap.

Urban Land Institute. THE PROHIBITION OF RESIDENTIAL DEVELOPMENTS IN
INDUSTRIAL DISTRICTS, by Seward H. Mott and Max S. Wehrly. (Technical
Bulletin no. 10). Washington, D.C.: 1948. 7p. pap.

Urban Land Institute. REDEVELOPMENT FOR INDUSTRIAL USE, by Robert B.
Garrabrant. (Technical Bulletin no. 25). Washington, D.C.: 1954. 32p.
illus., tables. pap.

Urban Land Institute. SPACE FOR INDUSTRY; AN ANALYSIS OF SITE AND
LOCATION REQUIREMENTS FOR MODERN MANUFACTURE, by Dorothy A.
Muncy. (Technical Bulletin no. 23). Washington, D.C.: 1954. 40p.
tables, charts. pap.

Urban Land Institute. WATER FOR INDUSTRY; A REVIEW OF WATER RESOURCES
AFFECTING INDUSTRIAL LOCATION. (Technical Bulletin no. 17). Washington, D.C.: 1951. charts, maps. pap.

Weber, Alfred. THEORY OF THE LOCATION OF INDUSTRIES. Translated
with an Introduction and Notes by Carl J. Friedrich. Chicago: University
of Chicago Press, 1929. 256p. diagrs.

West Virginia University. Bureau of Business Research. METHODS OF
PLANT SITE SELECTION AVAILABLE TO SMALL MANUFACTURING FIRMS,
by James H. Thompson. (Small Business Management Research Reports).
Morgantown: 1961. 151p. tables. pap.
    Prepared under the Small Business Administration Management
    Research, Grant Program. Includes a community check list
    and the questionnaire used in case studies for this project.

Wisconsin. University. Bureau of Business Research and Service. INDUS-
TRIAL LOCATION WITHIN THE URBAN AREA; A CASE STUDY OF THE
LOCATIONAL CHARACTERISTICS OF 905 MANUFACTURING PLANTS IN
MILWAUKEE COUNTY, by Norbert J. Stefaniak. (Wisconsin Commerce Reports,
vol. 6, no. 5, August 1962). Madison: 1962. 121p. tables, maps. pap.

Yaseen, Leonard C. PLANT LOCATION. Roslyn, N.Y.: Business Reports,
1952. 149p. tables, charts, maps. looseleaf. processed.
    Republished in 1956 in book form with new statistics and minor
    revisions of text by American Research Council, Inc., New York.
    226p. Includes "Hints for Industrial Development Groups."
    Practical. The author is the Senior Partner of Fantus Factory
    Locating Service.

Industrial Property—Bibliographies

California. University. Real Estate Research Program. INDUSTRIAL LOCA-
TION BIBLIOGRAPHY. Los Angeles: 1959. 82p. pap. processed.

Industrial Property—Bibliographies (continued)

Committee of Planning Librarians. PLANNED INDUSTRIAL DISTRICTS. (Exchange Bibliography no. 17). Oakland, Calif.: 6318 Thornhill Drive, zone 11, 1961. 15p. pap. processed.
    234 references; no annotations.

McDonald, Douglas Moore. A SELECT BIBLIOGRAPHY ON THE LOCATION OF INDUSTRY. (Social Science Research Bulletin no. 2). Montreal: McGill University, 1937. 82p. pap. processed.
    Canada, Great Britain, and the United States.

Syracuse. University. Business Research Center. A SURVEY OF THE LITERATURE ON INDUSTRIAL LOCATION. Syracuse, N.Y.: 1959. 111p.

Tax Foundation. FACTORS AFFECTING INDUSTRIAL LOCATION, A BIBLIOGRAPHY; SELECTED REFERENCES RELATING TO TAXES AND OTHER FACTORS AFFECTING THE CHOICE OF LOCATION BY INDUSTRY. New York: 1956. 8p. pap. processed.

U. S. Department of Commerce. Office of Area Development. SELECTED SOURCES ON PLANNED INDUSTRIAL PARKS. (An Area Development Aid; Industrial Location Series no. 1). Washington, D.C.: Government Printing Office, no date. 2p. pap.
    43 references, dated from 1944 to 1957.

Industrial Property—Periodicals

(See Appendix for complete information concerning these publications.)

AREA REDEVELOPMENT. INDUSTRIAL DEVELOPMENT AND MANUFACTURERS RECORD. INDUSTRIAL PROPERTY GUIDE. SOCIETY OF INDUSTRIAL REALTORS NEWSLETTER.

Section 21

NATURAL RESOURCES

Continental Oil Company. Denver Legal Staff. LANDMAN'S LEGAL HAND-
BOOK; A PRACTICAL GUIDE IN LEASING FOR OIL AND GAS, by A. T.
Smith et al. Denver: F. H. Gower, 2240 Mile High Center, 1957. 194p.
forms.
> "The legal aspects of land work in layman's language."

Falk, Harry W., Jr. TIMBER AND FOREST PRODUCTS LAW. Berkeley, Calif.:
Howell-North Press, 1958. 365p.

LAND AND WATER: PLANNING FOR ECONOMIC GROWTH, by Harold L.
Amoss and Roma K. McNickle. (Western Resources Papers, 1961). Boulder:
University of Colorado Press, 1962.
> Papers from third annual Western Resources Conference sponsored
> jointly by the Colorado School of Mines, Colorado State Univer-
> sity and the University of Colorado. Rapid urbanization and the
> competition for the use of land and water make necessary ade-
> quate planning for their use to ensure economic and orderly de-
> velopment.

National Institute for Petroleum Landmen. PROCEEDINGS, 1959. Albany,
N.Y.: Matthew Bender and Co., 1960.
> Oil and gas leases.

River Basin Development. LAW AND CONTEMPORARY PROBLEMS, vol. 22, no.
2. Spring, 1957. (entire issue).
> A Perspective, Some Engineering Aspects, the Economic Dy-
> namics, the Social Consequences, the Evaluation, the Politics,
> Basic Water Rights, Doctrines and their Implications, A Model
> State Water Code for River Basin Development.

WATER LAW AND POLICY IN THE SOUTHEAST; PAPERS PREPARED FOR PRESENTA-
TION AT THE SOUTHEASTERN WATER LAW CONFERENCE. Athens: Institute of
Law and Government, University of Georgia, 1962. 328p. pap. processed.
> Published in cooperation with the Farm Foundation and the
> Southeastern Land Tenure Research Committee.

Hoffman, Lewis Edwin. OIL AND GAS LEASING ON FEDERAL LANDS, 1st
rev. Denver: F. H. Gower, 2240 Mile High Center, 1957. 597p. forms.
> Traces "mineral leasing on the public lands and the submerged

lands of the outer continental shelf -", beginning with the
original leasing act of 1920. A discussion of laws, regulations,
and procedures, written by an official of the Bureau of Land
Management for the general reader.

U. S. Congress. Senate. Committee on Interior and Insular Affairs. RECORD-
ING OF FEDERAL OIL LEASES; HEARING BEFORE THE SUBCOMMITTEE ON
PUBLIC LANDS, 87th CONG., 2d SESS. ON S. 413. Washington, D.C.:
Government Printing Office, 1962. 41p. pap.
    A bill to amend the Mineral Leasing Act of 1920 in order to
    provide for the public records of oil and gas leases issued un-
    der such act and other instruments affecting title to such leases,
    and for other purposes.

U. S. Congress. Senate. Committee on Interior and Insular Affairs. MINERAL
LEASING REVENUES; HEARING BEFORE THE SUBCOMMITTEE ON PUBLIC
LANDS, 87th CONG., 2d SESS. ON S. 898. Washington, D.C.: Govern-
ment Printing Office, 1962. 33p. tables, charts. pap.
    A bill to amend Section 35 of the Mineral Leasing Act of 1920
    with respect to the disposition of the proceeds of sales, bonus-
    es, royalties and rentals under such act. May 15, 1962.

U. S. Department of Agriculture. LAND AND WATER RESOURCES; A POLICY
GUIDE. Washington, D.C.: Government Printing Office, 1962. 73p. tables,
charts. pap.
    Issued in May, 1962, slightly revised in September, 1962.
    Prepared by the Department's Land and Water Policy Commit-
    tee. An analysis of land and water problems of the United
    states and recommended policies and programs.

U. S. General Accounting Office. REVIEW OF SUPERVISION OF OIL AND
GAS OPERATIONS AND PRODUCTION ON GOVERNMENT AND INDIAN
LANDS, NOVEMBER 1958; REPORT TO THE CONGRESS OF THE UNITED
STATES BY THE COMPTROLLER GENERAL OF THE UNITED STATES. Wash-
ington, D.C.: 1959. 52p. tables. pap. processed.

U. S. President's Water Resources Council. POLICIES, STANDARDS, AND
PROCEDURES IN THE FORMULATION, EVALUATION, AND REVIEW OF
PLANS FOR USE AND DEVELOPMENT OF WATER AND RELATED LAND
RESOURCES. 87th CONG., 2D SESS. (Senate Document no. 97). Washing-
ton, D.C.: Government Printing Office, 1962. 13p. pap.

Section 22

PUBLIC LANDS

Calef, Wesley. PUBLIC GRAZING AND PUBLIC LANDS; STUDIES OF THE LAND MANAGEMENT OF THE TAYLOR GRAZING ACT. Chicago: University of Chicago Press, 1960. 292p. illus., tables, maps.
"The use and management of one class of western Federal public lands."

Carstensen, Vernon, ed. THE PUBLIC LANDS; STUDIES IN THE HISTORY OF THE PUBLIC DOMAIN. Madison: University of Wisconsin Press, 1963. 522p. tables, charts.
A collection of journal articles and seven appendices.

Clawson, Marion and Held, Burnell. THE FEDERAL LANDS: THEIR USE AND MANAGEMENT. Baltimore: Johns Hopkins Press, 1957. 501p. illus., tables, charts.
Published for Resources for the Future, Inc. Discusses the various nonurban lands held by the Federal government for purposes of management of natural resources--parks, forests, grazing districts, etc.

Food and Agriculture Organization. PUBLIC LANDS, by Andrew W. Ashby. (FAO Land Tenure Study). Rome: 1956. 47p. pap.
Discusses origins of public land ownership, types of public lands, and land policies. Bibliography: p. 46-7.

Foss, Phillip O. POLITICS AND GRASS; THE ADMINISTRATION OF GRAZING ON THE PUBLIC DOMAIN. Seattle: University of Washington Press, 1960. 236p. tables.
"History of the public domain and goes on to a more detailed examination of the formation and administration of public policy for the control and regulation of the Federal range under the Taylor Grazing Act."

Hibbard, Benjamin Horace. A HISTORY OF THE PUBLIC LAND POLICIES. (Land Economics Series). New York: Macmillan, 1924. 591p. tables, maps, charts.

Robbins, Roy M. OUR LANDED HERITAGE: THE PUBLIC DO,MAIN, 1776-1936. Princeton, N.J.: Princeton University Press, 1942. 450p. illus., tables, chart, maps.

U. S. Bureau of Land Management. ANNUAL REPORT OF THE DIRECTOR FOR THE FISCAL YEAR ENDED JUNE 30 .... Washington, D.C.: Government

Printing Office, 1947–
Issued as a section of the ANNUAL REPORT of the Secretary of
the Interior and separately. STATISTICAL APPENDIX to the
REPORT also issued.

U. S. Bureau of Land Management. GRAZING LAND POLICIES IN THE
UNITED STATES; A STUDY AND EVALUATION OF THE POLICIES, PRACTICES,
PROCEDURES AND VALUES PERTAINING TO GRAZING LANDS UNDER THE
CONTROL OF TEN WESTERN STATES, by Murray E. Morgan. Washington,
D.C.: 1961. 37p. Appendix. tables. pap. processed.
Includes leasing rate structures.

U. S. Bureau of Land Management. HISTORICAL HIGHLIGHTS OF PUBLIC
LAND MANAGEMENT. Washington, D.C.: Government Printing Office,
1962. 91p. pap.
A chronology from 1498 to 1962, with place name and subject
indexes.

U. S. Bureau of Land Management. THE HOMESTEAD LAW; A BRIEF SKETCH
IN UNITED STATES HISTORY. Washington D.C.: Government Printing Office,
1962. n.p. pap.
At head of title: 1862–1962, 100th Anniversary.

U. S. Bureau of Land Management. HOMESTEADS. Washington, D.C.:
Government Printing Office, 1962. 28p. tables. pap.
Homestead entry statistics by state, 1868–1961.

U. S. Bureau of Land Management. THE PUBLIC LAND RECORDS ... FOOT-
NOTES TO AMERICAN HISTORY. Washington, D.C.: Government Printing
Office, 1959. 32p. illus. pap.
Guide to the use of records begun in 1785, data on the public
domain and on lands transferred to private ownership.

U. S. Bureau of Land Management. SMALL TRACTS. Washington, D.C.:
Government Printing Office, 1958. 34p.
"This pamphlet tells how to obtain small parcels of vacant public
lands from the Federal government."

U. S. Congress. House. Committee on Interior and Insular Affairs. WITH-
DRAWAL, RESERVATION AND RESTRICTION OF PUBLIC LANDS; HEARINGS
BEFORE THE SUBCOMMITTEE ON PUBLIC LANDS, EIGHTY–SEVENTH CONGRESS,
SECOND SESSION ON H.R. 1785, H.R. 3342, H.R. 5252 AND H.R. 6377;
H.R. 4060; AND H.R. 8783. (Serial no. 25). Washington D.C.: Government
Printing Office, 1962. 153p. tables. pap.

U.S. General Land Office. ANNUAL REPORT OF THE COMMISSIONER.
Washington D.C.: Government Printing Office, 1812–1946.
STATISTICAL APPENDIX to the REPORT issued from 1941–1946.

U. S. Laws, Statutes, etc. OIL LAND LEASING ACT OF 1920; WITH
AMENDMENTS AND OTHER LAWS RELATING TO MINERAL LANDS, comp.
by Gilman G. Udell. Washington D.C.: Government Printing Office, 1960.
415p. pap.

Utah. University. Bureau of Economic and Business Research. UNIVERSITY
LANDS; THEIR HISTORY AND UNDEVELOPED POTENTIALS, by J.R. Mahoney.
(Utah Public Lands Research). Salt Lake City: 1961. 94p. charts. pap.

Public Lands—Bibliography

U.S. Bureau of Land Management. PUBLIC LANDS BIBLIOGRAPHY. Washington
D.C.: Government Printing Office, 1962. 106p. pap. processed.
   1,288 references containing "most of the known writing on public
   land activities, programs, and legislation previous to 1954."
   Arranged in three sections: Articles and monographs, laws and
   legislation, theses. Indicates library source and call number for
   each entry. Supplements to be issued.

Public Lands—Periodicals
(See Appendix for complete information concerning these publications.)

OUR PUBLIC LANDS.

Section 23

RECREATIONAL PROPERTY

American Public Health Association. RECOMMENDED PRACTICE FOR DESIGN, EQUIPMENT AND OPERATION OF SWIMMING POOLS AND OTHER PUBLIC BATHING PLACES, 10th ed. New York: 1957. 60p. pap.

American Society of Planning Officials. BOWLING ALLEYS. (Planning Advisory Service Information Report no. 110). Chicago: 1958. 30p. pap. processed.

American Society of Planning Officials. PRIVATE SWIMMING POOLS AND CLUBS. (Planning Advisory Service Information Report no. 65). Chicago: 1954. 28p. pap. processed.

American Society of Planning Officials. RECREATIONAL BOATING FACILITIES. (Planning Advisory Service Information Report no. 147). Chicago: 1961. 40p. pap. processed.
     Bibliography: p. 35-40.

An Analysis of a 36-Lane Bowling Alley. REAL ESTATE ANALYST APPRAISAL BULLETIN, vol. 29, no. 15, 1960. p. 155-60.

Chaney, Charles A. MARINAS; RECOMMENDATIONS FOR DESIGN, CONSTRUCTION AND MAINTENANCE. New York: National Association of Engine and Boat Manufacturers, 1961. 247p. illus., diagrs.

McReynolds, Tom. Bowling Alleys as Long-Term Investments. REAL ESTATE ANALYST APPRAISAL BULLETIN, vol. 25, no. 9, 1956, p. 83-6.

National Association of Engine and Boat Manufacturers. THE MODERN MARINA; A SOUND BUSINESS OPPORTUNITY FOR COMMUNITY, INVESTOR AND OPERATOR, 2nd rev. New York: 1960. 61p. pap.
    Intended as an aid to those who plan a facility.

National Golf Foundation. PLANNING AND BUILDING THE GOLF COURSE. Chicago: 407 South Dearborn Street, zone 5, no date. 32p. illus., diagrs., maps.

> "This Foundation also provides free consultant services to individuals or groups seriously considering the development of new or additional golf facilities, whether they be private clubs, commercial or municipal."

National Golf Foundation. PLANNING INFORMATION FOR PRIVATE GOLF CLUBS. Chicago: 407 South Dearborn Street, zone 5, no date. various paging. illus., tables, diagrs. pap. processed.

National Golf Foundation. PLANNING THE GOLF CLUBHOUSE, by Harold J. Cliffer. Chicago: 407 South Dearborn Street, zone 5, 1956. 96p. illus., diagrs.
> Supplement: GOLF CLUBHOUSE PLANNING AND EVALU-
> ATING CHECK LIST. 12p. pap. processed.

National Recreation Association. RECREATION AREAS; THEIR DESIGN AND EQUIPMENT, 2nd ed., prepared for the Association by George D. Butler. New York: Ronald Press, 1958. 174p. illus.
> Includes community swimming pool standards.

National Swimming Pool Institute. MINIMUM STANDARDS FOR PUBLIC AND SEMI-PUBLIC POOLS, rev. Harvard, Ill.: 1961. 17p. diagr. pap. processed.

National Swimming Pool Institute. MINIMUM STANDARDS FOR RESIDENTIAL POOLS. Harvard, Ill.: 1961. 13p. pap. processed.

Regional Plan Association. PARK, RECREATION AND OPEN SPACE PROJECT OF THE TRI-STATE NEW YORK METROPOLITAN REGION, 4 vols. New York: 1960. illus., tables, charts, diagrs., maps. pap.
> Vol. 1: THE LAW OF OPEN SPACE, by Shirley Adelson Siegel;
> Vol. 2: THE DYNAMICS OF PARK DEMAND; PRESENT AND
> FUTURE DEMAND FOR RECREATION AND OPEN SPACE IN
> THE TRI-STATE NEW YORK METROPOLITAN REGION AND
> THE NATION, by Marion Clawson; Vol. 3: NATURE IN
> THE METROPOLIS; CONSERVATION IN THE TRI-STATE NEW
> YORK METROPOLITAN REGION, by William A. Niering;
> Vol. 4: THE RACE FOR OPEN SPACE; FINAL REPORT OF THE
> PARK, RECREATION AND OPEN SPACE PROJECT. A joint
> undertaking of Metropolitan Regional Council and Regional Plan
> Association.

Salomon, Julian Harris. CAMP SITE DEVELOPMENT, 2d ed. New York: Girl Scouts of the United States of America, 830 Third Avenue, zone 22, 1959. 160p. diagrs.
> New and enlarged edition of the book first issued ten years
> ago. "Descriptions and typical plans for the facilities gener-
> ally needed in larger established camps, but the smaller, sim-
> pler and more temporary camps have not been forgotten."

U. S. Bureau of Outdoor Recreation. LIST OF AGENCIES ADMINISTERING STATE PARKS AND RELATED RECREATION AREAS. Washington, D.C.: 1962. 17p. pap. processed.

U. S. National Park Service. AREAS ADMINISTERED BY THE NATIONAL
PARK SERVICE AND TABULATION OF VISITORS TO AREAS ADMINISTERED
BY THE NATIONAL PARK SERVICE. Washington, D.C.: pap.
    Issued Annually.

U.S. Outdoor Recreation Resources Review Commission. OUTDOOR RECREATION
FOR AMERICA; A REPORT TO THE PRESIDENT AND TO THE CONGRESS.
Washington, D.C.: Government Printing Office, 1962. 246p. pap.
    Surveys our country's outdoor recreation resources, measures
    present and likely demands upon them over the next forty years,
    and recommends actions to insure their availability to all Amer-
    icans of present and future generations. The 26 study reports
    of the ORRRC listed in Appendix C, with annotations.

U.S. Outdoor Recreation Resources Review Commission. STUDY REPORTS, 27 vols.
Washington D.C.: Government Printing Office, 1962. tables, charts. pap.
    1: PUBLIC OUTDOOR RECREATION AREAS — ACREAGE, USE,
    POTENTIAL; 2: LIST OF PUBLIC OUTDOOR RECREATION
    AREAS — 1960; 3: WILDERNESS AND RECREATION — A
    REPORT ON RESOURCES, VALUES AND PROBLEMS; 4: SHORE-
    LINE RECREATION RESOURCES OF THE UNITED STATES; 5:
    THE QUALITY OF OUTDOOR RECREATION: AS EVIDENCED
    BY USER SATISFACTION; 6: HUNTING IN THE UNITED
    STATES — ITS PRESENT AND FUTURE ROLE; 7: SPORT FISH-
    ING — TODAY AND TOMORROW; 8: POTENTIAL NEW
    SITES FOR OUTDOOR RECREATION IN THE NORTHEAST; 9:
    ALASKA OUTDOOR RECREATION POTENTIAL; 10: WATER
    FOR RECREATION — VALUES AND OPPORTUNITIES; 11:
    PRIVATE OUTDOOR RECREATION FACILITIES; 12: FINANC-
    ING PUBLIC RECREATION FACILITIES; 13: FEDERAL AGEN-
    CIES AND OUTDOOR RECREATION; 14: DIRECTORY OF
    STATE OUTDOOR RECREATION ADMINISTRATION; 15: O-
    PEN SPACE ACTION; 16: LAND ACQUISITION FOR OUT-
    DOOR RECREATION — ANALYSIS OF SELECTED LEGAL PROB-
    LEMS; 17: MULTIPLE USE OF LAND AND WATER AREAS;
    18: A LOOK ABROAD: THE EFFECT OF FOREIGN TRAVEL
    ON DOMESTIC OUTDOOR RECREATION AND A BRIEF SUR-
    VEY OF OUTDOOR RECREATION IN SIX COUNTRIES; 19:
    NATIONAL RECREATION SURVEY; 20: PARTICIPATION IN
    OUTDOOR RECREATION: FACTORS AFFECTING DEMAND
    AMONG AMERICAN ADULTS; 21: THE FUTURE OF OUT-
    DOOR RECREATION IN METROPOLITAN REGIONS OF THE
    UNITED STATES; 22: TRENDS IN AMERICAN LIVING AND
    OUTDOOR RECREATION; 23: PROJECTIONS TO THE YEARS
    1976 AND 2000: ECONOMIC GROWTH, POPULATION, LA-
    BOR FORCE AND LEISURE, AND TRANSPORTATION; 24: E-
    CONOMIC STUDIES OF OUTDOOR RECREATION; 25: PUB-
    LIC EXPENDITURES FOR OUTDOOR RECREATION; 26: PRO-
    SPECTIVE DEMAND FOR OUTDOOR RECREATION; 27: OUT-
    DOOR RECREATION LITERATURE: A SURVEY.

U. S. Urban Renewal Administration. OPEN SPACE LAND PROGRAM GUIDE; POLICIES AND REQUIREMENTS UNDER TITLE VII FOR FEDERAL ASSISTANCE OF THE HOUSING ACT OF 1961. Washington, D.C.: Government Printing Office, 1962. various paging. charts. pap. processed.

Urban Land Institute. MARINAS — THEIR PLANNING AND DEVELOPMENT, by C. A. Chaney. (Technical Bulletin no. 14). Washington, D.C.: 1950. 23p. illus. pap.

Urban Land Institute. SECURING OPEN SPACE FOR URBAN AMERICA; CONSERVATION EASEMENTS, by William H. Whyte, Jr. (Technical Bulletin no. 36). Washington, D.C.: 1959. 67p. illus. pap.

Williams, Wayne R. RECREATION PLACES. New York: Reinhold, 1958. 302p. illus., tables, charts, plans.

Section 24

RESIDENTIAL PROPERTY

GENERAL

A list of Federal government agencies involved in housing and finance programs appears in Appendix D. The annual and special reports, administrative regulations, and miscellaneous publications of these agencies, as well as Congressional hearings and documents relating to the programs, are primary sources. THE MONTHLY CATALOG OF U.S. GOVERNMENT PUBLICATIONS lists such items.

Abrams, Charles. FORBIDDEN NEIGHBORS; A STUDY OF PREJUDICE IN HOUSING. New York: Harper, 1955. 404p.
> Written at the suggestion of the National Association for the Advancement of Colored People.

Abrams, Charles. THE FUTURE OF HOUSING. New York: Harper, 1946. 428p.
> "The housing question will come into its true perspective only when translated into its larger political and economic implications. With this in mind, the issues are framed, the aims stated, a program proffered to modify present legislation with the aim of securing good housing for the American people within the traditional framework of our economic and political patterns."

American Council To Improve Our Neighborhoods. AMERICAN HOUSING STATISTICS; CONDITION, SUPPLY, DEMAND. New York: no date. 28p. tables. pap.
> 1955 statistics latest used.

American Public Health Association. Committee on the Hygiene of Housing. AN APPRAISAL METHOD FOR MEASURING THE QUALITY OF HOUSING: A YARDSTICK FOR HEALTH OFFICERS, HOUSING OFFICIALS AND PLANNERS, 5 vols. New York: 1945-1950. tables, diagrs., maps. pap. processed. processed.
> Part I: NATURE AND USES OF THE METHOD; Part II: APPRAISAL OF DWELLING CONDITIONS; Vol. A: SURVEY DIRECTOR'S MANUAL, Vol. B: FIELD PROCEDURES; Vol. C: OFFICE PROCEDURES; Part III: APPRAISAL OF NEIGHBORHOOD ENVIRONMENT.

American Public Health Association. Committee on the Hygiene of Housing. BASIC PRINCIPLES OF HEALTHFUL HOUSING, 2d ed. New York: 1939.

34p. pap.
    Reprinted in 1954.

American Public Health Association. Committee on the Hygiene of Housing.
HOUSING AN AGING POPULATION; A CONTRIBUTION OF THE SUB-
COMMITTEE ON STANDARDS FOR HOUSING THE AGED AND INFIRM. New
York: 1953. 92p. pap.
    Identification of the problem and attempts to solve it. Includes
    European patterns of non-institutional housing for the aged.

American Public Health Association. Committee on the Hygiene of Housing.
HOUSING FOR HEALTH. New York: 1941. 221p. tables, charts. pap.

American Public Health Association. Committee on the Hygiene of Housing.
PRINCIPLES FOR HEALTHFUL RURAL HOUSING. New York: 1957. 29p. pap.
    "Standards for single-family homes and small apartment buildings,
    presented in 27 recommendations. Applicable to village, small-
    town, and urban-fringe dwellings, as well as rural."

American Public Health Association. Committee on the Hygiene of Housing.
A PROPOSED HOUSING ORDINANCE, REGULATING SUPPLIED FACILITIES,
MAINTENANCE AND OCCUPANCY OF DWELLINGS AND DWELLING UNITS.
New York: 1952. 24p. pap.

Architectural Record. APARTMENTS AND DORMITORIES. New York: F. W.
Dodge, 1958. 232p. illus., diagrs.

Banfield, Edward C. and Grodzins, Martin. GOVERNMENT AND HOUSING
IN METROPOLITAN AREAS. (ACTION Series in Housing and Community
Development). New York: McGraw-Hill, 1958. 177p.
    "Governmental structure as it affects the standard of housing in
    metropolitan areas."

Bauer, Catherine. MODERN HOUSING. Boston: Houghton Mifflin, 1934.
376p. illus., diagrs.
    An examination of the "modern housing" constructed in postwar
    Europe, as housing was removed from the speculative market and
    became a public utility. Includes National Housing Measures,
    1850-1934: England, Germany, Holland, Belgium, France,
    Austria, the Scandinavian countries, Switzerland. Bibliography.
    Appendix of photographs.

Berkman, H. G. DELINEATION AND STRUCTURE OF RENTAL HOUSING
AREAS. Madison: School of Commerce, University of Wisconsin, 1956. 144p.
pap.

Beyer, Glenn H. HOUSING: A FACTUAL ANALYSIS. New York: Macmillan, 1958. 355p. tables, charts, diagrs.
    "A statistical compendium of the non-technical aspects of hous-
    ing." Bibliography, p. 329-38.

Beyer, Glenn H. and Rose, J. Hugh. FARM HOUSING. (Census Monograph
Series). New York: John Wiley, 1957. 194p. tables, charts.

California. University. Real Estate Research Program. CASH OUTLAYS AND
ECONOMIC COSTS OF HOMEOWNERSHIP, by Fred E. Case. Los Angeles:
1957. 58p. tables. pap.

California. University. Real Estate Research Program. HOUSING MARKET
DATA FROM CENSUS MATERIALS - A STUDY OF CALIFORNIA AND THE BAY
AREA, by Wallace F. Smith. Berkeley: 1963. 104p. tables. processed.
    "An effort to improve the accessibility and significance of 1960
    census information, as that data relates to housing ... explores
    some current census resources in terms of certain major lines of
    interest in the housing field - population shifts; household;
    employment and income; and creation, use, and disposition of
    the housing stock."

Colean, Miles L. AMERICAN HOUSING; PROBLEMS AND PROSPECTS. New
York: Twentieth Century Fund, 1947. 466p. tables, charts.
    Production and marketing of housing. Program of action by the
    Fund Housing Committee based on findings by Miles Colean.
    Bibliography.

Colean, Miles L. and Kendall, Leon T. WHO BUYS THE HOUSES; A REPORT
ON THE CHARACTERISTICS OF SINGLE FAMILY HOME BUYERS. Chicago:
United States Savings and Loan League, 1958. 21p. tables. pap.

Commission on Race and Housing. PRIVATELY DEVELOPED INTERRACIAL
HOUSING; AN ANALYSIS OF EXPERIENCE, by Eunice and George Grier.
Berkeley and Los Angeles: University of California Press, 1960. 264p. tables.
    "...a few builders have ventured to break the 'cake of custom'
    and open their developments to white and nonwhite alike. This
    book is a study of these builders and of their interracial pro-
    jects." Bibliography includes list of unpublished research re-
    ports.

Commission on Race and Housing. PROPERTY VALUES AND RACE; STUDIES IN
SEVEN CITIES, BY Luigi Laurenti. Berkeley and Los Angeles: University of
California Press, 1960. 256p. tables, charts.
    "In addition to his original studies, Dr. Laurenti reviews the
    pertinent writings of real estate and appraisal experts and the
    findings of other studies."

Commission on Race and Housing. RESIDENCE AND RACE; FINAL AND COM-
PREHENSIVE REPORT TO THE COMMISSION ON RACE AND HOUSING, by
David McEntire. Berkeley and Los Angeles: University of California Press,
1960. 409p. tables, charts, maps.
    "The central focus of the study undertaken for the Commission
    was on the problem of inequality of housing opportunity connected
    with racial or ethnic distinctions...the research was national in
    scope and sought to comprehend all the more important aspects

GENERAL (continued)

and ramifications of a very complex, problem--its causes, impacts and consequence and directions of change."

"Other products of the research are unpublished but available in the library of the University of California at Berkeley." The Commission has published its own findings and recommendations under the title, WHERE SHALL WE LIVE?, based on the study.

Commission on Race and Housing. STUDIES IN HOUSING AND MINORITY GROUPS, ed. by Nathan Glazer and Davis McEntire. Berkeley and Los Angeles: University of California Press, 1960. 228p. tables, maps.
    Findings of seven local studies "which deal with special, local situations and try to suggest the wide range of factors which explain the outcome in terms of housing for different minority groups in different cities"; "deal with the special, rather than the general." Introduction by Glazer summarizing the main conclusions that emerge from this group of studies.

Commission on Race and Housing. WHERE SHALL WE LIVE? Berkeley and Los Angeles: University of California Press, 1958. 77p. pap.
    Report of findings and recommendations of the Commission. The main results of the entire study upon which the Commission based its own report are presented in RESIDENCE AND RACE.

Conference on Retirement Villages. RETIREMENT VILLAGES, ed. by Ernest W. Burgess. Ann Arbor: Division of Gerontology, University of Michigan, 1961. 1961. 156p. illus. pap.
    Papers, discussions, and recommendations for research presented at conference sponsored by the American Society for the Aged.

Cornell University, Center for Housing and Environmental Studies. ECONOMIC ASPECTS OF HOUSING FOR THE AGED, by Glenn H. Beyer. Ithaca, N.Y.: 1961. 59p. tables. pap.
    "One of the monographs being prepared on the problems of housing for the aged...others deal with the living and activity patterns and with the relationship of the aged to the community."

Cornell University Housing Research Center. HOUSES ARE FOR PEOPLE; A STUDY OF HOME BUYER MOTIVATIONS, by Glenn H. Beyer, et al. (Research Publication No. 3). Ithaca, N.Y.: 1955. 58p. tables, charts. pap.
    "This study is an attempt to bring into focus the fundamental human values reflected in patterns of living, so that designers can plan more rational shelter. It has attempted to find out what the real motiviations are that families have in buying a house."

Dean, John P. HOME OWNERSHIP: IS IT SOUND? New York: Harper, 1945. 215p.

GENERAL (continued)

Donahue, Wilma, ed. HOUSING THE AGING. Ann Arbor, Mich.: University of Michigan Press, 1954. 280p.
> Papers from the University of Michigan fifth annual Conference on Aging. Ann Arbor, July 24-26, 1952. Part I: The Problem; Part II: Housing Well Older People; Part III: Housing Older People Requiring Sheltered Care and Medical Supervision; Part IV: Financing Housing for the Aging; Part V: Getting Community Action.

Douglas Fir Plywood Association. NEW MARKET OPPORTUNITIES FOR YOU IN LEISURE HOMES. Tacoma, Wash: no date. n.p. pap.

Everard, Kenneth Eugene. AN IDENTIFICATION OF AREAS OF KNOWLEDGE ABOUT WHICH HOME BUYERS NEED UNDERSTANDING. Unpublished thesis, Indiana University, 1962.

Foote, Nelson N. et al. HOUSING CHOICES AND HOUSING CONSTRAINTS. (ACTION Series in Housing and Community Development). New York: McGraw-Hill, 1960. 450p. tables, charts.
> Knowledge about the values people attach to their housing and the degree to which they appear to be realizing or sacrificing those values.

Gray, George Herbert. HOUSING AND CITIZENSHIP...A STUDY OF LOW-COST HOUSING. New York: Reinhold, 1946. 254p. illus., tables, charts, plans.
> An historical review of activity in the United States and other countries, including defense and war housing programs. Appendix A: A Review and Appraisal of Accomplishments of Various Federal Housing Agencies.

Grebler, Leo. HOUSING ISSUES IN ECONOMIC STABILIZATION POLICY. (NBER Occasional Paper no. 72). New York: National Bureau of Economic Research, 1960. 129p. tables, charts.

Grebler, Leo. HOUSING MARKET BEHAVIOR IN A DECLINING AREA; LONG-TERM CHANGES IN INVENTORY AND UTILIZATION OF HOUSING ON NEW YORK'S LOWER EAST SIDE. (Publication of the Institute for Urban Land and Housing Studies, Columbia University). New York: Columbia University Press, 1952. 265p. tables, charts, maps.
> "This volume presents the first in a projected series of studies of the behavior of urban real estate markets."

Greenwald, William I. BUY OR RENT? New York: Twayne, 1958. 91p. charts, tables.

GENERAL (continued)

Housing Securities, Inc., Division of Housing Market Research. 75 HOUSING
AREAS, A HOUSING MARKET ANALYSIS; ANNUAL SUMMARY...SELECTED
DATA ON HOUSING, POPULATION, ECONOMIC INDICATORS AND MORT-
GAGE ACTIVITY. New York: 250 Park Avenue, zone 17, 1955-   . tables.
pap.

International Union of Family Organizations. Family Housing Commission.
MINIMUM HABITABLE SURFACES; INCREASE IN SIZE AND COST OF DWELL-
INGS IN RELATION TO THE SIZE OF THE FAMILY. Cologne: 1957. 31p.
pap
>Conclusions reached by the Rent and Family Income Standing
>Committee of the International Federation for Housing and Town
>Planning and the Family Housing Commission of I.U.F.O. dur-
>ing the 5th annual meeting of the I.U.F.O. Housing Commis-
>sion, April 11-12, 1957, at Cologne.

Kelly, Burnham, et al. DESIGN AND PRODUCTION OF HOUSES. (ACTION
Series in Housing and Community Development). New York: McGraw-Hill,
1959. 399p. illus., tables, charts.
>"Explores the roles of the builder, the labor union, the manu-
>facturer of building materials, the architect and the public of-
>ficial and points out ways in which their combined efforts can
>introduce many forms of improved design and technological in-
>novation into future home-building operations."

Kuchler, Frances W. H. LANDLORD, TENANT AND CO-OP HOUSING, Rev.
3d ed. New York: Oceana, 1960. 93p. pap.

Latty, E. R., ed. Housing. LAW AND CONTEMPORARY PROBLEMS. vol.
12, no. 1, Winter 1947, (entire issue).
>Contents: The Extent of the Housing Shortage; Technological
>Potentials in Home Construction; Changing Attitudes toward
>Property Ownership and Mortgage Finance; Real Property Law
>and Mass Housing Needs; Handicraft and Handcuffs - the Anat-
>omy of an Industry; Legal Requirements that Building Contrac-
>tors be Licensed; The Problem of Building Code Improvement;
>Administrative-Legal Methodologies in Elimination of Sub-Stand-
>ard Housing; Some Legal Aspects of Cooperative Housing; The
>Veterans Emergency Housing Program; Housing-Legislative
>Proposals; The Housing Crisis in a Free Economy.

Lowry, Ira Smith. RESIDENTIAL LOCATION IN URBAN AREAS. Unpublished
Ph.D. thesis, University of California, 1959.

Maisel, Sherman J. Changes in the Rate and Components of Household Formation. JOURNAL OF THE AMERICAN STATISTICAL ASSOCIATION, Vol. 55,
no. 290, June 1960, p. 268-83.
>Historical analysis and projections for 1965 and 1975.

GENERAL (continued)

Maisel, Sherman J. and Winnick, Louis. "Family Housing Expenditures; Elusive Laws and Intrusive Variances." p. 359-435. In CONFERENCE ON CONSUMPTION AND SAVING PROCEEDINGS. vol. 1. University of Pennsylvania, 1960. (Reprint no. 25, Real Estate Research Program, University of California, Berkeley).
> "Original data from the Wharton-Bureau of Labor Statistics Study of Consumer Expenditures."

Manheim, Uriel. LOCAL HOUSING DATA. New York: Housing Securities Inc., 250 Park Avenue, zone 17, 1958. 16p. tables. pap. processed.
> "Adaptation of an address before the First Annual National Housing Center Institute for Housing Statistics Users, Washington, D.C., Dec. 10, 1958."

Martini, Catherine E. Demand for Second Homes Grows; Four-Fold Increase in Sales Possible. REALTOR'S HEADLINES, July 4, 1960, Section 2, p.6.

Mathiasen, Geneva and Noakes, Edward H., eds. PLANNING HOMES FOR THE AGED. New York: F. W. Dodge, 1959. 119p. illus., tables.
> Bibliography included.

Meyerson, Martin, et al. HOUSING, PEOPLE AND CITIES. (ACTION Series in Housing and Community Development). New York: McGraw-Hill, 1962. 386p. tables, charts.
> Last of the series directed and edited by Martin Meyerson.
> "The culmination of a five year investigation of impediments to the improvement of housing and the urban environment."
> The setting, consumer, producer, investor, federal government and community.

Miami. University. Bureau of Business and Economic Research. FORECAST OF RESIDENTIAL NONFARM HOUSING STARTS FOR THE 12-MONTH PERIOD... Coral Gables, Fla., 195 - . tables, charts. pap. processed.
> Quarterly with five-year forecasts issued annually. Cover title: 12 MONTHS HOUSING FORECAST, UNITED STATES, REGIONS AND CITIES.

Michigan. University. Institute for Social Research. Survey Research Center. SURVEY OF CONSUMER FINANCES. 15th - . Ann Arbor: 1960- tables. pap.
> Survey Research Center of the University of Michigan for the Federal Reserve Board of Governors, 1946-1959. Annual. Appeared in Federal Reserve Bulletin 1946-1959. 1960 Survey published by Survey Research Center financed by business concerns, foundations and the center. 1960 covers data on intentions to buy housing for 1956 through 1959. Housing not repeated in 1961. Because these distributions usually change slowly, the data are not always collected annually. Nonfarm houses classified by price and mortgage debt, value of mortgaged and nonmortgaged, prices paid for new and used, additions and

repairs, rent payments, family income, age, occupation and
race of family head, equity.

Mobile Homes Research Foundation. TODAY'S MOBILE HOME PARK, IMPORT-
ANT TO YOUR COMMUNITY. Chicago: 1959. n.p. pap.
> Includes a Survey of the Mobile Home Consumer, made by Mich-
> igan State University, reprinted from TRAILER TOPICS Magazine.

National Association of Home Builders. THE APARTMENT PLAN, by James F.
Neville and Joseph Miller. Washington, D.C.: 1961. 40p. illus., diagrs.
pap.
> Includes an analysis of planning and design for housing for
> senior citizens and all illustrated designs are adaptable to this
> type. The terrace unit, court plan, townhouse, apartment home,
> low rise elevator, hillside site, split level, composite group
> plan, the neighborhood plan, retirement housing, planning
> considerations for the retired.

National Housing Center. ROUNDTABLE ON RETIREMENT HOUSING, WASH-
INGTON, D.C.: JUNE 22, 1961. Washington, D. C.: National Association
of Home Builders, 1961. 7p. pap. processed.

New York State. Division of Housing. HOME CARE AND HOUSING NEEDS
OF THE AGED. New York: March 1958. 56p. tables. pap. processed.
> A report on a study conducted by John G. Steinle and Associates.
> Bibliography included.

New York State, Division of Housing. HOUSING REQUIREMENTS OF THE
AGED; A STUDY OF DESIGN CRITERIA. New York: 1958. 124p. pap.
processed.
> By the Housing Research Center, Cornell University, Ithaca.

Nierstrasz, F.H.J., ed. BUILDING FOR THE AGED. Amsterdam: Published for Bouwcentrum by Elsevier, 1961. 187p. illus., diagrs. (Distr.
for U.S., Van Nostrand).
> The chapters dealing with the various forms of accommodation
> are based on reports compiled by the Bouwcentrum. Dwellings,
> nursing homes and provisions in a general hospital.

Perloff, Harvey S. NATIONAL PROGRAM OF RESEARCH IN HOUSING AND
URBAN DEVELOPMENT. Washington, D.C.: Resources for the Future, 1961.
32p. pap.

PRESIDENT'S CONFERENCE ON HOME BUILDING AND HOME OWNERSHIP,
11 vols. and general index, by John M. Gries and James Ford, general eds.
Washington, D.C.: 1932.
> Robert P. Lamont, Secretary of Commerce and Ray Lyman Wilbur,
> Secretary of the Interior, Joint Chairmen. Reports of committees
> Vol. 1: Planning for Residential Districts (City Planning, Sub-
> divisions, Utilities, Landscape Planning); Vol. 2: Home Finance

and Taxation (Loans, Assessments and Taxes on Residential Property); Vol. 3: Slums, Large-Scale Housing and Decentralization (Blighted Areas and Slums, Large Scale Operations, Business and Housing, Industrial Decentralization); Vol. 4: Home Ownership, Income and Types of Dwellings (Home Ownership and Renting, Investment Factors, Dwelling Types, Social and Economic Considerations, Income Levels and Home Purchase); Vol. 5: House Design, Construction and Equipment (Planning, Building Sanitation and Equipment of Dwellings); Vol. 6: Negro Housing (Physical aspects, Social and Economic Factors, Home Ownership and Financing); Vol 7: Farm and Village Housing (Housing Conditions and Problems, Design and Construction, Farmstead Planning, Beautification, Economic and Educational Aspects); Vol. 8: Housing and the Community. Home Repair and Remodeling (Relation of Housing to Health, Delinquency, Industrial Efficiency, Safety, Citizenship, Recreation. Home Improvement and Remodeling); Vol. 9: Household Management and Kitchens (Planning Household Activities, Equipment of Work Areas); Vol. 10: Homemaking, Home Furnishing and Information Services (Housing and Family Life, Furniture, Budgets and Design, Home Information Centers); Vol. 11: Housing objectives and Programs (Housing Problems. Technological Developments. Legislation, Standards, Objectives, Education, Service, Organizations. Housing Research); General Index to the Final Reports.

Quarterly Survey of Consumer Buying Intentions. FEDERAL RESERVE BULLETIN. Quarterly in various bulletin issues since 1959.
Measures changes over time in consumer intentions to buy durable goods by income and age groups.

Reid, Margaret G. HOUSING AND INCOME. Chicago: University of Chicago Press, 1962. 415p. tables, charts. processed.
Study of the relation of housing, its values and rents, to normal or expected long-run income; based on surveys and censuses for 1918 to 1960.

Rodwin, Lloyd. HOUSING AND ECONOMIC PROGRESS; A STUDY OF THE HOUSING EXPERIENCES OF BOSTON'S MIDDLE-INCOME FAMILIES. Cambridge: Harvard University Press & the Technology Press, 1961. 288p. tables, charts, maps.
Publication of the Joint Center for Urban Studies. "The principle theme of this book is that rising income and rising standards of demand, coupled with inadequate adjustments of housing supply in response to such rises in income and standards, are the sources of most of our vexatious problems of housing and neighborhood development."

Rosenman, Dorothy. A MILLION HOMES A YEAR. New York: Harcourt, Brace, 1945. 333p.

Rossi, Peter H. WHY FAMILIES MOVE; A STUDY IN THE SOCIAL PSYCHOL-
OGY OF URBAN RESIDENTIAL MOBILITY. Glencoe, Ill: Free Press, 1955.
220p.
> Jointly sponsored by Institute for Urban Land Use and Housing
> Studies and Bureau of Applied Social Research, Columbia Uni-
> versity. Financed under a contract with the Housing and Home
> Finance Agency. Area mobility, household mobility, and mov-
> ing decisions.

Sacramento State College. Real Estate Research Group. TRENDS IN MULTI-
FAMILY HOUSING, SACRAMENTO METROPOLITAN AREA, 1950-1970: A
CASE STUDY OF A DIRECTIONAL GROWTH PROBLEM IN THE METROPOLI-
TAN SACRAMENTO AREA. Sacramento: 1961. 272p. tables, charts. pap.
processed.
> Factors underlying the demand for and supply of apartment dwell-
> ing units with an empirical study of apartment house tenants.
> The investment experience of six Sacramento County income
> properties, examined in detail for the period 1949-1960 and
> compared with similar studies for New York, Chicago, Los
> Angeles, Washington, Detroit, and San Francisco. Apartment
> owner-manager survey of the buildings, vacancies and turnover,
> rentals and concessions, form and length of ownership.

Schultz, Robert E. LIFE INSURANCE HOUSING PROJECTS. (S. S. Huebner
Foundation for Insurance Education, University of Pennsylvania). Homewood,
Ill.: Richard D. Irwin, 1956. 154p. tables.
> Life insurance funds invested in the equity ownership of housing
> developments, covering the experience of all major housing projects
> together with an examination of the legal, economic and social
> implications.

United Nations. Economic and Social Council. Social Commission. REPORT
THE AD HOC GROUP OF EXPERTS ON HOUSING AND URBAN DEVELOP-
MENT. New York: 1962. 162p. pap. processed.
> Social Commission. 14th session. Item 4 of the Provisional
> Agenda. E/CN.5/367. March 16, 1962.

Straus, Nathan. TWO-THIRDS OF A NATION; A HOUSING PROGRAM.
New York: Knopf, 1952. 291p.

United Nations. Statistical Office. GENERAL PRINCIPLES FOR A HOUSING
CENSUS. (Statistical Papers, Series M, No. 28). New York: 1958. 14p.
pap. processed.
> A guide for taking a housing census or gathering housing infor-
> mation in connection with a census of population.

U. S. Bureau of the Census. HOUSING STARTS. (C-20 Series). Washington, D.C. Monthly.
   Estimates of the number of new housing units started, nonfarm and total, classified as follows: by ownership, and seasonally adjusted annual rate of private starts; by metropolitan–nonmetropolitan location and type of structure.

U. S. Bureau of the Census. HOUSING VACANCIES. (H-III Series). Washington, D.C. Quarterly.
   Rental and homeowner vacancy rates by geographical areas and housing characteristics. Current quarter compared with same quarter of preceding year.

U. S. Bureau of the Census. CENSUS OF HOUSING. Washington, D.C.: Government Printing Office.
   Information on the 1960 CENSUS OF HOUSING quoted from Catalog of United States Census Publications, January–June 1962: "A Census of Housing was taken as part of the Decennial Census of 1940 and 1950 and was conducted again in 1960. As a part of the 1960 Census of Housing, the Survey of Components of Inventory Change and Residential Finance (SCARF) was taken starting in late 1959 and extending into 1960. The Components of Inventory Change portion measures gains and losses in the housing inventory through new construction, conversion, demolition, and the like, since 1950, and changes since December 1956 when the National Housing Inventory was conducted. The Residential Finance portion presents data on method of financing purchase of property, the size of the outstanding mortgage debt, and detailed tabulations on such mortgage characteristics as amount of loan, interest rate, Government insurance status, method and amount of mortgage payments, and type of lender.

   "Current statistics on housing include quarterly data on vacancy rates and condition and characteristics of available housing vacancies for the country as a whole, for geographic regions, and inside and outside standard metropolitan statistical areas. Data on television sets for the Nation, regions and geographic divisions have been obtained from a series of supplements to the Current Population Surveys.

   "Results of the 1960 Census of Housing are being made available as they are tabulated and assembled. Preliminary figures have been issued as unbound multilithed reports identified as Series HC(P). Final figures are contained in advance reports HC(A1), HC(A2), HC(A3), etc., which began appearing late in 1960. Final detailed results are being published in separate series of reports HC(1), HC(3), HC(4), etc., which will constitute Volumes I, II, III, etc., of the 1960 Census of Housing. The description of the publication program and announcement and order forms for reports of the 1960 Census of Housing may be obtained on request from the Bureau of the Census."

HC(1) **STATES AND SMALL AREAS.** (55 reports) tables, map.
Series consists of a report for each State, the District
of Columbia, Puerto Rico, Guam, Virgin Islands, and
a United States summary.

The reports, which constitute Volume 1 of the 1960
Census of Housing, provide statistics on occupancy
characteristics, such as tenure, number of persons,
color of occupants, persons per room year moved into
the unit, and vacancy status; structural characteristics
such as number of rooms, bedrooms, year structure
built, number of units in the structure, and presence
of basement; condition of unit; plumbing facilities,
such as water supply, toilet and bathing facilities,
and number of bathrooms; equipment such as air conditioning, clothes dryers and washing machines, home
food freezers, radios, and television sets, availability
of telephone, and number of automobiles available;
cooking fuel, and water heating fuel; and financial
characteristics including value, contract rent, and
gross rent. Statistics are shown for States, counties,
SMSA's urbanized areas, places of 1,000 inhabitants
or more, and rural-farm and rural-nonfarm parts of
counties.

HC(3) CITY BLOCKS. (421) reports). various places, tables,
map.
Series consists of one report for each City or urban
place with a population of 50,000 or more, and for
172 places that have requested inclusion in the block
statistics program and have reimbursed the Bureau for
the cost of such inclusion, and constitutes Volume III
of the 1960 Census of Housing. Information shown for
occupied housing units in each block includes number
of owner-occupied and renter-occupied units, condition,
plumbing, average number of rooms, average contract
rent, average value, persons per room, number of units
occupied by nonwhite, and total population in each
block.

HC(4) COMPONENTS OF INVENTORY CHANGE. (18 reports).
various places, tables, map.

Part 1A 1950-1959 Components. (18 reports). various places,
tables, map.
This series of 18 reports constitutes Part 1A of Volume
IV of the 1960 Census of Housing. There will be a
separate report for the United States, by regions, and one

for each of 17 selected standard metropolitan
statistical areas (or standard consolidated areas).

The reports provide statistics on characteristics of
the housing inventory, including characteristics of
the present and previous residences of recent movers.
As in the case of Part 1A reports, above, the statistics for the Part 1B reports are based on results of
the December 1959 Components of Inventory. Change
survey, a part of the 1960 Census of Housing.

HC(S1) SPECIAL REPORTS FOR LOCAL HOUSING AUTHORITIES.
(140 reports). various paging.
 140 United States Summary. 37p.

Series consists of a report for each of 139 participating
localities, plus a summary, dealing with occupied housing
units defined as substandard by Public Housing Administration. Reports provide statistics by color of head of household and tenure on: Number of rooms, water supply,
toilet facilities, bathing facilities, condition and plumbing,
persons in household, persons per room, number of elderly
persons and non-relatives, numbers of persons and of minors
in primary family, and sex and age of family head. A
separate tabulation presents these characteristics for units
with a head of household 65 years and over. Gross rent,
contract rent, family income, and gross rent as a percent
of income are shown for units occupied by primary renter
families, classified by color of household head.

SURVEY OF COMPONENTS OF CHANGE AND RESIDENTIAL
FINANCE OF THE UNITED STATES CENSUS OF HOUSING, 1960:
PRINCIPAL DATA-COLLECTION FORMS AND PROCEDURES. 39p.
tables, exhibits. 1962.
 Includes reproductions of the enumeration forms used in
the Survey of Components of Change and Residential
Finance (SCARF), which was taken in connection with the
1960 Census of Housing. It also includes a brief description of the office and field procedures. A more complete
report on the enumeration and also on the data-processing
and publications activities of the SCARF program is to
be included in the history of the decennial census.

HC(A2) HOUSING CHARACTERISTICS - STANDARD METROPOLI-
TAN STATISTICAL AREAS. (49 reports). various paging, tables.
 Series consists of reports for the United States, the
District of Columbia, Puerto Rico, and each of the 46
States containing standard metropolitan statistical areas.
For each SMSA, the report presents data for the total
SMSA, constituent counties, places of 50,000 inhabit-
ants or more, urban balance, and rural total.

GENERAL (continued)

Information provided includes occupancy characteristics, such as tenure, color, vacancy status, population per occupied housing unit, number of persons,
and persons per room; structural characteristics, such
as number of rooms, number of bedrooms, type of
structure, year built, condition, and plumbing facilities; equipment and facilities, such as heating equipment, cooking and heating fuels, air conditioning,
source of water, radios, televisions, automobiles
available, etc; and financial characteristics, such as
contract rent, gross rent, and value.

HC(A3) HOUSING EQUIPMENT -- COUNTIES. (52 reports).
tables.

Series consists of a report for the United States and for each
State and the District of Columbia, showing data for
counties and independent cities. Information provided
includes a count of housing units and data on such equipment items as heating equipment, clothes washing machines
and dryers, home food freezers, telephones, automobiles,
air conditioning, television sets, and radios.

1960 CENSUSES OF POPULATION AND HOUSING. PHC(1)
CENSUS TRACTS. (180 reports). tables, map.
See entry on page 64 listing the reports in this series
and describing their contents. This entry is followed
by similar information on general reports based on both
the Population and the Housing censuses.

U. S. Commission on Civil Rights. HEARING HELD IN NEW ORLEANS,
SEPTEMBER 27 AND 28, 1960 AND MAY 5 and 6, 1961. Washington, D.C.:
Government Printing Office; 1961. 847p. tables, charts. pap.

U. S. Commission on Civil Rights. REPORT, 1961. Washington, D.C.:
Government Printing Office, 1961. 5 vols. pap.
Vol. 1; VOTING. Vol. 2; EDUCATION. Vol. 3; EMPLOY-
MENT. Vol. 4; HOUSING. Vol. 5; JUSTICE. HOUSING:
INTRODUCTION, EMERGENCE OF A POLICY, THE GOVERNMENT
AND HOUSING CREDIT, URBAN RENEWAL, OTHER FEDERAL
PROGRAMS, STATE AND LOCAL ACTION, OTHER.

U. S. Congress. Senate. Committee on Banking and Currency. Subcommittee
on Housing. REPORT ON INTERNATIONAL HOUSING PROGRAMS. (87th
Congress, 2d session, Committee Print). Washington, D. C.: Government
Printing Office, 1962. 72p. pap.

U. S. Congress. Senate. Committee on Banking and Currency. HOUSING
FOR FARM LABOR; HEARINGS BEFORE A SUBCOMMITTEE ON...BILLS TO
AMEND TITLE V OF THE HOUSING ACT OF 1949 TO ASSIST IN THE PRO-
VISIONS OF HOUSING FOR DOMESTIC FARM LABOR. 87th CONGRESS,

1st SESSION. Washington, D. C.: Government Printing Office, 1961. 107p. diagrs. pap.

U. S. Department of Commerce. Office of Technical Services. HOW TO MAKE AND INTERPRET LOCATIONAL STUDIES OF THE HOUSING MARKET, by Maurice Brewster, et al. Washington, D. C.: 1955. 66p. pap.

U. S. Federal Housing Administration. FOUR DECADES OF HOUSING WITH A LIMITED DIVIDEND CORPORATION. Washington, D. C.: 1939. 108p. tables, charts. pap.
    Investment experience.

U. S. Federal Housing Administration. HOMES IN METROPOLITAN DISTRICTS; CHARACTERISTICS OF MORTGAGES, HOMES, BORROWERS, UNDER THE FHA PLAN, 1934-1940. (FHA Form no. 2387). Washington, D. C.: Government Printing Office, 1942. 238p. pap.

U. S. Federal Housing Administration. Division of Research and Statistics. A SURVEY OF APARTMENT DWELLING OPERATING EXPERIENCE IN LARGE AMERICAN CITIES. Washington, D. C.: 1940. 138p. tables, charts. pap.

U. S. Federal Housing Administration. Economics and Statistics Division. THE STRUCTURE AND GROWTH OF RESIDENTIAL NEIGHBORHOODS IN AMERICAN CITIES, by Homer Hoyt. Washington, D. C.: 1939. 178p.
    "To suggest techniques through which certain generalizations on city structure and growth may be evolved. "

U. S. Housing and Home Finance Agency. HOUSING MARKET ANALYSIS; A STUDY OF THEORY AND METHODS, by Chester Rapkin, et al. Washington, D. C.: Government Printing Office, 1953. 92p. pap.

U. S. Housing and Home Finance Agency. STATE STATUTES AND LOCAL ORDINANCES AND RESOLUTIONS PROHIBITING DISCRIMINATION IN HOUSING AND URBAN RENEWAL OPERATIONS, prepared by the Intergroup Relations Service and the Office of the General Counsel, Rev. ed. Washinton, D.C.: 1961. 115p. pap.

U. S. Housing and Home Finance Agency. SURVEY OF HOUSING RESEARCH IN THE UNITED STATES, conducted for Building Research Advisory Board, National Research Council, by William H. Scheick, Washington D.C.: 1952. 723p. tables. (Sold by Government Printing Office).

U. S. Housing and Home Finance Agency. Division of Housing Research. HOW TO MAKE AND USE LOCAL HOUSING SURVEYS. Washington D.C.: Government Printing Office, 1954. 106p. illus., tables, charts, diagrs.
    Prepared by The Bureau of Business and Social Research, University of Denver.

U. S. Housing and Home Finance Agency. Office of the Administrator. FIRST PLANNING PAPER ON EMERGENCY HOUSING, by Milton B. Davis.

Washington D.C.: 1961. 53p.
    "Prepared...under an Agreement with the Office of Civil and
    Defense Mobilization."

U. S. Housing and Home Finance Agency. Office of the Administrator.
HOUSING INTERN PROGRAM GUIDE. Washington D.C.: 1961. 14p.
pap.

U. S. Housing and Home Finance Agency. Office of the Administrator. H.H.
F.A. PROGRAM PROGRESS REPORT; URBAN STUDIES AND HOUSING RESEARCH
PROGRAM, 1961-62. WASHINGTON D.C.: 1962.
    Annual.

U.S. President. Executive Order 11063: Equal Opportunity in Housing.
FEDERAL REGISTER, vol. 27, no. 228, November 24, 1962, p. 11527-30.

U. S. Public Housing Administration. AN INFORMAL SURVEY OF HOUSING
FOR THE ELDERLY IN NINE EUROPEAN COUNTRIES, by Mary Cleverly.
Washington D.C.: 1960. 113p. pap. processed.
    A report to the Housing Administrator. Methods and techniques.

U. S. Public Housing Administation. HOUSING FOR THE ELDERLY; ARCHI-
TECT'S CHECKLIST. Washington D.C.: 1962. 16p. pap. processed.

U. S. Works Progress Administration. Division of Social Research. URBAN
HOUSING; A SUMMARY OF REAL PROPERTY INVENTORIES CONDUCTED
AS WORK PROJECTS, 1934-1936, by Peyton Stapp, Washington D.C. Govern-
ment Printing Office, 1938. 326p. charts. pap.
    203 urban areas including over two-fifths of the urban families
    in the United States, "the most comprehensive data yet available
    on a considerable number of the physical and financial character-
    istics of urban dwelling units." Includes special reference in
    summary section to some of the most important findings on the
    extent and characteristics of substandard housing.

Urban Housing and Planning. LAW AND CONTEMPORARY PROBLEMS. vol. 20,
no. 3, Autumn 1955 (entire issue).
    Contents: The Master Plan: An Impermanent Constituion; Relation of
    Planning and Zoning to Housing Policy and Law; Conservation of
    Existing Housing; Private Enforcement of City Planning; Municipal
    Economy and Land Use Restrictions; New Developments in British Land
    Planning Law - 1954 and after; The Diminishing Fee.

Vacation Cabins. JOURNAL OF HOMEBUILDING. vol. 16, no. 8, August
1962, p. 61-6.

The Vacation Home. JOURNAL OF HOMEBUILDING. vol. 15, no. 7, July
1961, p. 71-7.
    Includes Selected Reading Matter on Vacation Homes, p. 77.

GENERAL (continued)

Van Ettinger, J. TOWARD A HABITABLE WORLD. Amsterdam: Published
for Bouwcentrum by Elsevier, 1960. 318p. illus., tables, diagrs. (Dist.
for U.S., Van Nostrand).

Veiller, Lawrence. A MODEL HOUSING LAW, Rev. ed., New York:
Russell Sage Foundation, 1920. 430p.
   1st edition, 1914, was a pioneer effort. A number of states
   and cities passed housing legislation based on it. "This
   new edition represents not only the experience of all the
   states and cities in the country which have enacted housing
   laws since 1914, but also the experience as well of the author
   in his capacity as Secretary of the National Housing Association in aiding in the drafting of such laws, in adapting them
   to local conditions and in meeting the difficulties that have
   arisen." Table of sections changed from first edition.

Wendt, Paul F. HOUSING POLICY - THE SEARCH FOR SOLUTIONS: A
COMPARISON OF THE UNITED KINGDOM, SWEDEN, WEST GERMANY,
AND THE UNITED STATES SINCE WORLD WAR II. Berkeley:
University of California Press, 1962. 283p.

(Roy) Wenzlick Research Corp. HOUSING FOR THE AGED. St. Louis:
1962. 45p. pap. processed.
   Case studies based on actual audited studies have been developed
   for a more complete understanding of the problems and costs
   involved. 1: Independent Housing: Single-Family Homes,
   Ranchette Apartments, Prefabricated Buildings, Elevator Apartments; 2: Resident Participation Facilities; 3: Nursing
   Homes; 4: Life Care Type Facilities.

White House Conference on Aging, Washington D.C. 1961. BACKGROUND
PAPER ON HOUSING. Washington, D.C.: 73p. tables. pap. processed.
   Housing needs and supply, current efforts affecting the housing
   supply, housing trends -- emerging patterns and current problems
   and issues.

Wilner, Daniel, et al. THE HOUSING ENVIRONMENT AND FAMILY LIFE;
A LONGITUDINAL STUDY OF THE EFFECTS OF HOUSING ON MORBIDITY
AND MENTAL HEALTH. Baltimore: Johns Hopkins Press, 1962. 338p. tables.
   Includes a review of the 40 previous studies and a selected
   bibliography.

Winnick, Louis. RENTAL HOUSING: OPPORTUNITIES FOR PRIVATE INVEST-
MENT. (ACTION Series in Housing and Community Development). New York:
McGraw-Hill, 1958. 295p.

Winnick, Louis. WEALTH ESTIMATES FOR RESIDENTIAL REAL ESTATE, 1890-
1950. Unpublished Ph.D. thesis, University of Michigan, 1953.

Winnick, Louis and Shilling, Ned. AMERICAN HOUSING AND ITS USE;
THE DEMAND FOR SHELTER SPACE. (Census Monograph Series). New York:

GENERAL (continued)

John Wiley, 1957. 143p. tables.
> For the Social Science Research Council in cooperation with the
> U.S. Department of Commerce, Bureau of the Census. Measuring
> the utilization of housing by the persons-per-room ratio, as
> determined by income, household size, value and rent, location
> and race. With a discussion of size of dwelling units and
> changes in household composition that occurred between 1940
> and 1950.

Woodbury, Coleman. APARTMENT HOUSE INCREASES AND ATTITUDES
TOWARD HOME OWNERSHIP. (Studies in Land Economics; Research
Monograph No. 4). Chicago: Institute for Economic Research, 1931. 74p.
tables, charts. pap.

TRAILER PARKS

Council of Planning Librarians. MOBILE HOME PARKS. (Exchange Bibliography No. 14). Oakland, Calif.: 6318 Thornhill Drive, zone 11, 1960.
20p. pap. processed.

American Society of Planning Officials. THE CHANGING FUNCTION OF
TRAILER PARKS. (Planning Advisory Service Information Report No. 84).
Chicago: 1956. 32p. pap. processed.

American Society of Planning Officials. REGULATION OF MOBILE HOME
SUBDIVISIONS. (Planning Advisory Service Information Report No. 145).
Chicago: 1961. 36p. pap. processed.

Bartley, Ernest R. and Bair, Frederick H. Jr. MOBILE HOME PARKS AND
COMPREHENSIVE PLANNING. Gainesville: Public Administration Clearing
Service, University of Florida, 1960. 147p. illus., diagrs. pap.
> Principles and references for location, regulation, operation, and
> site design of trailer parks.

Hodes, Barnet and Roberson, G. Gale. THE LAW OF MOBILE HOMES.
Chicago: Commerce Clearing House, 1957. 464p.
> Compilation of "cases involving mobile homes scattered through
> dozens of miscellaneous fields of law." Includes model ordinances
> and statutes.

Jones, Leslie M. Mobile Home Parks: Investment Potential. p. 143-7 In
National Real Estate Investor. NATIONAL REAL ESTATE HANDBOOK
DIRECTORY. New York: 1962.

Michelon, L.C. HOW TO BUILD AND OPERATE A MOBILE-HOME PARK.

TRAILER PARKS (continued)

Chicago: Mobile Home Manufacturers Association, 1955. 122p. illus., diagrs.
> Planning, building, and operating information based on a research program of actual development.

Mobile Home Manufacturers Association. A COMPREHENSIVE APPROACH TO MOBILE HOME PARK FINANCING, comp. by Leslie M. Jones. Chicago: 1962. various paging.
> Methods of financing and estimated developed costs.

Mobile Home Manufacturers Association. MOBILE HOMES INDUSTRY REPORT. Chicago, 1952- . pap.
> Present format established in the 9th survey covering 1959. Summary of information relating to the industry: industry, product, product placement, financial survey.

National Association of Real Estate Boards. MOBILE HOMES AND RESIDENTIAL LAND USE, by Dean W. Dittmer and Catherine E. Martini. Washington D.C.: 1960. 17p. pap. processed.
> Department of Research survey to determine increased use of trailers as dwellings and the relationship of trailer occupants and trailer parks to the community, for the Realtor-City Planners Committee.

U.S. Federal Housing Administration. MINIMUM PROPERTY REQUIREMENTS FOR MOBILE HOME COURTS, Rev. (FHA Form 2424). Washington, D.C.: 1961. 81p. diagrs. pap.

U.S. Federal Housing Administration. MOBILE HOME COURTS; SUGGESTIONS FOR SITE SELECTION, PLANNING AND IMPROVEMENTS. (Land Planning Bulletin 5). Washington, D.C.: 1955. 10p. pap.

U.S. Public Health Service. MOBILE HOME PARK SANITATION, WITH A SUGGESTED ORDINANCE, Rev. Chicago: Mobile Home Manufacturers Association, 1960. 28p. illus., diagrs. pap.
> Printed as a public service by Mobile Home Manufacturers Association and the Trailer Coach Association.

PUBLIC HOUSING

Eberstein, William. THE LAW OF PUBLIC HOUSING. Madison: University of Wisconsin Press, 1940. 150p.
> Contents: 1: The Elements of the Housing Problem; 2: Government and Housing; 3: Public Housing and the Law: Federal; 4: Public Housing and the Law: State; 5: Foreign Experiences and

PUBLIC HOUSING (continued)

Problems; Text of the United States Housing Act; Two Leading
Cases Relating to Public Housing; Table of cases.

Fisher, Robert Moore. TWENTY YEARS OF PUBLIC HOUSING; ECONOMIC
ASPECTS OF THE FEDERAL PROGRAM. New York: Harper, 1959. 303p.
tables.
> The study ... was originally undertaken in preparing a Ph.D.
> dissertation at Columbia University. "In analyzing certain
> economic aspects of the low-rent program, the book collects
> and interprets a variety of statistical information. Much of the
> data on federally aided public housing are published here for
> the first time." Bibliography; p. 282-8.

Georgia State College of Business Administration. Bureau of Business and
Economic Research. THE DEVELOPMENT OF THE PUBLIC HOUSING PRO-
GRAM IN THE UNITED STATES, by Robert K. Brown. (Studies in Business
and Economics, Bulletin No. 7). Atlanta: 1960. 92p. pap.
> Traces legislative action and its implementation.

Meyerson, Martin and Banfield, Edward C. POLITICS, PLANNING AND
THE PUBLIC INTEREST: THE CASE OF PUBLIC HOUSING IN CHICAGO.
Glencoe, Ill.: Free Press, 1955. 353p. maps.
> Focus on certain decisions made by the local and Federal agencies
> and on certain related decisions made in the local political
> structure, especially as related to location of projects and
> racial composition of occupancy, and to a small degree, archi-
> tectural type, to develop a perspective for the analysis of de-
> cision-making processes in general.

National Association of Real Estate Boards. Realtors' Washington Committee.
SOME FACTS, COMMENTS AND OPINION ABOUT PUBLIC HOUSING.
Washington D.C.: 1962. n.p. pap. processed.
> Reprints of newspaper articles primarily. "Some basic data
> about this controversial program for the use of local groups who
> are resisting the initiation of a public housing project ..."

National Housing Conference. THE HOUSING YEARBOOK. Washington,
D.C.: 1025 Connecticut Avenue, N.W., zone 6, 1954-

Schaffter, Dorothy. STATE HOUSING AGENCIES. New York: Columbia
University Press, 1942. 808p. tables.

Straus, Nathan. THE SEVEN MYTHS OF HOUSING. New York: Knopf,
1944. 313p.

U. S. Public Housing Administration. ANNUAL REPORT. Washington, D.C.:
Government Printing Office, 1947- . pap.
> From 1947 to date, issued as part of the Housing and Home Finance
> Agency ANNUAL REPORT and separately.

PUBLIC HOUSING (continued)

U.S. Public Housing Administration. INCOME LIMITS; A BULLETIN PREPARED BY A JOINT COMMITTEE OF THE PUBLIC HOUSING ADMINISTRATION AND THE NATIONAL ASSOCIATION OF HOUSING AND REDEVELOPMENT OFFICIALS. Washington, D.C.: 1961. 68p. pap.

Residential Property—Bibliography

Council of Planning Librarians. MOBILE HOME PARKS. (Exchange Bibliography no. 14). Oakland, Calif.: 6318 Thornhill Drive, zone 11, 1960. 20p. pap. processed.

Council of Planning Librarians. RESIDENTIAL DENSITIES. (Exchange Bibliography No. 18). Oakland, Calif.: 6318 Thornhill Drive, zone 11, 1961. 20p. pap. processed.

HOUSING AND PLANNING REFERENCES. U.S. Housing and Home Finance Agency Library, Washington 25, D.C.
        "A selected list of publications and an index of articles." Classified arrangement. Issued bi-monthly.

National Association of Housing and Redevelopment Officials. SELECTED REFERENCES ON HOUSING CODES. Chicago: 1959. folder. pap.

National Housing Center. Library. BIBLIOGRAPHY SERIES and REFERENCE LIST series. Washington, D.C.: National Association of Home Builders.

National Housing Center. Library. HOUSING AND CONSTRUCTION; BASIC TEXTS AND REFERENCE BOOKS. (Bibliography Series no. 2). Washington, D.C.: National Association of Home Builders, 1957. 52p. pap.
        239 annotated references plus list of periodicals.

National Housing Center. Library. HOUSING FOR OUR SENIOR CITIZENS; A LIST OF SELECTED REFERENCES PREPARED FOR THE INSTITUTE ON PRODUCING HOUSING FOR OLDER PEOPLE. NEW YORK CITY, 26-28 MARCH '61. (Reference List No. 35). Washington D.C.: National Association of Home Builders, 1961. 5p. pap. processed.

National Housing Center. Library. VACATION HOMES; A LIST OF SELECTED REFERENCES. Washington D.C.: National Association of Home Builders, 1960. 4p. pap. processed.

Smith, Thelma E. comp. Planning and Housing, 1960; a Selected Bibliography. NEW YORK MUNICIPAL REFERENCE LIBRARY NOTES, December, 1960, p. 389-93; January, 1961, p. 1-5; February, 1961, p. 13-8; March 1961, p. 26-30; April 1961, p. 37-41.

Residential Property—Bibliography (continued)

U. S. Bureau of the Budget. Central Statistical Board. CONSTRUCTION, HOUSING AND REAL PROPERTY; A SURVEY OF AVAILABLE BASIC STATIS- TICAL DATA, by Jean H. Williams. Washington D.C.: Government Printing Office, 1940. 169p. pap. processed.

U. S. Bureau of Labor Standards. SELECTED REFERENCES ON DOMESTIC MIGRATORY AGRECULTURAL WORKERS, THEIR FAMILIES, PROBLEMS, AND PROGRAMS, 1955-60. (Bulletin 225). Washington, D.C., 1961. 38p. pap.

U. S. Housing and Home Finance Agency, Office of the Administrator. A SPECIAL LIST OF HOUSING RESEARCH PUBLICATIONS, Rev. Washington D.C.: 1961. 2p. pap. processed.
> Earlier edition issued by Office of the Administrator, Division of Housing Research. The technical reports still available resulting from the general housing research program of the agency between 1948 and 1954.

U. S. Housing and Home Finance Agency. Office of the Administrator. Library. SELECTED READINGS FOR HOUSING INTERNS, Rev. Washington D.C.: 1960. 10p. pap. processed.

Residential Property—Periodicals
(See Appendix for complete information concerning these publications.)

APARTMENT JOURNAL, APARTMENT MANAGEMENT IN NEW ENGLAND, ARCHITECTURAL FORUM, ARCHITECTURAL RECORD, HOUSE & HOME, HOUSING, HOUSING AND URBAN AFFAIRS DAILY, HOUSING STATISTICS, HOUSING STARTS, HOUSING TRENDS, HOUSING VACANCIES, JOURNAL OF HOME- BUILDING, JOURNAL OF HOUSING, MANUFACTURED HOMES, REAL ESTATE ANALYST, RENTAL HOUSING, SALES OF NEW ONE-FAMILY HOMES, SAVINGS AND HOME OWNERSHIP, TOURIST COURT JOURNAL, TRENDS IN HOUSING.

APPENDIX A

PERIODICALS

AGRICULTURAL INDEX. H. W. Wilson Company, 950 University Avenue, New York 52, New York. 1916-
> Published monthly except September; cumulations issued. Includes periodicals, books, agricultural experiment station and extension service publications. Federal and state government publications, Food and Agriculture Organization reports.

ALL OPERATING SAVINGS AND LOAN ASSOCIATIONS, SELECTED BALANCE SHEET DATA AND FLOW OF SAVINGS AND MORTGAGE LENDING ACTIVITY. Federal Home Loan Bank Board, Washington 25, D.C.
> Monthly.

AMERICAN BUILDER. 30 Church Street, New York 7, New York.
> Three regional editions: Midwest, West Coast, Washington.
> Monthly.

AMERICAN CITY. 470 Park Avenue, South, New York 16, New York.
> Monthly.

AMERICAN INSTITUTE OF ARCHITECTS JOURNAL. 1735 New York Ave., N. W., Washington, D.C.
> Formerly JOURNAL OF THE AMERICAN INSTITUTE OF ARCHITECTS. Monthly.

AMERICAN MOTEL MAGAZINE. See HOSPITALITY.

ANNALS OF THE SOCIETY OF CHARTERED PROPERTY AND CASUALTY UNDERWRITERS. 266 Bryn Mawr Avenue, Bryn Mawr, Pennsylvania.
> Quarterly.

APARTMENT JOURNAL. 551 S. Oxford Avenue, Los Angeles 5, California.
> Official publication of the Apartment Association of Los Angeles County, Inc. Formerly WESTERN HOUSING. Monthly.

APARTMENT MANAGEMENT IN NEW ENGLAND. Middlesex Apartment Owners' Association, Inc., Box 224, Winchester, Massachusetts.
> Monthly. Controlled distribution.

APPRAISAL DIGEST. New York State Society of Real Estate Appraisers of New York State Association of Real Estate Boards, 210 State Street, Albany 10, New York.
> Quarterly.

APPRAISAL INSTITUTE MAGAZINE. Appraisal Institute of Canada, Inc., 909 Electric Railway Chambers, Winnipeg 2, Manitoba.
   Quarterly.

APPRAISAL JOURNAL. American Institute of Real Estate Appraisers, 36 South Wabash Avenue, Chicago 3, Illinois.
   Quarterly.

THE APPRAISER. American Institute of Real Estate Appraisers, 36 South Wabash Avenue, Chicago 3, Illinois.
   Monthly except July and August.

ARCHITECTURAL FORUM. Time, Inc., Time and Life Building, Rockefeller Center, New York 20, New York.
   Monthly.

ARCHITECTURAL INDEX. 517 Bridgeway, Sausalito, California.
   Annual. Index to ARTS AND ARCHITECTURE, ARCHITECTURAL FORUM, ARCHITECTURAL RECORD, HOUSE AND HOME, INTERIORS, and PROGRESSIVE ARCHITECTURE.

ARCHITECTURAL RECORD. F. W. Dodge Corporation, 119 West 40th Street, New York 18, New York.
   Monthly except May, when semi-monthly.

AREA REDEVELOPMENT. U.S. Department of Commerce, Washington 25, D.C. (Sold by Government Printing Office).
   Bi-monthly. Former title was AREA DEVELOPMENT BULLETIN.
   Redevelopment Library column includes brief annotations.

ASSESSORS' NEWSLETTER. International Association of Assessing Officers, 1313 East 60th Street, Chicago 37, Illinois.
   Monthly.

BANKERS RESEARCH. 28 Church Lane, Westport, Connecticut.
   Semi-monthly. Current developments in the mortgage market.

BARRON'S NATIONAL BUSINESS AND FINANCIAL WEEKLY. 200 Burnett Road, Chicopee Falls, Wisconsin.
   Weekly.

BEST'S INSURANCE NEWS. Fire and casualty edition. Alfred M. Best Company, 75 Fulton Street, New York 38, New York.
   Monthly.

BIBLIOGRAPHY OF AGRICULTURE. National Agricultural Library, Washington 25, D.C. (Sold by Government Printing Office).
   A monthly index of publications on agriculture and related subjects received in the National Agricultural Library.
   Lists approximately 100,000 items annually. Subtitle: A LIST OF RECENT U.S.D.A. PUBLICATIONS, STATE AGRICULTURAL EXPERIMENT STATION PUBLICATIONS, AGRICULTURAL EX-

TENSION SERVICE PUBLICATIONS, F.A.O. PUBLICATIONS,
AND AUTHOR INDEX.

BROKERS ROUND TABLE. National Institute of Real Estate Brokers, 36 South
Wabash Avenue, Chicago 3, Illinois.
>   Quarterly. Controlled distribution. Newsletter format with
>   each issue devoted to one brokerage topic.

BUILD AMERICA BETTER BULLETIN. National Association of Real Estate Boards,
Build America Better Committee, 1300 Connecticut Avenue, N.W., Washington 6, D.C.
>   Irregular. "Features up-to-the-minute information on renewal
>   from the nation's capital along with reports on conservation and
>   rehabilitation activities around the country."

BUILDING COSTS. E. H. Boeckh and Associates, 1406 M Street, N.W.,
Washington 5, D.C.
>   "Monthly publication giving current cost conversion factors or
>   indexes for the major metropolitan areas of the United States
>   and Canada. New cost studies on buildings to augment the
>   Manual. National trends and new techniques are regular
>   features." For users of Boeckh's MANUAL OF APPRAISALS and
>   INDEX CALCULATOR.

BUILDING PERMITS: NEW HOUSING UNITS AUTHORIZED BY LOCAL BUILD-
ING PERMITS. (Construction Reports. C-40 Series). U.S. Bureau of the
Census, Washington 25, D.C.
>   Monthly. 3,000 places (county, city, town, etc.). Includes
>   public housing units.

BUILDING PERMITS: NEW RESIDENTIAL CONSTRUCTION AUTHORIZED IN
PERMIT ISSUING PLACES. (Construction Reports. C-42 Series). U.S.
Bureau of the Census, Washington 25, D.C.
>   Monthly.

BUILDING SCIENCE ABSTRACTS. Building Research Station. Her Majesty's
Stationery Office, York House, Kingsway, London W.C. 2, England.
>   Monthly.

BUILDINGS. Stamats Publishing Company, 427 Sixth Avenue, S.E., Cedar
Rapids, Iowa.
>   Monthly. N.A.R.E.B. Roster issued in May as part of subscrip-
>   tion, 1959-1961; Separate publication, 1962- . November
>   issue: HANDBOOK OF BUILDING OPERATION; December,
>   issue: YEARBOOK OF REAL ESTATE AND MANAGEMENT.

BULLETIN OF THE PUBLIC AFFAIRS INFORMATION SERVICE. 11 West 40th
Street, New York 18, New York.
>   Weekly. Issued weekly with five periodic cumulations each
>   year culminating in an annual cumulative volume. Cites books,
>   periodicals, articles, pamphlets, government documents, and
>   miscellaneous reports.

BUSINESS PERIODICALS INDEX. H. W. Wilson Company, 950 University Avenue, New York 52, New York.
> Monthly.

BUSINESS STATISTICS. U.S. Department of Commerce, Office of Business Economics, Washington 25, D.C.
> Weekly. Supplement to SURVEY OF CURRENT BUSINESS.

BUSINESS TREND NEWS; BUILDING PERMIT VALUES. Dun and Bradstreet, Inc., 99 Church Street, New York 8, New York.
> Monthly. Values in 200 leading cities. Estimated building costs under permits issued including residential and non-residential buildings as well as additions, alterations and repairs. Land costs are not included.

CALIFORNIA REAL ESTATE MAGAZINE. California Real Estate Association, 117 West Ninth Street, Los Angeles 15, California.
> Monthly.

CANADIAN REALTOR. Canadian Association of Real Estate Boards, 20 Eglinton, East, Toronto 12, Ontario.
> Monthly.

CHAIN STORE AGE, 2 Park Avenue, New York 16, New York.
> Monthly. Annual survey each May of chain store leases in shopping centers.

CHARACTERISTICS OF HOME MORTGAGE LOANS, CHICAGO AREA. Federal Reserve Bank of Chicago, Research Department, Box 834, Chicago 90, Illinois.
> Monthly.

CHARTERED AUCTIONEER AND ESTATE AGENT. Chartered Auctioneers' and Estate Agents' Institute, 29 Lincoln's Inn Fields, London W.C. 2, England.
> Monthly.

CHARTERED SURVEYOR. Royal Institution of Chartered Surveyors, 12 Great George Street, Parliament Square, Westminister, S.W. 1, London, England.
> Monthly.

CHICAGO MARKET LETTER. Real Estate Research Corporation, 73 West Monroe Street, Chicago 3, Illinois.
> Monthly.

CHICAGOLAND HOUSING MARKET. Chicago Association of Commerce and Industry, Research Clearing House Committee, 30 West Monroe Street, Chicago 3, Illinois.
> Quarterly; Monthly supplements.

CLEARINGHOUSE FOR MEETING DATES. National Association of Real Estate Boards, Department of Education, 36 South Wabash Avenue, Chicago 3, Illinois.
> Irregular.

CLIENTS SERVICE BULLETIN. American Appraisal Company, 525 East Michigan, Milwaukee, Wisconsin.
>Bi-monthly.

COMMUNITY FACILITIES ADMINISTRATION NEWS. U. S. Community Facilities Administration, Washington 25, D.C.
>Irregular. 5 issues in 1961.

COMMUNITY PLANNING REVIEW. Community Planning Association of Canada, 425 Gloucester Street, Ottawa 4, Canada.
>Quarterly.

CONSTRUCTION ACTIVITY; VALUE OF NEW CONSTRUCTION PUT IN PLACE. (Construction Reports, C-30 Series). U.S. Bureau of the Census, Washington 25, D.C.
>Monthly.

CONSTRUCTION REVIEW. U.S. Department of Commerce, Office of Business Economics, Washington 25, D.C. (Sold by Government Printing Office).
>Monthly. Formerly published as U.S. Department of Commerce CONSTRUCTION AND BUILDING MATERIALS and Department of Labor CONSTRUCTION, which merged in 1955. Value of new construction, residential alterations and repairs; housing starts by ownership and type of structure, location and average cost, housing in government programs, vacancy rates; shipments of mobile homes; value and number of building permits by type of construction; contract awards; construction cost indexes, wholesale materials price indexes, union hourly wage scales; output of construction materials; contract construction employment.

CONVENTIONAL LOANS MADE IN EXCESS OF 80 PERCENT OF PROPERTY APPRAISAL, BY FEDERAL SAVINGS AND LOAN ASSOCIATIONS. Federal Home Loan Bank Board, Washington 25, D.C.
>Quarterly.

CONVENTIONAL LOANS MADE TO FINANCE ACQUISITION AND DEVELOPMENT OF LAND, FEDERAL SAVINGS AND LOAN ASSOCIATIONS. Federal Home Loan Bank Board, Washington 25, D.C.
>Quarterly. Tables of number and amount of loans for United States and the eleven F.H.L.B. districts.

DIRECTORS DIGEST. United States Savings and Loan League, 221 North LaSalle Street, Chicago 1, Illinois.
>Monthly.

DISCOUNT STORE NEWS, 2 Park Avenue, New York 16, New York.
>Bi-weekly.

DODGE REPORTS: CONSTRUCTION CONTRACTS STATISTICS. F. W. Dodge Corporation, 119 West 40th Street, New York 18, New York.
>Subscription available for all or one of three types of reports: General building service, House service, Engineering service. Price depends on selection of coverage by subscriber.

DOWNTOWN IDEA EXCHANGE. 125 East 23rd Street, New York 10, New York.
>Semi-monthly.

EASTERN UNDERWRITER. 232 Madison Avenue, New York 16, New York.
>Weekly.

ECONOMIC GEOGRAPHY. Clark University, Worcester 10, Massachusetts.
>Quarterly. W. Elmer Ekblaw Memorial Index to Economic Geography, volumes 1-25, 1925-1949. 1950.

EDUCATIONAL LETTER. National Association of Real Estate Boards, Department of Education, 36 South Wabash Avenue, Chicago 3, Illinois.
>Bimonthly.

EKISTICS: ABSTRACTS ON THE PROBLEMS AND SCIENCE OF HUMAN SETTLE-MENTS. Doxiadis Associates, 24 Strat. Syndesmou, Athens, Greece.
>Monthly.

EMPLOYMENT AND EARNINGS. U.S. Bureau of Labor Statistics, Washington 25, D.C. (Sold by Government Printing Office).
>Monthly. Contains statistics on gross hours and earnings of production workers in finance, insurance and real estate.

ENGINEERING NEWS-RECORD. 330 West 42nd Street, New York 36, New York.
>Weekly. E.N.R. building cost index.

ESTIMATED HOME MORTGAGE DEBT AND FINANCING ACTIVITY. Federal Home Loan Bank Board, Washington 25, D.C.
>Quarterly. " 'Home loans' include all mortgage loans on one-to-four-family nonfarm residences, regardless of occupancy status (owner-occupied, rented, and vacant)."

FARM COST SITUATION. U.S. Department of Agriculture, Economic Research Service, Washington 25, D.C.
>Triannually. Tables on farm property taxes and sales data.

FARM INDEX. U.S. Department of Agriculture, Economic Research Service, Washington 25, D.C. (Sold by Government Printing Office, Washington 25, D.C.). Monthly.

FARM-MORTGAGE LENDING EXPERIENCE. U.S. Department of Agriculture, Economic Research Service, Washington 25, D.C.
>Quarterly. Reports on twenty-one life insurance companies, the Federal land banks, and the Farmers Home Administration activity. (Was ARS--43 Series).

FARM REAL ESTATE MARKET DEVELOPMENTS. U.S. Department of Agriculture, Economic Research Service, Washington 25, D.C.
> Triannually. Formerly CURRENT DEVELOPMENTS IN THE FARM
> REAL ESTATE MARKET. Tables of estimated market value per
> acre by state and region and by major classes of land use.

FEDERAL HOME LOAN BANK BOARD DIGEST. Federal Home Loan Bank
Board, Washington 25, D.C.
> Monthly.

FHA MONTHLY REPORTS OF OPERATION. Federal Housing Administration,
Division of Research and Statistics, Statistics Section, Washington 25, D.C.
> Monthly. Applications received, committments issued, mort-
> gages insured for home mortgages, multifamily housing programs
> with total insured from the beginning of each program to date.

FEDERAL NATIONAL MORTGAGE ASSOCIATION NEWS. Federal National
Mortgage Association, Washington 25, D.C.
> Irregular.

FEDERAL RESERVE BULLETIN. Board of Governors of the Federal Reserve
System, Washington 25, D.C.
> Monthly. Includes quarterly survey of consumer buying inten-
> tions. Monthly reports on real estate credit and construction.

Federal reserve monthly bulletins of business conditions for the various districts.
> Monthly. Each district bank issues a monthly bulletin. The
> Research Departments may be an excellent source of information
> about land prices, mortgage market conditions, etc.

FSLIC INSURED SAVINGS AND LOAN ASSOCIATIONS; SAVINGS AND
MORTGAGE LENDING ACTIVITY--SELECTED BALANCE SHEET ITEMS.
Federal Home Loan Bank Board, Washington 25, D.C.
> Monthly. Figures for current month, preliminary; figures for
> previous month revised. Given for United States and for the
> eleven FHLB districts.

FROM THE STATE CAPITALS--REAL PROPERTY TAX TRENDS SUMMARIZED.
Bethune Jones, 234 River Road, Red Bank, New Jersey.
> Monthly. "A continuing and impartial analysis of state and
> municipal legislative and regulatory trends of nation wide
> significance."

FROM THE STATE CAPITALS--REVIEW OF REDEVELOPMENT AND HOUSING
LAW TRENDS. Bethune Jones, 234 River Road, Red Bank, New Jersey.
> Monthly.

FUNDAMENTALS AND STANDARDS BULLETIN. Institute of Real Estate Management, 36 South Wabash Avenue, Chicago 3, Illinois.
> Monthly. Numbers 1 to 4 issued as MANUALS. Each BULLETIN
> on a specific subject: practical aspects of materials, maintenance,
> personnel, equipment, etc.

HOMEBUILDING NEWS. National Association of Home Builders, 1625 L Street, N.W., Washington 6, D.C.
> Controlled distribution.

HORWATH ACCOUNTANT. Horwath and Horwath, 41 East 42nd Street, New York 17, New York.
> Monthly. Hotels, motels, restaurants, city and country clubs. Annual income and expense surveys.

HOSPITALITY--FOOD AND LODGING. (formerly AMERICAN MOTEL MAGAZINE AND AMERICAN RESTAURANT MAGAZINE). 5 South Wabash Avenue, Chicago 3, Illinois.
> Monthly. American Hotel-Motel-Resort Hospitality included in Food and Lodging. May be purchased as a separate publication for those with no interest in restaurants.

HOTEL AND APARTMENT MANAGER. Managers Hotel and Apartment Association, 1741 North Ivar Avenue, Los Angeles 28, California.
> Monthly.

HOUSE AND HOME. Time, Inc., Rockefeller Center, New York 20, New York.
> Monthly. Home building trade publication. News section includes national developments, market information of interest to any one in real estate. Articles for home builders. Mortgage market and housing stock. Market quotations.

HOUSING AND HOME FINANCE AGENCY WEEKLY NEWS SUMMARY, RELEASES ISSUED. U.S. Housing and Home Finance Agency, Washington 25, D.C.
> Weekly.

HOUSING AND URBAN AFFAIRS DAILY. National Housing Publications, Inc., 1120 National Press Building, Washington 4, D.C.
> Daily, except Saturday, Sunday and holidays. A regular feature is news of the housing agencies. Includes reports from the other Federal agencies and associations.

HOUSING AND PLANNING REFERENCES. U.S. Housing and Home Finance Agency, Library, Washington 25, D.C.
> Bi-monthly. Selected list of publications and index of articles on housing and planning in the libraries of HHFA, FHA, PHA, and FHLBB.

HOUSING STARTS. (Construction Reports, C-20 Series). U.S. Bureau of the Census, Washington 25, D.C.
> Monthly. Number of new units started by ownership, by metropolitan, non-metropolitan location and type of structure.

HOUSING STATISTICS. U.S. Housing and Home Finance Agency, Washington 25, D.C.
> Monthly. Historical supplement, October, 1961. Current statistics on housing production, construction costs, home financing, urban renewal, community facilities and specified housing programs of HHFA.

HOUSING TRENDS; THE LATEST TRENDS AFFECTING RESIDENTIAL CON-
STRUCTION. House and Garden Magazine, 420 Lexington Avenue, New York
17, New York.

HOUSING VACANCIES. (HOUSING REPORTS, H-111 SERIES). U.S. Bureau
of the Census, Washington 25, D.C.
> Quarterly. Rental and homeowner vacancy rates for U.S. re-
> gions and inside and outside standard metropolitan statistical
> areas. Percent distributions by condition and status.

IN THE FIELD. Society of Real Estate Appraisers, 7 South Dearborn Street,
Chicago 3, Illinois.
> Monthly newsletter.

INDEX TO LEGAL PERIODICALS. H. W. Wilson Company, 950 University
Avenue, New York 52, New York.
> Monthly.

INDUSTRIAL DEVELOPMENT AND MANUFACTURERS RECORD; THE INTER-
NATIONAL GUIDE TO INDUSTRIAL PLANNING AND EXPANSION. Conway
Publications, Inc., 2592 Apple Valley Road, Atlanta 19, Georgia.
> 13 issues per year. October issue: International Site Selection
> Handbook. Official publication of the Industrial Development
> Research Council. Includes cumulative index. A regular feature
> is Recent Releases, a listing with brief annotations of general
> reports and area reports, just published.

INDUSTRIAL PROPERTY GUIDE. Society of Industrial Realtors. Service Industries, Inc., Lincoln Building, Cleveland 14, Ohio.
> Controlled distribution.

INSURANCE LITERATURE. Special Libraries Association, Insurance Division,
31 East 10th Street, New York 3, New York.
> 10 issues per year. Lists new publications and selected period-
> ical articles in a classified arrangement.

JOURNAL OF THE AMERICAN INSTITUTE OF PLANNERS. 917 Fifteenth
Street, N. W., Washington 5, D.C.
> Quarterly.

JOURNAL OF AMERICAN INSURANCE. 20 North Wacker Drive, Chicago 6,
Illinois.
> Monthly.

JOURNAL OF THE AMERICAN SOCIETY OF FARM MANAGERS AND RURAL
APPRAISERS. Box 295, DeKalb, Illinois.
> Semi-annually.

JOURNAL OF FARM ECONOMICS. American Farm Economic Association,
Menasha, Wisconsin.
> 5 times a year.

JOURNAL OF FINANCE. American Finance Association, 5750 Ellis Avenue,

Chicago 37, Illinois.
Quarterly.

JOURNAL OF HOMEBUILDING. National Association of Home Builders,
1625 L Street, N.W., Washington 6, D.C.
Monthly. Controlled distribution.

JOURNAL OF HOUSING. National Association of Housing and Redevelopment
Officials, 1413 K Street, N.W., Washington 5, D.C.
10 issues per year. Public housing.

JOURNAL OF THE NATIONAL LEAGUE OF INSURED SAVINGS ASSOCIATIONS.
1200 18th Street, N.W., Washington 6, D.C.
Monthly. Controlled distribution. Formerly NATIONAL SAV-
INGS AND LOAN JOURNAL.

JOURNAL OF PROPERTY MANAGEMENT. Institute of Real Estate Management,
36 South Wabash Avenue, Chicago 3, Illinois.
Quarterly.

LAND ECONOMICS; A QUARTERLY JOURNAL OF PLANNING, HOUSING,
AND PUBLIC UTILITIES. University of Wisconsin, Sterling Hall, Madison 6,
Wisconsin.
Quarterly.

LEGAL BULLETIN; THE LAW AFFECTING SAVINGS ASSOCIATIONS. United
States Savings and Loan League, 221 North LaSalle Street, Chicago 1, Illinois.
Bi-monthly. Cumulative index, 1954-1960 in the November
1960 issue.

MANUFACTURED HOMES. Home Manufacturers Association, 117 Barr Building,
Washington 6, D.C.
Monthly.

MARINA, INCORPORATING MARINE DEALER. Marina Publications, Inc.,
75 Station Street, Southport, Connecticut.
Bi-monthly.

MARKETING INFORMATION SERVICE. U.S. Department of Commerce,
Business and Defense Services Administration, Washington 25, D.C. (Sold by
Government Printing Office).
Monthly. Listing of publications of Federal agencies, associ-
ations and commercial publishers in marketing.

MIDWEST HOUSING MARKETS; A STATISTICAL SUMMARY OF TEN KEY
METROPOLITAN AREAS. Advance Mortgage Corporation, First National
Building, Detroit 26, Michigan.
Quarterly, Regional, Chicago, Cincinnati, Cleveland, Columbus
Columbus, Dayton, Detroit, Grand Rapids, Indianapolis,
Milwaukee, Pittsburgh, U.S.A.

MONEY MAKING IDEAS FROM FELLOW REALTORS. National Institute of
Real Estate Brokers, 36 South Wabash Avenue, Chicago 3, Illinois.
Quarterly. Controlled distribution.

MONTHLY CATALOG OF U.S. GOVERNMENT PUBLICATIONS. U.S. Superintendent of Documents, Washington 25, D.C.
Monthly.

MONTHLY CHECKLIST OF STATE GOVERNMENT PUBLICATIONS. U.S. Library of Congress, Washington 25, D.C. (Sold by Government Printing Office).
Monthly.

MONTHLY LABOR REVIEW. U.S. Department of Labor, Bureau of Labor
Statistics, Washington 25, D.C. (Sold by Government Printing Office).
Monthly. Number of employees in real estate and operative
building.

MONTHLY TRADER. International Traders Club of the National Institute of
Real Estate Brokers, 36 South Wabash Avenue, Chicago 3, Illinois.
Monthly. Controlled distribution.

MORTGAGE BANKER. Mortgage Bankers Association of America, 111 West
Washington Street, Chicago 2, Illinois.
Monthly.

MORTGAGE BULLETIN FOR BANKS OF DEPOSIT. American Bankers Association, 12 East 36th Street, New York 6, New York.
Irregular. Includes regional mortgage market reports and general mortgage statistics for banks.

MORTGAGE INTEREST RATES ON CONVENTIONAL LOANS, LARGEST IN-
SURED SAVINGS AND LOAN ASSOCIATIONS. Federal Home Loan Bank
Board, Washington 25, D.C.
Monthly. U.S. totals only. Covers the first through the tenth
of each month. Current month compared with same month of
previous year and with previous month. Tables.

MORTGAGE MARKET. National Association of Real Estate Boards, Department of Research, 1300 Connecticut Avenue, N.W., Washington 6, D.C.
Semi-annually.

MORTGAGE RECORDING LETTER. Federal Home Loan Bank Board, Washington 25,
D.C.
Monthly. Tables for non-farm mortgages of $20,000 or less by
type of mortgagee, number and amount of mortgages, the eleven
FHLB districts and selected states.

MULTIPLE LISTING DIGESTAIRE. Executive Officers Council of the National
Association of Real Estate Boards, 36 South Wabash Avenue, Chicago 3, Illinois.
Triannually. Controlled distribution.

NAHB STATE LEGISLATIVE BULLETIN; LEGISLATIVE ACTIVITY IN THE STATE
CAPITALS ON PLANNING, LAND SUBDIVISION, ZONING AND URBAN
RENEWAL. National Association of Home Builders, State Associations Com-
mittee, 1625 L Street, N.W., Washington 6, D.C.
Irregular.

NATIONAL ASSOCIATION OF REAL ESTATE BOARDS NEWS SERVICE.
National Association of Real Estate Boards, Department of Public Relations,
1300 Connecticut Avenue, N.W., Washington 6, D.C.
>Irregular.

NATIONAL DELINQUENCY SURVEY. Mortgage Bankers Association of America,
111 West Washington Street, Chicago 2, Illinois.
>Quarterly.

NATIONAL HOME IMPROVEMENT COUNCIL NEWSLETTER. 87 Madison Avenue, New York 16, New York.
>Published by LIFE magazine as a service to the industry.

NATIONAL HOUSING CENTER LIBRARY BULLETIN. National Association of
Home Builders, 1625 L Street N.W., Washington 6, D.C.
>Monthly. An index of periodical articles of interest to builders.

NATIONAL LEGISLATIVE BULLETIN. National Association of Real Estate
Boards, Realtors' Washington Committee, 1300 Connecticut Avenue, N.W.,
Washington 6, D.C.
>Irregular. Prepared primarily for the use of local real estate
>boards.

NATIONAL MARKET LETTER. Real Estate Research Corporation, 73 West
Monroe Street, Chicago 3, Illinois.
>Monthly.

NATIONAL REAL ESTATE AND BUILDING JOURNAL. 1910--June, 1958.
Stamats Publishing Company, 427 Sixth Avenue, S.E., Cedar Rapids, Iowa.
>Earlier title, NATIONAL REAL ESTATE JOURNAL. Merged
>with BUILDINGS, July, 1958-

NATIONAL REAL ESTATE INVESTOR. 20 West 38th Street, New York 18,
New York.
>Monthly.

NATIONAL UNDERWRITER, FIRE AND CASUALTY EDITION, 175 West Jackson
Boulevard, Chicago 4, Illinois.
>Weekly.

NEW ZEALAND VALUER. New Zealand Institute of Valuers, G.P.O. Box
766, Wellington, New Zealand.
>Quarterly.

NON-FARM REAL ESTATE FORECLOSURE REPORT. Federal Home Loan Bank
Board, Washington 25, D.C.
>Quarterly. Foreclosure estimates based on data from approxi-
>mately, 1,700 counties, cities, townships or other governmental
>units. Statistics for U.S. as a whole.

NOTES FROM THE IDEA LABORATORY. Executive Officers Council of the
National Association of Real Estate Boards, 36 South Wabash Avenue, Chicago 3,
Illinois.
>Triannually. Controlled distribution.

NUMBER OF DWELLING UNITS REPRESENTED IN FHA OPERATIONS, BY
INSURING OFFICE AND ZONE. U.S. Federal Housing Administration,
Division of Research and Statistics, Washington 25, D.C.
  Applications received, insurance written, new units started.

OUR PUBLIC LANDS. U.S. Bureau of Land Management, Washington 25, D.C.
(Sold by Government Printing Office).
  Quarterly.

OWNERSHIP; UNDER ALL IS THE LAND. Stamats Publishing Company, 427
Sixth Avenue, S.E., Cedar Rapids, Iowa.
  Monthly. Franchised, public relations tool.

PARTICIPATION LOAN TRANSACTIONS, FSLIC INSURED SAVINGS AND
LOAN ASSOCIATIONS. Federal Home Loan Bank Board, Washington 25, D.C.
  Quarterly. Tables for U.S. and the eleven FHLB districts.
  Figures for amount of loans.

PERFECT HOME MAGAZINE. Stamats Publishing Company, 427 Sixth Avenue,
S.E., Cedar Rapids, Iowa.
  Monthly. Franchised, public relations tool.

PRACTICAL BUILDER. 5 South Wabash Avenue, Chicago 3, Illinois.
  Monthly.

PROGRESSIVE ARCHITECTURE. 430 Park Avenue, New York 22, New York.
  Monthly.

QUARTERLY ECONOMIC REPORT OF TRENDS IN THE MORTGAGE INDUSTRY.
Mortgage Bankers Association of America, 111 West Washington Street, Chicago
3, Illinois.
  Controlled distribution.

QUARTERLY LETTER ON SAVINGS AND HOME MORTGAGE LENDING.
United States Savings and Loan League, 221 North La Salle Street, Chicago,
Illinois.
  Quarterly. Controlled distribution. Includes data on home
  mortgage lending by savings associations, commercial banks,
  life insurance companies, mutual savings banks, individuals
  and other lenders, with total mortgage loans outstanding.

QUARTERLY REPORT ON FHA TRENDS. U.S. Federal Housing Administration,
Washington 25, D.C.
  Quarterly. Characteristics of home mortgage transactions insured by FHA under Section 203. Proposed and existing one-
  family homes and owner-occupied one-family homes. Characteristics of the properties and the mortgagors.

REAL ESTATE ANALYST SERVICE. Roy Wenzlick Research Corporation, 706
Chestnut Street, St. Louis 1, Missouri. Looseleaf service.
  59 bulletins and studies issued annually in several series:
  Agricultural Bulletin, Appraisal Bulletin, As We See, Construction Bulletin, Mortgage Bulletin, Real Estate Analyst,

Real Estate Trends, Real Estate Tax Bulletin. Analyses and
statistical compilations on vacancies, construction activity and
costs, mortgage markets, farm values, foreclosures and local
economic activity, etc. Annual index.

REAL ESTATE APPRAISER. Society of Real Estate Appraisers, 7 South Dearborn
Street, Chicago 3, Illinois.
Monthly. Formerly Residential Appraiser.

REAL ESTATE AND STOCK JOURNAL. Real Estate and Stock Institute of
Victoria, 6-8 Powlett Street, East Melbourne, Australia.
Monthly.

REAL ESTATE INVESTMENT LETTER. Institute for Business Planning, 2 West
13th Street, New York 11, New York.
Bi-monthly.

REAL ESTATE MARKET. National Association of Real Estate Boards, Department
of Research, 1300 Connecticut Avenue, N.W., Washington 6, D.C.
Semi-annually. Spring, 1962, the 73rd real estate market research study. Residential, commercial, industrial, and land-
farm property covered. "Information on supply and demand
factors, on prospects for the future, and on trends in price,
rate of transfers, and levels of rents and vacancies."

REAL ESTATE OPPORTUNITIES IN SELLING, BUYING, FINANCING, IN-
VESTMENTS, TAX SAVINGS. Prentice-Hall, Inc., Englewood Cliffs, New
Jersey.
Bi-weekly.

REALTOR'S HEADLINES. National Association of Real Estate Boards, 1300
Connecticut Avenue, N.W., Washington 6, D.C.
Weekly. Newsletter including association news, legislative
and market developments. Legal and tax columns. Quarterly
supplements include articles.

REALTY. Benenson Publications, Inc., 264 West 40th Street, New York,
New York.
Bi-weekly. Combined with SYNDICATION DIGEST. Includes
real estate stock indexes. New York real estate transactions
and news and short articles primarily with emphasis on syndication and investment information.

RENEWAL INFORMATION SERVICE NEWSLETTER. National Association of
Housing and Redevelopment Officials, 1413 K Street, N.W., Washington 5, D.C.

RENTAL HOUSING. National Apartment Owners Association, 1200 18th Street,
N.W., Washington 6, D.C.
Quarterly.

RESEARCH BULLETINS. See FUNDAMENTALS AND STANDARDS BULLETINS.

RESIDENTIAL ALTERATIONS AND REPAIRS. (Construction Reports, C-50 Series). Bureau of the Census, Washington 25, D.C.
>Quarterly. Additions, alterations, maintenance and repairs and replacements.

RIGHT OF WAY. American Right of Way Association, 7358 Beverly Boulevard, Los Angeles 36, California.
>Bi-monthly.

RURAL REALTOR. National Institute of Farm and Land Brokers, 36 South Wabash Avenue, Chicago 3, Illinois.
>Monthly. Controller distribution.

SAVINGS AND HOME OWNERSHIP. First Federal Savings and Loan Association of Chicago, 1 South Dearborn Street, Chicago 3, Illinois.
>Bi-monthly. Controlled distribution.

SAVINGS AND LOAN JOURNAL. California Savings and Loan League, P.O. Box R, Pasadena, California.
>Monthly.

SAVINGS AND LOAN NEWS. United States Savings and Loan League, 221 North LaSalle Street, Chicago 1, Illinois.
>Monthly.

SEARS URBAN OBSERVER. Sears Roebuck and Company, Community Planning Division, 925 South Homan Avenue, Chicago 7, Illinois.
>Quarterly. Formerly SEARS URBAN RENEWAL OBSERVER. "Dedicated to Community Redevelopment and Planning."

SECURITIES AND EXCHANGE COMMISSION NEWS DIGEST; A BRIEF SUMMARY OF FINANCIAL PROPOSALS FILED WITH AND ACTIONS BY THE SECURITIES AND EXCHANGE COMMISSION. U.S. Securities and Exchange Commission, Washington 25, D.C. (Sold by Government Printing Office).
>Daily. Keeps current the S.E.C. publication, REAL ESTATE INVESTMENT TRUSTS FILING UNDER THE SECURITIES ACT OF 1933. Issued Periodically.

SHOPPING CENTER AGE, 2 West Park Avenue, New York 16, New York.
>Monthly. Construction and management. Section on new centers under construction, planned additional construction and space available.

SHOPPING CENTER IDEA LABORATORY. National Research Bureau, Inc., 415 North Dearborn Street, Chicago 10, Illinois.
>Monthly. Includes SHOPPING CENTER NEWSLETTER. Advertising and promotion.

SKYSCRAPER MANAGEMENT. National Association of Building Owners and Managers, 134 South LaSalle Street, Chicago 3, Illinois.
>Monthly. Office buildings. Includes semi-annual occupancy survey.

SIR NEWSLETTER. Society of Industrial Realtors, 1300 Connecticut Avenue, N.W., Washington 6, D.C.
10 issues per year. Controlled distribution.

SOIL CONSERVATION. U.S. Department of Agriculture, Soil Conservation Service, Washington 25, D.C. (Sold by Government Printing Office).
Monthly.

SUMMARY OF CONGRESSIONAL AND EXECUTIVE ACTION OF INTEREST TO THE HOUSING AND HOME FINANCE AGENCY FROM CONGRESSIONAL RECORD AND FEDERAL REGISTER. U.S. Housing and Home Finance Agency, Washington 25, D.C.
Daily.

SUPER MARKET MERCHANDISING. 50 Emmett Street, Bristol, Connecticut.
Monthly.

SURVEY OF CURRENT BUSINESS. U.S. Department of Commerce, Office of Business Economics. Washington 25, D.C. (Sold by Government Printing Office).
Monthly, supplemented by weekly BUSINESS STATISTICS. Includes building cost indexes and mortgage applications and loans as part of the business statistical series.

SURVEYING AND MAPPING. American Congress on Surveying and Mapping, Box 470, Benjamin Franklin Station, Washington 4, D.C.
Quarterly. Regular features include, Surveying and Mapping Literature, Books in Review and Abstracts of Articles on Geodesy and Related Fields.

TAX INSTITUTE BOOKSHELF. 457 Nassau Street, Princeton, New Jersey.
Irregular. Index to periodical literature.

TAXES. Commerce Clearing House, 4025 West Peterson Avenue, Chicago 46, Illinois.
Monthly.

TECHNICAL VALUATION. American Society of Appraisers, 1028 Connecticut Avenue, N.W., Washington 6, D.C.
Tri-annually.

TITLE NEWS. American Land Title Association, 1725 I Street, N.W., Washington 6, D.C.
Monthly.

TOURIST COURT JOURNAL. 306 East Adams Avenue, Temple, Texas.
Monthly. July issue; Motel Financial Report.

TOWN AND COUNTRY PLANNING. 28 King Street, London, W.C. 2, England.
> Monthly. Official publication of Town and Country Planning Association.

TRAFFIC QUARTERLY. Eno Foundation for Highway Traffic Control Inc., Saugatuck, Connecticut.
> Quarterly.

TRENDS IN HOUSING. National Committee Against Discrimination in Housing, 426 West 58th Street, New York 19, New York.
> Bi-monthly.

TRENDS IN SAVINGS AND LENDING AT SAVINGS AND LOAN ASSOCIA-TIONS. United State Savings and Loan League, 221 North LaSalle Street, Chicago 1, Illinois.
> Monthly.

UNITED STATES SAVINGS AND LOAN LEAGUE MEMBERSHIP BULLETIN. United States Savings and Loan League, 221 North LaSalle Street, Chicago 1, Illinois.
> Irregular. Controlled distribution.

UNITED STATES SAVINGS AND LOAN LEAGUE SPECIAL MANAGEMENT BULLETIN. United States Savings and Loan League, 221 North LaSalle Street, Chicago 1, Illinois.
> Irregular. Controlled distribution.

URBAN LAND NEWS AND TRENDS IN CITY DEVELOPMENT. Urban Land Institute, 1200 18th Street, N.W., Washington 6, D.C.
> 11 issues per year. Controlled distribution.

URBAN RENEWAL NOTES. U.S. Urban Renewal Administration, Washington 25, D.C.
> Bi-monthly. Part of the Urban Renewal Service. Digest point-ing to good techniques and unusual approaches and successes, and including capsule form information on U.R.A. program de-velopments and publications.

THE VALUER; JOURNAL OF THE VALUERS INSTITUTE. 3 Cadogin Gate, London, S.W. 1, England.
> Bi-monthly. Controlled distribution. Lists government pub-lications and additions to the library.

THE VALUER. Commonwealth Institute of Valuers, 51-57 Pitt Street, Sydney, Australia.
> Quarterly.

WASHINGTON LETTER. Mortgage Bankers Association of America, 111 West Washington Street, Chicago 2, Illinois.
> Controlled distribution.

WASHINGTON LETTER.   National Association of Home Builders, 1625 L Street, N.W., Washington 6, D.C.
> Irregular. Controlled distribution.

WASHINGTON NOTES. United States Savings and Loan League, 13th Street and Pennsylvania Avenue, N.W., Washington 4, D.C.
> Irregular. Controlled distribution.

WHAT REAL ESTATE BOARDS ARE DOING. Executive Officers Council of the National Association of Real Estate Boards, 36 South Wabash Avenue, Chicago 3, Illinois.
> Irregular. Controlled distribution. Newsletter containing ideas and suggestions for worth-while board activities as gleaned from various boards across the country.

WHAT WOMEN REALTORS ARE DOING. Women's Council of the National Association of Real Estate Boards, 36 South Wabash Avenue, Chicago 3, Illinois.

Periodicals—Lists

U. S. Federal Housing Administration. Library. PERIODICALS RECEIVED IN FEDERAL HOUSING ADMINISTRATION LIBRARY, Rev. Washington, D. C.: 1961. 11p. pap. processed.

U. S. Housing and Home Finance Agency. Library. PERIODICALS CURRENTLY RECEIVED AND INDEX BY SUBJECTS, Rev. Washington, D. C.: 1962. 41p. pap. processed.

U. S. Public Housing Administration. Library. LIST OF PERIODICALS RECEIVED IN THE PHA LIBRARY. Washington, D. C.: 1961. 3p. pap. processed.

APPENDIX B

ASSOCIATIONS

In addition to the associations listed below, chambers of commerce and local real estate boards are good sources of information on local business and economic conditions and will refer inquirers to other organizations and offices in the locality from which specific kinds of data may be obtained. THE ENCYCLOPEDIA OF AMERICAN ASSOCIATIONS, published by the Gale Research Company, Detroit, in 1961, contains a list of state and local chambers of commerce. (This volume is the principal directory of associations.) The names and addresses of local real estate boards and state real estate associations are given in the OFFICIAL ROSTER OF REALTORS, published by the Stamats Publishing Company, 427 Sixth Avenue, S.E., Cedar Rapids, Iowa.

ACTION, Inc., 2 West 46th Street, New York 36, New York. Est. 1954. "The National Council for Good Cities." Formed in 1954 as the American Council to Improve our Neighborhoods; name changed in 1959 to ACTION, Inc. The four point program for the revitalization of our nation's cities, through organized citizen efforts at both local and national levels: good homes in good neighborhoods, efficient urban transportation, vigorous centers of commerce and culture, and adequate financing for public and private improvements. Publications: NEWS AND VIEWS ABOUT THE AMERICAN CITY FROM THE ACTION LIBRARY, bi-monthly, includes a listing of urban renewal projects seeking the participation of private enterprise; PUBLICATIONS AND PROGRAM MATERIALS; ACTION SERIES ON HOUSING AND COMMUNITY DEVELOPMENT, published in eight volumes by McGraw-Hill, is a comprehensive analysis of the nation's housing as it affects and is affected by the investor, consumer, the community, the producer and the government.

American Bankers Association, 12 East 36th Street, New York 16, New York. Est. 1875. The Savings and Mortgage Division has been active for fifty years. Its publication, THE MORTGAGE BULLETIN FOR BANKS OF DEPOSIT, reports the results of the three annual regional mortgage workshop meetings. The Committee on Real Estate Mortgages studies housing legislation which is reported in the BULLETIN. The activity of National Mortgage Market Com-

mittee made up of representatives from the various lending in-
dustries, the National Association of Home Builders and the
National Association of Real Estate Boards is reported in the
BULLETIN. The American Institute of Banking, a section of the
ABA since 1900 was organized to provide a program of educa-
tion through local chapters. Publications: HOME MORTGAGE
LOAN MANUAL; HUMAN SIDE OF MORTGAGE LOAN SERV-
ICING; and publications on construction loans, merchandising, mort-
gage credit, and mortgage lending.

American Congress on Surveying and Mapping, 733 15th Street, N.W., Washington, 5, D.C. Est. 1941.

Local sections and state societies affiliated. Membership of
licensed land surveyors in private and governmental practice,
exploration engineers, lawyers, cartographers, photogrammetric
specialists, teachers of surveying, instrument manufacturers, ti-
tlemen, etc. Six technical divisions: Cartography, Control
Surveys, Education, Instruments, Property Surveys, and Topog-
raphy. Publications: SURVEYING AND MAPPING, quarterly.

American Industrial Development Council, 230 Boylston Street, Boston 16,
Massachusetts. Est. 1944.

Organized in 1925 under the auspices of the Chamber of Commerce of the United States; in 1958 it became an independent,
incorporated association. Professional and lay men and women
in the United States and Canada engaged in promoting the industrial development of their areas to provide a medium for
conference and exchange of ideas on principles, practices and
ethics in the field of industrial development. Programs, conferences, seminars and institute publications: AID, bi-monthly
membership newsletter; CONFERENCE PROCEEDINGS, annual;
HANDBOOK ON INDUSTRIAL DEVELOPMENT; BIBLIOGRAPHY
AND SUPPLEMENT.

American Institute for Property and Liability Underwriters, 266 Bryn Mawr
Avenue, Bryn Mawr, Pennsylvania. Est. 1944.

Local chapters. CPCU (Chartered Property Casualty Underwriter) awarded upon successful completion of a four year program of study. Advanced educational program study aids include lists of suggested textbooks, topical outlines. Publications: CPCU ANNALS, quarterly, include papers from annual
seminars and regional institutes.

American Land Title Association, 1725 I Street, N.W., Washington 6, D.C.
Est. 1906.

Name changed from American Title Association in 1962. State
associations. Abstracters, title insurance companies and attorneys. Publications: TITLE NEWS, monthly, is mailed to all
accredited law libraries. AMERICAN LAND TITLE ASSOCI-
ATION ANSWERS IMPORTANT QUESTIONS includes information
about the associations and its members, with basic information
about the title industry and its service to the real estate buying public.

American Public Health Association, 1790 Broadway, New York 19, New York. Est. 1872.

> State societies affiliated. Committee on the Hygiene of Housing.
> Publications: AMERICAN JOURNAL OF PUBLIC HEALTH,
> monthly, included notice of publications and bibliographies.
> See RESIDENTIAL PROPERTY section for a listing of other pub-
> lications.

American Right of Way Association, 7358 Beverly Boulevard, Los Angeles 36, California. Est. 1934.

> 39 chapters. Professional organization of lawyers, appraisers,
> engineers, title examiners and right of way officials. National
> Pipeline, Utilities, Liaison, Land Economic Study, Highway,
> and Valuation Committees. Regional seminars by chapters. Pub-
> lications: RIGHT OF WAY, bimonthly; proceedings of the
> annual national seminar. See CONDEMNATION AND EMI-
> NENT DOMAIN section for citations of other publications.

American Society of Appraisers, Suite 1121 LaSalle Building, 1028 Connecticut Avenue, N.W., Washington 6, D.C.

> The American Society of Technical Appraisers and The Technical
> Valuation Society, both organized in 1939, were consolidated
> in August 1952, forming the American Society of Appraisers.
> Individual membership through local chapters drawn from the
> appraisal and engineering professions having to do with apprais-
> als and valuations of tangible and intangible property. Sen-
> ior members awarded the designation, ASA. Publications: pro-
> fessional journal, TECHNICAL VALUATION, tri-annual; AP-
> PRAISAL AND VALUATION MANUAL, annual; and a CON-
> DEMNATION APPRAISAL TEXT AND REFERENCE MANUAL.
> See APPRAISAL section for citations of other publications.

American Society of Farm Managers and Rural Appraisers, Post Office Box 295, DeKalb, Illinois. Est. 1929.

> Professional farm managers and rural appraisers devoting the
> major part of their time to the management and/or appraisal
> of rural property. Designations AFM and ARA (Accredited
> Farm Manager, Accredited Rural Appraiser) awarded those
> qualifying. Training schools, semiannual; conventions. Pub-
> lications: JOURNAL OF THE AMERICAN SOCIETY OF FARM
> MANAGERS AND RURAL APPRAISERS, semiannual, and peri-
> odic newsletters for members; THE AMERICAN SOCIETY OF
> FARM MANAGERS AND RURAL APPRAISERS, WHAT IT IS,
> WHAT IT DOES. Standard appraisal data, recommended price,
> and yield data have been made available since 1950.

Appraisal Institute of Canada, Inc., 909 Electric Railway Chambers, Winnipeg 2, Manitoba. Est. 1938.

> Affiliated with Canadian Association of Real Estate Boards.

AACI (Accredited Appraiser, Canadian Institute) awarded to those qualifying. Publications: APPRAISAL INSTITUTE MAGAZINE, quarterly. See APPRAISAL section for a citation of other publications.

Association of Real Estate Syndicators, 48 West 48th Street, Room 1309, New York 36, New York. Est. 1957.
New York membership of those professionals engaged in or affiliated or associated with the business of syndication of real estate investments. Publications: PROSPECTUS, quarterly.

Condemnation Law Bar Association, 117 Liberty Street, New York, New York.

Highway Research Board, National Research Council, 2101 Constitution Avenue, Washington 25, D.C. Est. 1920.
Cooperative organization of the highway technologists of America operating under the auspices of the Council and with the support of the several highway department, the Bureau of Public Roads and many other organizations. Economics publications: SOME EVALUATIONS OF HIGHWAY IMPROVEMENT IMPACTS (Bulletin 268); PARKING (Special report 28); LAND ACQUISITION AND CONTROL; and other publications on law, right of way, condemnation, etc.

Home Manufacturers Association, 1117 Barr Building, Washington 6, D.C. Est. 1943.
Member firms represent the major portion of homes manufactured in the United States. Includes Canadian and English home manufacturers. Associate members are principal suppliers for manufactured homes. The activities are geared to improve the design, engineering, production and on site erection of manufactured homes; generate wider use of the product among builders; increase interest among buyers; develop and coordinate projects of mutual benefit with related groups. Services include government liaison, technical services, public relations and publications: MANUFACTURED HOMES, monthly; MANUFACTURED HOMES DIRECTORY, annual; and PROFITS IN HOUSE PACKAGES, an annual publication for builder-dealers, are available to non-members. Statistical operating studies on the industry, technical bulletins on VA-FHA problems, architectural news, Standardization data, engineering bulletins and special news bulletins on production processes, cost saving ideas, etc. are available only to members.

Industrial Development Research Council, 2592 Apple Valley Road, Atlanta 19, Georgia. Est. 1961.
Executives of major manufacturing and distribution firms who have responsibilities in the areas of long range corporate planning, project feasibility analysis, facility planning, site selection and real estate management. INDUSTRIAL DEVELOPMENT AND MANUFACTURERS RECORD, monthly, is the official publication. Report on the Council: INDUSTRIAL DEVELOPMENT, vol. 131, no. 1, January 1962. p. 4-11.

International Association of Assessing Officers, 1313 East 60th Street, Chicago 37, Illinois. Est. 1934.

> Public officials engaged in the assessment of property for taxation, organized for the purpose of improving standards and developing better techniques in assessment administration. C.A.E. (Certified Assessment Evaluator) awarded to those qualifying. Publications: INTERNATIONAL CONFERENCE ON ASSESSMENT ADMINISTRATION PROCEEDINGS, annual; ACCESORS' NEWSLETTER, monthly; technical reports, assessment practice series and special information bulletins.

International Council of Shopping Centers, 342 Madison Avenue, New York 17, New York. Est. 1957.

> Shopping center owners, developers, managers and others whose business interests are involved in shopping centers. Associate Membership is available to those in a profession allied to the shopping center field. Merchant membership includes retailers, other tenants and merchants associations. Publications: newsletter for members, convention proceedings, SELECTED BIBLIOGRAPHY ON SHOPPING CENTERS, and a RECOMMENDED LEASE FORM for members only. Special conference and regional meetings information service management institutes, reference library, and a consultant service.

International Federation of Surveyors, 3 Krotenthallergasse, Vienna 8, Austria. Est. 1953.

> Federation Internationale des Geometres (F.I.G.) Constitution drafted in 1950 and 1951, adopted in 1953. Periodic international bulletin and congress proceedings in French. International congresses take place as a rule every four years. Organized to group the national associations or organizations of surveyors of all countries: "The surveyor is a professional man who identifies, determines the boundaries of, measures and values public or private landed property, whether urban or rural, and whether on the surface or below, as well as works executed thereon; and who arranges for the registration of the property and settles questions of ownership connected therewith. The surveyor also studies, plans and is responsible for land development and town country planning. He deals with the technical, legal, economic, agricultural and social aspects of the aforementioned." Members associations: ARGENTINA: Federacion Argentina de Agrimensores, Colon 684, Ciudad De San Luis; AUSTRIA: Osterreichischer Verein fur Vermessungswesen, Friedrich Schmidt-Platz 3, Wien 8; BELGIUM: Union Belge des Geometres-Experts Immobiliers, 76, Rue du Nord, Bruxelles; BULGARIA: Wissenschaftlich-Technischer Verein in Bulgarien, Sektion "Geodasie", Rakowskistr. 108, Sofia; CANADA: The Canadian Institute of Surveying, P.O.B. 3151, Postal Station C, Ottawa, Ont.; CZECHOSLOVAKIA: Cs. Vedeckotechnicka spolnecnost, sekce stavebnictvi - odborna

skupina, geodezie a kartografie, Siroka 5, Praha 1; DENMARK: Den Danske Landinspektorforening, H.C. Andersens Boulevard 5", Kobenhavn - V; FINLAND: Maanmittausinsinoorien Liitto r.y., (Union of Engineers on Land Surveying) Committee for Foreign Affairs, Adresse de correspondance: Dr. Mauno Kajamaa, Chairman, Kirkkokatu 3, Helsinki; FRANCE: Ordre des Geometres-Experts, Siege Social: Maison du Geometres, 40, Avenue Hoche, Paris - 8^e; GERMANY: Deutscher Verein fur Vermessungswesen e.V., Lavesstrave 77/78, Hannover; GREAT BRITAIN: The Royal Institution of Chartered Surveyors, 12, Great George Street, Parliament Square, Westminster, S.W.I.; HUNGARY: Geodeziai es Kartografiai Egyesulet, (Association de Geodesie et de Cartographie), Szabadsag ter. 17, Budapest, V.; ISRAEL: Association of Licensed Surveyors in Israel, Technion-Israel Institute of Technology, P.O.B. 4910, Haifa, c/o M. Geissler, Civ. Ing. Senior Lecturer; ITALY: Consiglio Nazionale dei Geometri, Corso Vitt. Emanuele, 269, Roma; LIBERIA: Liberian Surveyors Mutual Association, 29 Ashmun St., P.O.B. 415, Monrovia; LUXEMBOURG: Association des Geometres du, Grand Duche de Luxembourg, 54, avenue Gaston Diderich, Luxembourg; MOROCCO: Association Nationale des Ingenieurs, Geometres et Topographes, Rabat; NETHERLANDS: Nederlandse Landmeetkundige Federatie, Marnixstraat 44, Leeuwarden; POLAND: Stowarzyszenie Naukowo-Techniczne Geodetow Polskich, Zarzad Glowny, Czackiego 3-5, Warszawa; SWEDEN: Sveriges Lantmatareforening, Box 16027, Stockholm 6; SWITZERLAND: Societe Suisse Des Mensurations et Ameliorations Foncieres, 3, Croix-Rouges, Lausanne; YUGOSLAVIA: Savez geodetskih inzenjera i geometara FNRJ, Kneza Milosa 7/11, Beograd.

International Real Estate Federation, 53 Rue du Rocher, Paris, 8^e; American Chapter, 36 South Wabash Avenue, Chicago 3, Illinois. Est. 1951- Federation Internationale des Administrateurs de Biens Conseils Immobiliers (F.I.A.B.C.I.). The first meeting was held in 1948 to bring together the professional organizations whose principle activity is connected with property in the different countries. Their constitution was adopted in 1951. The Federation holds consultative status in the United Nations Economic and Social Council (ECOSOC) and FIABCI delegates regularly attend the sessions of the Housing Committee (E.C.E.). The F.I.A.B.C.I. meets annually in one of the member countries. Their publications in French, English and German include INTERNATIONAL YEARBOOK, Congress reports, quarterly BULLETIN. Affiliated national associations: AUSTRIA: Bundes-Innung der Gebaudeverwalter und Realitatenvermittler, Bauernmarkt 13, Wien 1; BELGIUM: Federation Nationale des Chambres Immobilieres de Belgique, 19, rue des Cultes, Bruxelles 1; CANADA: Canadian Association of Real Estate Boards, 20 Eglinton Avenue East, Toronto (Ontario); DENMARK: Annae Plads 6, Kobenhavn K.; FRANCE: Confederation Nationale des Administrateurs de Biens Syndics de Copropriete de France, 53, rue du Rocher, Paris-8^e; Federation

Nationale des Constructeurs Promoteurs, 106, rue de l'Universite, Paris-7^e; Chambre Syndicale Nationale des Agents Immobiliers de France, 163, rue St-Honore, Paris 1er; GERMANY: Ring Deutscher Makler, Breitestrasse 141, loln; ISRAEL: Association of Real Estate Boards Brokers in Israel, Maldan, 65, Ben Yehuda St., Tel-Aviv; ITALY: Federazione Italiana Mediatori Agenti d'Affari, Piazza G.G. Belli 2, Roma; JAPAN: All-Japan Real Estate Association, Zenrin-Gakusei-Kaikan, No 1-1, Koishikawa, Bunkyo-ku, Tokyo; NETHERLANDS: Makelaarsvereniging te Amsterdam, Rokin 24, Amsterdam; Nederlandse Bond van Makelaars de Ruyterstraat 65, den Haag; SPAIN: Junta Central de los Colegios Oficiales de Agentes de la Propiedad Inmobiliaria, Avenida Jose Antonio 70-3° Madrid; SWEDEN: Sveriges Fastighetsmaklares Riksforbund, Box 12280 Stockholm 16; SWITZER-LAND; Union Romande des Gerants et Courtiers en Immeubles, 1, rue du Temple, Geneve; Schweizerischer Verband der Immobilien Treuhander, Lettenstrasse 21, Saint-Gallen; UNITED KINGDOM: The Chartered Auctioneers' and Estate Agents' Institute, 29 Lincoln's Inn Fields, London W.C. 2; UNITED STATES: National Association of Real Estate Boards, 36 South Wabash Avenue, Chicago 3 (Illinois).

Lambda Alpha. Est. 1930.
Founded at Northwestern University. Four chapters; Chicago (Ely), New York, Los Angeles, and Washington D.C. (George Washington). Professional real estate fraternity organized to foster the study of land economics. Includes in its membership men actively engaged in some phase of the business of land utilization. Land Economics Foundation.

Land Improvement Contractors of America, 1818 Todd Avenue, Manhattan Kansas. Est. 1953.
State associations comprising a federation of land improvement and conservation contractors. Publications: USE OF LAND IM-PROVEMENT MAGAZINE, monthly.

Mortgage Bankers Association of America, 111 West Washington Street, Chicago 2, Illinois. Est. 1914.
Local associations. Membership composed of mortgage brokers and bankers, mutual savings and commercial banks, insurance companies and title companies. Special committees: Mortgage Market; FHA, GI and legislative; Farm Loan; Tax Loan Administration; Research; Conventional Loan; Insurance. Educational programs: mortgage conferences, loan administration clinics, seminars, schools and correspondence courses (11 planned for mortgage office employees). Publications: THE MORTGAGE BANKER, monthly; QUARTERLY ECONOMIC REPORT OF TRENDS IN THE MORT-GAGE INDUSTRY; and QUARTERLY DELINQUENCY SURVEY; the McGraw-Hill series sponsored by the MBA, listed in the FINANCE--MORTGAGES section.

Motel Brokers Association of America, 39 South LaSalle Street, Chicago 3, Illinois.

25 licensed brokers specializing in motel sales. Only one member accepted in a geographic area.

National Apartment Owners Association, Inc., 1200 18th Street, N.W., Washington 6, D.C. Est. 1939.

Combined with American Real Property Federation. Composed of rental property owners who have joined forces to protect their rights and the earning power of their properties. Assists state and local property owners associations. Publications: WASHINGTON LETTER; RENTAL HOUSING, quarterly.

National Association of Building Owners and Managers, 134 South LaSalle Street, Chicago 3, Illinois. Est. 1907.

Members include active members of federated associations in 60 cities whose executive officers form a national group known as Associated Secretaries. Members at large. The membership represents buildings containing over 300 million square feet of office space. Publications: SKYSCRAPER MANAGEMENT, monthly; OFFICE BUILDING EXPERIENCE EXCHANGE REPORT, annual; OPERATING HANDBOOK published in sections as completed; a fifty year history of the association and industry, OFFICES IN THE SKY, by Schultz and Simmons; a semi-annual survey of office building occupancy reported in SKYSCRAPER MANAGEMENT; LEGISLATIVE BULLETIN for member associations.

National Association of Home Builders of the United States, 1625 L Street, N.W., Washington 6, D.C. Est. 1942.

NAHB Headquarters is the National Housing Center. Formerly the Home Builders Institute affiliated with the National Association of Real Estate Boards. Dedicated to a strong housing economy, operating within a free enterprise system. Objectives: provision of adequate housing for all Americans; constant improvement of home building materials and techniques; encouragement of high professional and ethical standards. Publications: NAHB JOURNAL OF HOMEBUILDING, monthly; WASHINGTON LETTER; NATIONAL HOUSING CENTER NEWS; and LIBRARY BULLETIN a selective listing of 350 journals.

National Association of License Law Officials, 603-5 Berger Building, Pittsburgh 19, Pennsylvania. Est. 1930.

Membership is composed of license law officials charged with the administration and enforcement of real estate brokers' license laws in the various states and provinces of Canada. The association has been instrumental in raising standards of competency for real estate licensees, adopting uniform standards of procedure in interstate matters, the elimination of the advance fee rackets, regulation of subdivisions, and other real estate evils for the protection of the public and the betterment of the real estate industry.

National Association of Mutual Savings Banks, 200 Park Avenue, New York 17, New York. Est. 1920.

Membership composed of mutual savings banks and state associations of savings banks. Committee on Mortgage Investments publications: SAVINGS BANK JOURNAL, monthly, and MORTGAGE PORT- FOLIO ACTIVITIES OF MUTUAL SAVINGS BANKS and FACTS AND FIGURES, MUTUAL SAVINGS BANKING, annual studies.

THE NATIONAL ASSOCIATION OF REAL ESTATE BOARDS
AND RELATED INSTITUTES

National Association of Real Estate Boards, 36 South Wabash Avenue, Chicago 3, Illinois. Est. 1908.

The N.A.R.E.B. is a federation of over 1400 local real estate boards whose 72,000 active members use the term "Realtor," coined in 1916 and registered with the U.S. Patent Office as a property right of the Association. The N.A.R.E.B. is one of the largest trade and professional associations in the country. The original goals are still basic to the organization: the creation of unity in the real estate field, the compilation of information, the protection and promotion of property owner- ship and the establishment of professional standards of practice. The code of ethics was adopted in 1913. Publications: REAL- TOR'S HEADLINES, weekly, and NAREB AND INSTITUTE PUB- LICATIONS list.

The Institutes first started as divisions, beginning in 1923 as the educational arms of the association in the fields of special- ization in real estate. The activities in the early days in- cluded convention programming and exchange of ideas for those interested in the specializations. Starting with the American Institute of Real Estate Appraisers in 1932, several of the divisions reorganized as institutes of the association in order to become distinct groups requiring individuals to qualify for membership by demonstrating professional competence. They are:

American Chapter, International Real Estate Federation, 36 South Wabash Avenue, Chicago 3, Illinois. Est. 1956.

Assumed institute status in 1957. Membership is open to Realtors and individuals associated with Realtors. Objectives include: to further the education in inter- national affairs of persons in some phase of real estate; to encourage international real estate transactions and investments; and to encourage private ownership of real property and understanding of property rights and obliga- tions wherever possible. Membership in the chapter includes membership in the International Federation. Reports issued: REALTOR STUDIES IN EUROPEAN COUNTRIES; A BRIEF SUMMARY OF REAL ESTATE PRACTICES AND IN-FORMATION THERETO IS REVEALED DURING STUDY TOURS CONDUCTED WITHIN THE COUNTRIES, compiled and edited by Eugene P. Conser, 1961.

American Institute of Real Estate Appraisers, 36 South Wabash Avenue, Chicago 3, Illinois. Est. 1932.
Appraisers of real property demonstrating professional com-petence, are awarded the designation, MAI (Member, Appraisal Institute). Publications: Texts, case study prob-lems, demonstration reports; appraisal literature developed for use in the educational program of case study courses; THE APPRAISAL JOURNAL, quarterly; The APPRAISER, monthly newsletter of current professional topics; and news-letter for members. One of the American members of the International Federation of Surveyors. Research and Edu-cation Trust Fund. See APPRAISAL section for full listing.

American Society of Real Estate Counselors, 36 South Wabash Avenue, Chicago 3, Illinois. Est. 1953.
Membership includes those specialists who fulfill the soci-ety's definition of real estate counselor. Counselors are experts with a wide background of varied real estate expe-rience and knowledge rendering professional advice disinter-ested and independent of any direct, or contingent inter-est in the outcome or results of the situations in which they serve as advisors and whose compensation is a fee, paid by the client. Designation awarded to members, C.R.E. (Counselor in Real Estate). Objectives: to united those engaged in counseling; the certification, identification and qualification of experienced real estate counselors; enforcement of ethical standards; and the professional im-provement of its members. Publications: THE COUNSE-LOR; THE REALTOR'S ROLE IN COUNSELING; and THE AMERICAN SOCIETY OF REAL ESTATE COUNSELORS. Two publications in preparation listed in COUNSELING section.

Executive Officers Council, 36 South Wabash Avenue, Chicago 3, Illinois. Est. 1912.
Membership includes elected secretaries and, or, execu-tive staff personnel of real estate boards. Formerly, Sec-retaries Council, and earlier National Association of Real-tor Secretaries. Publications: triannual, WHAT REAL ESTATE BOARDS ARE DOING; NOTES FROM THE IDEA LABORATORY; MULTIPLE LISTING DIGESTAIRE; and re-search reports; THE REAL ESTATE BOARD OPERATION

N.A.R.E.B. INSTITUTES (continued)

MANUAL; BASIC OPERATING POLICIES OF REAL ESTATE
BOARDS; and EXTENSION COURSE IN REAL ESTATE BOARD
ADMINISTRATION described in BUSINESS--BOARDS sec-
tion. Annual Seminar of Real Estate Board Administration.

Institute of Real Estate Management, 36 South Wabash Avenue,
Chicago 3, Illinois. Est. 1934.
Organized to identify and qualify individuals and organizations in property management through certification of
individuals fulfilling professional requirements as C.P.M.s
(Certified Property Managers), and their firms which comply
with the requirements of A.M.O.s (Accredited Management
Organizations). Case study courses in property management
and texts developed by the members for an educational
program designed to help inexperienced individuals qual-
ify as property managers. Publications: JOURNAL OF
PROPERTY MANAGEMENT, quarterly; FUNDAMENTALS
AND STANDARDS BULLETINS, monthly; APARTMENT
BUILDING EXPERIENCE EXCHANGE REPORT, special an-
nual issue of the JOURNAL; COOPERATIVE APARTMENTS
BULLETIN. Annual Management Seminar in connection
with the May meetings of the Institute. See PROPERTY
MANAGEMENT section for full listing.

National Institute of Farm and Land Brokers, 36 South Wabash
Avenue, Chicago 3, Illinois. Est. 1944.
Name changed from National Institute of Farm Brokers in
1963. A.F.B. (Accredited Farm Broker) awarded to active
member having fulfilled requirements of the Institute.
Membership is composed of Realtors specializing in rural
property. Publications: THE RURAL REALTOR, monthly;
FARM AND RANCH BROKERS MANUAL; and ADVANTAGES
IN TAXES by Robert Weir. See FARM PROPERTY section.

National Institute of Real Estate Brokers, 36 South Wabash Avenue,
Chicago 3, Illinois. Est. 1942.
Membership is composed of Realtors and their salesmen.
Educational program is residential and commercial broker-
age with publications and educational conferences. An-
nual Commercial and Residential Property Clinics, each
May. Publications: Bulletin Service, quarterly; MONEY
MAKING IDEAS FROM FELLOW REALTORS, and BRO-
KERS ROUND TABLE, quarterly newsletters; COMMERCIAL
PROPERTY CLINIC, PROCEEDINGS; SHOPPING CENTER
PANEL TRANSCRIPT annual convention session. Inter-
national Traders Club of the National Institute of Real
Estate Brokers offers an educational program for those NI
REB members electing membership in the club in exchang-
ing. Publications: MONTHLY TRADER and the REAL
ESTATE TRADERS HANDBOOK.

N.A.R.E.B. INSTITUTES (continued)

Society of Industrial Realtors, 1300 Connecticut Avenue, N.W.,
Washington, 6, D.C. Est. 1941.
> Those Realtors specializing in the appraisal, management,
> and sale of industrial property with a record of eight or
> more years successful and ethical performance as industrial
> property brokers, who can satisfy the Society as to their
> technical knowledge of the industrial field. Members a-
> warded S.I.R. designation. Publications: INDUSTRIAL
> MARKET LETTER, monthly listing of plants and requests
> for plants, by members; STANDARD BROCHURE, uniform
> method of presenting essential data on available plants
> and sites; SIR NEWSLETTER, monthly for members; SPOT
> SURVEYS, preliminary studies within 24-48 hours of any
> or all areas for plants or sites meeting particular require-
> ments, available to members. INDUSTRIAL REAL ESTATE;
> A COURSE SYLLABUS by William M. Shenkel.

Women's Council, 36 South Wabash Avenue, Chicago 3, Illinois.
Est. 1938.
> Organized to provide women Realtors and their sales wo-
> men an opportunity for closer contact with other women
> in their goal toward professional self-improvement.
> Local board councils for the purpose of providing leader-
> ship training and to augment the educational program of
> local boards. Publications: WHAT WOMEN REALTORS
> ARE DOING, monthly newsletter; educational program
> furnished to local chapters; annual report of the activities
> of local chapters. THE STATUS OF WOMEN IN REAL
> ESTATE.

National Association of Insured Savings Associations, 1200 18th Street,
N.W., Washington 6, D.C. Est. 1943.
> Formerly National Savings and Loan League. Savings and loan
> associations, building and loan associations, and homestead
> associations, insured by the Federal Savings and Loan Insurance
> Corporation. Publication: JOURNAL OF THE NATIONAL
> LEAGUE OF INSURED SAVINGS ASSOCIATIONS, monthly.

National Association of Real Estate Brokers, 529 North Hill Street, South Bend 17,
Indiana. Est. 1948.
> Address changes each year with the elected officers providing
> office space. Association of Negro real estate brokers. Pub-
> lications: NAREB REPORT, bi-monthly.

National Association of Real Estate Editors, 901 Lakeside Drive, Cleveland 14, Ohio. Est. 1928.

Membership includes those engaged in writing or editing real estate building or home news or editorial matter in any regularly published newspaper or periodical of general circulation. Meetings scheduled to coincide with national conventions in the building, mortgage lending or realty fields. Publication: THE REALTY EDITOR, monthly newsletter of news handling ideas and interesting excerpts from various newspapers.

National Association of Real Estate Investment Funds, 213 Transportation Building, Washington 6, D.C. Est. 1960.

Trustees, officers and managers of real estate investment trusts organized to preserve and improve the system of investing funds in real property through the medium of real estate investment trusts; to encourage among its members sound business practices and methods in the origination and management of real estate investments; to raise and improve the ideals and standards established by those engaged in the real estate investment trust industry; and to provide a medium through which its membership may be enabled to confer, consult and cooperate with governmental and other agencies in the solution of problems affecting investors, the public, and the real estate investment trust industry.

National Industrial Zoning Committee, 2459 Dorset Road, Columbus 21, Ohio. Est. 1951.

Federation of zoning committees from national organizations to improve the techniques and practice of zoning as applied to land for industry as a part of comprehensive community planning. Publications: Pamphlet series includes: STEPS TO SECURE SOUND ZONING, PRINCIPLES OF OFF-STREET PARKING AND LOADING, PLANNED HIGHWAYS CREATE INDUSTRIAL ZONING, and PERFORMANCE STANDARDS IN INDUSTRIAL ZONING.

National Parking Association, 711 - 14th Street, N.W., Washington 5, D.C. Est. 1950.

Offstreet parking operational methods, construction and design, financing, legal rulings, business promotion, public relations, information on Park-and-Shop, citywide validation program; PARKING MAGAZINE, quarterly; OPERATING COST SURVEY, biennial.

Pan American Union of Appraisers Associations. (Union Panamericana de Asociaciones de Valuadores).

Biennial congress. The address of the association is that of the
current president, elected usually for one year. Contact the
American Institute of Real Estate Appraisers, the U.S. affiliate,
for the current listing. Member organizations are: ARGENTINA:
Instituto Argentino de Tasaciones; BOLIVIA: Cuerpo Tecnico de
Tasaciones de Bolivia; MEXICO: Instituto Mexicano de Valuacion;
PERU: Cuerpo Tecnico de Tasaciones del Peru; PUERTO RICO:
Instituto de Evaluadores de Puerto Rico; UNITED STATES: Amer-
ican Institute of Real Estate Appraisers, 36 South Wabash, Chicago 3,
Illinois.

Property Owners Association of American, Rialto Building, Kansas City, Missouri.
Est. 1947.

Organized to protect free enterprise, private ownership of property
and freedom of contract; to oppose public housing. Formerly,
National Association of Property Owners of America.

Real Estate Certificate Institute, 276 East Duane Avenue, Sunnyvale, California.
Those individuals having completed the Real Estate Certificate
Program of the University of California. Publication: RECI
NEWSLETTER, issued periodically.

Rho Epsilon, c/o College of Business Administration, University of Omaha,
Omaha 1, Nebraska. Est. 1947.

Professional fraternity in real estate. 10 chapters. Publication:
THE BINDER, issued periodically.

Society of Real Estate Appraisers, 7 South Dearborn Street, Chicago 3, Illinois.
Est. 1935.

Name changed from Society of Residential Appraisers in
1963. S.R.E.A. (Senior Real Estate Appraiser) awarded
upon successful completion of requirements. Courses and
regional conferences offered. Publications: REAL ESTATE
APPRAISER, monthly; APPRAISAL PRINCIPLES AND TER-
MINOLOGY; and APPRAISAL GUIDE. Society publications
cited in APPRAISAL section.

United Nations. Economic and Social Council. Committee on Housing, Building and Planning.

First meeting to be January 1963.

United States Savings and Loan League, 221 North LaSalle Street, Chicago 1,
Illinois. Est. 1892.

State and local leagues. Membership is composed of savings and
loan associations and cooperative banks, with the objectives of
support of thrift promotion, the encouragement of private investment in the purchase of homes; development of safe, efficient
operating methods; and the improvement of statutes and regulations affecting the savings and loan business and the public interest. Society of Savings and Loan Controllers, and the Savings and Loan Institute, the educational and training arm of the
League are affiliated organizations. Publications: QUARTERLY
LETTER ON SAVINGS AND HOME MORTGAGE LENDING,
quarterly; LEGAL BULLETIN; THE LAW AFFECTING SAVINGS

ASSOCIATIONS, bi-monthly; SAVINGS AND LOAN NEWS, monthly; WASHINGTON NOTES, periodic; SAVINGS AND LOAN FACT BOOK, annual; and SAVINGS AND LOAN AN- NALS, annual. See FINANCE SECTION and APPENDIX A: Periodicals for Citations.

Urban Land Institute, 1200 18th Street, N.W., Washington 6, D.C. Est. 1936. Membership composed of firms, corporations, associations, public agencies and individuals. The Institute is an independent, non- profit, research organization founded to promote the better plan- ning, development and redevelopment of urban areas. The Insti- tute studies, analyzes and reports on trends which influence the development and use of land. The organization includes a Community Builders Council, and Industrial Council and a Cen- tral City Council. Publications: URBAN LAND NEWS AND TRENDS, monthly, a monograph series, and a technical bulletin series. A history of the Institute has been published, OF LAND AND MEN; THE BIRTH AND GROWTH OF AN IDEA, by Garnett L. Eskew. Washington, D.C.: The Institute, 1959. 206p. See LAND USE section for the listing of technical bulletins.

APPENDIX C

GOVERNMENT AGENCIES

FEDERAL

THE U.S. GOVERNMENT ORGANIZATION MANUAL, published annually by
the Office of the Federal Register and sold by the Government Printing Office,
is the best one-volume reference book on the agencies of the Federal government. Under the name of each is given address, names of chief officials,
statutory and executive authority, purpose, organization, field office addresses.
Appendix A: Executive Agencies and Functions of the Federal Government
Abolished, Transferred, or Terminated Subsequent to March 4, 1933.

U.S. Army Corps of Engineers, The Pentagon, Washington 25, D.C.
In charge of engineering, construction, and real estate services
for the Army and the Air Force and for other Federal agencies,
as directed; conducts an extensive mapping program; administers
all real estate and construction matters necessary for improvement
of rivers, harbors, navigable waterways, and shore protection;
develops nuclear power plants for the three armed services.

Board of Governors of the Federal Reserve System, 20th Street and Constitution
Avenue, N.W., Washington 25, D.C.
Est. 1913. The Board and the twelve Federal Reserve Banks
are excellent sources of data on economic conditions, mortgage
activity, etc. in the various regions.

U.S. Bureau of Indian Affairs (Department of the Interior), 18th and C Streets,
N.W., Washington 25, D.C.
Est. 1824. Serves as trustee of Indian lands.

U.S. Bureau of Land Management (Department of the Interior), 18th and C
Streets, N.W., Washington 25, D.C.
Est. 1946 as a consolidation of the General Land Office, es-
tablished 1812, and the Grazing Service, established 1934.
Responsible for lands in the public domain, granting of graz-
ing permits, forest management, mineral leasing.

U.S. Bureau of Mines (Department of the Interior), 18th and C Streets, N.W.,
Washington 25, D.C.
Est. 1910. Concerned with the development and conservation of
mineral resources. Bureau publications a fundamental source of
economic and statistical data on minerals and production.

U.S. Bureau of Outdoor Recreation. (Department of the Interior), 18th and C

Streets, N.W., Washington 25, D.C.
Est. 1962. Charged with the formulation of a national plan
for the creation and conservation of outdoor recreational facilities, encouragement of interstate and regional programs, assistance to states, and research. List of reports in RECREATIONAL
PROPERTY section.

U.S. Bureau of Public Roads (Department of Commerce), 1717 H Street, N.W.,
Washington 25, D.C.
Est. 1894. The principal road-building agency of the Federal
government. Administers Federal aid to state and interstate
highway programs. Also conducts planning and research on all
phases of highway improvement and safety.

U.S. Community Facilities Administration (Housing and Home Finance Agency),
1626 K Street, N.W., Washington 25, D.C.
Est. 1954. Furnishes financial and technical assistance to
state and local public agencies, nonprofit educational and
other groups for planning and construction of group housing and
such public works as water facilities; administers direct loan
program for construction of private nonprofit housing for the
elderly.

U.S. Department of Agriculture, Economic Research Service, 14th Street and
Independence Avenue, S.W., Washington 25, D.C.
Est. 1961. Continues many of the statistical reports on farm
real estate values, taxes, mortgage debt, etc.; originally issued
by the Agricultural Research Service.

U.S. Department of Justice, Lands Division, 10th Street and Constitution
Avenue, N.W., Washington 25, D.C.
Supervises all suits in state courts, the Court of Claims, and
Federal district courts relating to Federal condemnation proceed-
ings on real property, including land, water, and natural re-
sources; passes on titles of all real property acquired by the
Federal government; represents the United States in all suits
involving Indian claims.

U.S. Farmers Home Administration (Department of Agriculture), 14th Street and
Independence Avenue, S.W., Washington 25, D.C.
Est. 1946. A direct loan and loan insurance program for farm
ownership loans. Direct loans through the agency's field offices
to individuals unable to obtain credit at reasonable rates else-
where.

Federal Home Loan Bank Board and System, 101 Indiana Avenue, N.W., Washington 25, D.C.
Board established as an independent agency in 1955; the System
of twelve banks est. 1932. Provides credit reserves for savings
and home-financing institutions.

U.S. Federal Housing Administration (Housing and Home Finance Agency), 811 Vermont Avenue, N.W., Washington 25, D.C.
>Est. 1934; independent agency until 1947. Administers premium-financed program of insurance for approved loans: home mortgage loans, property improvement loans, co-operative, rental, and armed services housing. Publishes standards and research reports. Insuring and service offices in all states, the District of Columbia, and Puerto Rico.

Federal Land Bank System, c/o U.S. Farm Credit Administration, 14th Street and Constitution Avenue, N.W., Washington 25, D.C.
>Est. 1916. Long-term mortgage loans from the twelve land banks through Federal Land Bank Associations.

Federal National Mortgage Association (Housing and Home Finance Agency), 811 Vermont Avenue, N.W., Washington 25, D.C.
>Est. 1938, rechartered 1954. Supplementary assistance to the secondary market for home mortgages by providing a degree of liquidity for mortgage investments and special financing assistance under certain conditions. Five regional offices.

Federal Savings and Loan Insurance Corporation, 101 Indiana Avenue, N.W., Washington 25, D.C.
>Est. 1947. Insures savings and credited earnings in approved savings and loan associations, etc.

U.S. Forest Service (Department of Agriculture), 14th Street and Independence Avenue, S.W., Washington 25, D.C.
>Est. 1905. Administers National forests and grasslands, applying scientific principles of management and conservation. Source for leasing and grazing information.

U.S. General Services Administration, 18th and F Streets, N.W., Washington 25, D.C.
>Est. 1949. Responsible for the procurement, maintenance, and disposal of real property for Federal agencies, except for the Post Office Department and the Armed Forces. The Public Buildings Service responsible for acquisition, utilization, custody, and accountability for real property under the jurisdiction of GSA.

U.S. Geological Survey (Department of the Interior), 18th and F Streets, N.W., Washington 25, D.C.
>Est. 1879. Surveys, maps, and research on topography, geology, mineral and water resources of the United States; charged with the enforcement of the Department's regulations on oil, gas, and mineral leasing.

U.S. Housing and Home Finance Agency, 1626 K Street, N.W., Washington 25, D.C.
>Est. 1947. A single, permanent agency responsible for principal housing program of the Federal government. Consists of

Office of the Administrator, Community Facilities Administration, Federal Housing Administration, Federal National Mortgage Association, Public Housing Administration, Urban Renewal Administration; also provides staff assistance to the Voluntary Home Mortgage Credit Program.

U.S. Post Office Department, 12th Street and Pennsylvania Avenue, N.W., Washington 25, D.C.
Est. 1872. The Bureau of Facilities in charge of acquisition, management, improvement, and disposal of real property occupied by the Department.

U.S. Public Housing Administration (Housing and Home Finance Agency), 1201 Connecticut Avenue, N.W., Washington 25, D.C.
Est. as a constituent agency of HHFA 1947; a successor to the Federal Public Housing Authority and U.S. Housing Authority. Administers the Federal aid program to low-cost public housing projects. Seven regional offices.

U.S. Bureau of Reclamation (Department of the Interior), 18th and C Streets, N.W., Washington 25, D.C.
Est 1923. Responsible for the reclamation of arid and semiarid lands through irrigation, flood control projects, prevention of water pollution, etc.

U.S. Small Business Administration, 811 Vermont Avenue, N.W., Washington 25, D.C.
Est. 1953. Offers counseling and makes loans to small business concerns for plant construction, expansion, or modernization and to victims of flood and other natural disasters for replacement of homes and businesses; charters, licenses, and makes loans to small business investment companies. Over fifty branch and regional offices.

U.S. Soil Conservation Service (Department of Agriculture), 14th Street and Independence Avenue, S.W., Washington 25, D.C.
Est. 1935. A permanent, nation-wide program for soil and water conservation, including flood control. Issues soil survey reports and maps for most areas of the United States.

U.S Urban Renewal Administration (Housing and Home Finance Agency), 1626 K Street, N.W., Washington 25, D.C.
Est. 1954. Administers Federal aid to approved slum clearance and urban renewal projects. Field operations carried on through HHFA regional offices.

U.S. Veterans Administration, Vermont Avenue and H Street, N.W., Washington 25, D.C.
Est. 1930. Loan Guaranty Service responsible for administration of direct and indirect Federal aid for purchase or construction

FEDERAL (continued)

of homes by eligible veterans. Regional offices throughout country.

Voluntary Home Mortgage Credit Program, 1626 K Street, N.W., Washington 25, D.C.
Est. 1954. Charged with the responsibility of obtaining private mortgage credit for FHA-insured and VA-guaranteed loans in areas in which such capital is not readily available or is not equally available to all groups.

STATE REAL ESTATE COMMISSIONS

Alabama Real Estate Commission
State Capitol
Montgomery, Alabama

Commissioner of Real Estate
Box 2259
Juneau, Alaska

Commissioner of Real Estate
Capitol Building
Phoenix, Arizona

Arkansas Real Estate Commission
Pyramid Life Building
Little Rock, Arkansas

State Real Estate Commissioner
1015 L Street
Sacramento 14, California

Colorado Real Estate Broker's Board
115 State Services Building
Denver, Colorado

Director of Licenses
State Office Building
Hartford 15, Connecticut

Delaware Real Estate Commission
511 West 12th Street
Wilmington 1, Delaware

Real Estate Commission
1145 19th Street, N.W.
Washington 6, D.C.

Florida Real Estate Commission
State Office Building
Winter Park, Orlando, Florida

Georgia Real Estate Commission
221 State Capitol
Atlanta, Georgia

Real Estate Commission
Empire Building -- Room 205
Honolulu 13, Hawaii

Idaho Real Estate Commission
715 Grove Street
Boise, Idaho

Department of Registration & Education
Capitol Building
Springfield, Illinois

Indiana Real Estate Commission
100 N. Senate Avenue, Room 1022
Indianapolis, Indiana

Iowa Real Estate Commission
State Capitol
Des Moines 19, Iowa

STATE REAL ESTATE COMMISSIONS (continued)

Kansas Real Estate Commission
State Office Building
Topeka, Kansas

Kentucky State Real Estate Commission
1403 Kentucky Home Life Building
Louisville, Kentucky

Louisiana Real Estate Commission
State Capitol, Box 4095
Baton Rouge, Louisiana

Maine Real Estate Commission
State Office Building
Augusta, Maine

Real Estate Commission of Maryland
504 State Office Building
Baltimore 1, Maryland

Board of Registration of Real Estate
    Brokers and Salesmen
18 Tremont Street
Boston 8, Massachusetts

Michigan Corporation and Securities
    Commission
300 E. Michigan Avenue
Lansing, Michigan

Real Estate Section
Securities Division
State Office Building
St. Paul 1, Minnesota

Real Estate Commission
Milner Building -- Suite 1070
Jackson, Mississippi

Missouri Real Estate Commission
222 Monroe Street
Jefferson City, Missouri

Montana Real Estate Commission
Helena,
Montana

Nebraska Real Estate Commission
State House
Lincoln, Nebraska

Nevada Real Estate Commission
11 W. Telegraph Street -- Room 204
P.O. Drawer C.
Carson City, Nevada

New Hampshire Real Estate Commission
State House Annex
Concord, New Hampshire

New Jersey Real Estate Commission
1100 Raymond Boulevard
Newark, New Jersey

New Mexico Real Estate Commission
1013 Simms Building
Albuquerque, New Mexico

New York Division of Licenses
Department of State
270 Broadway
New York 7, New York

North Carolina Real Estate Commission
711 First Citizens Bank Building
Raleigh, North Carolina

North Dakota Real Estate Commission
410 Thayer Avenue
Bismarck, North Dakota

Ohio Real Estate Commission
22 E. Gay Street
Columbus 15, Ohio

Oklahoma Real Estate Commission
804 Commerce Exchange Building
Oklahoma City, Oklahoma

Oregon Real Estate Commission
Labor & Industries Building
Salem, Oregon

Pennsylvania Real Estate Commission
Education Building
Room 566
Harrisburg, Pennsylvania

Rhode Island Real Estate Commission
Division of Business Regulation
49 Westminster Street
Providence, Rhode Island

STATE REAL ESTATE COMMISSIONS (continued)

South Carolina Real Estate Commission
1007-1009 Carolina Life Building
Columbia, South Carolina

South Dakota Real Estate Commission
107 N. Main Avenue
Sioux Falls, South Dakota

Tennessee Real Estate Commission
209 Stahlman Building
Nashville, Tennessee

Texas Real Estate Commission
Drawer F, Capitol Station
Austin, Texas

Securities Commission
Real Estate Division
314 State Capitol
Salt Lake City, Utah

Vermont Real Estate Commission
Hardwick, Vermont

Virginia Real Estate Commission
1312 E. Grace Street -- Room 211
P.O. Box 1-X
Richmond 2, Virginia

Real Estate Division
Department of Licenses
130 Civic Business Center
550 Mercer Street
Seattle, Washington

West Virginia Real Estate Commission
207 Pioneer Building
Charleston 1, West Virginia

Wisconsin Real Estate Commission
308 W. North Avenue
Milwaukee 12, Wisconsin

Wyoming Real Estate Board
308 Capitol Building
Cheyenne, Wyoming

CANADA

Commissioner of Real Estate
Natural Resources Building
Edmonton, Alberta

Real Estate Council
401-207 W. Hastings Street
Vancouver 3, British Columbia

Real Estate Agents Act
The Public Utilities Board
116 Edmonton Street
Winnipeg 1, Manitoba

Real Estate and Business Brokers Act
Ontario Government Building
145 Queen Street, West
Toronto, Ontario

OTHER STATE AGENCIES

Agricultural experiment stations

Departments of agriculture

Departments of mines, natural resources, geological surveys, etc.

Forestry services

Highway departments

Tax equalization boards

LOCAL

Reports of recorded real estate instruments, based on public records, are issued by non-governmental organizations in many cities. These reports, which may appear in periodicals or be issued as separate publications, include such information as location of property, names of grantor and grantee, date of instrument, and value of revenue stamps attached. The transactions involved include deed transfers and mortgage and lease recordings. The following are examples of publications of this type: Akron Area Board of Realtors. DEED TRANSFER REFERENCE MANUAL, 1957-1961; Real Estate Board of New York. Research Department. MANHATTAN REAL ESTATE -- OPEN MARKET SALES, FIRST HALF 1962; REAL ESTATE RECORD AND BUILDERS GUIDE. F.W. Dodge Corporation, New York, New York (weekly) -- for Manhattan and the Bronx; REALTY AND BUILDING. 2 East Grand Avenue, Chicago 11, Illinois. (weekly). -- for Chicago. State document stamp information is contained in the STATE TAX GUIDE, published by Commerce Clearing House.

Other sources of local real estate information are:

Building code and building permit offices

City and county assessors	-- real property taxes, special assessments, ownership
City and county clerks	-- land ownership records, former owners, dates of transfer
City and county engineers	-- roads, utilities, rights of way
City and county recorders	-- transfers
Planning and zoning commissions	-- land use, regulations, etc.
Registrars of deeds	-- land title records
Surveyors	--survey land in dispute and charge fees

APPENDIX D

A STATEMENT ON
LIBRARY RESOURCES

The library collections of colleges and universities offering courses in real estate and related fields are often available to individuals outside the institutions by special arrangement. A list of these institutions is available from the Department of Education, National Association of Real Estate Boards, 36 South Wabash Avenue, Chicago 3, Illinois.

Some local real estate boards have established libraries and municipal reference libraries exist in many cities. Both types of collection usually contain statistical and other data on local housing, real estate, and business conditions of interest to the real estate researcher. Special collections frequently exist in city planning departments, chambers of commerce, and such commercial establishments as banks and utility companies. Most Federal agencies maintain special libraries in their Washington, D.C. offices.

The following libraries are mentioned as collections of special interest and as examples.

American Institute of Architects
1735 New York Avenue, N.W.
Washington 6, D. C.

Central Mortgage and Housing Corporation
Montreal Road
Ottawa, Canada

Division of Building Research
National Research Council of Canada
Ottawa, Canada

Federal Home Loan Bank Board
101 Indiana Avenue, N. W.
Washington 25, D. C.

Herbert U. Nelson Memorial Library and Information Center
National Association of Real EstateBoards
36 South Wabash Avenue
Chicago 3, Illinois

National Agricultural Library
14th Street and Independence Avenue S. W.
Washington 25, D. C.

National Housing Center
1625 L Street N. W.
Washington 6, D. C.

National Research Council
National Academy of Sciences
2101 Constitution Avenue N. W.
Washington 25, D. C.

Tri-State Transportation Committee
100 Church Street
New York 7, New York

U. S. Federal Housing Administration
811 Vermont Avenue N. W.
Washington 25, D. C.

U. S. Housing and Home Finance Agency
1626 K Street N. W.
Washington 25, D. C.

U. S. Public Housing Administration
1201 Connecticut Avenue N. W.
Washington 25, D. C.

Real Estate Research Program
Graduate School of Business Administration
University of California
Berkeley and Los Angeles, California

Technical Information Division
Office of Technical Services
U. S. Department of Commerce
Washington 25, D. C.

APPENDIX E

FORMS

The following books, and many others on real estate law, brokerage, etc., contain specimen froms offered to serve only as guides and information. Legal counsel should be sought before using the forms cited. Local real estate associations are additional sources of information on this subject.

Business Forms for Builders, prepared as an industry service by the Business Management Committee of the National Association of Home Builders in cooperation with the United States Gypsum Company. JOURNAL OF HOMEBUILDING, vol. 16, no. 12, pt. 1, December 1962, p. A1-24; vol. 17, no. 1, January 1963, p. B1-40; vol. 17, no. 2, February 1963, p. C1-16.
> The three sections deal with forms for the pre-construction, construction, and post-construction and legal phases of the builder's operations. Reprint available from United States Gypsum Company, 300 West Adams Street, Chicago 6, Illinois.

Casey, William J. REAL ESTATE INVESTMENT DEALS, IDEAS, FORMS, 2 vols. New York: Institute for Business Planning, 1959- . processed. looseleaf.
> A looseleaf service, supplemented monthly. Specimen froms printed in sections on forms of ownership, real estate transfers, leases, etc. Includes bimonthly REAL ESTATE INVESTMENT LETTER.

Casey, William J. TAX TESTED FORMS OF AGREEMENT, RESOLUTIONS AND PLANS, 2 vols. New York: Institute for Business Planning, 1958- . processed. looseleaf.
> Section 6700: Real Estate Transfers; Section 6800: Leases; Section 7100: Oil and Natural Resources Transactions.

Crocker, George U. NOTES ON COMMON FORMS, 7th ed., by Roger Swaim. Boston: Little, Brown, 1955. 678p.
> Discussion and case references on deeds, mortgages, leases and tenancies, eminent domain, zoning and building laws, etc. Appendix: Mechanics of Title Examination in Massachusetts, by Richard B. Johnson.

Friedman, Edith J. HANDBOOK OF REAL ESTATE FORMS. Englewood Cliffs, N.J.: Prentice-Hall, 1957. 441p.
> 248 specimens "required in every branch of real estate activity ... selected for their clarity, legal soundness, effectiveness."

Gordon, Saul. STANDARD ANNOTATED REAL ESTATE FORMS. Englewood Cliffs, N.J.: Prentice-Hall, 1947. 1343p.
> A comprehensive collection of forms that have been tested in cases.

McMichael, Stanley L. and O'Keefe, Paul T. LEASES: PERCENTAGE, SHORT AND LONG TERM, 5th ed. Englewood Cliffs, N.J.: Prentice-Hall, 1959. 511p.
> Contains specimen lease forms of many types.

Parker, William Stanley and Adams, Faneuil. THE A.I.A. STANDARD CONTRACT FORMS AND THE LAW. Boston: Little, Brown, 1954. 147p.
> Part 1: Agreements between owner and architect; Part 11: Agreements between owner and contractor.

Thompson, George W. COMPLETE FORMS FOR REAL PROPERTY TRANSACTIONS, ALPHABETICALLY ARRANGED, WITH PIN-POINT INDEX; FORMS FOR ORDINARY USE AND CLAUSES FOR UNUSUAL REQUIREMENTS. Indianapolis: Bobbs-Merrill, 1941.
> Constitutes volume 11 of THOMPSON ON REAL PROPERTY. Supplemental pocket parts issued periodically. First edition published in 1924 as CYCLOPEDIA OF REAL ESTATE FORMS.

APPENDIX F

TABLES

Ellwood, L.W. ELLWOOD TABLES FOR REAL ESTATE APPRAISING AND FI-
NANCING. Ridgewood, N.J.: 374 Hamilton Road, 1959. 330p.

Financial Publishing Co. DIRECT REDUCTION LOAN AMORTIZATION SCHED-
ULES FOR LOANS WITH QUARTERLY, SEMIANNUAL AND ANNUAL PAY-
MENTS, 3d ed. Boston: 1954. various paging.

Financial Publishing Co. FINANCIAL COMPOUND INTEREST AND ANNUITY
TABLES. Boston: 1942. 900p.

Financial Publishing Co. MONTHLY PAYMENT DIRECT REDUCTION LOAN
AMORTIZATION SCHEDULES, SHOWING EQUAL MONTHLY PAYMENTS
NECESSARY TO AMORTIZE A LOAN OF $1,000; ALSO THE AMOUNT OF
INTEREST AND PRINCIPAL IN EACH PAYMENT, AND THE BALANCE OUT-
STANDING AT ANY TIME DURING THE LIFE OF THE LOAN, 9th ed.
Boston: 1958. various paging.

Frankel, Perry and Livingstone, Robert. BOOK OF YIELD TABLES FOR DIS-
COUNTED TRUST DEEDS AND MORTGAGES. Los Angeles: P-R Publishing
Co., 1961. 132p.

Inwood, William. TABLES OF INTEREST AND MORTALITY FOR THE PURCHAS-
ING OF ESTATES AND VALUATION OF PROPERTIES INCLUDING LOGARITHMS
OF NATURAL NUMBERS AND LOGARITHMIC INTEREST AND ANNUITY TA-
BLES AND MONEYLENDERS' TABLES, 33d ed. by William Schooling. London:
C. Lockwood and Son, 1930.

Kent, Frederick C. and Kent, Maude E. COMPOUND INTEREST AND ANNU-
ITY TABLES; CONVERSION FACTORS AND LOGARITHMS. (VALUES OF ALL
FUNCTIONS TO TEN DECIMAL PLACES FOR 1-100, 1-200, 1-300 YEARS, RATES OF
INTEREST 1/4 OF 1 PER CENT TO 10 1/2 PER CENT). New York: McGraw-
Hill, 1926. 214p.

Parry, Richard. THE APPLICATION, USE AND CONSTRUCTION OF VALUATION
TABLES, 4th ed., edited by Leonard Barton Gumbrell. London: Estates Gazette,
1936. 236p.
> 1st edition written as part of VALUATION TABLES. Text of
> the College of Estate Management.

Parry, Richard. VALUATION TABLES FOR THE USE OF SURVEYORS, VALUERS,
LAND AGENTS, AUCTIONEERS, CIVIL ENGINEERS AND OTHERS INTER-
ESTED IN THE VALUATION OF IMMEDIATE AND REVERSIONARY INTERESTS
IN FREEHOLD, LEASEHOLD AND LIFEHOLD PROPERTY, MINERAL AND

OTHER RIGHTS; ALSO FOR THE USE OF VALUERS OF COMMERCIAL UNDER-
TAKINGS, 7th ed., rev. and enl. by William R. Jenkins, London: Estates
Gazette, 1949. 253p.
    A Text of the College of Estate Management.

Schmutz, George L. CAPITALIZATION TABLES WITH PROBLEMS. Chicago:
American Institute of Real Estate Appraisers, 1936. 38p. pap. processed.
    Inwood compound interest and Haskold sinking fund valuation
    premises: Present worth of one dollar per annum, present worth
    of one dollar, amortization ratio for sinking funds, future worth
    of one dollar, future worth of one dollar per annum.

Smith E. Sawyer. THE PRACTICAL PRORATOR. (Brokers Institute Bulletin
Service). Chicago: National Institute of Real Estate Brokers, 1938. 48p.
    Distributed to members under special arrangement with the Prac-
    tical Prorator Co., Winnetka, Illinois. Tables to prorate in-
    surance premiums, taxes, interest charges, annual rents, etc.,
    by years, months, and days.

U.S. Federal Housing Administration. AMORTIZATION AND INSURANCE
PREMIUM TABLES FOR HOME IMPROVEMENT AND REHABILITATION LOANS
TO BE USED UNDER THE NATIONAL HOUSING ACT. (FHA no. 2008).
Washington, D.C.: 1961. 81p. pap. (Sold by Government Printing Office).

U.S. Federal Housing Administration. AMORTIZATION AND INSURANCE
PREMIUM TABLES; FOR HOME MORTGAGES AND LOANS TO BE INSURED
UNDER THE NATIONAL HOUSING ACT. (FHA no. 2025, which supercedes
FHA no. 20243). Washington, D.C.: 1961. 153p. pap. (Sold by Govern-
ment Printing Office).

APPENDIX G

MAPS

Maps of interest to the real estate man are available from both governmental and private sources. A discussion of the various types and offices from which they may be obtained appears on pages 107-11 in ENCYCLOPEDIA OF REAL ESTATE APPRAISING, edited by Edith J. Friedman, 1959. Maps issued by various agencies of the Federal government are listed in the MONTHLY CATALOG OF UNITED STATES GOVERNMENT PUBLICATIONS and in special lists of the Superintendent of Documents, Washington 25, D.C., such as PRICE LIST 53, which is revised regularly. Included in the group of Federal agencies from which maps are available are the following: Soil Conservation Service--county soil surveys (cited in PRICE LIST 46, Superintendent of Documents, Washington 25, D.C.); Coast and Geodetic Survey--coastal and harbor charts; Geological Survey--quadrangle maps of the entire United States; Army Corps of Engineers--rivers, navigable waters, dams, etc.; Forest Service--national forests, leased areas, etc.; State departments of highways, agriculture, and natural resources, and other department maps are listed in the MONTHLY CHECKLIST OF STATE PUBLICATIONS, Library of Congress, Washington 25, D.C.. Local government agencies from which certain maps are obtainable include the offices of the county and city engineers--cadastral, drainage, substructure, right of way maps; and regional, county and city planning and zoning commissions--land use and zoning maps.

Utility and transportation companies, chambers of commerce, and commercial publishers offer additional maps, many of a highly specialized nature. Examples are cited below.

Sanborn Map Co., Inc., 629 Fifth Avenue, Pelham, New York.
THE SANBORN MAP: "Virtually every town in the United States with a population of 2,000 or more is included in the more than 11,000 communities mapped." Diagrams of blocks showing lots, lot sizes, building sizes and uses, age of commercial structures, etc. Residential, commercial, and industrial property included. Revised about once a year.
Brewster Mapping Co., 5110 Huntington Drive, Los Angeles 32, California.
1960 Census Tract Report Maps of Los Angeles County: Home Values: 1961. 4 color 23x29 map showing median value of owner-occupied. 5 gradations for median value ranges under $11,000; 11-12,900, 13-19,900; 20-24,900,

25 and over. Other maps in the Series will cover median age, Negro population, rental values, condition of housing, income, Spanish-white population, educational status, age of housing, and mobility of population.

G.W. Bromley & Co., 325 Spring Street, New York 13, New York.

5 Manhattan atlases (Scale 80' to the unit) Manhattan Land Book (160' to the unit), 2 Bronx atlases (scale 100' to the inch), 2 Bronx Land Books (150' and 160 feet to the inch). Correction service on a subscription basis.

Chicago Real Estate Board, Renting and Management Division, 105 West Madison Street, Chicago 2, Illinois.

Occupancy maps of thirty major shopping areas in Chicago, first floor occupancy shown. Revised annually.

Nirenstein's National Realty Map Co., P.O. Box 454, 377 Dwight Street, Springfield 3, Massachusetts.

Regional atlases of maps for central business districts and shopping centers. Size, type, use, value, etc., shown for buildings.

Sidwell Studio, Inc., 28W240 North Avenue, West Chicago, Illinois.

Legal description atlases, aerial maps, etc.

SURVEYING AND MAPPING, the quarterly journal of the American Congress on surveying and Mapping, notes the availability of new maps in the "Map Information" department in each issue.

APPENDIX H

FILMS AND RECORDINGS

FILMS

California Real Estate Association. CLOSING MR. SELLER. 16mm, black and white, sound, 12 minutes. 117 West Ninth Street, Los Angeles 15, California.

California Real Estate Association. LISTING AND EVALUATING A PROPERTY. 35mm filmstrip with sound platter, black and white, sound, 15 minutes.

California Real Estate Association. PROSPECTING. 16mm, black and white, sound, 12 minutes.

California Real Estate Association. SHOWING A PROPERTY. 35mm filmstrip with sound platter, black and white, sound, 15 minutes.

California Real Estate Association. SIGNING UP THE BUYER. 16mm, black and white, sound, 12 minutes.

California Real Estate Association. SOCIAL AND ECONOMIC SIGNIFICANCE OF REAL ESTATE. 35mm filmstrip with sound platter, black and white, sound, 15 minutes.

California Real Estate Association. TRADING EVOLUTION IN REAL ESTATE. 35mm filmstrip with sound platter, 20 minutes

Industrial Sound Films, Inc. BLUEPRINT FOR PROGRESS. 16mm, color, sound, 25 minutes.
> An affiliate of Conway Publications, Inc., 2592 Apple Valley Road, Atlanta 19, Ga. Produced with technical supervision by the editors of INDUSTRIAL DEVELOPMENT. "A new motion picture about industrial zoning for communities."

Industrial Sound Films, Inc. GOLD MINE ON MAIN STREET. 16mm, color, sound, 25 minutes.
> Produced with technical supervision by the editors of INDUSTRIAL DEVELOPMENT. "A new motion picture about the benefits of industrial development to a community."

National Association of Real Estate Boards. YOUR STAFF AT WORK. 33mm filmstrip with script, color. 36 South Wabash Avenue, Chicago 3, Illinois.

Real Estate Training, Inc. THE TRADING EVOLUTION IN REAL ESTATE. 16mm slide film with sound platter. Detroit: Instructional Arts, Inc.

FILMS (continued)

Case history of the trading operation conducted by the Gordon
Williamson Company. To accompany the film: handbook of
"ground rules", TRADING IN REAL ESTATE. 24p. illus. pap.

United States Savings and Loan League. WHAT YOU SHOULD KNOW BEFORE
YOU BUY A HOME. 16mm, color, sound, 27 1/2 minutes. 221 North
LaSalle Street, Chicago 1, Illinois.
Produced by the United States Savings and Loan League in co-
operation with the National Association of Home Builders and
the National Association of Real Estate Boards. "Home Buyer's
Checklist" booklet Teachers Guide created especially for use
by Savings and Loan Associations for showings to the general
public or to a specific group.

Films—Lists

American Society of Planning Officials. MOTION PICTURE FILMS ON PLAN-
NING AND HOUSING; A BIBLIOGRAPHY, Rev. ed. Chicago: 1957. 13p.
pap. processed.

National Association of Real Estate Boards. Department of Education. MO-
TION PICTURES AND SLIDE FILMS; HOW AND WHERE THEY MAY BE SE-
CURED FOR POSSIBLE SHOWINGS AT REAL ESTATE BOARD MEETINGS.
Chicago: 1961. 35p. pap. processed.
Purchase and rental information for films on architecture, city
planning, free enterprise, home ownership, office techniques
and procedures, real estate training, rehabilitation and sales
training, general. Revised periodically.

United Nations. Department of Economic and Social Affairs. HOUSING,
BUILDING, PLANNING; AN INTERNATIONAL FILM CATALOGUE. (ST/SOA/
SER. H/5). New York: 1956. 246p. pap. processed.
A subject index of films, with alphabetical lists of titles, pro-
ducers and distributors, sources of information.

U.S. Housing and Home Finance Agency. Office of International Housing.
LIST OF FILMS AVAILABLE IN FILM LIBRARY. Washington: 1961. 9p. pap.

RECORDINGS

THE CODE OF ETHICS. LaSalle Research, Box 6175, Minneapolis 24, Minne-

RECORDINGS (continued)

apolis 24, Minnesota. 33-1/3 r.p.m. 7" record.
> A presentation of the National Association of Real Estate Boards
> Code of Ethics.

Hudson, George W. REALTOR AND PUBLIC RELATIONS. Delaware Broadcasting Co., 920 King Street, Wilmington, Delaware. 12"--2 sides, 33-1/3 r.p.m.

Krueger, Cliff W. SUCCESSFUL REAL ESTATE SELLING. Success Motivation Institute, Waco, Texas, Album of 4 sides, 33-1/3 r.p.m.
> Accompanied by script.

National Association of Home Builders. SALES ACSELLERATOR COURSE.
Home Facts Research, Inc., New Canaan, Conn. 13 records, 33-1/3 r.p.m.
> Narrated and interpreted by Jim Mills. Minimum developed for
> 1 sales manager and 5 salesmen. "salesminders" weekly booklets;
> meeting bi-weekly outlines; records; area data cards; question-
> aires tabulated as the course progresses about how your sales-
> men and selling environment compare with others in the country;
> conference summary sheets. 52 week course.

REAL ESTATE RECORDINGS. Arthur E. Nall, Real Estate Recordings, 1019 Goodhue Building, Beaumont, Texas.
> Tape recordings of addresses and discussions before annual na-
> tional conventions of the National Association of Real Estate
> Boards and various state and regional meetings. Catalogue
> available.

REAL ESTATE WORKSHOP: KEYS TO SUCCESSFUL SELLING. LaSalle Research, Box 6175, Minneapolis 24, Minnesota.
> Two sets of five 12" records, 33-1/3 r.p.m. Descriptive folder
> available.

AUTHOR INDEX

Boston University   188
Bouma, Donald Herbert   32
Bouwcentrum   66, 208, 217
Boyd, Joseph M., Jr.   126
Boyd, Osborne T.   91
Bradford, Lawrence A.   169
Bradshaw, Robert J.   52
Brasfield, Karney A.   167
Break, George F.   87
Brede, William J.   22, 50
Bredo, William   185
Brener, Stephen W.   52
Brett, Wyckoff, Potter, and Hamilton   115
Brewster, Maurice   215
Brewster Mapping Co.   270-1
Brimmer, Andrew F.   95
Bromley, G. W., and Company   271
Brown, Earle Palmer   188
Brown, Sam E.   58
Brown, Harry Gunnison   103
Brown, Robert K.   22, 220
Bryant, Willis R.   95, 171
Buckley, Ernest L.   66
Building Managers' Association of Chicago   115
Building Managers' Association of Chicago. Insurance Committee   112, 115
Building Research Station   225
Bundes-Innung der Gebaudeverwalter und Realitatenvermittler (Austria)   246
Burbank, Nelson L.   75
Bureau of Analyses   56
Burger, Lowell J.   155
Burgess, Ernest W.   204
Burke, Arthur E.   67
Burkhard, Paul L.   91
Burns, Ron J.   59
Bryce, Murray D.   185
Burrage, Robert H.   163
Burton, Hall   128
Burton, John E.   46
Butler, F. Elmore   110
Butler, George D.   198
Butwin, Stanley   112
Bye, Carl Rollinson   131

C

Cadwallader, Clyde T.   91, 92
Cal Pacific Estimators   67
Calef, Wesley   194
California Council of Civil Engineers and Land Surveyors   82, 139
California. Division of Highways   143
California Law Revision Commission   143
California Real Estate Association   27, 28, 32, 51, 92, 226, 272
California Real Estate Association. State Real Estate Institute   187
California Savings and Loan League   237
California. University. Agricultural Experiment Station   169
California. University. Bureau of Governmental Research   157
California. University. Bureau of Public Administration   122
California. University. Bureau of Public Administration   139
California. University. Extension Division   152, 185
California. University. Real Estate Certificate Program   254
California. University. Real Estate Research Program   13, 16, 41, 67, 92, 95, 96, 97, 98, 115, 122, 157, 158, 164, 190, 265
Callahan, Parnell   147
Cambridge University. College of: Estate Management   268
Cambridge University. Department of Estate Management   15, 181
Cambridge University. Estate Management Club   15
Canadian Association of Real Estate Boards   226, 246
Canadian Institute of Surveying   246
Carson, Eileen R.   67, 75
Carstensen, Vernon   194
Case, Frederick E.   22, 27, 92, 115, 158, 203
Case, Harold C. M.   169

I

J

K

L

N

National Association of Home
Builders. Business Management
Committee   266
National Association of Home Builders.
Community Facilities and Urban
Renewal Department   79, 125
National Association of Home Builders.
Rental Housing Department   79
National Association of Home Builders.
State Associations Committee   233
National Association of Housing and
Redevelopment Officials   123,
125, 126, 130, 221, 232, 236
National Association of Insurance
Agents   112
National Association of Insured Sav-
ings Associations   232, 253
National Association of License Law
Officials   21, 248
National Association of Mutual Sav-
ings Banks   99, 248
National Association of Property
Owners of America   254
National Association of Real Estate
Boards   25, 32, 33, 34, 45, 53,
63, 99, 150, 219, 236, 242, 247,
249-52, 272, 273, 274
National Association of Real Estate
Boards. Brokerage Management
Committee   53
National Association of Real Estate
Boards. Build America Better
Committee   71, 125, 225
National Association of Real Estate
Boards. Committee on Education
24, 36, 53
National Association of Real Estate
Boards. Committee on Multiple
Listing Policy   34
National Association of Real Estate
Boards. Committee on Professional
Standards   34
National Association of Real Estate
Boards. Department of Education
16, 29, 31, 36, 226, 228, 273
National Association of Real Estate
Boards. Department of Field
Services   34
National Association of Real Estate
Boards. Department of Public
Relations   31, 32, 34, 234
National Association of Real Estate

Boards. Department of Research
14, 219, 233, 236
National Association of Real Estate
Boards. Division of Research
189
National Association of Real Estate
Boards. General Counsel   35
National Association of Real Estate
Boards. Herbert U. Nelson Memo-
rial Library and Information Center
265
National Association of Real Estate
Boards. Industrial Property
Division   187
National Association of Real Estate
Boards. License Law Committee
21
National Association of Real Estate
Boards. Realtor-City Planners
Committee   219
National Association of Real Estate
Boards. Realtors' Washington
Committee   183, 220, 234
National Association of Real Estate
Boards. Secretaries Council   63
National Association of Real Estate
Boards. State Associations
Committee   35, 150
National Association of Real Estate
Boards. State Associations
Department   35
National Association of Real Estate
Brokers   252
National Association of Real Estate
Editors   253
National Association of Real Estate
Investment Funds   106, 253
National Association of Realtor
Secretaries   250
National Board of Fire Underwriters
113
National Bureau of Economic Research
13, 15, 85, 88, 89, 95, 98, 99,
100, 172, 205
National Committee Against Discrim-
ination in Housing   239
National District Heating Association
119
National Golf Foundation   197,
198
National Home Improvement Council
234

T

U

Washington State University. Agricultural Experiment Stations 180
Washington. University. Bureau of Governmental Research and Services 153
Wasserman, Paul 17
Watson, Howell H. 52
Watson, Jairus H. 145
Waugh, Herbert R. 75
Weaver School of Real Estate 23
Weber, Alfred 190
Wehrly, Max S. 81, 105, 136, 137, 142, 163, 166, 190
Wehrwein, George S. 132
Weimer, Arthur M. 26, 94, 138, 161
Weir, Robert H. 111, 180
Weismentel, William L. 139
Weiss, Shirley F. 160
Wendt, Paul F. 13, 47, 91, 102, 153, 157, 217
Wenzlick, Roy 15
Wenslick, Roy, Research Corporation 14, 47, 217, 235
West Virginia. University. Bureau of Business Research 190
Westcott, Roy D. 22
Wheaton, William L. C. 80
White House: Conference on Aging 217
Whitehead, Walter L. 46
Whitmer, Robert E. 27
Whyte, William H., Jr. 138, 200
Wickens, David L. 15
Wilbur, Albert A. 56
William, Jean H. 71
Williams, D. B. 169
Williams, Frank Backus 132, 142
Williams, Jean H. 222
Williams, Walter 112
Williams, Wayne R. 200
Williamson, Gordon 57, 273
Williamson, John C. 108
Williman, Glenn D. 34
Wilmette, Walter F. 39, 169
Wilner, Daniel 217
Wilt, H. S. 174
Winard, Arthur I. 153
Windsor, W. C., Jr. 117
Wingo, Lowdon, Jr. 139
Winnick, Louis 94, 207, 217

Wisconsin. University. Agricultural Experiment Station 180
Wisconsin. University. Bureau of Business Research and Service 190
Wisconsin. University. Institute for Research in Land Economics and Public Utilities 26, 52, 99
Wisconsin. University. School of Commerce 202
Wissenschaftlich-Technischer Verein in Bulgarien 245
Woessner, Charles 63
Wolff, Lewis N. 121
Women's Council of the National Association of Real Estate Boards 240, 252
Women's Council of the National Association of Real Estate Boards. Committee on Education 32
Wood, Ramsay 91
Woodbury, Coleman 129, 218
Woodbury, Wallace R. 59
Wright, Carroll 43
Wright, Ivan 102
Wunderlich, Gene 15
Wyckoff, Bradford 64

Y

Yang, W. Y. 175
Yaseen, Leonard C. 190
Yokley, E. C. 142

Z

Zuckerman, Solly 15

SUBJECT INDEX

F

U

Z

74
75
76
77
79
81
83
85
88